Praise for WHY I AM A CATHOLIC

"Among Wills's most memorable writings."
— *New York Review of Books*

"Elegant, electric with insight . . . [*Why I Am a Catholic*] could not be more timely." — *San Francisco Chronicle*

"One of our more muscular thinkers and prolific writers . . . explodes much of what passes as institutionalized Catholicism, the church's convenient use of Gospel, the pomp, the circumstance, the Pope-mobiles and . . . boils the question of why one could possibly be a Catholic down to its essentials." — *The Nation*

"Regardless of your beliefs, you'll come away from this book impressed with the fervor and sincerity of his examination of his faith."
— *Rocky Mountain News*

"Arguably the nation's most prominent liberal Catholic intellectual."
— *Washington Post Book World*

"A spiritual autobiography, in which Wills brings before us his most personal intellectual and spiritual influences." — *Houston Chronicle*

"An affirmation of Catholicism . . . The delight in reading Wills is found not only in the logic and phrasing of his arguments, but in the fact that he can pack more information into a few sentences than most writers put into whole chapters." — *Milwaukee Journal Sentinel*

"His loveliest writing and deepest thinking." — *Detroit News / Free Press*

"Eminently readable for anyone who has ever struggled with faith or even personal philosophy . . . Wills grapples with his old demon, the question of what constitutes reality, finds new meaning to replace childhood 'superstition,' discovers deeper layers of divinity in the everyday." — *Kansas City Star*

"Fascinating." — *Chicago Sun-Times*

WHY I AM A
CATHOLIC

GARRY WILLS

A MARINER BOOK
HOUGHTON MIFFLIN COMPANY
BOSTON • NEW YORK

First Mariner Books edition 2003

Copyright © 2002 by Garry Wills

Introduction to the Mariner Edition copyright © 2003 by Garry Wills
ALL RIGHTS RESERVED

For information about permission to reproduce selections from
this book, write to Permissions, Houghton Mifflin Company,
215 Park Avenue South, New York, New York 10003.

Visit our Web site: www.houghtonmifflinbooks.com.

Library of Congress Cataloging-in-Publication Data
is available.

ISBN 0-618-13429-8
ISBN 0-618-38048-5 (pbk.)

Printed in the United States of America

Book design by Robert Overholtzer

QUM 10 9 8 7 6 5 4 3 2 1

Excerpts from the poetry of G. K. Chesterton are reprinted with
the permission of A. P. Watt Ltd. on behalf of the Royal Literary Fund.

TO ANNE O'CONNOR
(*Sister John Joseph*)

CONTENTS

KEY TO BRIEF CITATIONS

ABD   *The Anchor Bible Dictionary,* edited by David Noel Freedman (Doubleday, 1992)

AAS   *Acta Apostolicae Sedis* (Typis Polyglottis Vaticanis, 1909–)

ASS   *Acta Sanctae Sedis* (Typis Polyglottis Vaticanis, 1865–1908)

F   W.H.C. Frend, *The Rise of Christianity* (Fortress Press, 1984)

H   Judith Herrin, *The Formation of Christendom* (Princeton University Press, 1987)

K   J.N.D. Kelly, *The Oxford Dictionary of Popes* (Oxford University Press, 1986)

M   Colin Morris, *The Papal Monarchy: The Western Church from 1050 to 1250* (Oxford University Press, 1989)

P   Peter Partner, *The Lands of Saint Peter: The Papal State in the Middle Ages and the Early Renaissance* (Methuen, 1972)

PL   Jacques-Paul Migne, *Patrologia Latina* (Paris, 1857–1867)

S   Klaus Schatz, S.J., *Papal Primacy, From Its Origins to the Present,* translated by John A. Otto and Linda Maloney (Liturgical Press, 1996)

Sch   Bernhard Schimmelpfennig, *The Papacy,* translated by James Sievert (Columbia University Press, 1992)

Unless otherwise specified, translations are by the author.

INTRODUCTION TO
THE MARINER EDITION

SOME WHO have read this book *still* ask why I am a Catholic. They must have a stereotypical view of what Catholics are, and I do not fit it. But neither do most Catholics. By large majorities they, too, differ from the pope on such things as contraception, married priests, women priests. They do not consider themselves non-Catholics, and neither do their priests.

But if I must spell out my loyalties in the most basic terms, I shall. I cannot leave the church because I would consider that a sin — a sin against the three theological virtues, a sin against faith, a sin against charity, a sin against hope.

It would be a sin against faith, because I would be saying that if the pope is wrong the church is wrong, and I must leave it. But I do not believe that the pope is the church. I never have, and neither have most Catholics through the ages. Neither did the Second Vatican Council. To act as if that were my belief would be a sin against my true belief in the church.

It would be a sin against charity, because I would be leaving my brothers and sisters in Christ. I have never had a religious belief, thought, or experience that did not come to me through the church. It has been the channel of every grace I have received. I have been formed and upheld by loving priests and nuns, by believing grandparents, parents, teachers, and friends. Why would I leave them? If the church is in difficulties now, that is a special reason for not leaving. And, as I say, most Catholics have the same difficulties with some current papal teachings that I have. We are in solidarity. To ignore that solidarity would be an affront to charity, to love for my fellow members of the body of Christ.

It would be a sin against hope, because I hope to be in communion with other Christians — Episcopalians, Lutherans, Eastern Orthodox, and others. The Second Vatican Council said that all baptized Christians are members of the mystical body of Christ. But I do not want to choose some other church as an individual, shopping around, saying this one is better than that, that my own is not a true church but some other is. That *would* be a "cafeteria" approach to religion. I hope to join with other Christians by the movement of my church as a whole. That has never been more possible than now, never since the Reformation. Pope Paul VI set up a process by which Catholic theologians worked out with Lutherans a joint statement on justification. It settled all the basic differences in theology that were at stake in the sixteenth century. Both sides admitted false emphases on their own side, true ones on the other side.

Joint ceremonies, studies, and activities go on at many levels between all the Christian churches now. There are no longer Protestant Bible scholars and Catholic ones. All who are any good are simply Bible scholars. There is a growing realization that the real scandal of Christianity has been the way Queen Elizabeth executed Jesuits and Queen Mary executed Protestants, or Catholics killed Huguenots, Calvinists killed Catholics. American Congregationalists hanged Quakers and American Protestants burned convents. See how these Christians kill one another. The prime task facing Christian churches, if they are to be truly Christian, is to find the Christ in each other. Most Christians now realize that. They are yearning for reunion, and even this pope has made many fine gestures in that direction.

But there, many say, is the rub: the pope. The papacy is what stands in the way. Other churches honor Saint Peter as first of the apostles, and there is no more obvious central point for a united Christianity than the site of Peter's execution. But Protestants, no matter how they revere Saint Peter, know that he was not the bishop of Rome (there was no such office at the time). They know as well that there has been no unilinear descent of popes from that non-existent office. (On two occasions there were three contending popes, and all were deposed. In one case, an emperor started the new line, in the other, a council did.)

The ecumenical problem is typified by Cardinal Ratzinger's decree that Anglican orders are not valid since their hierarchy does not branch from the papal descent. For once, Cardinal Ratzinger reminds me of the apostle John — but in one of John's less admirable moments:

> John said to him, "Teacher, we saw a man expelling demons in your name, but we stopped him, since he was not one of us." Jesus answered: "By no means stop him. No one who exercises power in my name can go on to speak ill of me. Whoever is with us is for us. Anyone who gives you a drink of water in my name, because you follow me, I tell you that person will not miss his reward."
>
> (Mark 9.38–41)

Anglicans have given far more than a cup of water in Christ's name. And their church is apostolic in the only sense that it had in the first centuries of Christian history, that it teaches what the six apostolic churches were agreed upon. It adheres to the early councils and creeds.

Papal infallibility would, indeed, seem an insurmountable obstacle — but for the fact that it is a religious irrelevancy. No Catholic belief or action is based on papal infallibility. There never was such a thing until 1870, when the First Vatican Council declared the pope infallible under certain conditions. John Henry Newman said then that it was a power too unwieldy to be used, and that has proved true. It has been used only once, to declare what the church already believed without that pronouncement. There were churches, Masses, liturgies, and artworks dedicated to the belief that the Virgin Mary was bodily assumed into heaven. It was celebrated in the fourth decade of the rosary all Catholics had prayed. The pope's addition of his own endorsement to this accepted belief made no real difference to the life of the church.

Why, then, all the attention given to papal infallibility? It is a red herring, brought up to stymie good relations between Christians. Among the conditions under which the council set for its exercise was this, that the pope can only exercise "that infallibility with which the divine Redeemer willed that his church should be endowed." Anything he might say beyond that is invalid. So understood, the papacy need pose no obstacle to reunion. All Christians can believe that anything anybody does is true to the gospel if it is only what Christ wished for his whole church. That is why the power has not been used beyond what the church had already accepted.

Papal infallibility is never more a red herring than when it is brought up in connection with things like abortion or birth control.

The Vatican itself says that the sanction against these is "natural law." That is all it can appeal to, since there is nothing about those subjects in Scripture, the creeds, the councils. They are not in the deposit of revealed truths. But if they are a matter of natural law, their truth should be accessible to natural reason, given good information and good faith. But people of good will and fine intelligence do not see the truth that Rome wants them to see. So, abandoning persuasion by natural reason, Cardinal Ratzinger says that papal pronouncements on the matter, though not technically infallible, are "irreversible." He has tried to create an "almost" infallibility. Vatican I set explicit standards for infallible definition so that there could be no more a quasi-infallibility than a quasi-pregnancy.

Most Catholics, as I say, agree with this. Not for the first time in history, the hierarchy has lagged behind the body of the faithful. Newman instanced the fidelity of the faithful in the fourth century, when most of the hierarchy, including Pope Liberius, defected to the Arians. The lag has always been corrected, and it will be again. Soon.

WHY I AM A
CATHOLIC

INTRODUCTION

THIS BOOK is an unintended sequel to my *Papal Sin* (2000) — unintended because I thought that book treated a narrowly defined and self-enclosed topic, the papacy's dishonesty in its recent (anti-modern) era. Some read the book as something else, which they indicated by changing the title, from *Papal Sin* to *Papal Sins* — as if I were covering the whole subject of papal misbehavior over the centuries. It is true that I dealt with a number of disparate things — from papal treatment of Jews to claims of priestly prerogative, from documents on gays to condemnations of artificial insemination. But these were brought up not for consideration in themselves, only for the way dishonesty was used, in recent times, to defend whatever papal position was involved. Some Catholics asked why I was exposing the church's "dirty linen," though I did not mention anything that had not been fully ventilated in public. The newspapers had been full of controversy over pedophile priests, or papal relations with Jews, or the dissent of Catholic women and gays. Those were all out in the open. I revealed nothing about them — in fact, some conservative critics of my book dismissed it as containing "nothing new."

What was, if not new, then somewhat different, was my argument that these matters should not be considered in isolation, as if exhibiting different vices within the hierarchy — its anti-Semitism, or anti-feminism, or homophobia, or even a secret sympathy with pedophilia. I do not believe the modern papacy is afflicted with these attitudes. There has, on the contrary, been a sincere reaching out to Jews and women and gays — but all these gestures have been checked or rendered abortive by a continuing nervous insistence that "the church" (by which these apologists mean the papacy) never really taught anything erroneous about these people. That is a claim that can be made only with the help of tendentious readings of history, suppression of evidence, or distortion of the evidence.

These maneuvers are justified — by those who think they must shoulder, all alone, the Spirit's role of protecting the church — as necessary measures to protect the mission of Christ. One of the most common objections to the book was the "everybody does it" argument — that is, leaders of every kind have to protect their organizations by stretching or evading or denying the exact truth about it. Those making this defense are the ones who do not really believe in the church, who think it can survive only by acting like any other political body. Admittedly, the rationale for such protective attitudes is different with church rulers — but only in the sense that they are protecting something more important than any mere earthly authority. This makes playing fast and loose with the truth more rather than less justifiable in their eyes. Anyone who doubts that this is the attitude should consider the long and energetic efforts of the hierarchy to cover up cases of priestly pedophilia. Abusing young innocence is not only a crime but a particularly vile crime, and covering it up is a crime added to a crime. Are the church authorities who did this moral monsters? What can have been their motive? They reasoned this way: since the saving truth of the gospel will reach more souls in need of it if they feel that priests bringing it to them are holy, it is necessary — for the good of souls and the honor of God — to maintain the priestly aura with deception. That is: the truth must be served with lies. There can even be a certain moral pride in the sacrifice of one's own repugnance to the crime, a sacrifice in service to the higher good of the corporate body. The Holy Spirit must appreciate this aid brought to the cause.

Any other explanation for their behavior, I submit, does them an injustice. They *thought* they were doing the right thing — naturally, since covering up the truth is such an ingrained habit with them. I was often asked, about my book, "Do you really think the pope and the pope's men deliberately lie?" Not quite. That is why the book's subtitle is *Structures of Deceit*. Given the priority of protecting the divine aura, and the terrible consequences of allowing it to be tarnished, the authorities do not allow the separate issue of truthfulness to distract them from the exigencies of their task. It is a luxury forgone, kept out of view, to be postponed while they meet immediate emergencies.

My book traced the same attitude in other and less lurid suppressions of the truth. I did not claim, for instance, that Pius XII sympathized with Nazism; I do not think he did. I expressly stipulated that he might have had a justifiable fear that action on his part would hurt those it meant to help. I focused instead on his post-war claim that he had *not* been silent, that he had spoken out "several times" against the Holocaust. That was dishonest. That came within the scope of my book. (Some of his defenders find themselves in the odd position of saying that his silence was justified but that he did not, in fact, keep silent. If silence was justified, after all, he *should* have maintained it.)

In the same way, I did not deny that the priesthood is a legitimate development in the history of the church; I said only that Paul VI was wrong when *he* denied that it was a development, claiming that it was instituted during Christ's lifetime. Similarly, on the subject of priestly celibacy, Pope Paul relied on a fundamentalist reading of Matthew 19.11–12, which speaks of eunuchizing oneself, though he does not read in a fundamentalist way a similar passage like that recommending that one tear out an eye or cut off a hand (Mt 5.29–30). It was dishonest for the same pope to write a lengthy encyclical on celibacy while suppressing the most relevant text (1 Cor 9.5). It was what I called "intellectually contemptible" for the Vatican's Congregation for the Doctrine of the Faith to say women cannot be ordained because they do not *look like* Jesus (*Inter insigniores* 27).

I did not deny that there is a justification for the papacy — how could I, since I was praising John XXIII? I criticized a Curia that claims the papacy was *not* a development, that it was instituted in the New Testament, finding its first expression in Peter's (non-existent) role as Rome's first bishop. Strange to say, I was criticized as a fundamentalist when I pointed out that this fundamentalist argument is invalid. That did not mean, and I have never said, that there is no defense of the papacy. But that was not my book's topic. Dishonesty was.

I did not anticipate, though I should have, that people would write me, in large numbers, sincerely asking what *would* be a valid defense of the papacy. How does one remain a Catholic while criticizing some of the church's authority figures? I have never received mail of this kind or quantity in my forty years of writing. Most people who wrote me in the past were upset or outraged at something I had published. Those who agree with you just nod, most often, in silent agreement and move on; they have no need to vent their feeling. But in this case the overwhelming number — over ninety percent — of letters and calls and comments began or ended with a thank-you for expressing what the correspondents felt, for letting them know they are not alone or that their own views could be expressed. These correspondents included priests and nuns who welcomed the call for candor in the church. That made all the more compelling some requests that I expand my book's closing comments on what positive things the church does or can do. What, they asked explicitly or implicitly, are the grounds of my own hope? Why am I still a Catholic? This I took as their way of exploring why they remain in the church. They were asking to compare notes.

Naturally, there were negative reactions to the book — in some cases, extremely negative. These differed from the first and larger group of responses in many ways. For one thing, the writers expressing gratitude proved by their questions that they had read the book. But some of the angriest letters I got admitted that the writer had not read my book, only some review of it in a conservative publication on the Internet or elsewhere. (I had not realized there are so many right-wing Catholic organs, ones I had never heard of, nor had Catholic friends I asked about them.) The first group asked how I stayed in the church. The second asked why I did not leave. Those writing out of gratitude assumed that I shared their (sometimes baffled) love of the church. The accusatory group flatly informed me that I hate the church, that I stay in it only to harm it, that I should get out before I do it irreparable damage. (Despite their belief in the church's divine mandate, these people express a great anxiety over its fragility — another attitude that makes shoring up the church with any material, even lies, seem justified.) So this group, too, asked, why I am still a Catholic, but in a different tone of voice. They meant, "Why are you keeping up this pose?"

A third body of responses to the book was neither as approving nor as disapproving as the first two. This was made up of non-Catholics (and some ex-Catholics) who were puzzled or bemused by the book, and by responses to it. On the one hand, they assumed that Catholics cannot "get away with" criticism of church authorities, and wondered why I had not been expelled. Non-Catholics are more certain that the church is authoritarian than Catholics are. Since they do not believe that the church is the people of God, and not simply the pope, they equate criticism of the part with condemnation of the whole. On the other hand, they wondered why I bother arguing about the church, which is for them an irrelevancy, though an interesting one. These secular observers treated me as an anomaly, to be explained each in his preferred way. Martin Gardner in the *Los Angeles Times* said that I do not seem entirely nutty — I probably do not really believe, for instance, that a whale swallowed Jonah — so I must not be a Catholic after all. Richard Rorty in the *New York Times* thought I was right to criticize dishonesty in church leaders but wrong to expect anything else — if the church tried to tell the truth, he said, it would perish. Falsehood is its necessary foundation. They too had a different tone of voice in asking why I am still a Catholic. They meant, "How can anyone not clearly a nut remain there?"

Of course I do not believe that one has to be nutty in order to be a Catholic (though there are nutty Catholics, just as there are nutty secularists). Nor do I think church leaders must lie in order to keep their organization afloat (some have actually told the truth, and it made the bark more seaworthy). But it seems unlikely I will convince those who are sure that the Catholic church cannot be taken seriously. I will mainly address, therefore, those in the first two groups, those who do take the church seriously but wonder how I can still take it seriously after having criticized its leadership so pointedly.

When I was growing up, saying why one was a Catholic would not have focused so much on one's attitude toward the papacy. For Catholics in the middle of the twentieth century, the pope was a revered figure, but a distant one. We wondered why people like Paul Blanshard made so much of him, why Protestants and Others United for the Separation of Church and State were so sure that we followed his marching orders for the subversion of democracy. Actually, we didn't know much about the positions alleged against him. Our piety had other bases. But now the pope is a celebrity who has been given vast media coverage, especially when he visits our shores (something unthinkable when I was a child). Pope John XXIII's Second Vatican Council made Roman church politics a hot topic that literate people discussed — adverting, for instance, to the long *New Yorker* dispatches from the council. Papal attitudes came under a new degree of scrutiny — attitudes toward other hot topics, like women and sex. The church's historical relationship with Jews has become particularly contentious. And the pope is at the center of these debates. Vatican II was supposed to diffuse authority in the church, making it more collegial, a thing shared by the whole body of bishops. But John Paul II has been more the center of action than any pope of the modern era, thanks to his charm, intelligence, and energy — and thanks to the uncompromising stand he has taken on issue after issue. He is an intriguing combination of personal popularity in service to unpopular positions. He is un-ignorable.

I cannot go back to the era when the pope could be, if not ignored, at least not made so much of. I am not a Catholic because of the pope. I am a Catholic because of the creed. I believe in that, and it does not mention the pope. In fact, it was formulated before there was a pope — but even to say that involves one in long arguments on the history of the papacy. Some have asked, Why not just keep the creed but forget the pope? Why not go to the Episcopal or Lutheran church, or join Eastern Orthodox Christians? But the pope is one of the reasons I stay, not a reason for going. I continually read the New Testament, after all, so wherever I find Christ, I expect to find Peter close to him. But the Apostle's relationship to his savior, always close, is never quite the same from era to era, and its current form will no more be its permanent one than were any of the earlier embodiments. There have been many papacies, and reaching a reasoned relationship with the current one entails taking a long hard look at the history of the institution. It also means learning that no Christian church is perfect — not even the Episcopal or Lutheran or Orthodox. We flawed believers live with our flawed fellow believers, even with flawed brothers like the pope.

I feel a bit uncomfortable making this book so personal. The church is a big thing; it will survive; it does not need my small testimony. But the questions addressed to me were uncommonly personal. They make me think that I am speaking for the first group of people, who remain in the church despite their own criticisms of the papacy, against the charges of the second and third groups. If I am a false Catholic, an insincere or a nutty one, then so are they. If I am told to "get out," or to "wise up," then so are my fellow troubled believers. Troubled belief is not disbelief, though "true believers" take it for that. I began, like all born Catholics, with serene certitudes instilled in me by my family and teachers. But those cannot be sustained without change while the believer grows up. An unexamined faith is not a faith. It is a superstition. The process of questioning one's faith is one that I have undergone with many, if not most, believers, most certainly with the ones who said they shared my critical attitude toward the pope without losing their fundamental commitment to the church. Though I may not always be speaking for them, I think my own development as a Catholic is not peculiar to me but analogous to their experience. I am not a special case, but in many ways a typical one.

I begin, then, with my own experience of growing up Catholic. Critics of *Papal Sin* told me (and others) that I was expressing hatred for the church, reflecting no doubt some bitter experience with it, some resentment at what it did to me, some rebellion against what it asked of me. In fact, my experience with the church has been of a supporting and nurturing body, and I have never felt closer to it than I do now. I benefited from marvelous teachers, who taught me to question, and from a supportive family that was not disturbed by such questioning. I describe that world in this book's first part, establishing a background to answering the question, Why am I still a Catholic?

But it is only a background. Eventually, given the salience of the modern papacy, and the urgency of the many contentious issues it has addressed, my faith had to come to terms with the complex reality of the church's hierarchy. This leads to a long excursus on the history of Peter as a Gospel symbol, of the pope in the church (the first millennium of Catholicism) and of the pope above the church (the history of the second millennium) and of the church revitalizing the papacy (our modern condition). This excursus — a long one, but necessary for addressing the issue of the papacy as a historical (not just a dogmatic) reality — fills Parts II through IV of the book. Only when I have suggested how the creed can be integrated with acceptance of the papacy do I reach (in Part V) the real object of my belief, the creed. *That*, after all, is why I am a Catholic.

I

BORN CATHOLIC

In 1928, when Al Smith became the first Catholic to run for president of the United States, he was asked about certain anti-democratic statements in papal documents. He said he had never heard of the documents. Neither had most American Catholics. We thought our duty to the pope was discharged when we learned the catechism and donated to the annual "Peter's Pence" drive for the Vatican. The pope was not a daily presence in our lives. Pius XII was as much the pope for my generation as F.D.R. was the president. But I knew more and cared more for F.D.R. than for Pius XII. I presume there was a picture of Pius on our school wall, though I presume rather than remember it.

Roosevelt, who took office two years before I was born and served thirteen years, was part of my mental iconography all through World War II, when my father was in the army and my schoolmates and I were fighting the war in our games, very much aware that Roosevelt was leading the war effort. Pius, who became pope five years after I was born and held that office for nineteen years, never had the same claim on my imagination or that of my friends. Catholicism for us meant the local church and school, priests and nuns.

There seemed to be a good feeling about Catholic culture in America, reflected in the movies, which was undisturbed by disputes over the pope — a feeling true to our own sense of the situation, even though it was sentimentally commercialized. Nuns were played by the likes of Ingrid Bergman, Loretta Young, Celeste Holm, and Alida Valli. The priests were Barry Fitzgerald, Bing Crosby, Spencer Tracy, Frank Sinatra, and Montgomery Clift. The TV face of Catholicism was Fulton Sheen, complete with an angel as the eraser-boy for his blackboard. One of the few disso-

nant notes was struck by Mary McCarthy in Memories of a Catholic Girlhood, *and that book had little to do with the institutional church, for the simple reason that McCarthy had had little to do with the institutional church.*

In the 1960s, this saccharine view yielded to new memories of Catholic childhood, memories peopled with coercive nuns and creepy priests, not a single Bing Crosby type among them. Though I could see the sappiness of the old view, the new one did not reflect my own background. In 1964, while the Second Vatican Council was still in session, I was asked to contribute to an early volume of these souring recollections, The Generation of the Third Eye, *edited by Daniel Callahan, but I had to confess that I had no life-darkening experiences to provide. The only nun I mentioned was the one to whom this book is dedicated, Anne O'Connor, who was still reading my writings then, just as she had when I was in the eighth grade, and as she continued to do till her death thirty years later.*

Though I had encountered some less than admirable priests in my constant exposure to the church, I found fewer outright scoundrels there than I would later meet in the worlds of business and the academy and journalism. I could see the false note of forced jollity in The Bells of Saint Mary's, *but the Saint Mary's I attended as a grade school student had done me nothing but good. I learned to be critical of my Catholic training, in large part because of that Catholic training; but this never made me believe less in the church. It always was, and still is, a flawed carrier of the truths of the faith — nonetheless, it carries them. That is what makes it the church on earth and not a paradise that will need no church.*

1

Saint Mary's and Campion

THERE IS something eerie about having total strangers describe to you the inmost recesses of your soul. I opened letter after letter explaining to me in some detail why I hated my church, had it in for the Blessed Virgin, and dismissed the Holy Spirit. This was news to me, and would be to Catholics who know me, including the many nuns and priests who have been guides and helpers all my life. I am a born Catholic. I have never stopped going to Mass, saying the rosary, studying the Gospels. I have never even considered leaving the church. I would lose my faith in God before losing my faith in it. In fact, the closest I have come to disbelief in God was when I was deepest in the social coils of the church, as a seminarian studying to be a priest. Before that, my upbringing had made me as little questioning as most of the Catholics around me in the 1940s.

I had no reason to doubt the good will and piety of those who cared for me. It was the Catholic part of my life — the Irish Catholic side of the family — that was most supportive and stimulating. My younger sister and I much preferred our mother's parents, Con and Rose Collins of Atlanta, to our father's parents, Garry and Ginny Wills of Oak Park. The Willses were originally Episcopalians from Norfolk, but Garry was an agnostic and Ginny had become a Christian Scientist by the time we knew them. When our grandmother Wills babysat us, during our parents' absence, she tried very hard to improve us — our manners, our diction, our reading habits (out with the comic books). She loved us, I suppose, but in a cold and fussy way, a kind of love we found it hard to reciprocate.

The Irish side, by contrast, was all love and little improving. The

Collinses had their faults, some recognized (the drink), some not (the racism), but they made children feel instantly at home. They had thick Southern accents (my mother's returned when she went back home), outgoing ways, and an unpretentious but omnipresent piety. Their house contained a large statue of the Sacred Heart that awed us, and many pictures of the Virgin. In Lent and on holy days we knelt down and said the rosary together. It was a Catholic home, even in stereotypical ways. It held a large family — Rose had eight difficult childbirths, though four of the babies were either stillborn or died soon after delivery. Only one boy lived, Bernard. He entered a Jesuit college (Spring Hill) but had to withdraw almost at once, since Con lost his job during the Depression. Of the three sisters, only the youngest, Anne, finished high school, since the Depression was over by the time she reached her teens. The extended family on both the Collins and the Driscoll side was thick with priests, who dropped in for some of Rose's wonderful cooking, making friendly priests a part of my social world from the outset. When at Christmas or Thanksgiving we visited Atlanta — or later, when the Collinses moved there, Louisville — the house was webbed with aromas from Rose's kitchen, and there were more people than beds. My sister and I slept on the floor — we thought that a great adventure. The Wills home seemed sterile by contrast, full of boring classical music and of objets d'art we could not touch (Ginny was an amateur artist of some talent).

Though my father, Jack, was not a Catholic (he became one after we had grown up), he honored the pledge he took to raise his children in the church, so our mother, Mayno, brought us up in the atmosphere of the Collinses. After my birth in Atlanta, my father had to travel north looking for work in the Depression — first to Fort Wayne, then to Beloit (where my sister was born), then on to Albion, Michigan, and finally to Adrian, Michigan (just across the Ohio border from Toledo). In Albion, my parents ran a boardinghouse on the edge of Albion College, renting rooms to college boys. I was two at the time, and in the boarders I had a house full of big brothers who taught me to tie my shoes, throw a ball, and be a lure for neighborhood girls who came to gush over me and flirt with them. My mother was not happy at the fact that Albion had no Catholic grade school; but by the time for me to enter first grade we had moved to Adrian, which had a very good school (Saint Mary's), run by Dominican sisters whose mother house (Siena Heights) is in Adrian.

I was lucky to have a teacher there who remained a lifelong friend. She had been born on Bastille Day in Augusta, Georgia, and baptized Marie Antoinette in honor of the day — she went by the second name, but shortened it to the less pretentious Anne. Her father, John Joseph O'Connor, was a graduate of the Jesuit college at Spring Hill (the same one my uncle attended briefly), and she had worked for the Willys-Overland car company in Toledo before entering the convent in Adrian. In honor of her father she took as her religious name Sister John Joseph (we kids called her Johnny-Joe behind her back). She was in her thirties when she taught me. In her fifties, when she had resumed her own name, she became the provincial superior of her order in California, and she had to steer women's colleges through the stormy sixties, which she did with a wise flexibility.

Most of my childhood memories revolve around the Adrian parish of Saint Mary's and the school attached to it. I later tried to re-create my days there in an essay, "Memories of Catholic Boyhood," which I included in my book *Bare Ruined Choirs*. It was an exercise in nostalgia that obviously spoke to many who had shared my experience, since I have had more requests to reprint it, or get copies of it, than for anything else I have written. Some excerpts will give a sense of the upbringing I am trying to describe now. Of going to pre-school Mass on a weekday, I wrote:

We came, in winter, out of the dark into vestibule semidark, where peeled-off galoshes spread a slush across the floor. We took off gloves and scarves, hands still too cold to dip them in the holy water font. Already the children's tin lunch boxes, left to steam on the bare radiator, emanated smells of painted metal, of heated bananas, of bologna and mayonnaise . . . Girls without hats hair-pinned Kleenex to their heads — it fluttered as they strode to the communion rail, like a raffish dove ill-perched on each sharer in the mystery . . . Scapulars like big postage stamps glued here and there on kids in swimming pools. JMJ [for Jesus Mary Joseph] at the top of schoolwork. The sign of the cross before a foul shot. Fishing pennies and dimes out of pockets pebbled with the fifty-nine beads and assorted medallions of a rosary . . . Nuns who moved in their long habits with stately calm, like statues rocking. The deferential "ster" pinned to all sentences ("Yester" for "Yes, Sister") . . . Holy cards of saints with eyes so strenuously upturned as to be almost all white. The Infant of Prague bulkily packaged in "real" clothes. The sight, in darkened churches, of a shadowy Virgin with hands held palm-out at the level of her hips, plaster cape flowing down from those hands toward blue votive lights unsteady under her like troubled water. Sand under the votive candles for putting out tapers; and a box of large kitchen matches, for lighting tapers, stuck into the sand. The momentary waxen strangle of St. Blaise day, as crossed candles bless one's throat.

I concluded, fondly: "It was a ghetto, but not a bad ghetto to grow up in."

Beneath this weave of churchy incense at the school, there was a strict discipline supporting good teachers who stressed the basics. Grammar was instilled by endless outlining of sentences. Rhetoric was shaped by giving rhythmic breakdowns of the same sentences. In a way, this system worked almost too well with me. When, at age ten, I had to transfer to a public school, I was so far ahead of those who missed this kind of drill that another of my very good teachers, Mildred Byfuss (later Mrs. Duckworth), pitied my boredom in class (and countered my tendency to fool around for lack of other occupation), telling me to go to the school library and read books she suggested to keep me busy. Teachers, I suppose, could not get away with that today.

Though I loved to read, I missed the nuns — I was back in Albion, where, since there was still no Catholic school, we were sent to Saturday catechism classes taught by laymen. My father had been drafted, despite his two children, for the final stages of World War II. This meant he could no longer commute from his Adrian job (selling gas appliances) to maintain the boardinghouse in Albion. So my parents rented the house in Adrian, and my mother moved back to Albion, where, helped by her sister, she could look after the boardinghouse. I acquired again that protective huddle of older brothers from the college, who now rode me around on the handlebars of their bikes and let me play catch with them on the college campus, just across the street from our house. (These days, I suppose, my mother would be criticized for letting the college boys give me rides without a helmet.) I had older friends than those I was going to school with — an arrangement that was repeated, in a milder way, when Miss Byfuss persuaded my mother to let me skip sixth grade.

But when we returned to Adrian, after a year, the private reading Miss Byfuss had directed put me ahead of my fellow students at Saint Mary's, and Sister John Joseph said I should skip another grade. My parents, rightly opposed to my getting too far out of my age group, said no to this. She then recommended that I go to a more demanding school. She idolized her older brother, who was a Jesuit priest, so she suggested that I be sent to a Jesuit boarding school, Campion, in Prairie du Chien, Wisconsin. I began my freshman year there in 1947.

Campion

The Dominican nuns, who had treated me well, sent me on to the Jesuits, who were even better to me. For one thing, they dispelled any notion I might have that I was precocious. At Campion there were many people as smart as I or smarter, and I was privileged to have a number of them as friends. Some who went on to distinguished careers are Joe Schorck as a classical scholar, Bill Birdsall as an economist at the University of Michigan, Greg Lucey as a university president, Bob Baker in the CIA, Lewis Ellingham as a poet. We were given an anachronistic education in humane letters, part of the Jesuits' already-fading Renaissance traditions. Those of us in the honors program had four years of Latin and two years of Greek. We were back to outlining sentences, but in two new languages. There was great emphasis on memorizing, elocution, and debate. We were among the last to have this kind of training, since the key factor in it — Jesuit "scholastics" — has now disappeared. Scholastics were Jesuit seminarians who interrupted, after the seventh year, their thirteen-year preparation for ordination to the priesthood. They were given time out to teach for three years in a Jesuit high school. Now there are too few Jesuit seminarians to sustain such a system, and the training of those who still exist has been shortened or altered to meet other needs, making the hiatus for high school teaching a rare exception instead of a regular part of the training. But while that system lasted, it was a great way to inspire and test adolescent boys.

The scholastics — men still in their twenties, immersed in studies they enjoyed, highly motivated, many of them athletic enough to play with us (and beat us at will) in sports — made ideal teachers. They were not only bright and hardworking in the regular classes. They had energy left over to run informal seminars on things like music appreciation, or to conduct reading groups, or to give extra-credit courses in everything from theater to theology. They got us interested in new books as well as old. When the article on which Evelyn Waugh based *The Loved One* ran in a special edition of *Life,* the scholastics quickly passed it around to each other and to those of us they thought would like it. Almost all my later interests — in Greek drama, in the New Testament, in Shakespeare, in opera, in movies, in authors like Newman and Ruskin and Chesterton — were initiated or accelerated by my four years at Campion.

I didn't love everything about Campion. Compulsory ROTC courses were taught by military hacks, whose dullness was made more grating by contrast with the scholastics in our regular classrooms. As a freshman, I joined the debate team, whose star was Bill Sullivan, then in his senior year — he would soon enter the Jesuits and became a distinguished theologian (later the president of Seattle College). My first day out for ROTC drill, when I saw Bill Sullivan, my fellow debater, strutting about in an officer's uniform with a silly-looking saber, I snatched the sword and made him run after me to get it back — which he did not think very funny. He didn't think much, either, of my dating his sister Kathy (the Sullivans lived in Prairie du Chien). When I met Kathy as a sophomore, I asked after Bill, who was by then a novice at the Jesuit seminary. She told me she was amused by the way novices addressed each other in Latin as Carissime ("dear fellow"), which they pronounced Criss-Me. Since *Kiss Me, Kate* was still a new show then, I addressed my first letter to her as "Criss-Me Kate." I wrote her on Sundays whenever I could not go into town to see her because I had a "lost weekend."

That was another problem for me at Campion — its system of "jugs" and "lost weekends." A jug punished minor infractions by depriving the culprit of recreation time, consigning him instead to the memorization of long poems, which he must recite in order to be released. (I still remember scraps of those many verses.) A certain number of jugs within a week led to a lost weekend — in which all one's recreation time on Saturday and Sunday (the only days we could go into Prairie du Chien) was spent sitting in a chair in the hallway outside the office of the school's president, Carl Reinert, S.J. I ran up record totals of jugs, often because I had missed daily Mass, for which we were forced to rise at six A.M. I was insomniac in my youth — doctors in those carefree days of pharmacology gave me strange mixtures of medicines for it — so I often ended up, after early lights-out, in the one room lit on each floor, the john, reading in a stall, lifting my legs when anyone entered, in case it was a Jesuit checking the room. Then I would sleep through Mass in the morning. After my jugs reached a certain total, I was expelled from the senior residence hall, where we got private rooms in our fourth year, and sent back to the juniors' dormitory.

That experience led me to a realization that my idolized scholastics were not all "the best and the brightest" men that the church had to offer. There was one genuine psychopath among them — he did not last long, I was later told, but I wondered how he had got that far. He had a grudge against the "honors boys," which he took out in naked hostility. One night he caught me, after my expulsion from the senior residence, roaming its halls after dinner, when the building was out of bounds for all but its inhabitants. He said with manic glee, "Now I really have you." He had been part of my getting expelled in the first place, and I did not know what new penalty he could inflict, but I was undoubtedly obnoxious when I laughed at him and said, "No you don't." I produced a written permission for me to be there preparing for a debate with my partner, Bill Birdsall. The scholastic's face was instantly contorted with pure hate, and he lunged at me. I ran down the stairs to the first floor, out onto the porch and down its stairs, and off across the length of the football field that lay beside the hall. Sheer panic gave me speed, since he was clearly in a murderous mood and he just kept coming. At last I wore him down (he was not one of the athletic Jesuits). It was a bitter winter night, and I had left my coat in Birdsall's room, but I stayed out for as long as I could bear the cold, and then circled the long way back to my dorm, in case he was lying in wait for me (I think he was).

This one exception to the general excellence did not tarnish my view of the scholastics. Nor did I ponder much the difference between these young men and the older Jesuits, already priests, who held administrative and some teaching posts at the school. The energy and curiosity of the seminarians had faded into odd hobbies or rote performance of duty in many of these elders. It is true that the president, Father Reinert, had great vigor, but much of it was expressed in bullying, not only of students but of the scholastics, so we had an unspoken sympathy for each other's plight. I did not know then, but learned later, that the year before I came to Campion, Father Reinert had forced reluctant scholastics, under holy obedience, to become informers on a group of students who protested an unfair example of mass punishment.

My admiration for the scholastics was so common with others that many of us considered joining them in the Jesuit order. Though I had applied and been admitted to Marquette University, in Milwaukee, with a vague notion of becoming a lawyer, I asked what entering the

Jesuit novitiate at Florissant, Missouri, would entail. I was drawn to this inquiry in part because of a book that had been recommended to me, a two-volume life of an Italian controversialist of the Renaissance, Saint (then Blessed) Robert Bellarmine. The book, written in a genial style by the Irish Jesuit James Brodrick, was the first scholarly work I had ever read — by scholarly I mean one working from archives and citing sources in the original tongues (without translation). I could not read the Italian passages, but I wrestled, after my four years of Latin, with the Renaissance language of debate. Father Brodrick made the ideal of consecrating one's intellect to the service of God very appealing — though the book was hagiographical, it was not entirely sicklied over with piety. (Brodrick admitted, in a later and better edition of the work, that he had whitewashed certain aspects of Bellarmine's activities — e.g., his role in the trial of his friend Galileo.)

When I asked about entering the Jesuits, I was given a physical exam. There was no psychological evaluation in those days (there is now), but there was a good deal of questioning about my number of jugs, to decide if they reflected some deep rebelliousness. Apparently it was concluded that they did not, and I said a sad goodbye to Kathy Sullivan, hoping to follow what seemed to me the highest calling I had been exposed to. It was a trial for me when Kathy showed up occasionally to visit her brother, who was farther along in the seminary but still on the same grounds. She later entered the convent of a teaching order of nuns and became a professor of mathematics.

2

Jesuit Days

I WAS NOT the only aspiring Jesuit in my class at Campion. Bill Birdsall and Greg Lucey went with me to Saint Stanislaus, the novitiate house at Florissant, Missouri (just outside St. Louis). Greg Lucey joined and stayed. This was the early 1950s, a high point in the post–World War II religiosity of American culture in general, and an especially flourishing period for Catholics. New seminaries had to be built, old ones expanded. The group who entered with me in the Jesuit province of Missouri exceeded sixty in 1951 (one or two from an equivalent area would be considered a lucky draw today). The retreat that began our life as novices — thirty straight days of silence while we underwent the "Spiritual Exercises" of Saint Ignatius — had to be given, for the first time, in two shifts, to cope with our numbers.

The novitiate was a shock. We had been attracted to the place by the breezy yet serious openness of the scholastics, their respect for things of the mind as well as for the mysteries of the faith. The novitiate of that dark pre–Vatican II era was a determinedly anti-intellectual place, a place where to be intellectual was to be humbled. We kept up the Latin that was one requirement for our entry (and even spoke a mangled version at all times except recreation). But there was no real course of study, not even in the Bible or church history. For a full two years, our reading was to be pious and lachrymose — hagiographical celebrations of submissive saints, especially two vapid young Jesuits who had died during their seminary years, Saint Stanislaus Kostka (after whom the novitiate was named) and Saint Aloysius Gonzaga. Our main reading was a book on European spirituality by a sixteenth-century Spanish Jesuit named Rodriguez, who told stories of miraculous rebukes to worldly figures, worm-eaten hunger artists, and other masters of masochistic asceticism. We were supposed to imitate these antics with "the discipline" (a little whip we used on ourselves after lights-out on prescribed nights) and with prickly chains worn around our waists on prescribed mornings.

We were encouraged to try various "mortifications" on our own, like walking with pebbles in our shoes, or choosing only the foods we liked least at the dining room, or seeing how long we could go without ever lifting our eyes. This regimen had come into the order after its founder's death, as part of a Spanish reaction to the free-wheeling early days of the Jesuits, and it had festered away in secret for centuries. (We were ordered not to tell outsiders, including our parents, about the discipline or the chain — "They will not understand." It was an unnecessary precaution, since we were not anxious to say something that would make us look like nuts.)

How did we, fairly normal American young men of our time, survive the weird two years of this novitiate? Largely by treating it as a joke, a form of hazing to keep the weak out of our mysterious club. We knew the antics had no significant afterlife, since the scholastics we had known survived it. If anything, the infliction of these exercises from an alien culture made it hard for Jesuits, afterwards, to take real asceticism as a serious matter. But though most of us made the nonsense bearable by a kind of gallows humor (discipline jokes were a staple), the whole experience was deeply puzzling to us, and psychologically disturbing to the scrupulous (those who tried to take it all literally, without a saving skepticism). Weeding out these "misfits" was considered a triumph of the system by people like our novice master, Father Gschwend — and was a further indication to the rest of us that it was dangerous to take the spiritual life itself entirely seriously.

I had a special problem. After reading James Brodrick's life of Bellarmine at Campion, I had — while thinking about joining the Jesuits — gone on to Brodrick's two more popular books on the founding of the Jesuits. He documented that Saint Ignatius wanted his order to be adaptable, mobile, responding to the crises of the church — unlike the monastic and mendicant orders of the past. His training of Jesuits lacked any precise timetable or set of uniform requirements. He trained men by a series of "experiments" fitted to each candidate's needs and talents. The "Spiritual Exercises" he had invented were given to an individual by an individual, their suggested four weeks of reflection and resolution lengthened or shortened according to the response of the person going through them. (The pacing of a whole group through a prescribed calendar was not at all what Ignatius had in mind.) Then the candidate was tested by being sent out to tend the sick, make a pilgrimage, teach catechism, or whatever suited his particular situation. There was no single period of a rigidly scheduled novitiate, a policy that has been restored in recent years.

But Ignatius's approach was too unstructured for those among the early Jesuits — especially some Spaniards, like Saint Francis Borgia — who kept trying to reintroduce communal prayer, monastic daily schedules, and dramatic asceticism. Ignatius actually punished, or threatened with expulsion, those who kept trying to alter his vision. He won battle after battle with these forces while he lived, but lost the war after his death to men who created the mentality of our novitiate. Though Brodrick's books were considered too "intellectual" to be part of our novitiate reading (even literate works about Saint Ignatius were excluded), I remembered enough of them to take my problem with the novitiate to Father Gschwend, my assigned confessor. He answered that the wisdom of the order over the ages had perfected this training — who did I think I was to come in and call for changes after brief exposure to it? — and assured me I would come to understand it if I just trusted my superiors and prayed harder. This was a customary way of answering questions by not answering them.

When the assistant novice master, Joseph P. Fisher, S.J., noticed my frustration with the place, he asked what was bothering me. I told him what I had told Gschwend, and Father Fisher tactfully granted that the novitiate was a place where old and outmoded thinking still held sway, though he assured me that later parts of the training would right the balance. That made sense to me as I remembered the scholastics I knew. They had spent five years in the order after leaving the novitiate, and its effects seemed to have worn off. What Fisher could not tell me, but what became obvious in a short time, was that he had been sent to the novitiate in order to start that righting of the balance. He was quietly de-kooking the place. Gschwend's superiors in the order realized that he was driving too many of his charges crazy. By the end of my first year, Gschwend would be out as master and Fisher in. Enough of us perceived the situation to enjoy the way Fisher undermined Gschwend without overt challenge or uncharitable comments about him. We caught on during the building of the swimming pool.

Fisher's effort to return us to something like a young people's normal world included building a swimming pool for escaping Missouri's summer heat. Gschwend was opposed to this, since it would strip novices to the semi-nudity of swimming trunks. (An obsessive fear of homosexuality in the novitiate led to panicky regulations that made some of us, products of pious Catholic homes, aware of homosexuality for the first time.) Fisher said, "No problem *ther*-er" (his favorite saying, delivered with an amused lilt of the voice and a semi-goofy grin). While swimming, he told Gschwend, the novices could be required to wear, above their bathing trunks, T-shirts with half-sleeves. Gschwend reluctantly yielded, so long as that condition were observed. Fisher, who liked manual labor (his father was a carpenter), led novices in digging the pool and laying the concrete, a task rapidly completed. As soon as the pool was in use, Fisher went to Gschwend and said that lint from the T-shirts was clogging the filters, so the T-shirts came off.

Though Fisher took over by the time my second year began, saving institutional face meant that changes could not be made too overtly or rapidly — which might suggest error in what had preceded, and would arouse conservative members of the order, who felt that "coddling" the new men devalued the "boot camp" they had endured. (These, too, were typical of the responses I would find to any changes in the church.) So even when Fisher became our superior, he had to bend the rules gradually, almost by stealth. When I, a compulsive bookworm since grade school, said that I was starving for something more than the dreary books in the small novitiate library, he asked what I would like to be reading. I answered, "Chesterton." When, at Campion, I had read his book on Charles Dickens, it made me plow through the Dickens novels in chronological order (Chesterton liked the early novels best, especially *Pickwick*). His *The Victorian Age in Literature* made me start reading Ruskin. These were still out of bounds, even for Fisher, though he said that some of Chesterton could be counted "spiritual reading" (the only thing allowed us). "No problem there," said Fisher, who also liked Chesterton, and he got *Orthodoxy* and *The Everlasting Man* to me — I almost memorized the two books, for lack of anything equally stimulating within reach. But he told me it would be better not to tell others what I was reading. As my frustrations deepened into depression, Fisher broadened my reading further. His favorite poet was Wordsworth ("definitely a spiritual writer," he assured me). So Wordsworth was included (though I found him boring). Before long we had agreed that Shakespeare is also a spiritual author.

My discontent did not go away, despite the changed atmosphere under Fisher. He contrived to give me, in effect, some vacations from the confining routine by extending my "experiments." A token remnant of the experiments that Ignatius had made central — the observation of applicants in actual conditions of ministry — sent us away from the novitiate, in small groups, to work for several weeks as orderlies in a Catholic hospital, or as house cleaners at a Catholic retreat house. The rule had heretofore been not to send anyone on successive experiments with the same partners, and to assign the partners, not allowing for choice in the matter (to prevent the "particular friendships" that could lead to homosexual liaisons). But Fisher asked me whom I would like to go out with (we were sent in overlapping pairs of two). I answered, "Jack Peradotto," since I found him a breath of sanity in the place; so I went on both my experiments with him. (Jack, a friend now for over half a century, would leave the order at almost the same time I did, to become a classicist, president of the American Philological Association, and founding editor of the journal *Arethusa* — I became his daughter's godfather.)

The experiments, whether in retreat house or hospital, took us off the novitiate grounds and permitted us to do things forbidden there — read newspapers, listen to classical music on the radio, see some television. Besides, we liked the work. Our labor at the retreat house involved making beds and shoveling sidewalks, but we had time to talk with the guests and to join the priests giving the retreats at breakfast, where we saw *The Today Show* for the first time. Our orderly service was in a St. Louis hospital with predominantly black patients. We made beds in the men's wing (there was such a thing in a Catholic institution), gave the men their baths, rubbed on cream to prevent bedsores, and washed the bodies of those who died. But this left us time to talk with the patients, to listen to the gospel music on their radios (Jack, an excellent singer, took to the music at once, though he and I were mainly opera fans).

One of our duties was to say the rosary every night after visiting hours. We knelt on a stair landing between floors, so anyone who wanted to join in could assemble on the floor above or the one below. A devout Protestant patient said he would never do such an idolatrous thing; the plain Bible was good enough for him, not any of this papistical stuff. I argued that the repeated Hail Marys of the rosary were made up, in large part, of gospel verses. The prayer begins "Hail Mary, full of grace, the Lord is with thee," which is simply the angel's greeting at Lk 1.28. And the next sentence of the prayer, "Blessed art thou, and blessed is the fruit of thy womb" is Lk 1.42. Besides, each decade of the rosary is devoted to an episode in Christ's life, offering an occasion to meditate on gospel events. I think the man may have come to one rosary, but I did not convince him. Instead, I convinced myself. The arguments still seem good to me, so I have maintained the lifelong habit of saying the rosary that began in the Collins household in Atlanta. (One of the critics of *Papal Sin*, who kept calling me though she admitted that she had not read the book, sent me a medical prescription container with a "Spiritual Healing" label pasted on it. Inside, instead of pills, it held a little plastic rosary. I suppose she would not believe me if I said it was a dosage I had never slackened.)

Since we quickly got to know all our patients, the only sad part of our service was when one of them died. We had to wash the body before it was moved to the morgue (where we attended one autopsy and never felt tempted to see another). Once, when we had washed a man up, his bowels relaxed further and we had to clean him up all over. No sooner had we done that than the bowels played their trick on us again. To end this cycle, we turned him over on his back, and Jack put both palms flat on his abdomen and pushed till the body was emptied out.

Another experiment did not take me away from the novitiate overnight but only into the town of Florissant, for an hour or two, where we taught catechism to Catholic grade schoolers. Since I had taken piano lessons in grade and high school, I would play tunes while Ted Cunningham, the only black novice in our group, led the children in chanted lyrics from the catechism. We enjoyed this activity so much that later, when we moved into St. Louis for the philosophy stage of our training, Ted and I did something similar on weekends at the hospital where I had been an orderly. Ted told me of the obstacles the order had put in the way of his joining — he was bluntly told that Southerners in the novitiate would resent his presence. I told him I had observed the same attitudes in Atlanta, where my grandmother, saintly in other ways, once walked out of church when a black priest came out of the sanctuary to celebrate Mass. Ted and I became good friends, and when he died (young) after leaving the order, I corresponded with his widow.

Despite the incremental changes Father Fisher was making in the novitiate, I found the place more and more distressing. Though I had considered leaving almost from my first day there, it was alarming when I stopped thinking of that. I now felt that life must be empty no matter where I went to live it. Part of this, I suppose, was the normal moodiness of adolescence, but more acutely it was the morbidity of being isolated with one's thoughts for most of the day and all of the night, feeding on doubts — doubts not only about God's existence (which seemed to me a fond dream) but about the existence of anything (which seemed a pointless dream). The training was meant to separate us from "the world," and it was working so well as to disconnect my mind from the cosmos and make me wonder if it would ever find a thing to reconnect with, or if such a thing existed at all. John Henry Newman, I later learned, thought this was a kind of depression common to those trying to take God seriously and live according to his will:

> Moreover, it is a question whether that strange and painful feeling of unreality, which religious men experience from time to time, when nothing seems true, or good, or right, or profitable, when Faith seems a name, and duty a mockery, and all endeavors to do right, absurd and hopeless, and all things forlorn and dreary, as if religion were wiped out from the world, may not be the direct effect of the temporary obscuration of some master vision, which unconsciously supplies the mind with spiritual life and peace.[1]

There is an autobiographical feel to those weary cadences. But it was Chesterton, not Newman, who came to my rescue in the seminary.

Father Fisher, who was now my confessor, pointed me to specific passages in *Orthodoxy* that seemed to be describing my condition with an eerie exactitude. Chesterton, I would learn, had gone through a solipsistic, even suicidal, period in his own adolescence. One chapter in *Orthodoxy* is called "The Suicide of Thought." As I read it then, Chesterton's breezy public manner did not hide from my morbidly receptive state the private experience from which he wrote it — an experience he described in his *Autobiography:* "I had thought my way back to thought itself. It is a very dreadful thing to do; for it may lead to thinking that there is nothing but thought . . . While dull atheists came and explained that there was nothing but matter, I listened with a sort of calm horror of detachment, suspecting that there was nothing but mind."[2]

Chesterton's path out of this mental cul-de-sac followed what he called the "mystical minimum" of being. If there is nothing but one's own dream of a senseless world, the dream itself exists, and that is an inexplicable miracle. The dream of a void is outside the void. Even if it is a vision of evil, the evil can be there only because it has attached it-self to something good, to existence. Pure evil, since it would be purely destructive, must (in its purity) annihilate itself. I soon learned that Augustine used a similar argument in his struggle to free himself from Manichaeism.

Chesterton, without knowing Augustine's work, echoed his views in an early poem, "The Wild Knight." A poet is trying to convince the her-oine of this mini-melodrama that nature is clean, not terrible, even though a villain named Orm is hounding her.

> This hour
> I see with mortal eyes as in one flash
> The whole divine democracy of things . . .
> Weave we green crowns — how noble and how high,
> Fling we white flowers — how radiant and how pure
> Is he, whoe'er he be, who next shall cross this scrap of grass.
> [Enter Orm][3]

The poet cannot live by his own teaching when faced with Orm; but an ascetic knight, who has been seeking a vision of God, comes on the scene and God at last reveals himself — in Orm. In Chesterton's solip-sistic funk, the mere existence of anything outside his own mind — and especially of any other person, however distant from him — was a reve-lation. One poem tells of a man fleeing about in a hall of mirrors where he can see nothing but himself — till he wakes in a tavern and sees across the tables

> The sight of all my life most full of grace.
> A gin-damned drunkard's wan half-witted face.[4]

In a sense, all of Chesterton's later work grew out of the early intu-ition he called "the mystical minimum." When he tried, for instance, to understand the humility of Saint Francis of Assisi, he did it this way: "It was by this deliberate idea of starting from zero, from the dark nothingness of his own deserts, that he did come to enjoy even earthly things as few people have enjoyed them; and they are in themselves the best working example of the idea. For there is no way in which a man can earn a star or deserve a sunset."[5]

I cannot honestly say how much of this I saw or intuited in Chesterton at the time, and how much I reflected on while reading more of him later. But I saw enough to pull myself out of the depression of my second year in the novitiate — not least because Joe Fisher had the Chestertonian attitude. I got as much of it from him, at that point, as from *Orthodoxy*. This is what he saw in the nature mysticism of Wordsworth. Fisher had a bemused wonder at things, at anything, reflected in the quirky wry smile with which he greeted apparent setbacks. He was balding, but what hair he had would curl up in funny ringlets, like those of Mr. Dick in *David Copperfield*. He loped along with bent knees — his walk needed little exaggeration to turn into a passing imitation of Groucho Marx's. But this almost elfin manner could not hide his extraordinarily disciplined mind. When he had to speak to us as a group, he would come in, take his watch off and put it on the desk, tell us he would take only ten minutes of our time, and then do exactly that, using no notes, leaving no obscurities in what he had to tell us. Yet when you sought him out for advice, he was even better at listening than at speaking. He did not rush you, or give the impression that you were intruding on his timetable. I never heard him raise his voice. I never saw him insult another in his presence or disparage another in his absence. The Wild Knight saw God in Orm. Fisher saw God in Gschwend.

Later, when I had left the seminary, I kept in touch with Fisher as he held higher offices in the order; but he had always wanted to be a missionary in some poor country — less to preach the gospel than to serve the afflicted. When he at last escaped administration and went to Honduras, he began building homes for the poor, returning to the manual labor he saw as a way of carrying on God's creative labor in the world. He wrote me that he could house a large family for only a hundred dollars. I sent him some money, and wrote an appeal for more in several Catholic newspapers, and he was pleased when checks started arriving. I was pleased that at last I could do a little thing for the man who did so much for me. He stayed in Honduras for a decade and a half, returning only as he was about to turn seventy.

If I had any suspicion that I had exaggerated Fisher's qualities in the glow of retrospect, it was removed when I dedicated *Papal Sin* to "Joseph P. Fisher, S.J. — the sanest guide." Jesuits and ex-Jesuits called me or wrote to say that this was the part of the book they liked best, since he had been the sanest guide for them in various crises of their own life. Fisher, who died in 1997, was not the only proof that wise and holy men could transcend the stultifying effects of an outmoded system — I knew and know others — but he is the most stunning proof of that fact. The scholastics at Campion inspired me to enter the seminary. Fisher inspired me to stay there — for a while.

3

Chesterton

THOUGH I HAD RECOVERED, in my second year of the novitiate, from the only time when I have seriously disbelieved in the existence of God (and the existence of everything else, for that matter), the recovery had not settled my attitude toward the seminary. As I said earlier, I had begun to think of leaving almost from the moment I arrived, though I had been distracted from the question while dealing with the more urgent matter of my depression. Now I had to make a decision, since first vows (of poverty, chastity, and obedience) are taken at the end of the second year. These are not the solemn vows sworn later, but they are sufficient to make one canonically "a religious," formally a member of the Society of Jesus (up to then, we had just been applicants). Poverty was not a problem — I had never wanted to own anything but books. But the same could not be said for the other two. Obedience would probably, at certain times, mean obeying people like Gschwend, even at the cost of intellectual integrity.

As for chastity (more properly celibacy), the scholastics I had known seemed to be healthy young men unscarred by their sexual abstinence. They were not prudes about our dates at Campion — one of them even helped smuggle me back onto the grounds after I had gone AWOL to see Kathy Sullivan perform in *The Mikado*. But to the normal sexual desires of youth I had added, in my solipsistic interlude at the novitiate, a great fear of loneliness: I did not know if a Jesuit community could supply the kind of affection and warmth I connected with the Collins home in Atlanta. I voiced these misgivings to Father Fisher, and he took them seriously. But he assured me that it would be easy to get a dispensation from first vows (which are a kind of tryout for the "real" ones) if I found these problems persisting. He thought I should take the vows, in order to sample the next stage of training, which I might find more congenial. So I went ahead. But as we novices knelt in the sanctuary to recite our vows during Mass, Fisher watched me quizzically from the altar as I missed my cue, so absorbed was I in my quandary. The silence around me at last nudged me into a step I was still not certain of.

Fisher was right about the next stage — the juniorate — being more congenial. We were still on the same grounds (in Florissant) with the novitiate, but the atmosphere was entirely different. The world of books opened up. We could listen to music again. Interrupted interests were resumed. From a starvation diet we went to intellectual force-feeding. The effects of this revivifying were what I had observed, without knowing it, in the intellectual enthusiasm of the scholastics at Campion. I was able to go back to serious study of Greek and Latin. I also became absorbed in reading Shakespeare and Shakespeare criticism. I had sped through all his plays (in my marked-up three-volume Readers Library edition) during the summer between junior and senior years at Campion, but that had been a superficial and somewhat mechanical exercise. Now I tried to read in a more serious and systematic way, helped by a good teacher who had us act out scenes from the plays (I was Richard II for the abdication scene). We were encouraged to try out various theatrical exercises, which might stretch our preaching skills. Jack Peradotto was a powerful Samson in a cut-down version we worked out for Milton's *Samson Agonistes* (we had to do without Dalila, of course). Milton gave me a title, down the road, for one of my books, *Nixon Agonistes*.

My enjoyment of this literary immersion does not alter the fact that it made little sense, coming where it did, in training me and my fellows to be priests. One of the sillier Renaissance notions that had persisted in the Society of Jesus was that one should learn subjects in the order of their dignity on a "ladder" of knowledge. So we began with an "infancy" or pre-learning stage of discipline in the novitiate, then went on (in the two years of juniorate) to study humane letters, followed by three years of natural knowledge (the philosophate), at last attaining the level of supernatural knowledge in the crowning three years of the theologate. What this meant is that people who wanted to serve Christ never even seriously studied Scripture, theology, or church history until they had been in the order for ten years, counting time out between philosophy and theology to teach in high school as a scholastic.

It is true that we spent endless hours in prayerful meditation on Gospel events, according to the Ignatian method of the "Spiritual Exercises." In that discipline, you imagine yourself, as vividly as possible, in one particular story told by a Gospel, and then imagine Christ speaking directly to you within that context. This literal, even fundamentalist, reading of the Gospels was natural to Ignatius, in whose time there was no such thing as Scripture scholarship in the modern sense. But to act, in our time, as if such a thing did not exist or did not matter was to separate piety from the intellectual quest for God — a separation that the rest of the training just deepened, and one not entirely bridged by the delayed scriptural studies in the final years of the course. We novices and juniors of the 1950s were not equipped with even the most basic knowledge of the Bible's symbolic systems or its various layers of meaning. A freshman who now takes an introductory course in Bible study at a Catholic university is better equipped than we would be for many years in our course of training as Jesuits.

The evil effects of this approach were far-reaching, though rarely adverted to. The idea that theological knowledge is for specialists only, at the end of long preparation, explains how non-intellectual, when not anti-intellectual, were most sermons, even those preached by the "intellectual" Jesuits. If even the professionals could not be introduced at once to knowledge of the saving truths, how could mere laypeople be expected to understand them? The "ordinary folk" must be content with submissive belief in the mysteries and practical application of them — which reduced sermons to Bible narrative and exemplary anecdotes.

Two further consequences followed. The keepers of the mysteries were led to think of themselves as an elite group of "initiates," who dispensed knowledge on their own authority, not on the basis of convincing explanation. Concomitantly, no layperson could challenge anything about church teachings — he or she did not have the hard-acquired tools for it. The laity must leave these matters to their betters, a position taken by some critics of *Papal Sin*. One sincere fellow who came to one of my book signings asked me how I could criticize people in Rome who have far more extensive theological libraries at their disposal than I do. I was reminded of President Lyndon Johnson, telling

Americans that if we knew all the arcane things he read in classified documents, we would realize that the Vietnam War was a wise venture — but unfortunately we could not be inducted into the "cleared" priesthood of those who kept such secrets. Publication of the Pentagon Papers revealed, in fact, what Robert McNamara later confessed, that there were no secrets that justified the Vietnam folly. The Nixon administration resisted that publication on national security grounds, but actually to keep the secret that there was no secret.

It dawned on me only gradually that it was odd to sequester theology at the end of a long process meant to instill submission before indulging questions. When it did occur to me, the effect was shattering. The Jesuits had the reputation of being the intellectuals of the church, and in some ways they were, especially in America, where the level of theological knowledge was low throughout the priesthood. But it was clear that there were many forces blunting original thought in this system shackled to stale Renaissance maxims. It seems odd at first, though it makes sense on reflection, that Walter Ong, one of the truly original Jesuits I encountered in my seminary years (by serving as acolyte at his early morning Mass), was a Renaissance scholar — he brushed away the empty maxims with genuine knowledge, which frees the mind instead of binding it. I would find the same thing true of another Jesuit scholar of the Renaissance, whom I came to know after publishing *Papal Sin* — John O'Malley at Fordham. There are, needless to say, many Jesuits I have known and know who have circumvented the worst effects of the system they were trained in. That does not mean that the system itself was not deeply flawed — and fortunately the whole system has been changed since Vatican II.

One of the things I could do in the juniorate was get access to more of Chesterton's work, and especially to Maisie Ward's biography of him. Unsatisfactory as that book is in certain ways, it is full of wonderful quotations from his private letters and early notebooks — which confirmed Fisher's claim that what I had undergone in the novitiate was something like Chesterton's adolescent depression, though his had been more severe, and had led to the brilliance of his escape from it. This continued interest in Chesterton helped me at the next stage of our training, the philosophate, for which we moved from our Florissant isolation to the city campus of St. Louis University.

American Jesuits had brought over from France the "existentialist Thomism" of Etienne Gilson and others. Men like George Klubertanz taught this version of Saint Thomas with a missionary zeal. They were not much interested in the *Summa*'s famous five proofs for the existence of God, which they saw as partial and misleading reflections of the "real" argument for God — Thomas's distinction between *esse* (to-be-ness) and *essentia* (being-a-what). A unicorn has essence but not *esse*. In some theological arguments over, say, evolution, the relation between *what* a primate is and *what* a human is seemed important. Not so, said Klubertanz. What matters is *that* they are (unlike unicorns), and the fact that both *are* is not the same as *what* they are. If so, the unicorn, simply by being a definable thing, would generate its own *esse* from its own *essentia*. Instead, the source of being is outside anything's being-what. The argument from order in the universe, or from causal impact of thing on thing, is a shuffling of essences about in jigsaw patterns. But where they fit does not get to the problem of whether or how they *are* (if they are). Being is a gift, given aside from *what* a thing is, an act of divine will extrinsic to the mere ordering of things once brought into existence.

All this seemed a bit technical to some of my fellows, but it sounded like simple Chesterton to me. The "mystical minimum" of being, present in every stone and worm, is a creative act by which God continually draws everything up out of the abyss of nothingness. Interrupt that act, and the whole cosmos would blink off, like a light bulb when the switch is turned. This approach to God does not find him back in the past, at the origin of things — we are always at the origin of being, present to us as God's continuing act. It does not find him off in the mental future, at the end of a chain of syllogisms or tenuous mental connections. It begins within, by a wonder at the moment-by-moment continuance of one's own being. As Chesterton said, "There is at the back of all our lives an abyss of light, more blinding and unfathomable than any abyss of darkness; and it is the abyss of actuality, of existence, of the fact that things truly are, and that we are ourselves incredibly and sometimes almost incredulously real."[1]

Klubertanz and our other Thomist professors did not connect Saint Thomas with Chesterton. They preferred to think of him as anticipating the "Christian existentialism" of men like Gabriel Marcel and Henri Bergson. I gave those authors a try, along with my Chesterton. (In fact I was still reading Bergson on an airplane, after I had left the seminary, when a woman told me I looked too young to be reading that. This was a conversation that clearly had to be continued off the plane, where it took a while for me to convince her that I was not too young to marry her. Forty-five years later, the conversation is still going on.)

The philosophate's emphasis on Thomist philosophy (and, later, theology) made some seminarians aspire to major in Thomistic philosophy or theology — among other things, this would guarantee that any post-graduate training would take place in Rome. But Peradotto and I continued to be more interested in the classics (he in Greek epic, I in Greek drama), and we were able to squeeze in some graduate credits in Greek while doing the basic philosophy courses. These latter courses were taught from Latin texts and notes, which gave some of the seminarians trouble. But since we did not have to struggle with the Latin, we found the actual content of the courses repetitive and not very challenging. For all the emphasis on the "existential" core of Thomism, scholastic method was still mechanical and sterile. I was getting restless with classes that ran on beyond useful elaboration, so I hid poetry texts behind the mimeographed notes from which we followed our lecturers. One priest caught me at this and was angered that I did not hang on his every word.

It was getting harder to distract myself with study from considering whether I should leave the seminary. I was still insomniac, and I used to sneak down after lights-out to listen to opera records in the middle of the night. This made me start missing Mass again, to what I considered the somewhat melodramatic horror of our house disciplinarian. I went to Father Fisher, who was now the provincial superior, and said that I felt I had given the whole course of study a fair trial. He began the procedure for gaining my release from vows, which had to come from the office of the Society's general in Rome. Seminarians were not supposed to tell their fellows they were leaving — the ideal was to have them buy a "civilian" suit on a secret trip to a clothier, and disappear overnight without a word to their friends. This was the culminating aspect of a general insistence that we not discuss our disagreements with the seminary or its ways, since that might "shake others in their vocation." This inhibition of frank discussion about what mattered most to one's fellows helped create the pattern of pretense for the good of the institution that is traceable in larger "structures of deceit." It also helps explain what occurred when I left in 1957. Like most of those leaving, I told my friends I was getting "processed out" in Rome, and the rumor spread — and enough people were "shaken in their vocation" that there was a pronounced exodus of some I had been close to.

This was not because I was the one leaving. If any of those in my circle had left, some of the rest would have followed. Since we had been inhibited from discussion of our problems, anyone tempted to leave could think he must be alone in his objections to the system. There was a feeling that "if So-and-so can hang in here, I guess I can." That argument lost its force as soon as So-and-so left. The great emptying out of the seminaries would occur only after the end of the Second Vatican Council (1965). But already, toward the end of the fifties, there was a reversal of the trend that had brought so many of us into the seminaries at the beginning of that decade. Soon buildings raised or expanded to cope with our overflow classes would have to be closed down and sold. A small harbinger of that was the spurt of departures after mine. When I married, two years after leaving, two friends who had left the seminary in that interval were at the wedding (one of them, Bill Dolan, was my best man), and two others who had left (including Jack Peradotto) sent gifts. Others left shortly after that, though my high school friend Bill Birdsall stayed on for a time. Of course, some of my friends stayed — including my best friend, Frank Higgins. Trained as a lawyer, he wanted to work for the rights of Native Americans out of a Jesuit parish in the reservations, though he died too young to realize his dream. Other friends who stayed were Dick Costigan and Tom Steele. My own relations with Jesuits, old friends and new, have always been cordial, and a number of Jesuits, including theologians and superiors in the order, expressed admiration for *Papal Sin*. Three Jesuit universities have given me honorary degrees — including one of my almae matres, Xavier University in Cincinnati.

I left with no regrets, nor with anything but gratitude toward the many teachers who had been helpful to me, certainly with no weakening of my faith in God, Christianity, or the church. When it became known to the faculty that my case was being processed in Rome, they could not have been kinder. A priest who had blown up at me, when he found me listening to phonograph records after lights-out, now assured me that he would not be patrolling that room henceforth. The delay in getting my release from Rome (a deliberate stalling to prevent rash impulses to leave) made it impossible for me to apply to graduate schools, so my Greek teacher arranged for me to get an overnight scholarship in the classics department run by a fellow Jesuit at Xavier University. There I was made an assistant to the professor who was editing John Chrysostom's baptismal sermons.

I left St. Louis in May of 1957, not returning for the awarding of a B.A. from the university in June, and went directly to Xavier, where I spent the summer collating Chrysostom manuscripts from microfilms, tedious work in a room without air conditioning. But my luck held out again when regular courses began in the fall. Another of the Jesuits who have given me important guidance, John Felton, had just returned from doing graduate work at Oxford. He had concentrated on the Athenian empire's tribute lists, the study of which had revolutionized Thucydides scholarship. He repeated the one-on-one tutorials he had received there for me, as I wrote a different paper on Thucydides every week. Under him I received a master's degree in one year (catching up on the academic work slowed in the seminary), and he recommended me for the fellowship I was given the next year at Yale.

After I finished the first year of graduate work at Yale (and received a second master's degree), I took time off in the summer of 1959 to do what I had long wanted to — to go over Chesterton's notebooks from his time of crisis. Maisie Ward's tantalizing quotations from these in her biography made me want to learn more about them. I knew they had been left, along with all his papers, to his secretary and executrix, Dorothy Collins, who lived in his house at Beaconsfield after his death. My friend Frank Meyer had got me a small grant for travel to London, which would be my base as I traveled out to Beaconsfield. Miss Collins resisted my project, since she had had some bad experiences with people who used the papers and marked them up or otherwise damaged them. But Wilfred Sheed, who had edited some of my book reviews for *Commonweal,* wrote Maisie Ward (his mother), asking her to intercede for me, and that was successful.

When my wife and I, newlyweds then, arrived in London, we went to thank Maisie Ward at her office in the publishing firm of Sheed and Ward. She came down to meet us at the reception desk, carrying a bulky photo album, and then launched into a hurried but efficient evaluation of the apartments pictured in the album — she had the impression that we were one of the poor young couples she helped find cheap housing. It was a sign of her concentration on the poor, and of her absentmindedness, that we had great difficulty explaining that we were there on a different errand. There was no such problem when we went out to Beaconsfield. Dorothy Collins knew who we were and was expecting us, though we had to sit down with her and her companion to watch "our telly show" (*I Love Lucy*), which was just coming on. Afterward, she served us a large English tea, which we had to complete before I could get down — or, rather, up — to work. The papers were in the flies of the theater that Chesterton had converted into his home. Letters and notebooks and drawings were thrown around as if they were discarded scripts from actors in that theater. But the authors of some of these scraps were such Chesterton correspondents as Bernard Shaw, H. G. Wells, and T. S. Eliot.

I sifted through the mass of material, isolating (as much as I could in this first survey) the early writings I was after. I asked Miss Collins why there were no letters from Hilaire Belloc, Chesterton's supposed great friend and ally. She explained that they rarely had any dealings with each other — only when Belloc, perpetually impoverished, came out to Beaconsfield, in order to tell Chesterton the plot of a novel he was planning to write. Chesterton, who had been trained at the Slade School of Art, would sketch illustrations for the tale as Belloc spun it out, and those drawings, turned over to Belloc gratis, became the basis on which he got his book advance. Unused drawings were sent back to Chesterton by the publisher, and at the end of the summer I tried to buy one of these, but Miss Collins generously gave it to me. It hangs in a place of honor in our home.

I asked Miss Collins how I could work on the papers with least disturbance to her. She said she would lend me a suitcase and I could just take anything I wanted back to our flat in London, and pick up a new batch each time I brought the suitcase back. That was not a procedure to be recommended for preserving irreplaceable manuscripts (I realized how earlier users of the papers had abused their privilege), but I was grateful for the way it eased my task. My wife typed copies of the material I needed from the suitcase while I worked in the reading room of the British Museum on the Chesterton holdings there and the writings of friends from his student period at Saint Paul's and the Slade School.

I meant, at the outset, to write nothing more than an essay on the importance of Chesterton's response to his early crisis — how the insight gained at that time informed much of his later work. But the temptation to use the rich material being ferried back by the suitcaseful made me attempt a survey of all his writings — not a biography (though some reviewers called it that), but a kind of intellectual portrait. This led me into areas not strictly connected with my main point, where I was too lenient on Chesterton's decided weaknesses — his anti-Semitism and anti-feminism, the glorification of war, the romanticizing of the Middle Ages. Though I expressed misgivings on those points, my own political views were not formed enough for me to be equally skeptical about his general political creed, clumsily called Distributism. This was a cluster of beliefs greatly influenced by the "social encyclicals" of Pope Leo XIII and Pope Pius XI (mainly *Rerum Novarum* of 1891 and *Quadragesimo Anno* of 1931).

The name Distributism came from the goal of distributing property more broadly than the concentrations of industrial capital would allow, without weakening the doctrine of private property that socialism would entail. Like the encyclicals themselves, the Distributists were better at describing the evils of unchecked capitalism and state socialism than in providing practical alternatives to them. The early Distributists — Dominican Father Vincent McNabb, Arthur Penty, Eric Gill, Hilaire Belloc, Cecil Chesterton (Gilbert's brother), Peter Maurin — glorified agrarian life in Jeffersonian ways (a note picked up by America's Southern "Fugitives," who admired Distributism). Chesterton's agrarianism led him to idealize medieval peasants, calling them freer than modern "wage slaves," which is an absurd historical claim. Some in the movement reverted to Luddism (Father McNabb wrote everything in longhand so his words would not be tainted by a machine like the typewriter). Since the encyclicals supported labor unions with references to medieval guilds, Chesterton praised the guilds without recognizing that they were monopolies close in spirit to the modern cartels he attacked. The encyclicals' emphasis on community, as opposed to the exaggerated individualism of a capitalist order, led some Catholics (including Chesterton) to defend the "corporate state" that Mussolini pretended to be forming.

For a while, under Chesterton's influence, I called myself a Distributist, and I still agree with much of the movement's critique of capitalism on the one hand and of socialism on the other. I also admire those — including Dorothy Day and her Distributist partner at the *Catholic Worker,* Peter Maurin — who tried to live up to their ideals, though the communal farms were the least lasting or effective part of the *Worker* activity. Maisie Ward herself tried to become a farmer in response to Chesterton's agrarianism (her son is caustic on the experience). When I first became interested in Distributism and voiced my views to Joe Fisher, he looked at me with that amused expression of his and said, "I don't think I'll see the day when you become a farmer." It had occurred even to me that Chesterton was the most urban of creatures himself.

Since I already knew, in 1959, all the published work of Chesterton, I was able to absorb the manuscript material from Beaconsfield rapidly and write most of my first book during that summer in England. Frank Meyer, who had helped me get to England in the first place, hoped to help me again with a review of the book by my favorite living prose stylist. Frank was the book review editor of *National Review,* and he asked Bill Buckley to wangle a review out of Evelyn Waugh. He did not tell me about this, since he was not sure he could bring it off, and if he did, he wanted to surprise me. But he was the surprised one when Waugh sent a review that dismissed the book on two grounds — he did not like academic dissertations, and he did not think one should expound the work of contemporaries, who are perfectly able to explain themselves. The book was not a dissertation, but I was already at work on my dissertation (on Aeschylus, safely non-contemporary), and there *is* a stiltedness about my book. I was trying (unsuccessfully) to disguise my enthusiasm with an "objective" tone, and I wanted to document the sources of unpublished material I was using. (The real academic dissertation on Chesterton was written by Hugh Kenner, under the direction of Marshall McLuhan.) As for Chesterton's being my contemporary, he died when I was two. Waugh himself wrote an interpretive biography of Ronald Knox, who died when Waugh was fifty-four.

Still, I do not want to defend the book, which has all the faults of a young man's first effort — and I would certainly not challenge Waugh's judgment of style. Frank, out of friendship, offered to kill the review, but I said that was unthinkable. I did not feel I had done Chesterton justice, or that I was finished with him. Others have wished I were. Some reviewers of my books have complained that I quote Chesterton too much. A friend even told me to lay off the man, since one could trivialize oneself by association with a writer often disparaged as an empty paradox-monger. Despite the admiration for Chesterton expressed by Kafka and Borges, by Eliot and Auden, his huge body of superficial journalism has hidden the core of his thinking. Yet I believe in paying intellectual debts, and one of my largest debts was to him.

That is why I served for a time as an adviser to the *Chesterton Newsletter,* and helped direct a dissertation on Chesterton at Northwestern University. Whatever things I disapprove of in Chesterton (and there are many), I still admire what it is not too pretentious to call his theological writings — as I hope to explain in Part V below. My Catholic upbringing would have been very different but for him. I now think I can go farther into the mysteries of faith with Augustine for a guide. But Chesterton was the Virgil to Augustine's Beatrice in my own journey up from Inferno.

4

Encyclicals

DURING THE LONG WEEKS when I was waiting for release from my vows to come from Rome, I had written several articles — on literature and art — I hoped to submit to journals. I would soon be free of the restrictions placed on writing for publication in the seminary. Three of the articles I sent to Catholic journals (the ones I was familiar with then), and all were rejected. A fourth I sent to *National Review,* making fun of the style of *Time* magazine (an ancient sport). Willi Schlamm, a veteran of the *Time* empire, was Bill Buckley's fellow editor at *National Review,* and he liked my piece so much that Buckley called me in Cincinnati, where I was just finishing up my summer's Chrysostom collations, and invited me to come see him in New York. When I met him in his office, he asked if I was a conservative. "Is a Distributist a conservative?" I answered. "Alas, no," he said. Distributism's dark view of capitalism disqualified it. (Bill knew about Distributism from Philip Burnham, the Catholic brother of another editor at *National Review,* Jim Burnham.)

Though I was unsound on capitalism, I pleased Bill by my Catholicism. Bill, who had recently started the magazine, was buying articles from any new talent he could find for cultural commentary, without setting hard ideological requirements — my fellows from that time would include John Leonard, Joan Didion, Arlene Croce, and Renata Adler. But I was the only Catholic in the bunch, and John Leonard told Buckley's biographer, John Judis, that this formed a tie with Bill that Leonard himself, along with the others, felt he did not experience.[1] I think that may be right, since Bill takes his religion very seriously and liked the idea that I did too. He is almost super-Catholic, which made it more than odd that in 1961, when I was in graduate school at Yale, almost every Catholic journal in America lined up to fire salvo after salvo against him as an anti-Catholic, an encourager of disrespect for the faith, a saboteur of the church. The *New York Times* ran a headline (August 13, 1961), "Jesuits Attack Buckley." The editor of the Jesuit journal *America* publicly announced that he would not accept advertising from *National Review,* and that no Catholic college should ever let Buckley speak on campus: "We will not publish advertisements for a journal which, in our opinion, seriously and consistently undercuts positions which we judge central to our faith." Another Jesuit, the columnist William J. Smith, sputtered that Buckley's writings were "the stuff from which seedling schisms sprout." The published attacks on my *Papal Sin* would be minor and sporadic compared with this barrage of indignation fired at Buckley's editorial.

What could have caused such an uproar? Bill had written disrespectfully about a 1960 papal encyclical. It is hard, now, to recall what a cult was made of those papal letters in the 1950s, at least by Catholic liberals. The attitude was caught in a 1956 article for the *Catholic Mind* called "How Binding Are Encyclicals?" The author, a priest named Norman Galloway, concluded: "The possibility of error in these documents is so utterly remote that it is practically non-existent, even as a possibility." The desire to inflate the binding nature of encyclicals came from the fact that the Vatican's anti-democratic record under Pius IX and Pius X had been partly softened by the social encyclicals that the Distributists (among others) welcomed. In America, *Rerum Novarum* was taken as a charter for the legitimacy of unions, indeed for all the progressive programs of the Democratic party. Younger Catholics protected themselves against their elders, formed in the ethos of Pius X, by citing the social encyclicals. These were supposed to have wiped out the church's reactionary past and made it officially "leftist." As one prominent liberal, John Cort, one of those who had attacked Buckley in 1961, confessed in 1971 (*Commonweal,* January 8), "We wrapped ourselves in the papal encyclicals, especially *Rerum Novarum* of Leo XIII and *Quadragesimo Anno* of Pius XI, and when we weren't wrapping ourselves in them we were beating our Catholic adversaries over the head with them in a manner that, since *Humanae Vitae,* I have come to resent in others." Several others who beat up on Buckley then have said in print or to me that they were not only mistaken on the nature of encyclicals but were attacking free speech in the church. They had, after all, supported the idea that Buckley, a popular speaker on campuses at the time, should be banned from all Catholic colleges.

If encyclicals in general were favorite reading for Catholic liberals, the one Buckley criticized, *Mater et Magistra* ("Mother and Teacher"), was an especially sacred utterance. This was John XXIII's first signal that he was opening up the church to the modern world, ending the long anti-modern papacy of Pius IX and his successors. The world-wide response of non-Catholics was enthusiastically welcoming. Robert Hutchins's Center for the Study of Democracy even sponsored a world conference on its importance. All this was a heady experience for American Catholics, who felt they were at last escaping the suspicion — bitterly expressed in Paul Blanshard's bestseller of the 1950s, *American Freedom and Catholic Power* — that they were opposed to freedom of conscience and liberal democracy. Only in this context can we understand the hysterical reaction of Catholic liberals to Buckley's comments on the encyclical.[2] He seemed to them to be undoing this long-overdue validation of Catholic liberalism when he wrote, in a *National Review* editorial (July 19, 1961), "[*Mater et Magistra*] may, in the years to come, be considered central to the social teaching of the Catholic Church or, like Pius IX's *Syllabus of Errors*, it may become the source of embarrassed explanations. Whatever its final effect, it must strike many as a venture in triviality coming at this particular [cold war] time in our history." The words "venture in triviality" caused the trouble. The cult of encyclicals had made these letters so sacrosanct that many people read this as saying Catholicism itself must be a venture in triviality.

This was not the beginning of Buckley's trouble with Catholics over the church's social teaching. Even before *Mater et Magistra,* encyclicals had been cited to show that he was not a true Catholic on political matters. In the late 1950s he had participated in a series of public debates on Catholic social doctrine with Bill Clancy of *Commonweal.* Buckley called me at Yale to ask for help in preparing for those debates. He thought I knew more about encyclicals than I did; but when I told him about my ignorance, he answered that no one else seemed to know much either — a condition I would find to be true. I told him I would do some homework before he came to New Haven to go over the first results of my hasty study.

I had taken part in reading groups on the social encyclicals, both at Campion and in the seminary, and I had read them more carefully when I was tracing their influence on the Distributists, but I was totally ignorant about the early history of encyclicals as a genre. Their formal status and binding force were far from clear. Those who cited them so blithely loved to inflate their authority, but had not bothered to find out what (if anything) made them compelling. To my astonishment I found that there was no book in English on the history of encyclicals. The major work on the subject, Dom Paul Nau's *Une source doctrinale: les encycliques* (1952), was never quoted in American commentary. The most commonly cited collection of encyclicals in their English translation, by Anne Fremantle, was full of errors that were parroted by others, leading to such headlines as this, in the *New York Times* for July 15, 1961: "Encyclicals Issued for Twenty Centuries."[3]

The first papal encyclical, Benedict XIV's *Ubi Primum,* was not issued until 1740. There had been encyclicals ("circulating letters") in the patristic period (the age of "the fathers," in the fourth and fifth centuries), but they were not papal documents. Originating mainly in Egypt, these were missives sent around by bishops to establish, with their accumulating signatures, the orthodox response to Arians and other heretics. Benedict XIV, a scholar of the early church, used this form in a new way, hoping to suggest a more collegial method of communing with bishops, though the *joint* authority of the originals was lacking. The pope, under this polite form of address, was not asking for others to endorse what he was saying. He was telling them what they should think or do. As other popes continued the issuing of such letters, the early (patristic) form was entirely forgotten, and encyclicals became direct exercises of papal prerogative.

Encyclicals were used by different popes for different purposes, so they did not have a single degree of authority derived from the format in itself. Some of them were merely celebratory (e.g., on a saint's feast); others were moral exhortations (e.g., recommending prayer). Some dealt with doctrine, some with practical matters. Those dealing with politics were dependent on the common knowledge of any particular era, or on the expertise available to the pope, and not on revealed truths (the deposit of faith). Church teaching could err in such matters, as when sanctifying monarchical forms of government before democracy was a realistic alternative. The example of this that has been best explored (by John Noonan) was the church's condemnation, over a period of centuries, of the taking of interest (usury), based as that was on faulty views of natural law and of economics. As Thomas Aquinas put it, "In judgments concerned with particular matters of fact, as in the settlement of property, the judgment of crimes, and such matters, the judgment of the church can be erroneous because of false witnesses [*propter falsos testes*]."[4]

When I showed this text to Buckley, he said, "Isn't *testis* also the word for 'testicle'?" It is. In Roman law a *testis* was a "standby" who gave supporting testimony, and one testicle "stands by" the other. (The same two meanings are contained in the Greek word for "standby witness" and for "testicle," *parastatēs*.) That conversation came back to me later, when Bill phoned to ask about some other point of church teaching. I said I thought it was an uncertain matter, but he wanted to take a public position on it anyway. I asked why he did not just avoid the issue. "Because I do not have *falsos testes*," he said with a laugh.

I learned more of his swashbuckling ways during the controversy over *Mater et Magistra*. Bill came back to me for information on other encyclicals when that storm arose, and I asked him over the phone, "Why not just say your position is 'Mater sí, Magistra no'?" It was a play on Cuban exiles' slogan of the time, "Cuba sí, Castro no." Bill repeated the crack to others, who spread it. But I did not expect to see it in print until I read — in a little *National Review* feature called "For the Record" — these words: "Going the rounds in Catholic circles, 'Mater sí, Magistra no.'"

This set off a new barrage of attacks on Bill. Some accused him of slandering his fellow Catholics by claiming that any of them would have said anything so vile as this. It was, on the contrary, his own personal attack on the church's teaching authority. This certitude about what Catholics are capable of saying might have been unsettled (or might not) if they learned what my friends still in the seminary told me in 1961, when John XXIII issued an apostolic constitution, *Veterum Sapientia* ("The Elders' Wisdom"), ordering increased use of Latin in the seminaries. "Veterum sí, Sapientia no" was soon "going the rounds" in the seminary.

The hysteria over Buckley and the church was getting out of hand, and Bill's friend Neil McCaffrey had been charting its wilder arabesques. Clipping samples of the attacks and scribbling caustic marginalia on them, McCaffrey sent them on to Bill for his amusement. Neil, one of the early direct-mail masters and the founder of the Conservative Book Club, had soon put in so much time on this effort that he asked Bill if he might publish a dossier on the attacks, along with Bill's responses to them. Bill agreed, and Neil brought in an astonishing amount of material, documenting Catholic liberals' positive obsession with Buckley. But the resulting dossier was endlessly repetitive, and Neil's running commentary was so bitter that Bill thought softening the rancor would not show *falsos testes*. He first suggested that Neil add an essay by me on the history of encyclicals (I had pursued the subject with the help of Dom Nau). And when that proved insufficient to detoxify the whole, he asked Neil to let me incorporate a selection of his material in a longer essay on the force of encyclicals. It took all of Bill's charm and talent to ease Neil into abandoning his project; and though the episode did not immediately cause a break between them, it contributed to Neil's suspicion that Bill lacked the intransigence of a true conservative. (I softened the edges of this transaction when describing it in *Confessions of a Conservative*, since Neil was still alive then, and not as harshly reactionary as he became by the end of his life.)

I called my book-length essay on encyclicals, from which all the anti-Buckley quotes above are taken, *Politics and Catholic Freedom* (1964). The title was a deliberate play on Blanshard's *American Freedom and Catholic Power*. I was arguing, against Blanshard, that there could be freedom of speech and openness of debate among Catholics, that encyclicals were not a form of instruction that closed political questions to further inquiry. It was the Catholic liberals, of all people, who were making Blanshard's point for him when they said that Buckley should shut up the minute an encyclical appeared. But *Politics and Catholic Freedom* was a shot fired after the battle was over. The liberals had changed their tune overnight. In the wake of the Second Vatican Council, it was no longer fashionable to cite or stress papal authority. The liberals now called for independent initiatives by bishops and the laity, not slavish dependence on papal dicta.

But the controversy over *Mater et Magistra* had taught me a number of things that led indirectly to the writing of *Papal Sin*. For one thing, I had seen in this case what the Jesuit church historian Klaus Schatz calls a recurrent impulse by papal outsiders to up the ante on papal pronouncements. When this occurs, assertions of authority come less from the popes themselves than from the exigencies of those wanting to use the popes for some purpose of their own. Catholic liberals of the 1950s found it convenient to inflate the pope's power when it served their purpose, though they recoiled from the consequences of their claims when that purpose had been achieved. Similarly, in the ninth century, bishops called for papal approval as a way of circumventing the authority of their local metropolitans (S 70). Religious orders, with their trans-diocesan structure, would do the same thing in order to escape control by the "ordinaries" (diocesan bishops). In fact, the historian Brian Tierney has claimed that the concept of papal infallibility was not invented until the thirteenth century, when the Franciscan Peter Olivi tried to use it to freeze in infallible terms a papal dispensation for his order.[5] Alexis de Tocqueville was on to something when he wrote in 1856: "The pope is driven more by the faithful to become an absolute ruler of the Church than they are impelled by him to submit to his rule" (S 181). This is what Schatz calls centralization orchestrated from the periphery, not the center (S 176). The papolators hounding Buckley were a perfect example of this.

Aside from the instruction I derived from writing *Politics and Catholic Freedom* at Bill's request, there were several more concrete results of its publication. For one thing, it prompted Hillel Black of the William Morrow publishing house to ask me for a book on Catholicism as part of a series he was editing on major American religions. Before that book was written, Ken McCormick of Doubleday bought it away from Black in order to put together a multi-book contract with me. The volume finally appeared as *Bare Ruined Choirs* (1972), in which I described the impact of Vatican II on Catholic life. D. H. Lawrence said that the "dirty little secret" of American puritans was sex. I argued that the dirty little secret of American Catholics was change. We had been brought up with the false notion that our church had always been the same. Any basis for that notion was swept away by the changes initiated or encouraged by Vatican II, and by the historical arguments made to justify these changes.

Another consequence of my book on the encyclicals was an invitation from Bob Hoyt to contribute a regular column to the newspaper he was about to launch, the *National Catholic Reporter*. He was lining up an ecumenical spread of columnists — one of them Protestant (Martin Marty), one Jewish (Arthur Hertzberg), and — in an exercise of intra-ecclesial ecumenism — one a liberal Catholic (John Leo, then of *Commonweal*) and one a conservative Catholic (me). The conflict he envisaged between John and me never quite came off. For one thing, we quickly became good friends. For another, we had begun that convergence to a common position that became in time a reversal of positions, so that John now writes a conservative column for *U.S. News & World Report* and I write regularly for the liberal *New York Review of*

Books. On some of the Catholic issues that seemed big at the time, I had never taken the stock conservative position — I supported changing the liturgy to English, for instance, and lifting the ban on contraception. On issues in the larger (secular) society, I was becoming an advocate for the civil rights movement and the anti-war movement.

These issues were clarifying the differences with Buckley that had been foreshadowed when he said a Distributist could not be a conservative. My admiration for Dr. King came up against *National Review*'s sense that the civil rights movement diminished America's moral leadership in the cold war. Harping on injustices at home was a luxury the nation could not afford when it was engaged in a death grapple with the Soviet Union. This attitude closely resembles the one I would criticize in *Papal Sin,* that the moral mission of the church should not be compromised by admission of its own past wrongs, or even of present crimes like priestly pedophilia. Flaws should be covered up or denied to keep the enterprise strong in apparent righteousness.

The first serious argument I had with Bill came early on in my *National Catholic Reporter* days, when Leo and I both signed a letter in the *New York Times* deploring the fact that Cardinal Spellman had exiled Dan Berrigan, the social-activist Jesuit, from the New York archdiocese. Bill thought I showed disrespect for the cardinal. I thought it was a case of freedom of speech within the church — just as his own criticism of *Mater et Magistra* had been. Relations with Bill remained amicable, but others at *National Review* resented things I was writing. It was my old friend Frank Meyer who tried to kill my coverage of the 1968 Democratic convention in Chicago, on the grounds that I was too sympathetic to protesters in the street. Bill resisted that pressure, but when I wrote an article critical of the Vietnam War he told me that it would upset his readers too much for him to run it. That was the effective end of our association.

The letter supporting Dan Berrigan was the beginning of a new friendship with him and his brother Philip, leaders of the Catholic anti-war effort, which I soon joined. I still did not think of myself as a liberal. In fact, I often argued (in respectful ways) with the liberal Paulist priest who led the Catholic community on campus at Johns Hopkins, where I taught from 1961 to 1980. Phil Cunningham was an ardent disciple of Teilhard de Chardin, the Jesuit paleontologist, who impressed me as a vaporous diluter of the Gospels' challenge. Phil, in turn, thought my interest in Augustine retrograde and anti-progres-

sive. I was happy to use ammunition against Teilhard from my con-
versations with William Albright, the great biblical archeologist at
Hopkins, who had known Teilhard in China. Albright, a genial man
very sympathetic to Catholics (his son, a convert, had entered a religious order), strongly disliked Teilhard. He found him totally uninterested in Chinese culture, in the people around him, and in the world in
general. Teilhard's lofty involvement in his own hieratic formulations
left him no time for social concerns of any sort.

Up to this point, all of my writings about the Catholic church had
been accidental, in the sense that others requested them. Bill had done
this for *Politics and Catholic Freedom,* Hillel Black for *Bare Ruined
Choirs,* and Bob Hoyt for the *NCR* column. When I wrote, on my own
initiative, a book about religion in American politics, *Under God,* some
reviewers complained that there was practically nothing in it about Catholicism (I was giving the subject a rest). Much of the modern fer-
ment in Catholicism passed me by during my forty years in churches
on campuses where I taught, since the sermons did not mention Vatican campaigns against homosexuality, feminism, divorce, contraception, or abortion. Yet even we, at the non-Catholic universities where I
taught (Johns Hopkins and Northwestern), had to be aware of some
problems in the church — the dwindling numbers of priests and nuns,
the pressures on seminaries and Catholic universities to silence dissent,
the way Vatican II reforms were being reversed or coming under siege.
I was often quizzed about these matters by journalists or non-Catholic
friends.

When I was asked to contribute a volume to a new series of short bi-
ographies, I chose my own hero, Augustine, as the topic for my volume.
While working on it, I re-read the two treatises on deception that Augustine wrote to counter what he found particularly false to the gospel,
deception used to promote the Catholic church. That crystalized what
I had been feeling about the papacy during its modern phase, so I un-
dertook a first book about Catholicism that was not requested by others but reflected my own sense of urgency. The heart of *Papal Sin* is its
final section, dealing with Augustine's timeless call for honesty in the
church. The book wrote itself "from the back" in that sense. I began by
collecting data to show that Augustine's problem in the fourth century
was just as pressing in our own time.

That book's narrow focus led others to ask the larger questions this
book addresses — how one can remain a Catholic at a time when the

papacy seems opposed to basic freedoms, and even to the council that Pope John XXIII assembled; what attitude a Catholic should take toward papal statements on such matters; whether Catholics who disregard papal teaching on contraceptives, divorce, gay rights, married priests, ordained women, and other issues must be considered disloyal; whether disregard of some teachings amounts to rebellion against the whole concept of the papacy. I must perforce answer these and similar questions in order to give an account of why I am a Catholic at this time. But this involves looking at the meaning of Peter in the Gospels and in history, at how the papacy has developed over the centuries, at how it has made many different claims, some of them rejected by every modern Catholic (e.g., that a purely secular state is illegitimate). By what norms do we judge the papacy? We cannot know that until we try to pin down what the papacy is. And the only way to do that is to take a long look at what it has been at various times in the past. Only by considering how its claims have — some of them — been self-contradictory or self-canceling can we get to the substrate remaining throughout all these changes, the Petrine charism of church unity.

II

CHURCH WITHOUT
PAPAL PRIMACY

The papacy did not come into existence at the same time as the church. In the words of John Henry Newman, "While Apostles were on earth, there was the display neither of Bishop nor Pope."[1] Peter was not a bishop in Rome. There were no bishops in Rome for at least a hundred years after the death of Christ. The very term "pope" (papa, daddy) was not reserved for the bishop of Rome until the fifth century — before then it was used of any bishop (S 89). To call even earlier bishops of Rome popes is a matter of later custom, followed here, even though it is misleading. Dating the inception of the papacy depends on how you define its essential powers. If Rome's bishop must have teaching and ruling primacy over all other bishops in order to be a "real" pope, then the church got along without real popes for a very long time.

How long a time? Newman thought the papacy could not, at the earliest, arise until after the fourth century, when the Nicene Council exercised the power that the popes would later claim: "I say then the Pope is the heir of the Ecumenical Hierarchy of the fourth century, as being, what I may call, heir by default."[2] The power exercised without the pope at Nicaea only became his power when there was no obvious other vehicle for that authority. "That which in substance was possessed by the Nicene Hierarchy, that the Pope claims now."[3] This happened by what Newman calls "a process of concentration," the pope taking up, for lack of any other organ, the powers that were previously diffused throughout the church.

This was not a usurpation, he says, since it was forced on the pope by "the changes of times and the vicissitude of nations."[4] The so-called words of institution ("You are Cephas, and on this stone . . .") did not actually institute the power, but predicted that it would arise at some time. The words were "prophecies and promises, promises to be accomplished by Him who made them, prophecies to be fulfilled according to the need, and to be interpreted by the event."[5] These prophecies were not fulfilled until some time (he is vague about what specific time) in the Middle Ages. Modern papalists do not agree with him. They find the primacy implicit in earlier acts. They try to reduce the period when the church got along without it. This section looks at the period before any clear primacy of teaching or governing authority was established and accepted.

5

Peter

> When Christ at a symbolic moment was establishing His great society, He chose for its corner stone neither the brilliant Paul nor the mystic John, but a shuffler, a snob, a coward — in a word, a man. And upon this rock He has built His church, and the gates of hell have not prevailed against it. All the empires and the kingdoms have failed, because of this inherent and continual weakness, that they were founded by strong men and upon strong men. But this one thing, the historic Christian Church, was founded on a weak man, and for that reason it is indestructible. For no chain is stronger than its weakest link.
>
> — G. K. Chesterton[1]

CHESTERTON CALLS Peter a snob and a coward — which is small potatoes by the standard of the New Testament, where Paul calls him a hypocrite (Gal 2.13), a "so-called pillar" (Gal 2.9), and perhaps, dismissively, a "big-shot apostle" (2 Cor 11.5). Jesus himself is much harsher on Peter, calling him not only an obstacle blocking his mission (Mt 16.23) but "Satan" (Mk 8.33).

Peter is unique in the Gospels — both a highly symbolic figure and the only realistically drawn individual in them. The other disciples are stock figures, reacting like a Greek chorus to the wonder-working protagonist. Judas is a stock villain. The "disciple Jesus loved" is a stock admirer. Mary Magdalene is so little individual that she blends into and is confused with two other characters in the narrative. As for the main figure, Jesus, he is hieratic, moving through events as an embodied mystery, without any human psychology to be probed — though nineteenth-century rationalists thought they could retrieve a nice liberal moralizer from this tale of one grappling with demons and striding over stars: "Before Abraham came to be, I am" (Jn 8.58). As Chesterton says, clouds gather or are scattered around his head, far above the spiritual weather system through which his followers move.[2] One challenge the Gospels pose is this: who could have been sophisticated enough to present the mystery of divinity so persuasively under cover of naïve narration?

But if Jesus is a walking mystery, and the other characters in the story are what artists call "lay figures," Peter is a recognizably complex human being. Into a story that has sometimes the air of a fairy tale and sometimes that of a nightmare, he seems to have come straight out of the pages of a Dostoevski novel. He is the comic boaster who bungles everything. His fourth-century cultists, as we shall see, tried to make him the new Moses. But the Gospels make him less a Moses than Mister Magoo. A man of action, he invariably takes the wrong action. In the garden where Jesus is arrested, he is not only inept but ridiculous. With armed soldiers collaring his leader, he attacks a nearby servant — in the ear. As a journalist I know would say, this does not show an instinct for the jugular but an instinct for the capillary. It is as if Peter said, "I am so mad at you that I am going to shoot your dog — in the paw." Pure Dostoevski.

The man is unaware of his own instability. Quick to commit himself, he is just as quick to abandon his commitment, and even quicker to repent the abandoning. He likes to offer his leader suggestions, even to contradict him. When he tells Jesus not to wash his feet and Jesus insists anyway, he says, "Okay, then, not only my feet but my head and hands, too" (Jn 13.8). He luckily stops short of ordering a shave and a manicure. When Jesus says that all the disciples will betray him, Peter abruptly tells him he is misinformed. He in effect thumps his chest with the emphatic last three words of Mk 14.29 (*all' ouk ego*): "Sure, the others may stumble over what you say — *but I? Never.*" Even after his fall and repentance, he has not learned his lesson. When the risen Jesus appears walking on water, Peter jumps impulsively out of the boat to do the same thing — and just as quickly sinks (Mt 14.30).

Peter the coward is easier to bear than Peter the wise man, who favors Jesus with his advice. The words at Mk 16.22 and Mk 8.32 are, literally, "He [Peter] took him [Jesus] apart from the others and tried to straighten him out." No wonder Jesus jerks away (*strapheis*) from this pompous counselor and says "before the other followers" the terrifying words, "Get out of my path, Satan, you are a stone blocking it." It is a long way from this stumbling stone (*skandalon*) to the stone of foundation at Mt 16.18: "I say that you are Stone, a stone on which I shall build up my community [*ekklesia*]."

We know what Peter's ideas of foundation are. When Jesus is seen in visionary discourse with symbols of the beginning and the end, Moses and Elijah, Peter takes charge of the dream's consequences and becomes an ecclesiastical contractor. He is going to build a triple shrine on the spot (Mt 17.4). He seems to think that Jesus has been promoted into exalted company. He cannot grasp the far more revolutionary hint that the great prophets are come to show reverence to what they prophesied.

The Gospel portrait of Peter as a vacillating figure gets stunning confirmation from the one contemporary report of an encounter with the historical person, Paul's words at Gal 1.13. When Peter comes out to the Hellenized Christian Jews at Antioch, he joins them in abandoning kosher discipline. But when the Christian ruler of Jerusalem, James the brother of the Lord, sends emissaries to investigate this development, Peter falls in line with the newcomers. For this Paul openly calls him a hypocrite, even though this means that he (Paul) will lose his evangelizing companion Barnabas. Peter is later back at home among the Hellenizers, showing that he can recoil from timidity as he does from precipitancy. Whether he is rushing ahead or lagging behind, it seems, you just have to wait a short time for him to change course. This tergiversating aspect of the man is even built into his commission from Christ: "After you have reversed yourself [*epistrepsas*], uphold your brothers" (Lk 22.32). And Galatians is not the only place where Paul has hard words for Peter. He defends himself against a "party of Cephas" in 1 Cor, which makes some scholars believe that Peter or his followers are the "big-shot apostles" at 2 Cor 11.5.[3]

Paul presents Peter not only as a human figure, but as a safely bourgeois one. Unlike Paul, who has cut his ties with all lesser community than discipleship, Peter travels about with his wife (1 Cor 9.5). In fact, though Jesus has said his followers should renounce their families, even hate them, Peter is uxorious enough to take Jesus to his sick mother-in-law — and Jesus heals her (Mk 1.30). Peter the family man would long be remembered in Rome, where there was a cult of his wife and of his daughter, Saint Petronilla. The relics of Petronilla were still being reverenced by popes in the eighth century (K 93). Charlemagne, during his first visit to Rome, stayed at the shrine of Saint Petronilla, to whom he was devoted (H 375, 399).

Does it make any sense that the Peter of the Gospels, a weathervane at the mercy of every wind, should be made the unshakeable stone underneath the whole church? The Gospels seem to have created their only realistic figure just to place unrealistic demands on him. The least provident of the disciples is made a provider for the others. Or was Jesus teasing Peter when he called him "Rocky," naming him *ab opposito,* as when one calls a not-so-bright person Einstein? One Catholic exegete, Brian Stock, thinks that Jesus was, indeed, being ironic: "It is not an exaggeration to say that the image of Peter which Matthew presents is anything but that of a bedrock. On the contrary, Peter is presented as a vacillating figure on whom Jesus could not build . . . Matthew's overall description of Peter suggests that he might more fittingly be likened to the loose sand of 7.24–27 that cannot bear the weight of a house."[4]

One reason to hesitate over calling Peter "Stone" in earnest is that this seems a usurpation. Everywhere else in the New Testament, Jesus is the stone of foundation. Peter himself says this at Acts 4.11: "This stone, which the architects rejected, is placed at the corner of honor." At 1 Pt 4.5–8, Christians are "living stones" built up from Christ, who is the cornerstone (*lithon akrogōniaion*) referred to by Isaiah (28.16). Once again Peter says this stone was rejected by the architects — so he is a "stone for stunning them" (*lithos proskommatos*) and a "rock to make them stumble" (*petra skandalou*).

Three Pauline passages call Christ a stone. At 1 Cor 10.4, the stone *(petra)* from which Moses struck water is a type of Christ. At Eph 2.19, Christians "are built upon the foundation — that is, the apostles and the prophets — with Christ as the stone at the corner" (*akrogōniaiou*). Rom 9.33 quotes the same passage from Isaiah that Acts 4.11 does, on the "stone that stuns them and the rock that makes them stumble." The images of a cornerstone and a stumbling block are linked in these passages about Christ, in exactly the way they are combined in Mt 16, where Christ first calls Peter the stone of foundation (18) *and* a *skandalon* (23). This pattern led Max Wilcox, in an important article, to suggest that Matthew applies the Christic language to Peter in order to protect his position as the first of the apostles:

May we therefore dare to suggest that in Matthew 1.16 a piece of "stone/rock" midrash relating to the foundation of the Church upon the (rejected) Son has been skillfully reinterpreted, by way of the word-play *Petros-petra*, to make it clear that it is the Church or community whose leader is Peter that is the Church of Jesus and the true heir to the kingdom; the Church built upon the *lithos proskommatos* (Jesus) and the *petra skandalou* (Peter).[5]

There would be good reason to bolster Peter's claims, since Galatians shows him as a shuttlecock between James, speaking for the Temple Christians, and Paul, speaking for the non-Temple Christians. Corinthians represents him as the leader of a faction, like Apollo. Some modern exegetes have concluded that Matthew or Mark or both mount subtle attacks on Peter.[6] Others find the same prejudice against him in the Johannine writings.[7]

Anti-Petrine Gnosticism

The historical attacks on Peter came early and were intensified in some Gnostics' condemnation of him. Whether or not Paul called Peter a posturing "big-shot" apostle, second-century Gnostics like the Marcionites felt that was just what he was. Weak human Peter was the very antithesis of the enlightened soul with its secret knowledge (*gnosis*) that was the ideal of various Gnostic sects. What was a credential in the eyes of some — Peter's early and leading role as a witness to Christ's life — was a fatal flaw for those who believed that the real Jesus, the risen one, rejected his own earthly career, with its inferior Jewish roots. The risen Jesus preached a higher God than Jahweh, one revealed to the select few who had visions of him. A favorite recipient of these revelations was Mary Magdalene, to whom Jesus first appeared after the Resurrection (ABD 4.581–84). The *Gospel of Mary* presents Magdalene as the object of Peter's scorn, since he is too earthbound to understand her higher wisdom.[8] It was a recommendation, in the eyes of these Gnostics, for one to have clashed with Peter — which helps explain why Simon Magus, defeated by Peter at Acts 8, became a Gnostic seer (F 195–97). Another favored visionary was the apostle Thomas, who was right to question the physical reality of the risen Jesus — the nickname "Twin" given Thomas in John's Gospel was taken to mean he was the twin brother of *Jesus* (ABD 6.528–44).

But the preferred carrier of Gnostic wisdom was Paul, whose escape from Jewish law was the touchstone for many things beyond the rejection of Peter. Paul was the guiding light of the greatest organizer of a Gnostic sect — Marcion, born in the first century in Syria and expelled from the church at Rome in the early second century (ABD 4.514–21). He reduced Christian Scripture to ten letters of Paul and the most Pauline parts of the Gospel of Luke (who was supposed to have been a fellow missionary with Paul). This selection (*hairesis*) of parts of the tradition one liked was typical of the Gnostic revelations that swept over the empire within a half-century of Christ's death. People emphasized a favorite apostle, or set of sayings, or school of mysticism, and rejected the rest. For this reason men were branded as "selecters," heretics, *hairesioi.* The church organized to meet this challenge by defending the *whole* revelation, the *entire* body of apostles, the *inclusive* history of the church (including its Jewish component). This panoply of institutions and standards was needed in order to condemn the alarming pullulation of second-century heretics.

Some see this rise of an authoritarian emphasis in the church as a betrayal of the charismatic freedom defended by Gnostics. Dogmatism was expelling dissent. It should be seen, rather, as a rescue of things expelled by the heretics themselves. It was a defense, not only of Peter, but of the apostles generally, and of communities derived from them. The orthodox excluded a few heretics only because the latter had excluded whole chunks of history, large bodies of believers, and vast amounts of Jewish and Christian writing. In this contest, the orthodox were the includers, the heretics were the excluders. This was the first great example of what Newman called the development of doctrine. For the development at this time, four interrelated elements were necessary — apostolic succession, the Scripture canon, the creeds, and bishop-presbyter government. All four were new, and were needed to protect the old things of the faith. Each was tailored to its time, and to the specific challenge mounted by the Gnostics.

Responses to Gnosticism

1. *Apostolic succession.* This has become, in some modern versions, a linear descent of all bishops from the bishop of Rome. That was far from the sense given to the concept in the second century (when there was still no bishop in Rome). It referred to the joint testimony of the

six outstanding communities of the early church, the ones that claimed foundation from the apostolic period — Antioch, Philippi, Ephesus, Corinth, Thessalonica, and Rome (S 7, 8, 11). Apostolic teaching was whatever these churches agreed on. The church was a community of communities, opposed to the private revelations and charismatic individualism of the Gnostics. *Joint* authority is the essential note, as the Jesuit historian Karl Schatz emphasizes: "A judicial superiority of one church over another, or certainly anything like papal primacy of jurisdiction, was completely foreign to Ignatius or Irenaeus [in the second century], or even Augustine [in the fourth] . . . In particular, all kinds of thinking in categories of hierarchical subordination or superiority will lead us astray" (S 3). Of the six apostolic churches, Rome was the only one in the West. Since the empire was declining in the West and becoming stronger in the East, Rome would be on the edge of the action for the early centuries of Christian life, playing a minor role, if any, in the formation of the creeds and canon, in the growth of the bishopric, and — later on — in the great councils that hammered out doctrinal definitions of the Trinity and the Incarnation.

In the second century, as W.H.C. Frend says, orthodoxy was held together not by a Roman primate but by "like-minded Greek-speaking bishops" in the major churches of the East (F 251). The emphasis was on the agreement between the apostolic churches and those in union with them. Thus Tertullian, defending the whole Gospel of Luke against Marcion's selections from it, said that this was endorsed "not only by the apostolic churches, but by all those joined with them in the fellowship of the revealed faith."[9] The apostolic churches are to be looked to — not only one of them (Rome) but the one in whose region any community dwells, as Tertullian said: "If Achaea is close by, you have Corinth. If Macedonia is not far off, you have Philippi or you have Thessalonica. If you can reach Asia, you have Antioch. If, however, Italy is your neighbor, you have Rome, which is also the authority handiest [*praesto*] to us [in Africa]."[10]

2. *The canon.* If Marcion accepted only parts of the Gospel of Luke as authoritative teaching, the Ebionites accepted only the Gospel of Matthew (F 250). Marcion accepted ten of the letters of Paul, but other churches rejected Pauline or Johannine writings, in part because they were favored by the Gnostics. And, of course, many Gnostics rejected the whole of Hebrew Scripture. The only way the apostolic churches could oppose this pick-and-choose use of texts was to reach an agree-

ment on what constituted authoritative scripture. It is not true, as some have argued, that Marcion's slender but well-analyzed canon caused the church to create its broader canon on reasoned principles.[11] But Marcion probably hastened a process that would have occurred in a less focused way. Lists were circulated, like the Muratorian Canon of the late second century; claims were debated, some texts added, some dropped. Paul had to be rescued from the Gnostics by showing how he could be reconciled with the other parts of the New Testament (Tertullian was a leader in this effort). Protestants who would later say that only the Bible should be trusted, not the church, forgot how the Bible was created *by* the church during this time of sifting, to reach apostolic consensus. The Bible was what the church (the six apostolic communities) said it was.

3. *Creeds.* The private visions of the Gnostics had to be answered with the public body of beliefs that were apostolic. Just as the canon was formed by circulation of lists in the network of churches, so the agreed-on beliefs were listed with a growing authority. The creeds, like the canon, were shaped to respond to the Gnostic challenge, as we can see from this proclamation of the universal creed by Irenaeus in his book *Answer to Heresies* (1.10):

> The church, though dispersed out to the ends of the habitable earth, preserves what it received from the apostles and their schools, a faith in one God, all powerful, creator of heaven, earth, sea, and all that is in them; and in one messiah, Jesus, the son of God who took flesh for our rescue; and in the Holy Spirit, who inspired the stages [*oikonomias*] of revelation, such as the descent [of Christ], birth from a virgin, death and rising from the dead, and bodily reception into heaven as the beloved Son, messiah Jesus our Lord, coming again in glory from the Father for the cosmic restoration, the resurrection of all human flesh — so that to Christ Jesus our Lord and God and savior and king, by God the invisible Father's will, every knee shall bend, of those on earth, over earth, under earth, and every tongue shall testify in agreement to him as he judges all things rightly, the spirits of evil sending to endless fire, whether angels who sinned and were defeated in rebellion, or humans who are godless, sinful, anarchic and blaspheming; while he will freely give life unfailing and a halo of glory to the virtuous and holy, who observe his rules and abide in his love, some of them from the outset, others by returning to him. Having received this message and this faith, the church guards it earnestly, as if supervising a single

household, however scattered (as I said) over all the earth. And since it believes these truths with one mind and one heart, in unity it preaches and teaches and hands on the truths as with one mouth.[12]

The emphasis on the creator of heaven *and earth* is a direct answer to Marcionite claims that Jahweh was a secondary and inferior creator of the material universe. The birth from Mary's flesh and the bodily ascent to heaven answer the claim that the risen Christ was a spiritual being not tainted with mortal flesh. The punishing of *spiritual* evil goes against the claims of the elite to have a higher revelation. The talk of some returning to the faith counters the Gnostics' claims that the purified do not fall. This and similar creeds were used to assert the inclusive apostolic teaching — Tertullian gives three variants in his writings.[13]

4. *Government by bishops.* The churches described in Paul's letters had a range of ministries, with no single structure of authority. This arrangement could not survive much beyond any division of a local church into factions. Activities of the church at Rome, for instance, were conducted until the middle of the second century by a group of elders (presbyters). But in one of the apostolic churches, Antioch, a faction of Docetists formed its own circle for celebrating the eucharistic meal, in defiance of Ignatius, the man holding the recently established office of community "overseer" (*epi-skopos*) at the beginning of the second century. Docetism was a variant of Gnostic spiritualism, claiming that Christ merely *seemed* (Greek *edokēse*) to have a human body. This faction convinced the imperial authorities at Antioch that Ignatius had been the cause of civil turmoil, because of his opposition to the Docetists. He was taken to Rome to be executed. Along the way he wrote to other cities in Asia Minor, asking his fellow bishops to intervene on his behalf — not to save him from martyrdom in Rome (which he ecstatically anticipated) but to restore him to the good graces of his own community in Antioch — a plea that succeeded.[14] One interesting aspect of his famous letters is that all his pleading with bishops in other places had no parallel when he wrote ahead to Rome, the one place where he could not address a bishop (they still had none in the first decade of the second century).

The role of heresy in the creation of the bishop as a center of authority in each community comes out in Ignatius's anti-Docetist arguments. He writes to the Smyrneans, for instance, that Jesus is truly [not seemingly] born in the flesh to David's line, though he is God's son by his will and that will's enactment; truly brought forth of the virgin, baptized by John to observe all aspects of the law [not rejecting it]; for our sake truly nailed through the flesh under the tetrarch Pontius Pilate, an ordeal whose beneficiaries we are by God's blessing, so that he could raise an eternal standard for sanctified believers in him, whether Jewish or Gentile, all united in the church's single body. All these things he suffered for our rescue, suffered truly, just as he rose again truly — not merely seeming [*dokein*] to suffer, as some doubters say, who merely seem themselves, since their opinion will be fulfilled in them when they suffer as mere bodiless shades. But he was still in the flesh, even after his resurrection — as I know and believe.[15]

The bishops Ignatius described were not consecrated by Peter's successors (or any other apostle's). They were, like him, elected by their own communities. What made them apostolic was their election by Christians in the apostolic faith, as that was warranted by the apostolic churches. This public and communal aspect of authority was meant to contrast with the self-selecting and esoteric nature of authority among the Gnostics.

The Symbol of Peter

These four interlocking measures, adopted in the course of the second century, made for huge changes in the church's life. None of the four — not the canon, the creed, the office of bishop, nor the need for concord between the apostolic churches — is in Scripture. No text in the New Testament gives a list of the other New Testament books to be considered authoritative. If it had, the apostolic churches' long effort at sifting the candidates for inclusion would have been unnecessary. That was a task for the churches, not a Scripture task. Nor was it a task for Peter, or for the church in Rome, which played a small part in these developments. No single church could at that time speak for *the* church.

Yet the Gnostics were right to make Peter the object of their criticism. He is the weak and often mistaken man for whom the church exists, one who does not have a secret gnosis. Christ did not come to save the special, the extraordinary, the strong. Chesterton put this point in one of his Father Brown stories. An acolyte of a spiritualist leader praises her guru's "wonderful spiritual powers." Spoken like a good

Gnostic. Father Brown answers: "I don't care for spiritual powers much myself. I've got much more sympathy with spiritual weaknesses."[16] Spoken like a true champion of orthodoxy. The New Testament does not fudge the record of Peter — his lapses, his silliness, his vanity. No Gnostic gospel presents its leading visionary as a buffoon. The writers of these texts were interested in "spiritual powers." But in the canonical Gospels Peter is the first of the disciples — first called, most mentioned, made central. If he is not included in the church, who has the right to be?

In John's Gospel, the commission to Peter is not based on superior knowledge, insight, or vision. It is a simple test: "Do you love me more than these do?" (Jn 21.15). The question is asked three times, to counter Peter's three denials. And then his mission is given to him: "Pasture my flock" (verse 17). The relation of this verse to the commission in Matthew is clarified by the problems the church was already experiencing when the Gospels were written, during the latter part of the first century. The norms for inclusion in the church were being posed in terms of gnosis. Who can be included in the church? Only the elite, only those with special vision? That is the question being answered when Christ tells Peter: "I shall give you the keys to heaven's kingdom. Whatever you tie [*deseis*] on earth will have been tied in heaven, and whatever you untie [*lyseis*] on earth will have been untied in heaven" (Mt 16.19).

At a first reading, this passage presents us with the same problem as the description of Peter as a stone, the problem of usurping Christ's own role. *Jesus* is the bearer of the key at Rev 1.18, and he is the one who unties (*lythenai*) a woman tied up (*edēsen*) by the devil at Lk 13.16. But Jesus says that what Peter binds on earth "will *have been* bound in heaven" (future perfect). Peter does not work the binding or loosing himself, but reports what is accomplished already. The language of binding and loosing was used in Greek magic texts. But scholars rightly connect the terms rather with Jewish usage — as when Jesus says that scribes and Pharisees tie [*desmeuousin*] heavy burdens on others (Mt 23.4). The ability to set rules is indicated, and the connection with the "keys" indicates that these are the rules for inclusion in or exclusion from the community:

The verse is evocative of Isa 22.15–25, where Shebna, prime minister of King Hezekiah of Judah, is deposed and replaced by Eliakim, on whose shoulder God places "the key of David: he shall open . . . and he shall shut." The power of the key of the Davidic kingdom is the power to open and to shut, i.e., the prime minister's power to allow or refuse entrance to the palace, which involves access to the king.[17]

This is precisely the activity of the church in deciding norms of inclusion — whether that of non-Temple observers in Jerusalem (Acts 7.48), non-kosher Christians in Antioch (Gal 2.12), or Gnostics in the time when Matthew's and John's Gospels were written.

This power of inclusion or exclusion is given to Peter, as first of the apostles — but not exclusively to him. In fact, he was on the wrong side of the inclusion issue at Antioch. All the disciples are included in Jesus' words at Mt 18.18: "Solemnly I tell you [hymōn, plural] this: Whatever you tie on earth will have been tied in heaven, and whatever you untie on earth will have been untied in heaven." This power cannot be primarily a teaching role, since Jesus, in this very Gospel of Matthew (23.10), tells the disciples: "Do not take the title of expositors [kathēgētai] — you have a single expositor, the Messiah [Christos]." Nor can the language of tying and untying refer to papal primacy or Rome's bishop — neither existed at the time.

The verses have a pastoral sense. The brothers must support each other, keep the wolf from the fold, and confirm their unanimity of belief. Even one of the apostolic churches could need brotherly correction, as we saw in the case of Ignatius. Antioch itself was divided, and Ignatius appealed to the surrounding churches (not, that is, to Rome) to restore unity there. There is a powerful expression of the centrality of shepherds in Luke's nativity story. Men pasturing their flocks are the first to have the message of Christ's birth brought to them. They precede the learned, the wise men from the East, just as Peter's choice preceded that of Paul. Peter is the central figure among the disciples, the grounded one, the common man. Jesus was not like any human founder of an organization, who must have a strong successor or representative. There can be no successor or substitute for Jesus.

There would, in time, be many different uses for the symbol of Peter, including the papacy itself. But in the early days it was his Jewishness, his love, his return to Christ that were important. To defend these was to defy the Gnostics' claim that the Jewish background of Christianity had to be renounced, that the perfect do not fall, that those who do fall cannot be welcomed back. Peter was already a symbol of unity because he was a symbol of inclusion. The Christian community followed the rule set by a criminal for his gang in the movie *There Was a Crooked Man:* "You're only as good as your worst man." Chesterton put it more tactfully: a chain is only as strong as its weakest link. Peter holds the chain together.

6

Paul

IF PETER WAS SUSPECT to many in the early church, Paul was far more so, and for a longer period. He was, after all, the apostle who had never known Christ in his lifetime, who had persecuted Christians, who had defied the Jerusalem leader James, who had clashed with Peter in Antioch (and perhaps in Corinth), who was favored by many Gnostics, who seemed to be attacking the Jewish law, and whose daring speculations were obscure, if not unsettling, to more conventional minds. Even Peter's critics admitted that he had been favored by Christ in his lifetime. But Paul could only assert that the risen Jesus had appeared to him personally (just what made the Gnostics like him so much). With all these liabilities, the writings of Paul were like radioactive material, to be handled with special instruments.

No wonder some preferred not to handle them at all. In a surprising amount of the earliest Christian literature, Paul might as well not have existed.

> The silence of the so-called Epistle of Barnabas and the Didache concerning Paul's activity, the eclipse of his influence that seems to underlie such passages as Rev 2.2, 9, 14–15, 20–24; 3.9; 21.27; 2 Peter 3.16; James 2.17, and the negligible use made of the epistles by Justin Martyr, point to the conclusion that by Marcion's day the gospel of Paul was in clear danger of being forsaken altogether.[1]

Hegesippus, in the second century, ignores Paul. So does his elder, Papias:

When we move back from Hegesippus to one of similar stripe, Papias, and ask what this bishop of a community that belonged to the regions reached by the Apostle to the gentiles, and was already in existence during Paul's lifetime (Col 4.13), [says about Paul], it appears to me that again only one answer is possible — nothing . . . When the *Ecclesiastical History* [of Eusebius] 3.39.12–17 informs us that Papias valued the Apocalypse quite highly, that he used the apostolic gospels of Matthew and of Mark/Peter along with other traditional material from the circle of the twelve, and finally that he also cites from 1 John and 1 Peter, while in the same context various persons of the apostolic age to whom Papias appealed are mentioned by name (3.39.2–10), its silence about Paul and his letters is completely clear.[2]

If Peter is called Satan by Jesus, Paul seems to have been given the same title by the author of Revelation. Modern scholars find a reference to him at Rev 2.9 and 3.9, where it is said that those who reject the Jewish synagogue make themselves members of "Satan's synagogue."[3] In the pseudo-Pauline 2 Tim 1.15, Paul is made to complain that "everyone in Asia [Minor] has turned away from me," better describing a situation at the end of the first century than during Paul's lifetime. Others find an anti-Pauline bias in the Johannine writings.[4]

It is not surprising that Peter would be pressed into service in the discrediting of Paul, especially since there was a (minority) Petrine school of Jewish Gnosticism that found expression in the early church. This variant of Gnosticism could not, with Marcion, reject the whole of Hebrew Scripture; so Peter was made the Christian champion of it against Paul, especially in the pseudo-Clementine *Peter's Announcements* (*Kērygmata Petrou*), an apocryphal text from the beginning of the second century.[5] This purports to be a gospel of Peter as reported in a narrative by Clement, his successor in Rome. Peter is made to say, among other things, that his mission to Rome followed that of Paul, "as light follows darkness, as Gnosis follows ignorance, as healing follows sickness."[6]

The Christians addressed by *Peter's Announcements* were apparently descendents of the false brothers the apostle [Paul] did battle with in his letter to the Galatians. We have seen that the Pauline letters generally oppose the exponents of a Jewish gnosticism, and it is very likely that those adversaries belonged to approximately the same circle as the

false brothers who came [to Antioch] from Jerusalem. We have estab-
lished, in fact, that there were bound to be different emphases at the
core of Jewish Christianity — James representing one of these, and
Peter's Announcements a different one. One group emphasized the
Gnosis, while the other shied from such speculation. But they made
common cause against Paul. The letter of James and our gnostic text
[*Announcements*], each in its own way, mounted an attack on him.
Origen among others made no distinction between the two groups of
Jewish Christians, united as they were in a common antipathy toward
the apostle Paul.[7]

The attacks on Paul made Tertullian and other fathers look more
deeply into Paul's writings, trying to save them for the orthodox community. The touchiness of this operation comes out in a late letter
attributed to Peter which was included in the canon of the New Testament. This text warily endorses Paul — but only if he is properly understood. In a context of controversy over the End Time, Peter is made
to say (3.15–17):

> Consider that the Lord's long forbearance is for your rescue, as our
> loved brother Paul, out of the wisdom vouchsafed him, wrote to you
> whenever in his writings he spoke on this subject [the End Time] —
> though there are difficult points [on the subject] which the ignorant
> and ill-grounded twist from their true meaning, as they do his other
> writings, to their own bane.[8] But you, loved ones, since you are advised
> beforehand, be on your guard. Do not be dislodged from your own
> firm grounding, as if swayed by the waywardness of the fickle.

The imagery of "grounding" is appropriate here. A sound instinct told
the orthodox that the way to save the lofty Paul from misinterpreta-
tion was to ground him in the earthiness of Peter. Tertullian labors
mightily to reconcile the two. He says, for instance, that there was no
real disagreement between them at Antioch — a position that Augustine would stoutly deny in a later century.[9] Though Paul says he was
swept up to the third heaven, Tertullian argues that this does not mean
he received a secret gospel like that of the Gnostics.[10] Marcion is rebuked for pitting apostle against apostle: "Happily Peter and Paul became equal by their martyrdom."[11]

This shared death in Rome became a powerful fact for the early
church. We have seen earlier that Rome was the only apostolic church

in the West, out of the mainstream of early church activity. But it was also the one community that could boast of two apostles who ended their lives together. And these two were the figureheads for opposing tendencies in the church. If they could be maneuvered into an embrace (a common depiction of them in early Roman art), they would give warrant for each other's orthodoxy, each bringing in his own symbolic constituency. It is with an obvious sense of relief that Tertullian says, "To the Romans Peter and Paul entrusted their gospel, marked with the seal of their blood."[12] The two men's reconciliation was probably real, if we are to believe Raymond Brown's and Oscar Cullmann's interpretation of Tacitus's *Annals* 15.44, which says that Christians turned in other Christians during the Neronian persecution.[13] The informers would have been Judaizing Christians, whose status was recognized in Rome and who feared that the non-Jewish forms of Christianity would jeopardize that status — which puts Peter in the opposite (Paul's) camp.[14] After his lapse in Antioch, Peter returned to the missionary inclusiveness of Paul.

The martyrdoms of Peter and Paul are not described in the New Testament — presumably because the internal conflict of the Christian community, which led to the apostles' betrayal, was too embarrassing to be officially recorded. But a reference to the circumstances of their death is the only thing that makes sense of a letter sent three decades later from the Roman community to Corinth. The amanuensis of the community, presbyter Clement, urges the Christians of Corinth to heal their inner division (*schisma, stasis, eris*) caused by "rivalrous grudges" (the hendiadys *zēlos kai phthonos*). Near the outset of the letter, a rhetorical set piece, structured by anaphora, describes the bane of internal strife:

A *rivalrous grudge* caused the fratricide [of Abel by Cain]. From *rivalry* our father Jacob fled the reach of his brother Esau. *Rivalry* caused Joseph to be threatened with death and given over into slavery. *Rivalry* forced Moses to flee Pharaoh's reach when those of his own blood asked, "Who gave you rule over us?" . . . *Rivalry* ostracised Aaron and Miriam from the encampment. *Rivalry* carried Dathan and Abiram, while still living, into Hades, since they sowed division [*stasis*] among the followers of Moses, who was God's servant. From *rivalry* David suffered not only the foreigners' grudge [*phthonos*] but was hounded by Saul, who was Israel's own king. (1 Clement 4, emphasis added)

All these are examples of betrayal by one's own — by a brother (Abel, Jacob, Joseph), or by one's people (all the rest). With this preparation, we reach the climax of Clement's list of wrongs inflicted *by one's own* — the death of Peter and Paul:

> But enough of ancient cases. Turn we now to the glorious prizewinners [*athlētai*] of recent time; take we up the models of our own age. From a *rivalrous grudge* our most prominent and approved pillars were hounded, and they won the prize [*ēthlēsan*] of death. Put we before your gaze our own apostles. From evil *rivalry* Peter suffered not one or two but many ordeals and, offering his life as witness, achieved his merited rank of honor. From *rivalrous strife* [*phthonos kai eris*] Paul won the trophy for endurance. Though seven times in captivity, though put to flight, this herald of the faith in both the East and the West won the high fame of his faith for preaching redemption through all the world — while traveling toward the far term of the West, he offered the authorities the witness of his life, escaped this world, and entered the sacred precinct, the very prototype of endurance. (1 Clement 5, emphasis added)[15]

Clement, who is asking the Corinthians to mend their inner wounds, bares the brotherly betrayals in Rome's own past, to show that a community can overcome self-inflicted wounds and reach the harmony (*homonoia*) recommended by Clement in almost rapturous ways. The polished rhetoric against discord, like the wealth of studied examples marshaled to support the argument, seems not to be invented for this one occasion, but to reflect long consideration and mutual exhortation in Rome's struggle to overcome the shame of Christian complicity in the death of the church's greatest apostles. Peter and Paul were united not only by their martyrdom but by the *cause* of their martyrdom — resentment at Paul's opposition to Jewish Christian practices, an opposition to which Peter had "defected." The Rome of Clement has rallied back to the two apostles, who are now held in joint honor. (Paul even seems to have an edge on Peter, placed as he is in the climactic position, and with more fulsome praise than that given Peter.)

It is a touching fact that the Roman community, torn by a strife that sacrificed many Christians along with Peter and Paul, became a symbol of unity and wholeness precisely because the two apostles, along with what each stood for, were reconciled there. That alone was enough to make Rome a place special and holy, despite its latecomer status among the apostolic churches. Its importance was bound to grow as people reflected on all that was involved in the union of Peter with Paul. This would draw pilgrims, century after century, to the execution sites of the two men. Even now, it makes me feel like a pilgrim every time I enter again the traffic-clogged modern city.

Almost all early references to the Roman church praise it as the community of Peter *and* Paul. One without the other lacked the aura that made Rome distinctive. Ignatius of Antioch, who realizes there is no bishop in Rome, and who does not ask its church to intervene for him, is still deferential to it as the church of Peter and Paul (Letter to the Romans 5). Irenaeus refers to "the church established and structured by the two most illustrious apostles, Peter and Paul."[16] Even a later believer in papal primacy like Pope Leo I could say that Christian Rome was founded by a more benign version of ancient Rome's founders, Romulus and Remus (Sermon 5.2). For many centuries, the importance of Rome would be marked because of its dyarchy — a condominium of power (S 57, 65, 89, 184).[17]

In the third and fourth centuries, despite the fact that the myth of Peter as bishop had already been developed, portrait busts of him alone were rare — Peter and Paul were paired, as the stunning exhibit of early materials at the Quirinal Palace in 2000 graphically demonstrated.[18] As a contributor to the catalogue of that exhibit says, "Their cult was a single one, indivisible."[19] There is a division of labor between the two men — Peter is shown as a stereotypical senator and Paul as the conventional philosopher.[20] Their equality is celebrated in representations of Christ giving his charter to the church (*traditio legis*). This visual device shows both men kneeling before Christ. Peter is often on Christ's favored right side, receiving the keys, but sometimes Paul is in that position, receiving a scroll — signs that Peter is the leader, Paul the teacher.[21] The men are treated as equals, as Bernhard Schimmelpfennig says:

As a result of a further unfolding of older traditions recognized in Rome since the first century, both apostles were now considered to be the forefathers of the bishop of Rome, the [later] bishops inheriting from the one the position of chief shepherd, from the other the supreme authority on doctrine. Thus the festival on June 29, when both apostles were commemorated, grew in significance for the solidification of the episcopate. (Sch 27)

Actually, neither man founded the church in Rome, which had existed for two decades before they arrived there. When Paul writes ahead to the Romans, before his arrival among them, he mentions all those he knows (or knows of) in the community (Rom 16.1–17), and Peter is not there yet. These latecomers became co-founders in the second century, when all the apostolic churches were inventing or emphasizing their apostolic connections. And by the fourth century Peter had acquired at least one iconographic indicator that he was the founder *par excellence.* This pictorial image arose mysteriously, flourished with many exemplars, and disappeared almost as suddenly as it had popped up. Its effective life was limited to the fourth century.

The image depicts the "miraculous font," or miracle of the rock. It shows a rock that gushes water when Peter strikes it with a wand.[22] This seemed an obvious reference to the miracle of Moses in the desert (Ex 17.6), and for a time scholars thought Moses was the figure being depicted. But then some examples were found with "Peter" inscribed on them. The next clue was that two men were shown drinking from the fountain. Since these men were garbed as Roman soldiers, they must be part of the legend of Peter's escape from prison in Rome, effected when he works the miracle of the rock to baptize his two captors, Processus and Martinianus. (Once escaped, Peter runs away, following his characterization in the Gospels; but he meets the risen Jesus on the road, who asks him where he is going — *Quo vadis?* — and he turns back to face his death.)

We know the written version of the miracle of the rock from the sixth-century *Acts of Saint Processus and Martinianus* (by "Linus"), but the elements of the myth obviously existed in lost earlier texts.[23] In fact Augustine, in the fourth century, had already made the connection between Moses striking the stone and Peter's nickname "the Stone." Expounding the passage in Paul (1 Cor 10.5) that says Christ is the rock, he compares the doubting of Moses (told to strike the rock) with the denials of Peter.[24] This is precisely the conflation of rock imagery that Max Wilcox found behind the story of Peter's renaming in Matthew (p. 60 above).

This miracle of the rock, so popular in Rome, where over four dozen examples of it survive, was not picked up by the church at large, and even Rome dropped it after the fourth century. It is clear why this should be so. The new Moses is not Peter but Christ, who delivers the Sermon on the Mount, just as Moses brought the tablets down from Mount Sinai. To make Peter a substitute for Christ was too close to blasphemy. But the artifacts show that Peter's claims were being exalted within Rome, and precisely in terms of folk piety (the tale of the escape with his prison guards). Tertullian had said that Peter and Paul were equalized in the shedding of their blood. But over a long course of time Peter would be given the more eminent place. The *church* of Peter and Paul became the *seat* (see) of Peter — which made Walter Bauer claim that Rome "cut in half the apostolic foundation of its own church."[25]

7

Rome Mediating

I REFERRED in the introduction to the way *Papal Sin* was criticized for biblical fundamentalism — for not allowing any development of doctrine. But the crucial four changes of the second century were developments that clearly went beyond Scripture, and are clearly the basis for later beliefs I accept. Even later developments of the fourth and fifth centuries — principally the elaboration of the doctrines of the Trinity and the Incarnation — are not in Scripture.[1] In that sense the creed I profess goes beyond Scripture (without betraying it). These vital developments took place before the papacy existed. Even the Roman church had little to do with them. The church of Rome did not formulate the canon, establish the creed, or set up the episcopate. On the last point, Ignatius describes the system of bishops before Rome had one of its own. The Apostles' Creed was based on the liturgical practice of Rome, but that too took shape before there was a bishop there, and it was presented as originating not in Rome but in Jerusalem (see Chapter 23).

The great doctrines of the Trinity and the Incarnation were debated and resolved in the East, under imperial direction from Constantinople (see Chapter 9). It is important to remember how much of the church took shape before or apart from the papacy. The Catholic historian Eric John, who recognizes the legitimacy of the papacy, nevertheless warns us against equating the church with this function of the later church:

No pope created the episcopate or priesthood, not even Peter. The canon of the Bible owes nothing to any pope. The canon of the mass was established with next to no assistance from the pope; the great

creeds owe a little but not very much to the popes of their day. Even
the codification of canon law was largely done by private enterprise
and popes had to be shown just how effectively the judicial authority
they claimed could be deployed in practice. Some things, like the addition of the *filioque* to the Nicene creed, were done in the teeth of papal
prohibition. In missions, the development of theological studies, the
creation of religious orders, everywhere we see private initiative and a
scattering of the gifts of the Holy Spirit random enough to satisfy the
most extreme pentecostal sect.[2]

Rome, though never irrelevant, was often not central to what was happening in the church, even in its own sphere, the West. In the sixth century, says Peter Brown, "The most dramatic religious change to occur
in the western Mediterranean — the final adoption of Catholicism as
the religion of the Visigothic state, in 589 — took place in almost total
independence of the bishops of Rome."[3]

Some who maximize later papal claims say that primacy was implied
in early actions taken or statements made by Roman bishops. And it is
natural to wonder just what the church of Rome *was* doing while all
the early developments were taking place outside its scope. For the
most part, it was performing a collaborative role with the other five apostolic churches. But when it tried — as others sometimes did — to assert itself outside that collaborative framework, it was sharply rebuked,
often by people now honored as saints. I shall save the rebukes for the
next chapter and describe here the essentially mediating powers that
Rome exercised in the early centuries.

1. I have already mentioned the first known example of Rome acting
as mediator. Even before it had a bishop of its own, the church sent a
letter, drafted by presbyter Clement, to the fractious Corinthian Christians. It was doing just what Ignatius of Antioch had done when he
warned the churches of Asia Minor against the divisiveness that had
afflicted his church. The Romans told the Corinthians: "Your splinter-
ing [*schisma*] has misled many, dejected many, puzzled many, and sad-
dened us all — yet your division [*stasis*] continues" (1 Clement 46). The
letter speaks church-to-church. It is not signed, and it does not name
anyone living in either Corinth or Rome. Though some try to present
this as an early *papal* statement (even "the first papal encyclical"), establishing Rome's authority over another church, the letter issues a
plea (*enteuxin*, 63), not an order. James Jeffers observes:

First Clement was written not as an affirmation of Roman primacy, but as the action of one sister church helping another restore peace and unity. The author states in 63.4 that the letter is directed "to your speedy attainment of peace." He never asserts the authority of the Roman church, nor does he appeal to it as an example. Rather he writes as an interested friend who appeals to commonly held beliefs.[4]

As we saw earlier, Jeffers is not quite right in saying the letter does not offer Rome as an example — but it is a negative example, based on the division *in Rome* at the time when Peter and Paul were killed. This, however, just makes the nature of the letter more evident — as expressing fraternal solidarity in the need for repentance and for unity in the Lord.

2. In the second century, Polycarp, the bishop of Smyrna who had been praised in Ignatius's letter to the Smyrnaeans, took up the intermediating role that Ignatius had called for when he responded to a request from Philippi that he help bring peace to that riven community (Polycarp, Letter to the Philippians 3).

3. In the middle of the third century, Africa's Saint Cyprian asked Rome to intervene as mediator in a sister church's troubles. The bishop of Arles had refused to accept back into the church any who defected under persecution. A man in Lyons wrote to both Bishop Stephen in Rome and Bishop Cyprian in Carthage, asking for their help in reconciling opposed factions. Cyprian deferred to Rome, as the church closer to Arles, but urged Stephen (Letter 68) to take action. As we shall see in the next chapter, this had nothing to do with a judicial primacy in Rome, which Cyprian heatedly denied when that was claimed.

4. Early in the 260s, Christians in Alexandria suspected the trinitarian views of their patriarch, Dionysius, and asked that they be scrutinized by the pope, who was also named Dionysius (they entered their respective churches' calendars as "Saint Dionysius," and the episode is known as "the affair of the two Dionysiuses"). The pope did condemn the views of his namesake, but backed off when the Alexandrian explained to the Roman that he had misunderstood his position (F 383–84 — see also Chapter 9).

5. In the fourth century (313), just when the emperor Constantine recognized the Christian church, the puritanical Donatus in Africa asked him to intervene in a quarrel with the bishop of Carthage. Constantine committed the adjudication to Miltiades, the bishop of

Rome, who summoned other bishops to confer with him in the Lateran Palace (which Constantine had turned over to the popes). This has been called the Lateran Synod, and represented as an early exercise of papal primacy. But when Donatus continued to protest the judgment of Miltiades, Constantine called a new synod at Arles, since "the emperor did not consider his [the pope's] verdict final" (K 27). Schimmelpfennig (36) concludes that "[Pope] Miltiades was of significance for Constantine only as bishop of his empire's capital, but was not considered the highest judge in matters concerning the Christian congregations in the West [not to mention the East]."

6. In 339, the Nicene enemies of Athanasius asked Pope Julius I to join them in condemning that champion of the Nicene Creed. The pope went into the matter more thoroughly than they had anticipated, letting Athanasius defend himself before a Roman synod. When that group cleared Athanasius, Julius wrote to protest the unapostolical procedures of the men who had called on him to join them. He said that complaints against a bishop of Athanasius's standing "should have been addressed to *all* of us [in apostolic sees], so that what was right could have been determined by *all*" (S 23 — emphasis added). The bishops of the East had not followed "the instructions of Paul [who founded the Eastern churches] or the things the Fathers handed down to us . . . or what we received from the blessed apostle Peter" (S 24). The Arians had invited him late into a consultative process they had not been faithful to themselves.

7. In the fifth century, the mediating role of Rome was still important, as one sees from a recently discovered letter of Augustine (Letter *22). An African bishop, Honorius, had tried to transfer himself to a different see, against the canons of the Council of Nicea. When this was opposed by his fellow African bishops, Honorius took his case to Rome.[5] Augustine wrote his friend Alypius, who was in Italy at the time, that Rome would be the best venue for adjudication — not because Rome had any primacy of jurisdiction, but because a neutral arbiter was called for: "Since it is impracticable to conclude the matter here, personal animosity and the force of circumstance [*necessitas*] commit the matter to the apostolic see." Besides, Augustine is sure Rome will just confirm what the Africans had told Honorius: "We are not worried about Rome judging the matter, because we are confident how that see will decide."[6] This is just the kind of situation in which sister churches can play a mutually strengthening role.

8. In 429, a fierce dispute over the nature of Christ broke out between Eastern patriarchs, Cyril of Alexandria and Nestorius of Constantinople, both of whom appealed to the West for arbitration. Pope Celestine I, heeding the advice of the theologian John Cassian, sided with Cyril and called on him to act as his agent in disciplining Nestorius. But, as W.H.C. Frend says, "it was he [Cyril] and not Celestine who called the tune" (F 756). Cyril sent a letter to Nestorius demanding that he renounce twelve anathematized positions, and Nestorius responded with twelve counter-anathemas. The emperor Theodosius II called for a council to assemble at Ephesus, in 431, to decide whether the patriarch of his own capital was a heretic. He appointed his officer, Count Candidian, to preside over the council, but it was clear by the end of its session that "Cyril himself had run the proceedings from start to finish and reduced Count Candidian to a cipher" (F 760), steering through a condemnation of Nestorius, who was ousted from his see in Constantinople. Cyril began the council without waiting for the pope's legates to arrive, and the council record was not submitted to the pope, who nonetheless expressed approval of it (K 42).

9. In 448, another Alexandrian, the monk Eutyches, appealed to Rome after being condemned in the East. This gave Pope Leo the Great one of the West's rare opportunities to influence Eastern councils of the church, since he found against Eutyches and sent his findings to the East in a letter (known as the *Tomus*), which was read and approved at the Council of Chalcedon in 451, where someone present said, "Peter has spoken through Leo." Leo had addressed his letter to Patriarch Flavian of Constantinople, who was deposed by supporters of Eutyches at a rump council ("Ephesus II"). Leo, with a savage pun, called that council "not an assembly but a dissembly" (*latrocinium, non concilium*). Flavian, with the help of Leo's letter, prevailed at Chalcedon. Papal apologists have tried to make of this letter an early example of a papal ruling accepted just for being that. But the council fathers accepted it on the grounds Leo himself gave — as intermediation by one of the apostolic churches.

When Leo's legate read the pope's position, which also conformed to the intentions of the members of the synod, they were happy to have found a speaker who was neutral on the internal bickerings in the East, and they applauded him, exclaiming: "Peter has spoken through Leo." From this Leo derived the magisterium for all Christians, as did later popes to an even greater degree. But the council fathers also showed that they would only accept the Roman line if it corresponded to their own views. They did so by granting the patriarch of Constantinople the same position in the Eastern empire that the patriarch in Rome held in the West, just as their predecessors had done in 381. Little wonder that both of the decrees drawn up in Chalcedon on this point were not accepted in Rome. (Sch 48)

Father Schatz agrees:

Certainly one cannot read out of it [the council's adoption of Leo's letter] an unconditional formal authority, and definitely not an "infallibility" of papal teaching documents. Leo's letter was by no means accepted without discussion of its content, and it created serious difficulties for some individual fathers. This, in fact, was not contrary to Leo's instructions, which called for agreement based on discussion and accommodation among the fathers. (S 44)

Frend says that Leo's communication borrowed from rather than lent authority to an even more important letter, that which Cyril of Alexandria sent to Nestorius. The twelve anathemas in that letter had been accepted as norms of belief at the Council of Ephesus, and it was still invoked at Chalcedon: "Cyril indeed presided in absentia. His teaching was orthodox. All else, including Leo's *Tomus*, had to stand the test of agreement with him" (F 770).

All the cases described here show Rome's interventions being accepted when they were efforts at unity undertaken by one apostolic church — doing what all the apostolic churches did when they were called on for this service. Schatz points out that Rome was well positioned to act as an arbiter in this period, since it had largely been left out of the internal conflicts of the East, and could be seen as an outsider listening to all sides. This made it a "refuge in critical situations" (S 26). But Schimmelpfennig observes that other churches in the West had the same advantage, so that patriarchs of Antioch or Alexandria also called on Carthage and Milan to adjudicate their disputes (Sch 49). And Rome was not necessarily more successful than those churches at discharging a mediator's office: "As would frequently be the case in centuries to come, the expectation of finding assistance in Rome far exceeded the ability of Rome to meet that expectation. Rome often lacked both competence and adequate information about the difficult problems of the East, nor did it have any real ability to carry through on its decisions" (S 26).

Still, as Schatz says, Rome was a symbol of unity at a time of bitter divisions. This was an appropriate symbolic role for Peter, who had tried (though ineffectually) to mediate between Paul and James at Antioch. Peter was a man in the middle, the mean between extremes.

8

Rome Meddling

WELCOME AS Rome was as a mediator with her sister churches, attempts to claim a superiority over them were rebuked, often severely, and the Roman bishop had to retreat. Consider what happened to Popes Victor I, Stephen, Zosimus, and Celestine.

1. When (c. 195) Pope Victor I tried to impose a single date for Easter on the churches of Asia Minor, they refused his intervention and he excommunicated them all. Not only did these churches themselves resist. Irenaeus of Lyons stepped in as a mediator between Rome and the East. He had a history of such diplomatic interventions with Rome. Before he became the bishop of Lyons, he had been sent as a presbyter to make his church's appeal to one of Victor's predecessors, recommending more lenient treatment for those accused of Montanist "rigorism." Now he opposed Victor's excommunication, stating that diversity in ritual was a long established practice, endorsed by previous bishops of Rome as well as by many bishops throughout the church. He saw in this no challenge to the essential truths of the faith. If people agreed on the meaning of the Resurrection, why was it heretical to celebrate that meaning a day or a week earlier or later? Agreement on essentials should actually protect difference on accidentals. "The fact that we differ about the [Easter] fast just proves that we are at one in the faith."[1] This is a maxim that could be applied to many of the issues confronting the church today.

Irenaeus was, as his name implies, irenic in his appeal. The affected bishops in Asia Minor were not so equable. Writing for them, Polycarp of Ephesus pointed out that their combined churches were, like Rome, the carriers of tradition derived from two apostles (Philip and John), and the home of many martyrs and saints who had celebrated Easter in their way. Polycarp brusquely remarks, "I do not panic because others have been struck silly."[2]

2. Pope Stephen I was defied on two occasions by the African church, led by Saint Cyprian. We saw in the last chapter how Cyprian *appealed* to Rome to act as a mediator in the troubles of Arles. But when in 254 the pope ordered two Spanish communities to take back bishops who had deserted the faith under persecution, those communities, which had appointed their own successors to the fallen bishops, appealed to Cyprian to arbitrate the conflict. The bishop of Carthage called a council of thirty-seven bishops to decide the case (F 353–54). They concluded that the pope had acted unwisely, but only because he was misinformed about the facts of the case — Thomas Aquinas's *propter falsos testes* (K 20). The pope's directive was ignored.

3. A far more serious clash between Stephen and Cyprian took place when the pope ordered African and Asia Minor churches not to rebaptize those who had defected from the faith under persecution. Stephen was not acting, now, as a mediator with his fellow bishops, or as the spokesman for a Roman synod, but imposing an *ipse dixi*. He not only intruded in a very sensitive process going forward in Africa, but acted in response to difficulties in his own situation in Rome. The problem in both places had been caused by the empire-wide persecution launched by the emperor Decius in 250. In Rome, Pope Fabian was arrested, and died in prison. When Stephen was elected pope, he adopted a policy of bringing *lapsi* (those who defected from the faith during the persecution) back into the church on easy terms. The prominent Roman presbyter Novatian said this was a policy that disqualified Stephen to be pope, and had himself elected in his stead.

Things were even worse in Carthage, where three rival bishops emerged from the ordeal of the persecutors. Cyprian, the bishop when the persecution began, knew that its aim was to kill the Christian leaders first, so their followers would be disanimated. So he went into hiding and governed the church from underground lairs. Though he would die bravely as a martyr in a later persecution, his conduct in this one allowed his well-placed enemies to portray him as deserting his flock. Cyprian, a wealthy aristocrat, had been elected by the people of his diocese, who loved him for his many charities. He incurred the enmity of five men who had greater seniority as presbyters. These disappointed priests joined with the professors of the faith (*confessores*) who were in prison, saying that those who had not fled should judge the terms on which defectors could be readmitted to communion. They began to issue their own certificates, pardoning those *lapsi* who would join in opposing Cyprian.

When Cyprian came out of hiding, he could forge a new consensus only by calling a series of councils with other African bishops. This led one presbyter, Novatus, with a harsher line on *lapsi,* to be consecrated as a rival bishop — and he was soon joined by a third anti-bishop taking a more lenient view. "Thus Cyprian was in fact meeting two diametrically opposed movements, the extremes of laxity and of rigorism."³

The councils called by Cyprian had to deal with four main categories of the lapsed:

A. Those who offered sacrifice to idols: There was a strong effort to exclude these "quislings" entirely, though Cyprian was able to work out readmission to the church after a lifetime of repentance — with instant access to the sacraments whenever death threatened any *lapsus.*

B. Those who did not sacrifice, but who bribed Roman officials to give them certificates recording that they did. These could be readmitted after a period of repentance, its length depending on individual circumstances. As Cyprian said (Letter 55.113–14), some bought the certificates to save their families, or used them to shelter others threatened with death: "Different is the attitude of the philosophers and Stoics, dear brother, who say that all sins are equal, and that the man of character must not give way to softness. But between philosopher and Christian there is a world of difference."⁴

C. Those who, whether or not they had sacrificed or bought certificates, were baptized by the schismatic bishops — Novatian (in Rome), Novatus (in Africa), or any who had joined with them. In Rome, Stephen admitted these people as having been validly baptized, and he ordered the churches in Africa and Asia Minor to do the same. But Cyprian, like the Asian bishops, said that local councils had jurisdiction over their own flocks, and that baptism outside the church was not valid.⁵ Those wanting readmission would have to be rebaptized — or, rather, be validly baptized for the first time.

D. Those in any of the above categories who refused to acknowledge their guilt. These could not be readmitted to the church at all.

Pope Stephen, to give his order greater force, made the first known use of the text on Peter as "Stone" (Mt 16.18), claiming that it gave Rome jurisdiction over other churches. Up to this time, the Matthew text was seen as addressed to all bishops, with Peter as their representative — or even to all Christians. As Origen said, in his commentary on the verse: "Anyone who imitates Christ is a stone . . . and on such a stone is built every declaration of the church . . . for the church is being built up of each [person] who is redeemed." This accords with Peter's own alleged words at 1 Peter 2.5: "You, like him [Jesus], must be living stones built into the spiritual fabric of a holy structure."

Stephen's use of the Matthew passage to claim a new power made Cyprian alter what he had written about the chair of Peter in the first edition of his treatise, *The Catholic Church's Unity.*[6] In that edition, he said that Peter was a symbol of unity for all Christians — that was what distinguished him:

> Though [Jesus] gives equal authority to all the apostles, yet he estab-lished only a single chair, and he authoritatively made it the beginning and the characteristic of such unity. The rest of the apostles were in-deed just what Peter was, yet the first place [*primatus*] was granted to Peter, making manifest that there is only one church and one chair. This demonstrates that there is only one flock, though there are many shepherds, who are all to be of one mind in feeding the flock.[7]

Though it is a scholarly convention to call this "the primacy text" be-cause of its use of the word *primatus,* nothing like later claims of pri-macy is contained in it. Peter is the symbol of unity, but in every other way all apostles are equal: "When Cyprian ascribes a *primatus* to Peter — and he is the earliest writer so to do — he means that Peter was the first of the apostles to be chosen, his 'primacy' is a priority in time and not a supremacy of jurisdiction."[8] To emphasize this fact, under the challenge offered by Stephen's reading of Matthew, Cyprian removed *primatus* from his second edition, and spelled out his meaning even more clearly: "The other apostles were exactly what Peter was, en-dowed with equal amounts of honor and authority . . . there is only one apostolic office, each aspect of which, in each individual, is ordered to the entirety [of its exercise]."[9] Or, as Cyprian put it in his Letter

55.24, "The episcopate is one, spread out in the concordant fellowship of its many bishops."[10]

Cyprian's treatise is the first major theological work on the authority of the Roman see. To back it up, he engaged in a sharp exchange of letters with Stephen. An even harsher response came from Asia Minor. Bishop Firmilian of Cappadocia wrote to call Stephen "patently ignorant . . . bold and insolent . . . a disgrace to Peter and Paul."[11] Cyprian wrote to a fellow bishop in Africa, Pompeius: "There is much that is arrogant, irrelevant, self-contradictory, ill-considered and inept in what he [Stephen] has written."[12] Stephen, for his part, thundered accusations at Cyprian, calling him "a false Christ" (F 336). When Cyprian sent to Rome a delegation to discuss the matter, Stephen refused to receive it. He probably, according to J. D. Merdinger, excommunicated Cyprian. But Stephen died almost immediately after this rash act, and Cyprian was martyred a year later. Pious legend, trying to restore Stephen's status vis-à-vis his African foe, said that the pope too had been martyred, but the early bishop lists of Rome do not rank him with the martyrs (K 21). He was nonetheless given his own feast day as a saint.

4. In 417, an African council had condemned Pelagius as a heretic, but Pelagius appealed to Rome as to a higher court. Pope Zosimus sent a letter to Carthage (*Magnum pondus,* 417) ordering the Africans to reconsider, and to justify themselves before his tribunal. This was not a matter of mediation between sister churches. It was a command from on high: "I urge you to do so as much by the authority of the Apostolic See as by the mutual concord that exists between our two churches."[13] While, as Merdinger puts it, "Augustine was fuming" over this letter, the pope quickly followed it up with a second one (*Postquam a nobis*) praising Pelagius and denouncing the Africans for introducing tempests into the church.[14] When the Africans did not comply, the pope sent a third letter (*Quamvis patrum,* 418) asserting that Rome has final authority on all matters of doctrine and practice.[15] The Africans — under their leaders Aurelius, Augustine, and Alypius — not only scheduled a new council to condemn Pelagius, but sent a secret delegation to the emperor Honorius in Ravenna, asking him to enforce their decision. When Honorius did so, Zosimus had to back down and join in the condemnation.

This papal defeat was misrepresented later as a papal victory. When Zosimus was forced to issue his condemnation of Pelagius, Augustine is supposed to have said, "Rome has spoken, the matter is ended"

(*Roma locutus est, causa finita est*). He did not say that; but even if he
had, the maxim would not have indicated a Roman primacy, since
Zosimus's real initiative, his exoneration of Pelagius, had not "ended
the matter." What Augustine actually said, at the end of the struggle,
was "In this proceeding [*causa*], two council findings were sent to the
Apostolic See, and a report has come back. The proceeding is ended —
I wish the heresy were" (Sermon 131.10). It is the victory of Africa's two
councils that he is celebrating — a victory sealed when even the pope
had to comply with them, despite his reluctance.

5. Pope Zosimus found himself in conflict with the African churches
again in 419, when a troublemaking priest, Apiarius, tried to reverse his
excommunication in Africa by going over the heads of local bishops
with an appeal to the pope. When investigators sent by the pope arrived in Carthage, the Africans denied that the pope had any jurisdiction in the matter. The delegates cited a canon from the Council of
Nicea to authorize their mission, but Augustine said that it was not an
authentic part of that council's legislation. Since the delegates would
not accept Augustine's document, he offered to send a mission to the
East to ask for a record of the council's proceedings.

Pending that, the pope's men would not be allowed to conduct any
investigation. They went home stymied. "The matter was ended" —
not because the pope had spoken, but because he had (in his emissaries) been silenced. The reports from Constantinople confirmed that
what the pope was citing was not a Nicene canon but words from a
council (Sardica, not recognized by the Eastern church) that had been
inserted into the Nicene record to bolster papal innovations.[16]

6. Six years after this clash, the occasion for it, the conduct of
Apiarius, caused new trouble. Apiarius had been deprived of his office
as bishop in 419, but remained a priest, and in that capacity committed
a sexual crime so heinous that the record is mute about its details.
Condemned again in Africa, he went again to Rome. A new pope,
Celestine, let the leader of the former delegation, Faustinus, return to
Africa to accomplish what he had not in his first attempt. The Africans
proved, all over again, that the pope was relying on a defective understanding of his authority under the canons of Nicea, and sent a blistering letter (*Optaremus*), telling the pope to keep Faustinus at home
and send no more emissaries. "We do not find it authorized in any
council of the fathers that delegates can be sent from your Holiness . . .

Do not send delegates, do not take up any cases, lest we appear to introduce the acrid pride of the world into the light of Christ's church . . . We are sure that never again will Africa have to put up with him [Faustinus]."[17]

As a result of his own experiences with the popes, Augustine repeated Cyprian's progress from the preceding century — he, too, made it clearer over time that he did not admit any claim of jurisdiction based on Mt 16.18. In the words of Robert Markus,

> Thus the favorite proof-text on which the Popes were building their claims, "You are Peter and upon this rock (*super hanc petram*) I will build my church" (Matt. 16.18), was silent, for Augustine, on the Roman claims to primacy. He had changed his mind, he informs us, about the interpretation of this verse. Originally, he took it as referring to Peter, though to him as "representing the whole Church"; but, as if even this interpretation might seem to place man at the foundation of the Church, he came to prefer another. So later, he tells us, "most often" he interpreted the verse in a sense such as to mean that the Church was founded on Him whom Peter had confessed as the Messiah: "Thus Peter, so named by that rock (*petra*), would represent the person of the Church which is built upon the rock. He was not called *petra* but *Peter;* the *petra* was Christ.[18]

Augustine saw the problem adverted to in Chapter 5 above — that everywhere else in the New Testament Christ is the stone of foundation for the church, and no man can usurp that role. So Augustine said that even in Mt 16.18, Christ must be the rock, and the church (symbolized by Peter) is built on him. As he said in *Interpreting John's Gospel* (124.5),

> Peter, because he was the first apostle, represented the person of the church by synecdoche.[19] As for his merely personal characteristics, he was a man by nature, a Christian by grace, an apostle and the first apostle by grace added to grace. But when he was told, "I will give you the keys of heaven's kingdom, and what you tie on earth will have been tied in heaven, what you untie on earth will have been untied in heaven," he was standing for [*significabat*] the entire church, which does not collapse though it is beaten, in this world, by every kind of trial, as if by rain, flood, and tempest. It is founded on a Stone [*Petra*], from which Peter took his name Stone-Founded [*Peter*] — for the Stone did not take its name from the Stone-Founded, but the Stone-

Founded from the Stone — as Christ does not take his name from Christians, but Christians from Christ . . . Because the stone was Christ.[20]

So even in the West (not to mention the East), papal primacy based on the Matthew text was denied, not by peripheral figures but by central Christian leaders like Saint Cyprian and Saint Augustine — and not only in the first three or four centuries but well into the fifth. And it should be noticed that both Zosimus and Celestine, though they asserted their own primacy, did not expect to persuade others by that assertion alone but by appeal to the decrees of the Council of Nicea. When that argument collapsed, so did their claim of primacy.

9

Rome and the East

IN THE fourth and fifth centuries, Rome was far from the center of theological action. All six of the early councils were held in the East, following the pattern established by the emperor Constantine when he took over the care of the church after giving it official status. He and his successors called, directed, promulgated, and enforced the councils, which were held at sites of their choosing — the first (325 C.E.) at Nicea, the emperor's summer palace, and two more in his capital, Constantinople. Though the fourth council was called for Nicea, the emperor Marcian shifted it to Chalcedon.

When the emperor did not preside in person, lay officials of his appointment did, nineteen of them at Chalcedon. By the seventh council, an empress (Irene) was the directing officer (H 411). As Frend says of Constantine's regional council of Tyre,

It was presided over by an imperial official, the count Dionysius, a former consul. The emperor had intervened directly in a matter of church discipline, and though sentence would be pronounced by the bishops, their proceedings would be supervised by a layman. This was to be the pattern for all the great councils of the patristic age. At Chalcedon, the papal delegates themselves had to address their speeches to a bench of lay assessors, and the emperor Marcian himself guided the deliberations of the bishops at the crucial sessions of the council . . . [Athanasius at Tyre] never questioned the rightness of the presence of the lay element there, even when the case went against him. (F 527)

No pope attended these councils. His delegates, when any were sent, sometimes arrived late, and took little part, often because they were unable to follow the debates in Greek. The only time a pope had any important contribution to make was the case considered earlier, when Leo I's letter (*Tomus*) was acclaimed at Chalcedon; but Leo also opposed one finding of that council, unsuccessfully; and Leo's letter was approved because it conformed to the twelve anathemas of the non-pope, Cyril (F 770).

There is nothing surprising about the defining of church doctrine in the East. Not only had Constantine shifted the seat of the Roman empire there. That is where most of the Christian churches were, and most of Christian learning, along with patriarchs and bishops and theologians. Rome had become an intellectual backwater by the fourth century, "a curiously obscure see" (F 330). Even when a separate and co-ordinate emperor was constituted for the West, he made his capital not in Rome, but in Milan (later shifted to Ravenna). Rome's isolation was deepened by the fact that Latin had become Rome's official language in the middle of the third century. Modern admirers of the Latin Mass claim that they are defending a universal language, the tongue of the Roman empire — but it was never that. The lingua franca of Roman rule was Greek (Rome had inherited the eastern territories conquered and settled by Alexander's Greek troops). Koine (pidgin Greek) was what merchants and bureaucrats used to communicate with the motley elements of the empire. Pilate and Jesus had to speak to each other in Koine, since one had no Aramaic and the other no Latin. Koine was the original language of the church — of the Gospels, of the liturgy, of Jews and Christians who traveled to Rome. Peter would not have spoken Latin, even in Rome, and Latin did not become the language of the Mass there until the third century.

Virgil, looking at the prospects of the Roman empire in a Greek-speaking world, had expressed a fear that Latin would be swallowed up in Greek. That fear might have seemed justified as the empire moved out from Rome to the East, or to Greek-speaking cities in Italy like Milan and Aquileia and Ravenna. In the fourth century, Ambrose of Milan was a far more influential Christian leader than Pope Damasus in Rome, and not only because Ambrose possessed the more forceful character. He also had the advantage of living in the imperial city, and of speaking Greek to its rulers. The papacy, left behind in the aban-

doned former capital, had to adjust to the needs of the people there —
of Latins who were neither cosmopolitan intellectuals speaking classical Greek nor immigrants from areas speaking Koine, but native speakers of the native tongue. Gradually popes with Latin names replaced
those with Greek ones — Telesphorus and Soter and Eleutherius of the
second century giving way to Victor and Urban and Fabian of the
third.

Rome's provincialism separated it from the rich theological culture
from which the doctrinal formulations of the fourth century emerged.
The gap between East and West was already apparent in the third
century, in the dispute between "the two Dionysiuses" (of Alexandria
and of Rome), mentioned in the last chapter. That debate went nowhere because each side ascribed to the other a position it did not
hold:

> The resulting correspondence (preserved by Athanasius) between Di-
> onysius of Rome and Dionysius of Alexandria always had the makings
> of a comedy of errors. Neither was fluent in the other's language . . .
> The meaning of the technical terms for "substance" (*ousia* and *sub-*
> *stantia*) became obscured. Dionysius of Rome thought his colleague
> believed the Trinity consisted in three different substances, while Dio-
> nysius of Alexandria regarded his namesake as an ally of the Cyrena-
> ican Modalist Monarchians. (F 383–84)

Rome simply did not have the resources — physical, intellectual, or
linguistic — to lead the church yet: "Traditions of public service, higher
education, and literacy were also more developed [in the East]. The
most distinguished schools of philosophy, law, and science were in
such cities as Athens, Beirut, and Alexandria" (H 25). The West had
nothing like the massed intellectual firepower of the East — of Athanasius, John Chrysostom, Basil the Great, Gregory of Nyssa, Gregory of
Nazianzus. The Roman church was so peripheral that it received only
broken reports of what was happening in the East, and had trouble understanding information that did reach it. "Rome had no complete
Latin version of the first four ecumenical councils until the early sixth
century. Full participation in the process of defining dogma and establishing ecclesiastical discipline was therefore denied to the see of St. Peter, for without complete knowledge of past rulings it was powerless"
(H 105). Schimmelpfennig puts it this way:

Two factors led to the popes having little say in matters of faith, compared to later local interpretations. First, Roman bishops, except for Leo I, were usually bad theologians in comparison to representatives of the Eastern church; second, important decisions were made at councils at which few representatives (Nicaea 325, Ephesus 431, Chalcedon 451) or none at all (Constantinople 381) from the West took part — an example of how little prominence the West held at that time in theological questions. (Sch 47–48)

Far from presiding over doctrine in these years, Rome was too much in the dark to figure out what was going on in the theological world. It suffered from what J.N.D. Kelly has called a doctrinal "blackout."[1] Hilary of Poitiers (c. 315–367) admitted that, even after he became a bishop, he did not for a long time know there was such a thing as the Nicene Creed, until he was sent into exile. That means that this supremely important document had been circulated for two decades before a highly educated Christian leader of the West knew about it.[2]

It is interesting to note that the Western churches had no firsthand knowledge of the principal texts expounding the Arian position — such texts as the letters of Arius and the letter of Eusebius of Nicomedia — until little short of a quarter of a century after the Council of Nicea. The year 355 is probably the earliest date to which the publication of the first Latin translations can be ascribed. Even more remarkable, however, is the fact that the corresponding orthodox documents were equally slow in coming to the notice of Western churchmen.[3]

Peter, though commonsensical and down-to-earth, was never learned; and what the church called for in the fourth century was learning of a very high order. The emperor was riding the storms of controversy that raged beyond Rome's horizon. To perform that function, emperors took it on themselves to proscribe heretics, to confirm the consecration of all bishops (including the bishop of Rome), and to tell the world what was the true faith. Constantine even bore the (pagan) title that would later be arrogated by popes — Pontifex Maximus, "Supreme Pontiff" (Sch 34). His successors were also known as Pontifex Inclitus, "Renowned Pontiff" (F 811).

Rome was not the only apostolic church to be demoted by the new city Constantine founded. Gradually the four Eastern patriarchs were supplanted by the patriarch of Constantinople, a city which had not even existed in apostolic times, so it could not have had an apostolic foundation. To promote its claims, Constantinople invented the legend of the apostle Andrew's martyrdom near the site of the city (H 174). The Council of Chalcedon declared that there were now only two leading sees in the world, Rome in the West and "New Rome" in Constantinople. That was the part of the council's canons that Leo would not accept. He and following popes tried to counterbalance "New Rome" with a claim that Old Rome actually had the combined force of *three* ancient churches behind it — not only Rome itself, but Antioch (since Peter had been there before he came to Rome, and later embroidery had made him a bishop in the first place as well as the second), and Alexandria (to which Peter had sent Mark as an emissary to a new foundation). This was the "Triad" (*Trias*) that Rome hoped would overshadow or at least counterbalance Constantinople as the center of the teaching church (S 49). But the claim amounted to no more than a futile gesture. It could take nothing from the growing authority of the imperial city.

From the time of Constantine, the church in Rome had been subject to the Eastern emperors and councils. But the fifth century showed that Constantinople could not always back up its authority over Rome with protection of the city, as northern tribes overran the Western empire. Alaric the Visigoth briefly captured Rome in 410 (the pope, Innocent I, was in Ravenna, trying to get imperial help for the city). In a situation where the empire could not be relied on, popes bargained with the new powers on their own. The act that became symbolic of this was Pope Leo I's trip to meet the invading army of Attila at Mantua in 455. In later legend, Leo froze Attila in his tracks with an assertion of spiritual authority. Raphael painted the scene in the Vatican *stanze* — Saints Peter and Paul streaking through the air to support Leo, with Attila shrinking from their airy menace. Actually Leo had come forth as part of a "greater delegation, also comprised of representatives from the upper classes [of Rome] and the secular administration" (Sch 32). And they did what the Eastern emperors were doing with the tribes menacing their half of the empire — bought Attila off with treasure, a sphere of his own, and the promise of a highborn bride (H 74).

Rome Under Gothic Rule

The Germanic occupation of Italy became stable when Odoacer, a Christian but an Arian, took over the peninsula in 476. Rome came to terms with him, and later popes would find an advantage in adversity, since the coming of a new temporal order gave them maneuvering room to defy the East. Three popes in succession showed this new independence, telling Constantinople it should have nothing to do with the Monophysite heretics of Syria and Egypt (though they, the popes, were forming accords with Arians). The three popes in question — Simplicius (468–483), Felix III (483–492), and Gelasius I (492–496) — were dealing with Acacius, the patriarch of Constantinople. Acacius involved Rome in the Monophysite controversy when he called on Pope Simplicius to back him in condemning the patriarch of Alexandria, Mongo. Simplicius did so. But widespread adherence to Monophysitism (which declared there was only one nature in Christ, not two) threatened Emperor Zeno's rule — he was expelled briefly from Constantinople by a Monophysite usurper, Basiliscus. Zeno sought a compromise formula to unite the Christian East. Acacius now entered into negotiations with his former enemy, Mongo, and they came up with an evasive formula called the Accord (*Henōsis*). Pope Felix, the successor to Simplicius, excommunicated Acacius, causing the first major break between East and West. The Acacian schism would last for over a third of a century (482–519).

When Gelasius succeeded Felix on the papal throne, a new emperor tried to reach a compromise with the new pope. But Gelasius, in a stunning letter, denied that the emperor had any authority over the church — though every emperor had successively exercised just that (and the emperor had, in fact, confirmed Gelasius in his office): "Two there are, my august emperor, by which the world is governed as by sovereigns [*principaliter = sicut principes*]: the consecrated authority [*auctoritas*] of bishops and the power [*potestas*] of princes. Of the two, the duty of bishops is the more weighty, since they must give an account even of princes at the time of God's judgment." While Gelasius was thus declaring his independence from Emperor Anastasius, he was coming to terms with Theodoric, the Ostrogoth who had replaced Odoacer as king of Italy. "Gelasius was markedly more polite to Theodoric than he was to Anastasius" (F 812). Popes were willing to play ball with the new rulers of the West in the hope of slipping out from the dominance of the East: "The papal situation was made easier by the fact that in this very period the popes were not subjects of the emperor because Rome was ruled by Odoacer (476–493) and then by the Ostrogoths (493–536) — Arians, but tolerant rulers. The great 'magna carta of Western church freedom,' the letter of Pope Gelasius to Emperor Anastasius in 494, could only have been written under such circumstances" (S 51–52).

Rome had for a long time chafed at its subordination to Constantinople — to the empire's representative in Ravenna as well as to the superiority of Byzantine culture:

> Underlying Gelasius's confident assertion [of independence] was the growing antipathy of the West for Byzantium as such. Gelasius shared this. He treated the Byzantines with contempt, and may even have planned to restore papal influence in the Latin-speaking province of the empire, at the expense of the emperors and Constantinople. Writing to the bishops of Dalmatia and Dardania (that is, the Balkan provinces of the empire) in February 493, he referred to their eastern brethren as "Greeks, among whom there is no doubt that heresies abound." He contrasted "the Greeks" at Constantinople with the "Roman senate" and the "Roman Church." (F 811)

In the brief reign of Gelasius's successor, Anastasius II (496–498), Theodoric used his good relations with Western Christians to win Constantinople's agreement to call him king of Italy. His authority was great enough for him to be called on to choose the next pope when rival factions elected two popes in 498, Lawrence and Symmachus. Theodoric, the Arian, chose Symmachus (498–515) — and soon came to regret the choice. Theodoric wanted peace in his realm, and Symmachus was a divisive figure. Those who had opposed his appointment complained to Theodoric about his fiscal and other crimes — among his female consorts was the infamous courtesan Conditaria (Spice Girl).[4] Theodoric summoned the pope to Ravenna for trial, and Symmachus set out from Rome. But when he heard of the witnesses prepared to testify against him — including his slaves — he turned back. Theodoric issued a preliminary verdict against him, though he knew it would have to be backed up by a synod of bishops. "The king was personally persuaded of Symmachus' guilt, or at least of the impossibility of his continuing in office, and felt it to be his duty to act in protection of the Catholic Church."[5]

Theodoric suspended the pope from his office, sent a regent (Peter of Altinum) to conduct church affairs at the Lateran, and ordered that an ecclesiastical trial be prepared in Rome. The pope refused to attend his own trial; the frustrated bishops tried to dissolve the court; Theodoric refused to let them. Finally, a rump group of bishops (about half of those in Rome) rendered a Scottish verdict, "not proved guilty," in 502 — a satirical pamphlet called it "the Synod of the Incongruous Absolution."[6] Theodoric, having failed to oust the man he had elevated in the first place, let the rival pope he had rejected (Lawrence) take over the Lateran and rule there for four years, while the unpopular Symmachus hid out from mob violence in St. Peter's. The first residence for a pope at the Vatican was built as a bunker by Symmachus. It was in this period that his busy counterfeiters created a small library of forged church documents proving that the pope cannot be tried or judged by any earthly authority — the Symmachan forgeries would be imbedded in canon law for centuries.[7] In 506, to bring peace to the unruly streets of Rome, Theodoric finally accepted the legitimacy of Symmachus.

The Emperor Justinian (527–565)

The Acacian schism was healed in 519 by a pyrrhic victory for Rome. The emperor Justin posthumously excommunicated Acacius, but he reasserted Eastern supremacy over Rome, and the patriarch of his capital see took the title Universal Patriarch for the first time (F 813). Justin's nephew, Justinian, took the reunion with Rome as just the first step toward a reconquest of the West from Germanic overlordship. But the popes were no longer sure they wanted that. They were finding it easier to assert religious authority over the Arian kings than over orthodox emperors. In fact, Pope Agapetus went to Constantinople in 536 to speak for his Gothic ally, Theodahad, asking Justinian to call off his campaign of reconquest in Italy. He felt it would simply cause a return of the sufferings of war after a modus vivendi had been reached.

Justinian, who was nothing if not determined, pushed ahead with his reconquest. His general, Belisarius, captured Rome while the pope was away on his mission. But Justinian, hoping perhaps to recruit more support for his campaign in the West, deferred to Agapetus's request that the patriarch of Constantinople be deposed as a Monophysite heretic. This angered the empress Theodora, who schemed with a clerical member of Agapetus's delegation, Vigilius, to restore the patriarch. If Vigilius helped her do that, she promised, she would make sure that he became pope on the death of the ailing Agapetus. But when Agapetus died, Theodahad in Rome promptly put his own man, Silverius, on the papal throne. Undaunted, Theodora sent Vigilius back to Rome, with instructions to Belisarius to seat her man. Silverius was deposed and exiled to Patara in the present Turkey; but the bishop of Patara, upset at this injustice, went to Constantinople to plead for Silverius.[8] Justinian ordered the deposed pope returned to Rome for a hearing on the validity of his election. Vigilius helped Belisarius rig the trial, and Silverius was exiled a second time.

Vigilius, now pope, was an object of detestation to the Western churches, not only for his ruthless scheming but for his cooperation with the Monophysites. Striving to win acceptance in the West, he now refused to join the emperor's efforts to reconcile the Monophysites with his regime. He could neither hold the West while submitting to the East nor retain his seat in the West if the East recalled him. When he reneged on his deal with Theodora, Justinian sent the imperial police to arrest him in the midst of a ceremony.[9] Brought forcibly to Constantinople, he predictably buckled under pressure, and endorsed the emperor's effort to reconcile Monophysites and the orthodox by condemning three theologians of the past who were unacceptable to the Monophysites. The theologians — whose supposed doctrines were described and condemned in a document called *The Three Chapters* — included the esteemed Theodore of Mopsuestia. Disgusted with Vigilius's tergiversations, a synod in Africa excommunicated the pope (F 852). Rebuked by his own deacon, Pelagius, Vigilius swerved back toward orthodoxy, and fled from the emperor's displeasure to the Bosphorus. Hardship there made him alter his course a final time, crawl back into Justinian's favor, and set off for Rome — where he would have faced an extremely hostile reception if he had not died on the way.

Vigilius's deacon, Pelagius, inherited Vigilius's dilemma when he succeeded him as pope. Despite his own misgivings, Pelagius had endorsed the council Justinian called (Constantinople II, 553 C.E.) to reach accord with the Monophysites. At this council of Constantinople "the bishops turned intellectual somersaults in their effort to uphold [the council of] Chalcedon yet condemn the *Three Chapters*" (F 853). Even Vigilius would not take part in the council (though he had first suggested it), and when Pelagius went back to Rome as the imperial choice, he was accused of conspiring in Vigilius' death. Before he could exercise any authority, he was forced to take an oath forswearing heretical views ("unheard of in papal history," Sch 67). Even after that, his endorsement of the council drove some Western churches into schism

— "that dividing Aquileia from Rome lasted in an acute form for forty years, and did not finally abate until A.D. 700" (F 853).

Pelagius could not defy the East by rejecting the council, though it was costing him so much in the West. Nor could his successors (even the saintly Gregory I) do more than come up with evasive formulations about the conciliar acts — with the anomalous result that "this council even nowadays is considered an ecumenical council, although its decrees contradict the main doctrines which are held in the West" (Sch 68).

Even more surprising is the fact that Vigilius was condemned and excommunicated at the council — after Silverius had been deposed to seat Vigilius in the first place. It was clear now that a pope could serve only at the pleasure of the emperor. As John Moorhead writes:

> Whereas the Gothic kings had sometimes exerted an influence on the election of a pope, they had never sought to depose one. Emperors did not behave in such a gentlemanly fashion: of the 52 patriarchs of Constantinople who held office from the reign of Justinian until that of Alexios Comnenos (1081–1118), 19 or 20 were deposed or forced into temporary retirement, and the fall of Silverius showed that popes were similarly at risk while Rome was part of the empire.[10]

The effort of Gelasius to separate church from empire proved abortive. In fact, "Justinian had clearly won a triumph over the papacy. Humiliated and thoroughly under the Emperor's thumb in all matters, from election to doctrine, it had been brought by Justinian to a new low as a dependency of the emperor in Constantinople. So it was to remain in one degree or another for more than a century."[11] Since Justinian's reconquest proved short-lived in all parts of the West except Sicily, he proved far more successful in subjugating the Western church than in controlling Western land.

Gregory I (590–604)

In 585 Pelagius II, trying to placate the schismatics in Aquileia, wrote one of the rare admissions by a pope that his predecessors — Vigilius and Pelagius — were wrong (on the Monophysite issue). This letter is stunning because it was composed for the pope by his deacon, Gregory

— who would become Pope Gregory the Great, one of the four fathers of the Western church. This is what he wrote, in Pelagius's name:

> Since Peter contradicted himself, should you tell him, "We refuse to hear what you are saying because you once said the opposite"? If . . . one position was held while truth was being sought, and a different position was adopted after truth had been found, why should a change of position be considered a crime in this See, which is humbly venerated by all in the person of its founder? One should not blame change in one's stand but inability to take a stand. So if the mind is firmly intent on seeking the truth, why will you criticize it when it sheds ignorance and fashions a better statement of the truth?[12]

For once the real Peter is invoked, deserving reverence but not providing a model of consistency. Yet even Gregory, when he became pope in 590, would not absolutely renounce Justinian's Fifth Ecumenical Council. In order to woo back the schismatics, he merely downplayed it by saying that the truly important councils were the first four ones, just as the truly important scriptures were the four Gospels (H 161). This nuanced stand did not end the schism. Instead, it exposed Gregory to some Western bishops' accusations of heresy (Sch 67).

Gregory could neither totally rely on nor totally defy either the Eastern emperor or the Western Lombards, who had replaced the Visigoths as the invading power in Italy. He tried to make and maintain truces with the Lombards, while arming defenders of Rome and calling on the empire for help. Despite his own great wealth, from which he fed the Romans, his city did not have the resources to do more than keep up an improvised defense. "In 604, Rome was centuries away from a self-sufficient authority to manage the spiritual life of the West. As Gregory's biographer makes clear, beyond the walls of Rome its bishop had little power. The papacy was still an almost exclusively local organization" (H 164).

Gregory had to maneuver for peace with the Lombards, working through King Agiluf's Catholic queen, Theodelinda. These efforts sometimes put him at odds with the emperor's policies toward the Lombards: "In his concern for the security of Rome, Gregory took no account either of constitutional propriety or of the Empire's strategic interests. This was what set him on a collision course with the Emperor and his officials in Italy."[13] While thus fighting for his city's very existence, Gregory could not afford to alienate the emperor. He did not challenge his right to make church law. When, for instance, Justinian set new norms for entry into monasteries, Gregory expressed his disagreement with the measure but loyally promulgated it. "A sharper contrast with Gelasius' protest to the emperor Anastasius, or Ambrose's to Theodosius, it would be hard to imagine . . . Gregory never questioned either the ideological foundations or the daily realities of the institutional framework of the Empire and the imperial church."[14] He therefore did not meddle in the affairs of Constantinople, where he had been the papal nuncio (*Apocrisiarius*) before he became pope — protesting neither the illegal ouster of its patriarch, Anastasius, nor the usurpation of the imperial throne by Phocas.

One practice in the East Gregory did object to, heatedly — Patriarch Eulogius's use of the title assumed during the Acacian schism: Universal Patriarch (Greek *patriarchēs oikumenikos*, Latin *patriarcha universalis*). He called this a proud and un-Christian title, an insult to the other apostolic churches. Strange to say, this has been taken to mean that Gregory was appropriating for Rome the title he denied to Constantinople — as if only the pope has a right to be proud and un-Christian. R. A. Markus shows how impossible is this interpretation of Gregory's letters. Gregory had written to the other apostolic churches with his complaint against Constantinople, and the patriarch of Alexandria responded by addressing Gregory as "universal pope." Gregory said he claimed no such title, which would derogate from the dignity of Alexandria:

> I said that neither to me *nor to anyone else* ought he [the patriarch of Constantinople] write in such terms; yet in the opening of your letter to me, who have forbidden this, you thought fit to include *the title of pride,* calling me "universal pope." Please, I implore your holiness, do this no more; for anything wrongly bestowed on one is taken from you . . . I am rightly honored when no one is deprived of the honor due to him. [Emphasis added][15]

Gregory no more wanted the title himself than he would put up with it in another. As Markus notes: "To use the title 'universal,' whichever bishop it was bestowed on, was to undercut the legitimate standing of each and every bishop in his own church: if any particular bishop was 'universal,' no bishop anywhere else could be in possession of full episcopal status."[16]

Honorius (625–638)

One reason the Western schism dragged on into the seventh century is that the Eastern empire kept trying to involve Rome in the effort to accommodate the Monophysites of Egypt and Syria. In Constantinople, Patriarch Sergius thought he had found a way. Instead of speaking of one nature in Christ, why not call it one "principle of action" (*energeia*)? In 634, Sergius asked Pope Honorius to endorse this position. The pope thought he had an even better formulation — that there was only one *will* in Christ. He promoted this concept in letters to other bishops as well as to Sergius — with the result that he was later condemned by a council for the heresy of Monothelitism (One-will-ism), a sentence that Pope Leo III ratified. "Because of this condemnation, henceforth every new pope before taking office had to acknowledge solemnly — as stated in the *Liber Diurnus* — the true faith, inclusive of the condemnation of Honorius" (Sch 68).

During the Middle Ages, the *Liber Diurnus* (the record of papal acts) fell into neglect, and people forgot that a pope had been condemned for heresy, a condemnation his immediate successors had to affirm. When the *Liber Diurnus* came back to light, some in the hierarchy tried to suppress this passage — or even the entire book (Sch 69). As Lord Acton wrote, at the time of the First Vatican Council, when it was called heretical to think of a pope as heretical:

> The inclination to get rid of evidence was specially associated with the doctrine of papal infallibility, because it is necessary that the Popes themselves should not testify against their own claim. They may be declared superior to all other authorities, but not to that of their own see. Their history is not irrelevant to the question of their rights. It could not be disregarded; and the provocation to alter or to deny its testimony was so urgent that men of piety and learning became a prey to the temptation of deceit. When it was discovered in the manuscript of the *Liber Diurnus* that the Popes had for centuries condemned Honorius in their profession of faith, Cardinal Bona, the most eminent man in Rome, advised that the book should be suppressed if the difficulty could not be got over; and it was suppressed accordingly.[17]

The papal party at Vatican I tried to dismiss the Honorius episode, saying that his remarks were merely made in a letter to the patriarch of

Constantinople, and did not constitute a considered position. But Leo's *Tomus* was also a letter to a patriarch of Constantinople, and papal supremicists make much of that. A council (Constantinople III) and a pope (Leo II) who were close to the case thought it official enough to call for official condemnation. "To the supporters of the Chalcedon Creed in the seventh century, Honorius was the perfect example of a heretical pope" (Sch 68–69). Father Schatz is clear on this point: "It is an undisputed fact that must be maintained against all attempts to water it down that the council and the subsequent popes clearly condemned Honorius as a heretic. In other words, they were absolutely convinced that a pope could fall into heresy" (S 55). In order to say that Honorius did *not* err on an essential of the faith, his defenders have to claim that Leo II *did* err on the same point. Papal inerrancy, in either case, disappears.

Honorius is not the only example of a pope who embraced heresy. Earlier (in the fourth century), Pope Liberius defied Constantius II when that emperor demanded that he submit to Arian doctrine. He was banished to Thrace for his refusal:

> Here, as the months slipped by and the local bishop worked on him, his morale collapsed and, in painful contrast to his previous resolute stand, he now acquiesced in Athanasius's excommunication, accepted the ambiguous First Creed of Sirmium (which omitted the Nicene "one in being with the Father"), and made an abject submission to the emperor. His capitulation is pathetically mirrored in four letters which he wrote from exile in spring 357 to Arianizing bishops, and which suggest that he was ready to pay almost any price to return home. Finally, brought to Sirmium (Mitrovica in Yugoslavia) in 358, he was content to sign a formula which, while rejecting the Nicene "one in being with the Father," declared the Son to be like the Father in being and indeed in everything. (K 30–31)

This latter position was an authoritatively anathematized one. Saint Jerome wrote, in his *Chronicle of Famous Men* (Number 941): "Liberius, conquered himself by the ordeal of exile, returned to Rome as if he were a conqueror by endorsing the heretical perversion."

John Henry Newman used Liberius as one of the supports for his argument that the faithful in general were better at preserving orthodoxy in the Arian period than was the hierarchy:

In that time of immense confusion, the divine dogma of our Lord's divinity was proclaimed, enforced, maintained, and (humanly speaking) preserved far more by the "Ecclesia docta" than by the "Ecclesia docens," that the body of the episcopate was unfaithful to its commission while the body of the laity was faithful to its baptism; that at one time the Pope, at other times the patriarchal, metropolitan and other great sees, at other times general councils, said what they should not have said, or did what obscured and compromised revealed truth; while, on the other hand, it was the Christian people who, under Providence, were the ecclesiastical strength of Athanasius, Hilary, Eusebius of Vercellae, and other great solitary confessors, who would have failed without them.[18]

The piety and fidelity of "the people of God" were not something disjunct from the importance of Saint Peter in the fourth century. On the contrary, the great exhibit of early Christian art for the Jubilee Year 2000 shows a veritable explosion of Petrine images at that time, indicating pious celebration by pilgrims to what was thought to be his tomb.[19] The *Liber Pontificalis* — that dry record of papal activities — gives a detailed record of the Roman churches built, restored, or expanded from this time on, when Rome had a pagan inner core going to ruin, while it was ringed with the shrines of martyrs (Sch 19). One could gain the impression from this chronicle that what popes did was mainly build churches in Rome — and in one sense this would be true. That activity did not occur in a vacuum. But for the influx of pilgrims and the growth of popular celebrations, there would have been no demand for this supply of holy places. Pilgrims went in procession from shrine to shrine, with Peter's shrine especially honored. The pope, it should be remembered, did not yet live at that shrine — he went there in procession with others, leaving his own palace and church, the Lateran, known already as "the head and mother of all churches" (Sch 19).

The pope was honored as the successor to Peter, not primarily for doctrinal matters (which had traditionally come from the East), but as the living representative of Peter the pastor, the symbol of unity, the strengthener of the piety that was adorning all the "pilgrim-station" churches of Rome. When the pope had few resources to lead or control the West (much less the universal church), pilgrims and ascetics attending the devotions at Rome took back practices of prayer and liturgy to their own lands. In their travels and litanies and processions, their movements wove a tapestry of union that had little to do with the papal struggle against emperors or Goths or Lombards. That unity is what Newman is talking about when he says that there was a popular orthodoxy, which grew out of popular devotion (*lex orandi lex credendi*).

In another place Newman noted that the church is the same, whichever part of it is preserving orthodoxy at the moment: "A triangle or parallelogram is the same in its substance and nature, whichever side is made its base."[20] To say that the church was based, at one point, more on the body of the faithful than on the hierarchy is not to deny that that was a *Petrine* base. Devotion to Peter was a principal inspiration of Western Christianity.

10

Rome Turns West

FOR FOUR CENTURIES after Constantine recognized Christianity, Rome was dominated, both spiritually and temporally, by the East. At first that meant, in the *spiritual* realm, accepting the orthodox faith hammered out at the major councils. But popes were later compromised by the need to get along with emperors who flirted with Arianism (Pope Liberius) or Monophysitism (Popes Vigilius, Pelagius, Honorius, even — to a degree — Gregory). Some of the *temporal* control was relaxed when Goths and Lombards took over much of Italy from the empire. But the need to strike bargains with the invaders meant that partial freedom from Constantinople came at a high price, and popes had to keep asking for aid from their former master. Then Justinian took back both temporal and spiritual authority. Though the only part of Justinian's reconquest that stayed firmly associated with the East was Sicily, that was enough to guarantee that some Greek popes — Agatho (678–681), Conon (686–687), Sergius I (687–701), Zacharias (741–752) — came from Sicily or its dependencies in Calabria.

Other Greek popes came from the Middle East — Theodore I (642–649), John V (685–686), Sisinnius (708), Constantine (708–715), Gregory III (731–741). One pope (Conon) was the son of a Byzantine general, and another (John VII, 705–707) was the son of a high Byzantine official. All these popes were still confirmed in office by the emperor, but their Greek names do not mean that they were all complaisant about imperial domination. The eighth century saw the beginnings of the iconoclasts' victories in Constantinople, and the popes, knowing how deep was devotion to sacred images in the West, stubbornly resisted the East on this point. Besides, Rome was caught in the middle, between Justinian's reassertion of authority and the need for a modus vivendi with Lombard kings, especially with Liutprand, who drove the Byzantine forces from their recaptured Italian capital of Ravenna (733). Pope Gregory II supported the imperial forces that reoccupied Ravenna, which broke his alliance with Liutprand. And when Liutprand's son, Aistulf, finally put Ravenna firmly in the grip of the Lombards, Rome was vulnerable to both the major forces in play, the imperial East and the Lombard West.

At this point, the popes made a brilliant move, connected with their missionary activities north of the Alps (like Gregory I's dispatch of Saint Augustine to England). They decided to introduce a third force into the centuries-old seesaw game that had kept them suspended between two masters. They appealed to a growing power north of the Alps, the Franks. In 739, and again in 740, Pope Gregory II sent a call to the Frankish leader, Charles Martel, inviting him to become the pope's protector in Italy (H 353). Charles would not do that, but he did promote the mission of Saint Boniface to the tribes of the north, in that process forging closer ties with the papacy. When Gregory's successor as pope, Zacharias (the last Greek pope), found himself at loggerheads with Aistulf's Lombards, he cultivated Charles's son Pepin III. In 751, at Soissons, Boniface consecrated Pepin as king, ending the Merovingian and beginning the Carolingian line of Frankish royalty. The next pope, Stephen II, decided to throw in his lot entirely with the Carolingians. He went north over the Alps in 753 — the first pope to do this — and for two years left Rome behind, in order to save Rome. He solemnly anointed Pepin with the title "Rome's Father-Figure" (Patricius). Pepin, for his part, promised to restore to Rome some of its dependencies taken by Aistulf. He fulfilled this promise, though sluggishly, and the destinies of the papacy and the Frankish empire were intertwined, giving birth — in the 750s or 760s — to a fake document whose influence would outlive the empire, the Donation of Constantine (H 85–87).

The Great Forgery

A modern audience can be shocked at the idea of a forgery's being used for centuries to give popes spiritual and temporal supremacy. But forgeries were an important part of life in late antiquity and the Middle

Ages. Anthony Grafton, in a study of the subject, concludes that "perhaps half the legal documents we possess from Merovingian times, and perhaps two-thirds of all documents issued to ecclesiastics before A.D. 1199, are fakes . . . The basic code of canon law, Gratian's *Decretum*, contains some five hundred forged legal texts."[1] In *Papal Sin*, I argued that deceit became a separate papal problem in the nineteenth century, because only then was documentary evidence put on a completely scholarly basis — though the popes kept using the laxer standards of earlier days.

In the early centuries, a forgery was an "as if" creation. In order to spell out what were considered true circumstances, the forgers supplied a basis for them *as if* these had been formally mandated. Pseudonymous creations pullulated in both pagan and Christian circles. The canon of Scripture holds some pseudonymous letters attributed to Peter, Paul, and John created by followers who felt they were acting *as if* under the apostles' guidance. They evidently thought this was excuse enough for signing their names to the new missives. The classical historians, from Herodotus on, wrote speeches for the actors in the story *as if* those speeches had literally been delivered. The papacy, which was claiming rights not generally recognized, found it especially useful to put those claims in the form of forged legal texts. At the beginning of the sixth century, as we have seen, there was a Stakhanovite forging of papal privileges for Symmachus (498–514). Precisely because he was put in office by the Arian Theodoric, and then removed from it by the same authority, he felt he had to declare the papacy beyond all such interference, so a body of phony precedents was written up for him in legal form.[2] In the ninth century, a body of Spanish forgeries would be created and attributed to Isidore of Seville (d. 636), to protect bishops from their metropolitan superiors by invoking papal privilege.[3] They are known as the False Decretals, and they were as successful as any of these forgeries, with the single exception of their distinguished predecessor, the Donation.

That document purports to be Constantine's own grant of spiritual and temporal authority to Pope Silvester and all his successor popes. It is hard at this point to appreciate the skill with which the forger worked. What seems to weaken it in our eyes actually strengthened it in the eighth century. The folktale miracle by which Silvester cured Constantine of leprosy was widely accepted on the authority of the popular *Legenda Sancti Silvestri*. That legend included the baptism of Constantine by the pope in 312 (rather than his actual baptism by the Arian bishop-historian Eusebius, which occurred in 337, when Constantine was on his deathbed). Aside from such legends, the Donation built on some real events, especially the fact that Constantine had given the popes their seat of government, the Lateran Palace, and built the Lateran Church, as well as the shrines to both Peter and Paul, showing a deep respect for the founding apostles and for the bishop of Rome.

The Donation was meant not merely to persuade others, but to formulate the exact nature of the grave step the popes were trying to take as they entirely severed themselves, for the first time, from Eastern domination. This was a declaration of independence, and it juggled with three sets of relationships — those between Rome and the East, between Rome and the Franks, and between the Franks and the East. To the East, the forger was saying that this was not a real break with history, or even with the East, since it was only what Constantine had himself decreed before setting up his new city of Constantinople. The implied praise of Constantine was an effort to disarm those in the city named for him. To the Franks, the Donation signaled that Constantine had already given what Pepin was only *restoring* to the pope. Rome did not want to wrestle itself free from one overlordship only to succumb to another. As for the relationship between the Franks and the East, the Donation's message was that Rome could not be a proper cause for conflict or tension between these powers, since it was just following an Eastern mandate in accepting Western assistance.

In light of these complex tasks to be performed, we can only admire the artfulness with which the Donation is constructed. It has five main parts.

1. *Creed.* "Constantine" begins with a confession of faith (Chapters 1– 5, lines 1–78).[4] This was meant to dispel the (justified) notion that Constantine's conversion to Christianity was partial, gradual, or not entirely orthodox, or that he had derived his creed from the council he presided over at Nicea. Here Constantine spells out his proper trinitarian views, and he attributes them to the personal instruction given him before Nicea was even thought of.

2. *Cure* (chapters 6–9, lines 79–139). The occasion for the pope's instruction is narrated. Having contracted leprosy, Constantine consulted the pagan priests in Rome, who said that he could be cured only by bathing in the blood of slaughtered children. When he re-

fused to murder the young innocents, Peter and Paul rewarded
him with a joint appearance in a dream, telling him to seek a cure
from the pope, who was hiding from Constantine's persecutors on
Mount Soracte. When Silvester was brought to him, Constantine
verified his dream by looking at pictures of Peter and Paul entrusted to the pope — they were the very visages he had seen in his
sleep. (This is a dig at the East's iconoclasts, who denied any use
for sacred images. See? — even their founding emperor had used
them.) At this, the emperor submitted to a course of fasting and
penance, in his Lateran palace, before being baptized. At the moment of baptism he saw a hand from heaven touch him, and the
leprosy disappeared.

3. *Spiritual supremacy* (chapters 10–13, lines 140–208). After Constantine's cure, the pope interpreted for the new convert the Matthew
text (16.18–19) on Peter as the stone, who was given the keys of
heaven. On this basis, Constantine declared that the church he
would build for Peter (at his Lateran Palace, not at St. Peter's) must
be the "head and peak of all churches on the entire globe." This
church would establish the authority of the apostles in the churches
of Antioch, Alexandria, Constantinople, and Jerusalem by exercising its own sway over "Judea, Greece, Asia, Thrace, Africa, Italy and
the islands besides."

4. *Temporal supremacy* (chapters 14–16, lines 209–260). After calling
the Lateran Church the head of all churches, Constantine gave Silvester the Lateran Palace to be "placed over and above all palaces in
the entire globe." To signify this temporal eminence, Constantine
bestowed on the pope the imperial insignia, and held the reins as he
walked beside Silvester's horse — a symbol of vassalage. This is a
breathtaking grant. It goes beyond even Gelasius's assertion of autonomy, since he claimed only spiritual supremacy, not temporal.

5. *Limits of supremacy* (chapters 17–20, lines 261–306). But Constantine, while conferring spiritual supremacy over all the churches,
limited the pope's temporal supremacy to one half of the world,
keeping the rest for himself. Silvester's sway extended to "Rome,
and all the sectors of Italy and western lands, their territory and cities." Constantine withdraws from these, to set up a new city in his
name, far from Rome, since "it is not right for an earthly emperor
to have power in the place where priestly authority and the supremacy of the Christian church has been established by heaven's emperor."

It will be seen how neatly the forger has disposed of a number of issues, clearing the way not only for separation from the East but for a "new deal" in the West, where Rome shall rule with the attributes of the emperor himself. It has puzzled people that this ambitious document, once drawn up, was not instantly invoked, but lay dormant for a period. The reason is that the Franks were not ready to play ball by these unilaterally formulated rules. In the next papacy, that of Paul I (757–767), Pepin did not so much subdue the Franks for Rome as bring the two parties to a forced settlement over disputed territories. And when Pepin's son succeeded him, he made it clear that he — Charles, known to us as Charles the Great (Carolus Magnus, or Charlemagne) — would set the rules.

Charlemagne

The first pope to deal with Charlemagne, Stephen III (768–772), was frightened by Charlemagne's marriage to the daughter of the Lombard king, Desiderius, into denunciations of Desiderius that collapsed into ineffectual sycophancy toward him — hardly the conduct of a man with full spiritual and temporal authority in the West. The second pope, Hadrian I (772–795), was frightened in 1781, when the empress-regent of the East, Irene, concluded a marriage between her son (the heir to the empire) and Charlemagne's daughter. Hadrian began to cultivate the East as well, sending legates to Irene's council (Nicea II), which condemned iconoclasm. Hadrian's emissaries tried to assert Roman ecclesiastical privilege at the council, but they were simply ignored on this point. When the pope accepted the council nonetheless, this irritated Charlemagne, who had not been invited to it. For a counter-council of his own, at Frankfurt (794), his theologians composed a document (the *Libri Carolini*) rejecting the council and its teachings.[5] Of this document Robert Folz wrote: "It is rightly considered a kind of doctrinal manifesto on the part of the Latin Church, and an assertion of its right to make its voice heard. It is equally true that the spokesman for this Church was the Frankish king; and holding the faith to be a trust committed to him, he showed himself to be its watchful and jealous guardian."[6] The teachings of the *Libri* were made formal at the Council of Frankfurt (794), which also condemned Adoptionism (the belief that Jesus was adopted into divinity, rather than held it of his own right) — a council that "took place solely on the initiative of the

Frankish court, which paid no heed to Pope Hadrian's efforts to salvage the decrees of the council of Nicaea."[7]

Charlemagne, it is clear, thought he should exercise all the authority that Constantine had in declaring church teaching and ruling church procedures. For this he had assembled his own team of theological advisers — from England (Alcuin), France (Theodulph), and Italy (Paulinus). He made Alcuin the abbot of St. Martin's at Tours, Theodulph the bishop of Orleans, and Paulinus the patriarch of Aquileia. With advice of this caliber, Charlemagne had his own creed drawn up for him.[8] "Alcuin believed that Charles was acting as 'the rector of the Christian people,' the divinely commanded leader of the churches within his domain" (H 435). Charles was determined to make one part of his own creed a tenet of the entire church — the assertion that the Holy Spirit proceeded from the Father *and the Son* (*filioque*), not from the Father *through* the Son. The third pope who dealt with Charlemagne, Leo III (795–816), resisted this addition to the creed, posting texts without it on silver plaques in St. Peter's (H 464). Gibbon wryly observed of this conflict: "In the correspondence of Charlemagne and Leo the Third, the Pope assumes the liberality of a statesman, and the prince descends to the passions and prejudices of a priest."[9]

The irrepressible Leo III was not one to give up hope even when dealing with a force like Charlemagne. He fecklessly aspired to lure Charles into playing the role marked out for kings in the Donation — or at least in the Silvester myth, which he had put in the form of two ideological mosaics decorating his new banquet hall at the Lateran Palace (H 450). Created in 796–798, the mosaics were variations on the *traditio legis* type we have already encountered (see Chapter 5). In that configuration, a seated Christ gave the sign of rule to Peter, on his right, and the sign of teaching authority to Paul, on his left. In Leo's triclinium, the first mosaic showed Christ on his throne bestowing a sign of authority (the pallium) on Pope Silvester, to his right, while giving the labarum, the battle ensign, to Constantine, on his left. In the companion mosaic, Saint Peter is shown giving Leo the pallium and Charles the labarum. The point is that Charlemagne should recognize the Donation that Constantine gave to Silvester.[10]

Unfortunately for Leo, soon after his grandiose vision was assembled in the tesserae of the two mosaics, he was reduced to scrambling for his chair. Enemies in Rome assaulted him in 799, and supposedly put out his eyes. Deposed by these forces, he retreated to a monastery, where his recovered vision was hailed as a miracle. But when he fled to Charles's court at Paderborn, Alcuin and others took very seriously the allegations against him, which included adultery and perjury (Sch 91). The disorder in Rome and in Constantinople (where Emperor Constantine VI, the former husband of Charlemagne's daughter, had been overthrown) proved to Alcuin that Charlemagne's "New Rome" was superior to both Old Rome and Second Rome (Constantinople): "It is to be ranked above the other two dignities for it eclipses them and surpasses them in wisdom."[11] Exercising this jurisdiction, Charles sent Leo back to Rome under guard. Investigation of the charges against the pope was a preparation for Charles's decision when he reached Rome to celebrate Christmas. On December 23, 800, Charles ended the judicial proceedings against Leo with a compromise between the accusers and the accused. The pope was compelled to take an oath of compurgation, "which was taken by the accused in Germanic law when the accusation could not be supported by any proof."[12]

Two days later occurred the famous Christmas crowning of Charles as emperor of the Romans. It was later said that the pope had surprised an unsuspecting Charles by putting the crown on him as he came up from the tomb of Saint Peter (H 455). But Charles was in charge of the whole proceeding in this state trip to Rome, and the tension with Leo probably reflects his resistance to accepting the role Leo had prescribed in his triumphalist mosaics. The order of dignity is clear from the fact that Leo prostrated himself to the emperor after the crowning, the first and last time a pope performed such a *proskynesis* — and a ceremony all the more striking because Charles had objected to the cult of images as a form of *proskynesis*.[13]

The conduct of Charlemagne's heirs to the throne just proved that Rome had not escaped imperial domination when it traded Eastern dominance for Western. The grand vision of the Donation had to bide its time while popes underwent humiliation at the pleasure of the "third Rome" of the Carolingians. The Western emperors, like the Eastern ones, called councils, seated and unseated bishops, and judged popes. In 844, when Sergius II became pope without Emperor Lothair's confirmation, an army was dispatched to try the new pope before a synod of twenty bishops before his title could be cleared by the emperor's representative, his son Louis (K 103). When Benedict III was deposed by his Roman opponents in 855, because his election had not been validated, Emperor Louis reinstalled the pope, but on condition that he submit to an overseer of the emperor's choice (K 105). On the death of Benedict, the emperor himself hastened to Rome to make sure that the election was under his supervision this time (K 107).

As the descendants of Charlemagne fell out among themselves over his inheritance, popes were caught between contending masters. In 875, Pope John VIII chose the wrong brother to crown, Charles the Bald, and the pope, like his supposed emperor, soon had to take flight from Charles's enemies, while he tried to find a more plausible person to crown. He resisted the claims of Carloman, and assisted instead at the ceremony of Louis the Stammerer in 878 — only to have him die at once. Not till his third try (in 881) did a coronation "take," with the elevation of Charles the Fat. (The flotilla of Charleses bobbing in the wake of Charlemagne made people sort them out with epithets less heroic than the one with which Charles the Great initiated the imperial succession.)

The Roman Captivity

As the Carolingian empire fell apart, the world of the popes contracted. In place of the Eastern or the Western emperors as its protector-overlords, Spoleto held dominance. Actually, the papacy's day-to-day fate hung upon the favor or enmity of a few clans struggling in the tiny cockpit of the city itself, making it "more and more a plaything of Roman families" (Sch 106). The contest of rival popes took its grimmest form in the infamous "cadaver synod" of 897, when the body of Pope Formosus, nine months dead, was exhumed by his successor Stephen VI, dressed in his former papal splendor, and put on trial for usurping the papal office. (Formosus had been bishop of Porto at a time when bishops were ineligible for the papacy, since they could not leave their dioceses.) Robert Browning did justice to the grotesque nature of Stephen's judgment on the corpse:

> "Strip me yon miscreant of those robes usurped,
> And clothe him with vile serge befitting such!
> Then hale the carrion to the market-place;
> Let the town-hangman chop from his right hand
> Those same three fingers which he blessed withal;
> Next cut the head off, once was crowned forsooth;
> And last go fling all, fingers, head and trunk,

In Tiber that my Christian fish may sup!"
(Either because of ICHTHUS, which means fish
And very aptly symbolizes Christ,
Or else because the Pope is Fisherman
And seals with the Fisher's signet.)[14]

A few months after this victory over his dead foe, Stephen was himself imprisoned and then strangled (P 77). The body of Formosus was retrieved and honored as a miracle-working relic.

The later move of the papacy to Avignon would be called its period of foreign captivity. But it was never more a captive than in Rome during the tenth century. Popes in this period were frequently deposed, often hobbled with the claims of anti-popes, and murdered with a dismal regularity. The roll call of papal homicides is grim. In a single century, Stephen VI was killed in 897, Benedict IV in 903, Leo V in 904, John X in 928, Stephen VIII in 942, Benedict VI in 974, John XIV in 984. In this suffocatingly close little arena, popes were at the mercy of the city they supposedly ruled. They became the wholly owned subsidiaries of a few families, especially that of Theophylact, the boss of both the civil and ecclesiastical sides of Rome, a consul and *patricius* of the state (where his wife, Theodora, was a senator) and the minister of papal finance. Nothing escaped this combination of controls.

Admittedly the three generations of rule by this family have been blackened by Liutprand of Cremona, the bishop who helped Emperor Otto I in his efforts to reform the situation in Rome. But the record is atrocious enough even on the most skeptical reading of it. Three popes in a row were simply Theophylact's creatures, ready to do things like consecrate a five-year-old son of a Theophylact favorite as archbishop (K 121). By the papacy of Leo VI (928), Marozia, Theophylact's daughter, had taken over the family business of the papacy, ruling from her eyrie in Castel Sant'Angelo. In her teens she had allegedly had an affair with one pope (Sergius III), father of her bastard child who became Pope John XI. In 928, she had Pope John X murdered for trying to escape the family's stranglehold (Sch 111). In his place she put her very own puppet-pope, Leo VI (K 122). When Leo died suddenly, she put in a stopgap figure, Stephen VII, to hold the chair until her son entered his twenties and could be put on the throne as John XI.

Marozia's son was installed to preside at her uncanonical marriage to her brother-in-law, to whom she "offered her somewhat bloodstained hand . . . In this iron age of politics, the obstacles of canon law did not stand in the way" (P 82). A legitimate son of Marozia by her first marriage, Alberic, did not like the dynastic implications of this union between his mother and his uncle-in-law, so he imprisoned the two, and his half-brother the pope as well. Marozia disappears at this point, perhaps murdered by Alberic, and the pope served out the rest of his term as the prisoner (some said slave) of Alberic. For over two decades, Alberic was the ruler of Rome and of the papacy. To make sure his own bastard became Pope John XII, he forced his predecessor, Pope Agapetus II, to stipulate (uncanonically) that John must follow him. The ill-educated John was eighteen when he took the throne. He performed an inadvertent service to the papacy when he invited the Saxon king, Otto, to Rome for consecration as Emperor Otto I — elevating the man who would assail his type of corruption. To impress Otto with the fact that the papacy had authority to grant power to emperors, he had a cardinal deacon named John draw up an ornate copy of the Donation of Constantine.

Pope John was so dissolute and treacherous that Otto returned to Rome and presided over a synod that deposed him, replacing him with Leo VIII. But when Otto left Rome, John raised a rebellion against Leo, who fled to Otto. Those who had supported Leo were savagely punished. One of them, the deacon who had made the copy of the Donation, had his fingers cut off, as no longer worthy of what they had done (P 89). When Otto's army moved back toward Rome, John fled to Campagna, where he died of a stroke, reportedly in the arms of a married woman. He was twenty-seven.

The Ottonian Era

The emergence of a new Holy Roman Empire under the Ottos and the Henrys signaled a renewed dominance over Rome, but one that promised reform and a release from the more local and sordid control of Theophylact's family. This went along with other forces of renewal and reform, including the vital monastic foundations and reforms of the tenth century, led by figures like Romuald, John of Gorze, and Abbot Odo of Cluny. These movements were international, transcending the local politics of single dioceses and jealous bishops. They also provided islands of order and peaceful discipline in an otherwise turbulent world. Attributes like this made them appealing to both the pope and the emperor, who extended patronage to them, gratefully accepted. In fact, the best thing that can be said of Theophylact's family is that it fostered the Cluniac movement, the reform of Monte Cassino, and the foundations of John of Gorze (P 84). Alberic was especially active in this cause, with the paradoxical result that he, a layman, was reforming the church while corrupting the papacy. A reform monastery was founded in the very Theophylact house where Alberic had been born (P 84).

The attempt of the Ottonian line to bring reform to Rome led to the appointment of some men of real stature. Perhaps the greatest of these was the scholarly French monk Gerbert, brought to the throne as Silvester II by Otto III. Though pope and emperor worked together for spiritual and temporal reform, "as Otto's conception of his role in the renewed Christian empire developed, Silvester was inevitably the junior partner" (K 137). Otto expressly branded the Donation of Constantine a forgery, unconnected with anything he might do for the papacy (P 100).

Not even the Ottonian interventions could bring an end to the struggle of Roman families for control of the papacy. After Otto deposed Alberic's son, John XII, two lines with relations to the Theophylacts, the Crescenzi and the Tuscolani (a branch of Theophylact's family), competed for the papacy, alternately rejecting and suing for imperial support. They frequently fielded rival popes, leading to a confusing series of depositions, reinstallations, and joint rules. The emperor's interventions were defied as soon as he withdrew to his northern territories. As Schimmelpfennig puts it: "There were now usually two competing popes, as there had been since 963. Though this may not present any problems to a historian, it certainly does to a dogmatist. Because there is a lack of criteria, it is difficult to decide who lawfully governed, and, by extension, who carried on the apostolic succession" (Sch 12).

One sequence will illustrate the problem. In 1012, the Tuscolani overthrew the Crescenzi by electing Benedict VIII, upon which the Crescenzi created their own pontiff, Gregory VI. When Benedict died, his layman brother was put in as John XIX, and when John XIX died, *his* brother elevated his own son as Benedict IX, in 1032. Benedict, dissolute and unpopular, was deposed and fled Rome. The Crescenzi were able to supplant him with their own man, Silvester III, upon which Benedict returned to Rome with an armed force, expelled his successor, and again took up residence in the Lateran Palace. But after a brief time he turned over the papacy, in return for a large sum of money, to his godfather, who became Gregory VI. "There were now three popes whose legitimacy was in dispute" — Benedict, Silvester, and Gregory (Sch 114). When Henry III went to Rome in 1046 for his coronation, there was no obviously legitimate pope to crown him, so he *deposed all three,* and put in a fourth man, Clement II. Question: who, at each point in this process, was the real pope? If Benedict's first term was valid, does that make his second term equally canonical? And if he could not legitimately sell the papacy after this second term, does that make his third term authentic too? Even the leaders of the nascent reform movement, which was about to come into power, could not agree on which pope, in this tangle of popes, was the legitimate one.

Clement II, the pope Henry III installed, was the first of four fellow Germans he put into the papacy. The Roman hold on the office was broken, and real reform could come at last, supported by the monastic advisers the four Germans shared with their imperial patron. Not till the papacy was put back on a sound moral and financial basis could it finally take the move that was signaled by the drafting, two centuries back, of the Donation of Constantine, and break free of imperial control whether Eastern *or* Western.

III

FORMS OF
PAPAL PRIMACY

F inally, after a millennium, something like the "plenitude of power" claimed for the papacy was about to become a reality, under the reforming popes Leo IX (1049–1054) and Gregory VII (1073–1085). The earlier attempt to escape the grip of the Eastern emperor had just landed the popes in the equally restrictive embrace of Charlemagne and his heirs. And that captivity, in turn, was broken only by a spiraling fall downward into the clutches of Spoletan dukes, Marozia's sordid relatives, and the murderous conflicts of the Crescenzi and Tuscolani. The assistance of German emperors was needed for the effort to climb back out of this pit. The Ottonian and Salian dynasties, working with monastic reformers, put the papacy back on a solid moral and financial base.

Now the project envisaged when the Donation of Constantine was forged could be pushed forward. The popes concluded, with strong reasons on their side, that spiritual primacy (of the sort claimed by Gelasius) could never succeed unless temporal primacy was claimed as well. After all, emperors of both the East and the West had not made a distinction between the two. When they exercised their secular rule over Rome, they presumed to speak on dogmatic matters as well. The only way to prevent that, it seemed, was to agree with the emperors that temporal and spiritual power go together — but to maintain that only the church should exercise them. This may have been a historical necessity for preservation of the papacy, justifiable on those grounds. But, of course, the actual seizure of power could not have taken place on such rational grounds. A powerful myth was needed to sway opinion in those days — a myth of the sort the Donation was deliberately tailored to provide. The end may have been justifiable, but the means used would be neither honest nor honorable, *considered in themselves. The only excuse for the popes is that, by this time, some of them had come to believe the myth themselves (incredible as it seems to us). A great deal of belief can come of* wanting *to believe. Whatever the motives of the popes at the time, they built a huge system on a substrate of falsehood. And it would last for centuries. We have entered the era of the forgeries.*

11

Forgeries and Populism

"Gregorian Reform"

OF THE FOUR German popes appointed by Henry III between 1046 and 1057, the most commanding was the third, Leo IX (1049–1054). As a clerical nobleman he had led troops for his kinsman, the emperor Conrad II. As bishop of Toul, he was energetic in the principal reform causes of his time — ridding the church of simony (bribery) in the appointment of bishops, enforcing clerical celibacy, and supporting the monastic movement. He took those concerns with him into the papacy, and gathered around him leading reformers, including the monk Hildebrand, who would become Gregory VII. But Leo's most trusted counselor was Humbert of Moyenmoutier (later cardinal-bishop of Silva Candida). In a burst of fresh energy and authority, Leo traveled through Italy, France, and Germany to hold synods of reform. He at first wanted to depose all bishops whose offices had been bought, but there were too many of them — the church would be decapitated by their removal. He settled for imposing penances on them, and he ordained again some priests ordained by bishops who were clearly guilty of simony, recognizing that the bishops' powers were null.

In order to prevent the appointment of bishops by bribeable authorities such as metropolitans, feudal lords, or emperors, Leo sought to return to the early church's practice of election "by the clergy and the people" (Sch 135). Of course, his campaign against appointment by the powerful called into question the way he was selected by Henry III — a problem he tried to finesse by going to Rome in answer to the emperor's appointment, but entering the city as a humble pilgrim, to be chosen by the local clergy (a formality, of course). In principle, he had to oppose the very process that had raised him. He was acting on the view of his authority spelled out in the Donation. He had to be careful about invoking it (Otto III had, after all, called it a forgery), but it was now in canon law (along with the Symmachan forgeries and the False Decretals of Pseudo-Isidore).[1] Leo acted on the Donation's provisions when he led a papal army into battle with Normans to take back "his" lands. Saint Peter Damian criticized Leo's willingness to shed blood (P 114), but the next great reform pope, Gregory VII, would be an even more ardent combatant.

It was only in a mission to the East, far from the sight of Henry, that Leo could fully unmask his batteries on the question of the Donation. In 1054, his most trusted aide, Humbert, took to Constantinople a defense of Roman primacy, expressly quoting the Donation and the Decretals.[2] When the patriarch of Constantinople would not submit, Humbert excommunicated him and placed the bull of excommunication on the altar of Hagia Sophia. The Donation was finally doing the work for which it was designed — to break the authority of the Eastern empire over Rome. "The schism between the Eastern and Western churches is conventionally dated from this event" (K 148).

When Hildebrand took office as Gregory VII (1073–1085), he did not send the customary notice to the emperor, though royal participation in the election was still required by a Roman synod of 1059.[3] "The proceedings were irregular, for the 1059 decree was totally disregarded: there was no preliminary discussion among the cardinal-bishops, and no consultation of the German court . . . The questionable character of the election was to figure among the many charges which Gregory's enemies would direct against him" (M 109).

Gregory was not going to bow to any other ruler. He had been an éminence grise in two preceding reigns (of Nicholas II and Alexander II). "Hildebrand and his party carried out the revolutionary move of electing a new pope outside Rome; at Siena, at the end of 1058, Gerard, Bishop of Florence, was elected pope as Nicholas II" (P 117). During the rule of the next pope (Alexander), Peter Damian acidly said that one must obey not the pope but the pope's master, Hildebrand (M 95). He also referred to him as "the Satan of our side" (*sanctus Satanas*).[4] As pope, Gregory dreamed of leading a crusade to the Holy Land before Urban II preached the First Crusade (M 148). He loved to quote a favorite biblical text, Jer 48.10 — "Cursed is he who keeps back his sword from bloodshed" (M 110). He strongly believed that the pope must maintain his own army, and his military operations drained the treasury of his patroness, Matilda of Tuscany. When he tried to convert church property to military uses, his own bishops in Rome blocked him (P 133).

Despite his enthusiasm for arms, he was notably inept in the campaign with which he opened his papacy. After he had excommunicated Robert Guiscard, the leader of Norman troops, he combined several armies to defeat him, though "they broke up ignominiously" before engaging the enemy (P 127–28). Gregory was in a hurry to assert his authority over almost everything within his ken, and he grasped at any tool for accomplishing it. When the hierarchy resisted his efforts to rid the church of simoniacal bishops, he publicly urged the laity not to obey unworthy clergymen — alienating even those friendly to reform (M 104). Churchmen of great stature, like Lanfranc in England, turned a cold shoulder to him (M 113). It has been discovered that "the terms *obedience* and *disobedience* are by far the most frequently encountered twin concepts in the more than four hundred extant letters of Gregory."[5]

Gregory conceived of himself as a reincarnation of Peter, whose personal authority was far above that of a sinful church, sinful clergy, sinful hierarchy: "His papal actions were direct actions of Peter himself . . . Thus it seemed self-evident to him that his papal activities should be free of all error on the basis of Christ's prayer for Peter."[6] An archbishop who disobeyed him was "Anti-Christ."[7] The famous *Dictatus Papae* (his draft of guides for canon law revision) asserts (Thesis 23) that any canonically elected pope is "without question holy" (*indubitanter sanctus*). And in a letter of 1081 he maintained that only seven priests had ever been saints, but a hundred popes were.[8] Though Gregory VII professed devotion to his papal namesake (and fellow monk), Gregory I, the *Dictatus* (Thesis 2) bestows on the pope the title that the earlier pontiff had condemned in the strongest terms — "universal patriarch." Gregory VII claimed to be restoring the practices of the early church, but he was a headlong innovator.[9] So extreme were the theses of the *Dictatus* that when they were cited later, "there was a tendency to tone them down and to adhere more closely to biblical or canonical precedents."[10]

His sweeping claims were not confined to spiritual primacy. With regard to the temporal sphere, the *Dictatus* asserts that "the pope alone can bear imperial insignia" (Thesis 8) and that princes should kiss no one's feet but the pope's (Thesis 9). Thesis 12 states that the pope has a right to depose emperors — an act Gregory performed in 1080, the first pope to do such a thing. Domenico Maffei finds, in the thesis on imperial insignia, a clear reference to the Donation of Constantine, and in any case a direct challenge to Emperor Henry IV.[11] Gregory's biographer, H.E.J. Cowdrey, thinks there is no overt reference to the Donation in Gregory's writings, but that it was the basis for his actions: "There can be little doubt that the papal claim [to Brittany] was tacitly founded upon the section of the *Constitutum Constantini* in which Constantine delivered to the papacy *omnes . . . occidentalium regionum provincias.*"[12]

Given his view of the relationship between emperor and pope, it is no surprise that Gregory abominated the ancient practice by which secular rulers bestowed on bishops the emblems of their spiritual authority ("lay investiture"). Gregory formally condemned the practice in 1075, and when Henry IV, acting with a majority of the church at Milan, invested his candidate as archbishop, Gregory sent him a threatening message. The emperor responded by calling a synod at Worms, where two archbishops and a majority of the German hierarchy deposed Gregory. The papal reaction was quick. Henry was excommunicated, and ordered not to exercise any royal functions. His subjects were dispensed from any obligation to obey him. German princes, worried that some subjects would refuse obedience at the pope's command, urged Henry to get the excommunication lifted. He did that by going to the pope, who was at Matilda's castle in Canossa, and performing public penance. This is a famous image of a pope humbling a secular ruler; but Colin Morris argues that it was "a coup" for Henry, which "transformed the situation" in his favor (M 116). It allowed him to solidify his support for further defiance of the pope. When Gregory realized that Canossa had not achieved what he wanted, he formally deposed Henry (his earlier act had been merely a suspension of royal activity) in 1080. Inspired to prophecy, the pope predicted "that if Henry did not repent within the year, he would be either dead or deposed — or he, Gregory, was no true pope."[13]

Henry countered this with a council at Brixen, which deposed Gregory and elected a new pope, Clement III. Henry marched on Rome and installed Clement in the Lateran (1084). Gregory had by now alienated so much of his support, even in Rome, that "thirteen cardinals, much of the staff of the Lateran palace, and even the papal chancellor changed their allegiance to Clement III" (M 120). But when Henry left the city, the Norman Robert Guiscard, now Gregory's ally, invaded Rome, drove out the emperor's soldiers, and rescued Gregory from his stronghold in Castel Sant'Angelo. In the process, the Normans devastated the city, destroying one whole sector and burning famous churches. The Romans were so enraged at this that Gregory had to flee from their anger and never returned to the city of his birth.

> When Gregory died at Salerno on 25 May, 1085, he was an apparent failure. He had alienated from his cause many who shared his desire for a renewal of the church, had failed to defeat Henry and had stirred up a civil war which did grave harm to the German churches. He left Rome, the city he loved, in disorder, damaged at the hands of his Norman allies. The western church was in schism and the once-fruitful co-operation between papacy and empire replaced by suspicion and hostility. (M 121)

Morris argues that the reforms Gregory espoused came to little — celibacy did not become the norm ("it remained common for country priests to have a family life and to pass their church to a son"); the simony issue was forgotten in the concentration on lay investiture. The investiture struggle dragged on for another thirty-seven years, to reach a compromised conclusion in the Concordat of Worms, where a pope (Callistus II) surrendered on "a range of privileges which offended Gregorian principles — the election of bishops in the presence of the king, royal control over disputed elections, and the performance of homage [to the king] before consecration" (M 172–73).

Nonetheless, pride had been returned to the papacy after the abasements of the clusters of Theophylact families. Squalid Marozia had been traded in for pious Matilda. Gregory promised more than he could deliver, and demanded more than would be given. But now he was the one making demands, not the one submitting to petty Roman puppet masters. His longer-term legacy — which some think a triumph — was that he set the standard for later popes, who tried to live up (or down) to the Donation of Constantine and other forgeries. These pontiffs would be inspired by his example to believe that papal armies are the sword of Peter, that political subjects can be dispensed from their obligations to any state out of communion with Rome, that only an imperial church can be Christ's church. His followers constructed an ideal derived from what they claimed was the primitive church. "The irony was that most of the material which was being used, although of this they had no conception, was the product of ninth-century forgery, and they were thus reconstructing, not the apostolic age, but a church order designed for polemical purposes by the imagination of a Carolingian author" (M 108). Gregory bequeathed to successors the papacy of the forgeries.

Twelfth-Century Populism

If the tenth century was the nadir of the papacy and the eleventh was an era of reform, the twelfth and thirteenth centuries would be a time of papal populism. Though pilgrimages and missions had, earlier on, given people the sense that they were dealing directly with Peter's heirs, most Christians could not see the distant papacy over the immediate horizon, filled as that was with local ecclesiastics, feudal overlords, and imperial armies. All this would change in the altered economic and cultural conditions producing what is now called the twelfth-century renaissance. The popes found means to appeal to ordinary Christians and make them feel close to Rome's energies and concerns. The means included crusades, indulgences, the Inquisition, mendicant religious orders, military orders, universities, penitential practices, a clarified canon law, and the deployment of powerful abbots (most famously, Bernard of Clairvaux) in service to the pope. It may surprise some to think of the Inquisition and canon law as populist programs, but that is what popes would make of them by the end of the twelfth century.

Returning to the immediate aftermath of Gregory VII's reign: the two popes who followed him could not at first function in Rome, since Henry's pope, Clement III, still held that city. The immediate successor to Gregory, Victor III (1087), was Desiderius, abbot of the monastery of Monte Cassino, where he had given Gregory shelter in the early days of his flight. Afterward, he accompanied him to Salerno and stayed there until Gregory's death. Desiderius was not one of the three men Gregory had recommended to follow him, and Gregorian extremists opposed him. For almost a year there was no hope of securing an election in Rome. When at last Norman protection allowed Desiderius to enter the city, he was elected over heated opposition, but had to flee before he could be consecrated. Not considering himself pope, he returned to his abbey. When, the next year, he called a synod at Capua, it was not as pope but as acting vicar. There he was persuaded to return to Rome under guard, where he was at last consecrated in 1087. Driven out of Rome twice more, he returned to Monte Cassino two more times, and that is where he died, after calling a council at Benevento that excommunicated not only the anti-pope Clement III but some extremists of Gregory's party.

Victor III could at least be elected in Rome, though he never had a secure purchase on the place. The next pope, Urban II (1088–1099), could not even get into the city for that process. He was chosen at Terracina, and it took him three years of hard and patient diplomacy to put together support for his entry into the city. Even when he was there, he could not acquire the Lateran Palace or Castel Sant'Angelo without weeks of negotiation supplemented by bribery (K 159). Urban softened or shelved the more intransigent items in Gregory's program, wooing back disaffected princes and bishops. Once he had secured his base, he traveled to an ambitious series of synods, culminating in the synod at Clermont, where he proclaimed the First Crusade.

This was the real beginning of the populist papacy. No king went on this crusade — the kings of France and Germany were excommunicated at the time — but a whole constellation of princes, leading their own troops, created a new international band of heroes marching under the pope's standard: Raymond of St. Gilles (Count of Toulouse), Duke Robert of Normandy, Counts Stephen of Blois and Robert of Flanders, Duke Godfrey of Lorraine with his brother Baldwin, and Bohemond of Taranto (M 150). Peter the Hermit and others preached the crusade to the masses. Wandering prophets, who would be suspected of heresy or condemned for it later, were now harnessed to the papal cause. "Above all it was the popular evangelists, themselves closely connected with the poverty movement which affected the lower classes, who took over the preaching. Robert d'Arbrissel (c. 1055–1117), one of the intellectual leaders of this group, which sought to imitate Christ in a life of complete poverty, preached in the Loire valley."[14] It has to be remembered that this was a society semi-permanently on pilgrimage, and the pilgrimage to the Holy Land was the most esteemed and meritorious journey, not only because it went to the sites where Jesus lived and died, but because it had always been difficult or dangerous. Now there was to be an *armed* pilgrimage, on which common folk could go, and for which high spiritual rewards were being offered.

Any emotional explosion like that of the First Crusade has more than a single source of its energy. Overlays of ignitable material had gradually been building up. There was the long campaign to check or reverse Turkish incursions into Middle Europe. There was the Muslim occupation of Spain and Sicily. There was also, and especially on Urban's part, a desire to unite Rome with the endangered churches of the East, with Constantinople and Alexandria, Cyprus and Antioch, to forge a common Christian front.[15] A brave thrust outward promised to heal inward wounds. Urban, who had been trying to bolster the Peace of God movement at home, denounced the internal wars of Europe, calling them "harms, not arms" (*malitia, non militia*). By turning their swords outward to a common foe, they could promote internal peace.[16] "Christendom," a new word of the twelfth century, would act as a whole, under its only international leader, the pope.

To cap it all, Urban offered a special indulgence for those going on crusade. This was a dangerous gift that would become a great curse to the church later on; but it, too, seemed a popular move at the time. In fact, the popular preachers gave Urban's words a scope he had not intended. The theology of indulgences had not yet been developed, and all that Urban had in mind was a remission of penitential acts imposed by the church in this life. But preachers of the crusade extended this to cover penalties to be performed in the afterlife (in purgatory). Once people acted on this understanding, it became impossible to back off from it, and theologians had to come up with a justification for this new papal power. What gave the pope authority to dispose of people's souls even in the afterlife? Peter Abelard said that no such justification could be found; and it was not until the next century that Hugh of Saint-Cher came up with a notion that became the official rationale — that the church has a "treasury of merit" earned by Christ and the saints, which can be drawn on to pay out to others.[17] Even the *New Catholic Encyclopedia* (s.v. "Indulgences") admits: "The theory of indulgences lagged more than a century behind the practice. It was not until the teaching of Hugh of Saint-Cher (c. 1230) that the source of the grant was related to the Church's treasury of merits."

The point here is that Urban had lit a populist fire, and the popes recognized the force of what was happening. By the time Bernard of Clairvaux preached the Second Crusade in 1146, "the indulgence, once a means to an end, had become an end in itself."[18] Indulgences were taking their place in a whole system of populist teachings that promoted what has been called "the pastoral revolution" (M 489). The doctrine of purgatory was just being clarified in the second half of the twelfth century, and it, too, was a popular success: "Purgatory made even more impressive headway with the populace than it did with the theologians and clergy."[19] To an age with vivid and omnipresent fears of hell, the idea that there was a less final destiny for sinners had to be appealing. Though Christians had prayed for the dead throughout the history of the church, and had come to use "purgatorial" as an adjective with a word like "pain" or "trial," there was no clear definition of its status or place. It was only in the 1170s that purgatory became a noun and theologians defined its nature.

The purgatory doctrine was a necessary adjunct to the theory of indulgences. Otherwise how could one set the exact times of release from purgatory? Another bit of teaching had to be added, and it was — a specification of what, exactly, was a venial sin. (Only venial sins could be punished in purgatory — mortal ones sent you to hell.) It is no wonder, then, that "the system in which mortal sins are contrasted to venial sins was fully worked out only in the second half of the twelfth century, by the disciples of the theologian Gilbert Porreta (Gilbert de la Porrée), who died in 1154."[20] This theology was also needed by the authors of penitentiaries, the guidebooks for priests, who were given new authority for the practices of the confessional: "The discipline of the confessional was formally established in the western church by canon 21 of Fourth Lateran [1215], *Omnis utriusque sexus,* which has been called with pardonable exaggeration 'perhaps the most important legislative act in the history of the church'" (M 491). This is when the formula "I absolve you of your sins" first came into use (M 492).

Confession, purgatory, indulgences, crusades, and a theology of venial sin made a tightly interlocking construct whose parts seemed to confirm each other. And their place in the system of Catholic thought was indicated in what R. W. Southern has called "the first masterpiece of scholastic humanism," Gratian's synthesis of the canon law collections.[21] Completed in 1141, this is generally known as the *Decretum,* though Gratian called it *A Reconciliation of Conflicting Canons.* Assembled by a brilliant legist in Bologna, it had been prompted not by the papacy, but by bishops dealing with vexed questions of procedure and rights. Nonetheless, it served the popes by making the system uniform. The *Decretum* was "populist" because it took much of the uncertainty and unpredictability out of daily matters like the rules for marriage and the other sacraments.[22]

Care for souls was signaled in all these developments — and in the greatly improved preaching skills of the time. Saint Bernard's Cistercians were popular orators who tried to imitate his great eloquence. The military orders (Templars and Hospitalers), set up to protect and minister to pilgrims to Jerusalem, were also popular services, and ones not connected with any single nation. The internationalism of the pastoral revolution strengthened Rome as the international center. Even universities, though in service to the elite, were international gathering places for the bodies of students called separate "nations." Charismatic teachers like Abelard drew disciples from all places, creating popular songs as well as knotty arguments. Chivalry and courtly love created an international audience that could be addressed by friars as well as troubadours.

All these elements were coming together by the beginning of the thirteenth century in the pontificate of Innocent III (1198–1216), whose Fourth Lateran Council (1215) legislated some of the elements into formal acceptance. Innocent also gave the first encouragement to Francis of Assisi and Dominic of Guzman, who would shortly found the mendicant orders of Franciscans and Dominicans. The two were itinerant preachers who resembled the "barefoot evangelizers" widely suspected of heresy. It was a risky thing Innocent did, supporting these "friars," who were bound neither to one monastic house (and the chanting of the office) nor to one bishop (with his diocesan discipline). Of course, the friars supplied the pope with a mobile support force, since Francis and Dominic had to rely solely on his guidance and protection; but that could backfire if they became an embarrassment (as some later Franciscans did).

Innocent was courageously open to new pastoral approaches. He actively sought and won reconciliation with other "barefoot evangelizers" who made up the populist new poverty movement — the Humiliati or "Poor Men," the Trinitarians.[23] Innocent even allowed lay preaching by a submissive branch of the Waldenses, though the larger body, still smarting from its treatment by an earlier pope (Alexander III), was irreconcilable.[24] With the Cathars of Languedoc, Dominic had enjoyed some preaching success, since he went among them practicing the asceticism their "perfect" members possessed. Innocent made this Dominic's mission. But when a Cathar who seemed connected with a prince (Raymond of Toulouse) killed a papal legate, Peter of Castelnau, the pope let himself be drawn into what was largely a struggle for territory. He mixed religion with the politics of that situation, inflaming territorial-religious strife like that in modern Palestine and Israel. Even worse, he was quick to use the powerful new weapon Urban II had invented, the crusade, with indulgences granted to the warriors of righteousness. What worked in the East could be tried in Europe — and the butchery that had followed on the first capture of Jerusalem was replicated in the countryside of Languedoc, where "crusaders" waged ruthless war on the people known in this region as Albigensians.

Innocent's successors Honorius III (1216–1227) and Gregory IX (1227–1241) would follow up on his initiatives, both the benign and the malignant ones. Honorius formally recognized the mendicant orders. Gregory sent papal investigators (*inquisitores*) into Languedoc — missions that would develop, eventually, into the institutionalized Inquisition. The church historian Richard Kieckhefer has argued that it is anachronistic to talk of "*the* Inquisition" when describing these first, targeted inquisitorial missions.[25] Different kinds of "inquisitions" are separated by time and space over the centuries after this early experiment. The historian Mark Gregory Pegg writes of "the great inquisition of 1245–1246":

> Part of the problem when one thinks about the early inquisitors and their methods, and so the necessity of having to stress that torture was not one of them, is that a vicious mythical beast known as *The Inquisition* prowls the modern imagination. Yet such mythologizing (or rather the unreflective acceptance of the fantasy for fact) is woefully misleading for a whole host of reasons. The most crucial error is that when one confuses the medieval inquisition with the Inquisition of the sixteenth and seventeenth centuries, especially the Spanish and Roman tribunals, and so makes a rather ordinary noun all too proper, a monolithic institution comes into being, a bureaucratic entity that lacks not only historical specificity but also historical reality.[26]

As fatal as the tool of inquisition would prove for later persecution, it should be recognized that even this was, in its origins, a populist development. Heretics are often extremely unpopular. They are elitists, who profess to have higher standards than ordinary Christians. The Cathars were "puritans" (from the Greek word for pure, *katharos*). As dualists who thought matter was diabolical, they denigrated marriage and the ordinary joys of life. Neighbors rarely look on such attitudes with composure. Besides, as challengers of orthodox belief, they often had to be secretive, evasive, or conspiratorial for their own safety. The popular American suspicion and hatred of Communists in the 1940s and 1950s is a partial parallel to this attitude. The same would be true of other targets of inquisition, like witches and Jews.

In fact, the early inquisitors, with their orderly procedure, sometimes calmed and controlled the frenzy against "subversives." One might compare them with the federal investigators and marshals sent in the 1950s and 1960s into the South, where, even when they were ineffective, they were at least more stabilizing than the local extremists. It is true that local authorities sometimes used or misled the FBI. But Kieckhefer points out that killing often went down after inquisitors began their investigations. And seventeenth-century Scotland and America would prove, in their witch hunts, that you need no Catholic inquisition to make witches the victims of mass hysteria. Colin Morris, when studying the early Albigensian inquisitions, writes: "There has been a reaction against the sweeping liberal condemnation of the inquisition, and it has been stressed that it was an orderly institution [Kieckhefer would make that noun plural] which was penitential in character, was inclined to be more merciful than lay powers, and only rarely surrendered the accused to the death penalty" (M 473).

This is not said to champion any or all inquisitions. Here the important point is to recognize that the inquisitions fit, like crusades and purgatory, into the widespread spiritual movement of the twelfth century that was both populist and papal.

"The Greatest of Centuries"

When I was in high school, a Jesuit recommended that I read *The Thirteenth, Greatest of Centuries,* by an Irish-American biologist, James J. Walsh. Unfortunately, I did — it made me susceptible, for a while, to Chesterton's sentimental celebrations of the Middle Ages. Though the book had been published in 1907, when the Knights of Columbus promoted its distribution, it maintained its popularity well into the 1940s, when I read it. For some Americans it had a tonic effect, arguing that almost all the humane things that came after grew from seeds planted in the thirteenth century by the Catholic church. Walsh even gave the church credit for Magna Carta, without bothering to mention that Innocent III, a backer of King John, had condemned it.[27] But for Catholics of an immigrant church whose loyalty was suspect, the book boosted morale.

Exaggerated though Walsh's claims were, the thirteenth century *is* a dazzling stretch of history. Gothic cathedrals were going up like flights of arrows. Architectonics of a different kind produced the huge structures of Thomas Aquinas in theology and of Dante in poetry. (Walsh included in the century men like Dante, who lived into the fourteenth century.) Aristotle was reabsorbed into the texture of Western thought. The universities flourished. Duccio and Cimabue, Giotto and Pietro Cavallini were painting. Great sculpture was being created by Nicola and Giovanni Pisano, Arnolfo di Cambio, Lorenzo Maitani. Vernacular literature burst entirely free of its Latin cerements, in the songs of the *trouvères* and the epics of Germany, France, and Spain. Chivalry and courtly love created a culture of their own, animating many arts.

The five crusades of the century did not succeed, but they brought back elements of a larger world — as did explorations like that of Marco Polo. These developments were made possible by the prosperity of the upper and upper-middle classes; but they continued the populist accent of the preceding century. The cathedrals were focal points for festivities and pilgrimage. They were boldly painted, inside and out; special tapestries and paintings were hung or uncovered for the processions of holy days. (Corbusier wrote a book called *When the Cathedrals Were White* — they never were.)[28] The courts of princes now vied with the church for popular spectacle. That is one reason popes were so opposed to jousting. They were critical of courtly love, too, not so much for its sexual content, but because it aped religion in its ceremonies.

Walsh, then, was not wrong in thinking the thirteenth century a high point in European culture, only in thinking that the church was the origin, object, or conduit of all that energy. Actually, the secular venues now began to surpass the principally sacred ones. Better Aristotelians could be found at the Sicilian court of Frederick II than in Rome. Frederick, in fact, founded the Neapolitan school in which Thomas Aquinas, the son of one of his nobles, was trained. Texts of Aristotle were leading men to realize that the state can be a secular institution competent to all its own purposes. Even sacred things could be wrested from the popes. The Fourth Crusade was "hijacked" by Venice, which diverted it toward Constantinople, against the pope's wishes. The Sixth

Crusade was taken over by Frederick II, who was actually in a state of excommunication when he recovered Jerusalem.

Frederick II was a sign of all the things that would go wrong for the church in the thirteenth century. He towers over the early part of the century, just as Philip the Fair of France does over its ending. Innocent III had been Frederick's guardian in his Sicilian childhood. But when Frederick took the throne of Germany, he pursued the Hohenstaufen policies that had led to his grandfather's and his father's excommunication. He would be excommunicated twice himself. The popes were terrified that he would add Lombard Italy to his holdings in Germany, Sicily, and the East. Pope Innocent IV (1243–1254), to escape Frederick's encompassing power, fled to Lyons, where he called a council, deposed Frederick, and had the mendicant orders preach a crusade against him.

The degradation of spiritual powers to temporal uses can be seen in this abuse of the indulgence weapon, by which Christians were promised rewards in the afterlife for killing fellow Christians. The result was "an ideological war which in fierceness, ferocity and depth of passion and disregard of all the accepted norms of warfare has few, if any, parallels in medieval history."[29] Pope Innocent also conspired with agents to murder Frederick; he deployed inquisitors; and he sold privileges shamelessly: "Innocent lowered the prestige of the papacy because he used his spiritual powers constantly to raise money, buy friends, and injure foes; he treated the endowments of the church as papal revenues, and his exploitation of the system of papal provisions to benefices (i.e., the pope's right to nominate to vacant benefices) aroused scandal" (K 19). This is hardly the stuff of James Walsh's "greatest century."

Innocent's successors were so intent on hounding Frederick's heirs — Manfred and Conradin — to death (which they accomplished) that they brought France into the struggle, "giving" Sicily to Charles, the brother of King Louis IX, with the task of taking it from Manfred. The result was that the Angevin line dominated the papacy as much during the last half of the century as the Hohenstaufen had during the first half. This produced a line of French popes who died and were elected outside Rome, in a series of disorderly elections that left growing gaps between reigns — four months (1265), six months (1281), eleven months (1288), twenty-seven months (1294).

This last delay was caused by the fact that Nicholas IV (1288–1292) felt so insecure in Rome (a city only intermittently inhabited by popes of the time) that he gave himself over to the protection of the Colonna family. This made other families unite behind the Orsini, rivals of the Colonna, deadlocking the election for over two years. Finally, as a compromise, a total outsider was chosen — the old (eighty-five) and saintly, but half-literate, hermit Pietro di Morrone, who became Celestine V. Charles II, king of Sicily, took Celestine to his castle in Naples, where he manipulated the pope's appointments and siphoned church funds into his personal coffers (P 287). When acting on his own initiative, not that of King Charles, Celestine clumsily promoted his own little religious order over the great established orders. The cardinals who had elected him were quickly disgusted by his incompetence and found a way to ease him out, pressuring him to resign. He was replaced with one of the men who had ousted him, Benedetto Caetani, who became Boniface VIII (1294–1303) and was as ruthless as Celestine had been dithery. Boniface ended the century with the first great jubilee year in Rome (1300), jamming the city with pilgrims enticed there by the increasingly overused spiritual bribe of indulgences. It seems an appropriately populist ending for the "greatest century." But Boniface was about to assert his own power in a way that subverted papal claims.

12

Rise of the Secular State
and the Church Council

BONIFACE VIII had a great gift for making people hate him. The most famous hater is Dante, whose party the pope drove out of Florence. In the *Inferno* (19.56–67), Boniface's arrival in hell is awaited with this cry:

> Nor did your tricks to win the Church, then, fail —
> You put Her holy body up for sale.

The Colonna faction, which helped put Boniface in office, soon grew tired of his arrogance — upon which he excommunicated two Colonna cardinals and proclaimed a crusade (with full indulgences) against their family and its allies. He sent out an army, led by Orsini family members, to destroy or confiscate the Colonna castles. Even Boniface's sympathetic biographer, T.S.R. Boase, admits: "It was grim warfare. Orders were given to devastate all hostile lands, to cut down the vineyards and destroy the crops, to drive off the cattle and to kill or capture the inhabitants."[1]

Dominicans hated Boniface and tried to have the University of Paris declare his election invalid.[2] Spiritual Franciscans (the Fraticelli) hated him even more, and supported the Colonna revolt against him. Ubertino of Casale called him "the angel of the abyss fraudulently ascended through the malicious procuring of spirits."[3] Jacopone da Todi, the Franciscan poet, wrote bitter verses against Boniface from the prison where he was confined for calling the pope's election a fraud.

But the great foe who brought Boniface down was Philip IV of France ("the Fair"). Philip harbored Boniface's foes at his court —

Colonna exiles, Dominicans, Franciscans — and mounted a great propaganda war against the very notion of papal primacy. Boniface's reaction was typically bold and foolish. After calling a council against Philip, he issued, on his own authority, the bull *Unam Sanctam* (1302), a digest of the most extreme claims of the papacy. Boase argues that there is nothing in the bull that had not been said before in one or other place. But Boniface pulled the claims together in a forceful manner, so compendiously that later popes were constantly tempted to draw arguments from this dangerous document. For one thing, he gave a succinct form to the popular "two swords" theory of papal power, which was based on a misreading of the Gospel of Luke, but which had a symbolic and preacherly elegance that made popes return to it again and again.

About to face his death, Jesus says there is nothing left to the disciples but "a sword," meaning spiritual struggle (Lk 22.36). When the typically muddle-headed Peter says, "Here, in fact, are two swords," Jesus resignedly answers, "That's enough of that" (*Hikanon esti*, 22.38). Jesus is not referring to physical swords, as he shows when Peter uses one at the arrest and Jesus has to tell him, "Put that back where it belongs. Those who take up the sword are destroyed by the sword" (Mt 26.52).

Here is what *Unam Sanctam* makes of those useless swords, which Jesus tells Peter *not* to use:

> We are informed by the texts of the gospels that in the church, placed in its charge, are two swords, the spiritual and the temporal. For when the Apostles say, "Look, here are two swords" — "here," that is to say, in the church, since it is apostles who are speaking — the Lord did not reply that there were too many, but that there were "enough." Certainly, the one who denies that the temporal sword is in the power of Peter has not listened closely to the Lord's word when he commands, "Put up your sword into its place." Both, therefore, the spiritual and the physical swords are subject to the church, though the spiritual is to be wielded *by* the church, the physical *for* the church; the former in the hand of God's priest, the latter in the hand of kings or generals acting by direction and permission [*ad nutum et patientiam*] of the priest.

The reference to not having "too many" swords is connected with what immediately follows in *Unam Sanctam* — a discussion of the divine economy in terms of the pseudo-Dionysius's concept of hierarchy, with all lower things aspiring upward through higher things, leaving nothing outside this magnetic alignment of filings acting under one ordinating influence.

As one sword must be [not pitted against but] subject to [*subesse*] the other, so the temporal authority must be in service [*subjici*] to the spiritual power. Since Saint Paul says, "There is no power not derived from God, and what is derived from God is set in order by him" (Rom 13.2), the swords would not be set in order if one were not in service to the other, and if the inferior one were not drawn upward through the superior one. By divine providence, as the holy Dionysius teaches, lowest things communicate with highest things only through intermediaries. By cosmic rule, then, things are not ordered separately and on their own, but the lowest by the intermediate, the inferior by the superior . . . If, therefore, a temporal power goes astray, it is to be corrected by the spiritual power. And if a lower spiritual power goes astray, it is to be corrected by a higher spiritual power; but if the highest power of all err, it can be corrected only by God, not by man . . . And this power, though given to a man and exercised by him, is not a human power but a divine one, since it was given by a divine charge to Peter and confirmed for him and his successors by the authority Peter recognized, the Lord, who told Peter, "What you tie on earth is tied in Heaven . . ." Therefore, whoever resists this power, after its establishment by God, resists God's command — unless, like Manichaeus, he pretends that there are two highest powers, a false and heretical notion. After all, Moses says that God created heaven and earth "in the beginning," not in the beginnings. Therefore we publish, declare, and define it, as a condition of salvation, that every human being must be subject [*subesse*] to the Roman pontiff.

Boniface's claim that God could not act on all things separately and directly, but only through their superiors, would remain for centuries a papal argument against democracy. Only deference to higher social orders can redeem the lower social orders. This is the crowning vision of the greatest of centuries — a pyramid with all things neatly arranged in a descending and broadening order; but also, of course, an ascending order, as the pyramid narrows more and more toward the top, with only a single figure at the pinnacle: the pope, to whom everything on earth is subjected.

Boniface issued this confident trumpet blast just as his own position was crumbling. King Philip sent officers to arrest Boniface in his hometown of Anagni, to bring him to trial before a council. Philip did not send many troops, since he knew Boniface had little support from anyone; but enough of the pope's hometown connections rallied to rescue him from custody, and he was taken back to die in Rome, a broken and rejected man. A new world, one invisible to him, had grown up around him, leaving him an anachronism.

The Secular State

James J. Walsh was right, in a way, when he said that the roots of modernity were in the thirteenth century. But he saw these as fostered by the church. In fact, the church was at deadly odds with what has been called "the new science of politics" hatched in the thirteenth century.[4] Political theory had in the recent past been of the pseudo-Dionysian sort — a hierarchical and theocratic theory. The rediscovered texts of Aristotle challenged such concepts in a fundamental way.[5] For Aristotle, the state does not reflect God's order *descending* through king and pope — it is, rather, built *up* from the family unit (*oikos*) till it reaches a level of organization capable of self-maintenance (*autarkeia*). The competent state is contained within itself (*princeps sibi*). This Aristotelian approach is evident in John of Paris's *On Royal and Papal Authority*, finished near the end of John's life (1306), of which Walter Ullmann writes: "This tract marked the entry of the concept of the State as an independent, autonomous entity into the arena of scholarly political discussion. Intellectual superiority of quite remarkable dimensions enabled John partly to ridicule, partly to destroy hierocratic arguments."[6]

A brilliant example of this new political science was written by Boniface's old enemy Dante. His book *Monarchy* (c. 1314) was publicly burned in 1329, and placed on the Index of Forbidden Books in 1554, where it remained until 1881.[7] Here Dante argues from Aristotle's definition of freedom, as "that which exists for its own sake," to assert the competence of a free state to establish and reach its own earthly goals.[8] Secular authority exists for secular advantages, and the church has no role in establishing those goals, or in choosing the means to reach them. Peter's keys were given him to deal with what belongs to him, and the state does not belong to him.[9] Dante admits that Constantine thought he could "donate" the state to Pope Silvester (like most of his contemporaries, Dante did not know that the Donation was a forgery); but he says that Constantine was a fool, and the gift is self-contradictory. If Constantine had a realm to give, then it could not have been derived from the popes in the first place. Besides, no ruler can give away his kingdom. He exists for it, not it for him.[10]

Dante was imagining a free state under a universal secular ruler. His follower, Marsiglio of Padua (who translated Dante's Latin treatise into Italian), went further. In his epochal *Guardian of the Peace* (*Defensor Pacis*) of 1324, he argued that all legitimate government is derived from consent of the governed:

> Let us, then, say in accordance with the truth and the counsel of Aristotle in the *Politics*, Book III, Chapter 6, that the legislator, or the primary and proper efficient cause of the laws, is the people or the whole body of citizens, or the weightier part thereof, through its election or will expressed by words in the general assembly of citizens, commanding or determining that something be done or omitted with regard to human civil acts, under temporal pain or punishment.[11]

Nothing could be further than this from the regnant papal claim — that the laity are to obey the pope as subjects are to obey princes, whose authority comes from God. The papacy would not catch up to Marsiglio until the Second Vatican Council.

The future belonged to Marsiglio. Already in the thirteenth century the elements for this were coming together. After Peter of Auvergne completed Thomas Aquinas's commentary on Aristotle's *Politics* (1274–1290), his emphasis on popular participation in government was picked up almost immediately by succeeding commentators.[12] By the time of Marsiglio, popular consent was one of those ideas whose time has come, so that it was expressed independently by two different thinkers, not only by Marsiglio but by his contemporary, Bartolus of Saxaferrato.[13] "With a few juristic strokes Bartolus provided within legal theory what Marsiglio had provided within political theory. To both it was axiomatic that there was no sovereign above the people. 'A free people is not subjected to anyone,' Bartolus had declared. And with this the concept of the subject also vanished, since a free people knew of no subjects, but only citizens."[14]

By the next century, Nicholas of Cusa would be endorsing the popular-consent thesis, and any pope risked looking ridiculous if he tried to blow again the tinny horn of *Unam Sanctam*.[15]

The General Council

The men sent to arrest Boniface in Anagni were going to take him to France for trial by a council. The idea of a council's superiority to the pope had been given a great boost by the accession of Boniface. Boniface's critics claimed that he had assembled false precedents to persuade Celestine that he could resign from the papacy. Ironically, some of those defending Boniface did so by applying "the new politics" to the papacy. John of Paris said that the papal office exists for the good of the whole body of Christians, and it can be given up if that will serve the corporate interest. So far that was a defense of Boniface's legitimacy, and an argument that Celestine's resignation had cleared the way for a normal succession. But John then went on to say that, by the same principle of corporate health for the whole body, a pope can be deposed for the good of the church.[16] That was a defense Boniface did not want to hear. If that was what his defenders were saying, what could he expect from his foes?

The answer was not long in coming. Marsiglio's *Guardian of the Peace* not only defined the "faithful legislator" of government as the whole people of a state, but defined the legislator of the church as the whole people, best represented in a general council:

> The church means the whole body [*universitas*] of the faithful, who believe in and invoke the name of Christ, and all the parts of this whole body in any community . . . Therefore all the Christian faithful, both priests and non-priests, are and should be called churchmen [*ecclesiastici*] according to this truest and most proper signification, because Christ purchased and redeemed all men with his blood . . . And for the same reason, those ministers — bishops or priests and deacons — are not alone "the church," which is Christ's bride, but they are rather a part of this bride, since it was for this bride that Christ gave himself.[17]

This anticipates Vatican II's definition of the church as "the people of God."

Marsiglio not only brands it a usurpation for church ministers to call themselves the church. He says those ministers go on to commit two further usurpations — embodied in crusades and in indulgences — which are attacked in his *Shorter Guardian* (*Defensor Minor*, c. 1340). The papacy cannot commandeer the resources and purposes of the secular order, which has authority over its own domain. A crusade usurps that power, letting the pope direct secular activity. If a pope can persuade competent legislators of the state to take certain actions, good in themselves, that is the extent of his authority. The secular power must make its own decision, based on its own norms, to undertake acts "meritorious for the sake of the peace and tranquility of all who live civilly."[18] If encroaching on the rightful temporal order is bad, it is worse to claim jurisdiction in the afterlife, which is God's domain — and that is what indulgences do. If the papacy cannot even punish in this world (which would be an infringement on the secular supervision of earthly penalties and rewards), how can it take things out of the hands of God himself? One can pray for the dead, but not legislate for them.[19]

The role of the hierarchy, formulated mainly by councils, is to establish the true faith from Scripture and provide for ministers of the sacraments, instructors in the faith, and rebukers of sin. To rebuke is not to punish — if sinners cause temporal disorder, the authority for punishing that lies with the temporal ruler. If sinners are not causing such disorder, but are believing wrong things, they cannot be coerced into belief. They must be persuaded and prayed for. If they persist in error, God will know how to handle that in the coming world.[20]

Marsiglio thinks the indulgence power not only invalid but trivializing, when it is not much worse. It trivializes when it makes pilgrimages and jubilees more important than acts of mercy and justice.

> For we do not find counsels or precepts about the making of such pilgrimages in Scripture, but one may locate clear counsels in the Old Law as well as the New about alms-giving and distribution of worldly goods or riches to the poor . . . He says in Matthew (25.42–43), "I was hungry, and you did not give me something to eat" . . . [while] nowhere is it written that He had said, "I was in Rome and Jerusalem and you did not visit me."[21]

But the whole crusade and indulgence system was far worse than trivializing, and Marsiglio gives us the terms in which to judge, retrospectively, the "greatest century." It was a time of great spiritual energy, but of the deepest spiritual corruption. The four crusades to the Holy Land were bloody enough, but the great scandal is the use of spiritual bribes to launch crusades not only against Cathars but against the supporters of Western rulers who were in the popes' way. More people were butchered in these parodies of holy war than in any inquisitions.

The use of indulgences to motivate temporal conquests for the papal state is far worse than the sordid little affairs carried on in what is thought of as the least great century, the tenth. Marozia's family had little effect on the Christian world at large. Crusade after crusade, pitting Christian against Christian, left a regularly rising toll of the dead, along with widows and orphans. The earth was being emptied in order to empty purgatory.

Avignon (1309–1378)

Marsiglio has been called the "founder of conciliarism."[22] But the popes were the real, if unintentional, promoters of that movement. The sad line of fourteenth-century pontiffs, with their rival papacies, fairly cried out for conciliar remedy. Boniface's successor, Benedict XI (1303–1304), at the mercy of Philip the Fair, withdrew all Boniface's condemnations of the king and pardoned that pope's attempted kidnappers. The next pope, Clement V (1305–1314), truckled even more ignominiously to Philip. The king, still unhappy that his arrest of Boniface had not succeeded, was determined to exhume the dead pontiff and put him on trial. Clement bought off the king's vengeance by calling a council (at Vienne) to satisfy another of Philip's demands — the dissolution of the Order of the Knights Templar, whose considerable property Philip had his eye on.

> After much undignified wrangling its [the order's] goods, estates, all its property, were by papal and conciliar decrees distributed amongst the Hospitallers and the French fisc. The price which the papacy paid for avoiding the trial against the dead Boniface was high indeed. No doubt the handling of this matter by the papacy must have gravely damaged its standing. It is surely legitimate to observe that only a modicum of statesmanship and a moderate implementation of some papal principles — which ironically enough had been proclaimed with such furor less than a decade before — could have saved a good deal of the pope's prestige.[23]

Clement also placated the king, the Colonna, and the Spiritual Franciscans by canonizing Celestine V, encouraging the view that Celestine had remained the "real" pope when Boniface seized power.

Since Clement was a Frenchman and promptly created nine French cardinals (including four of his own nephews), he had no desire to re-

turn from Lyons, where he had been crowned, to a faction-riddled Italy, and especially not to a hostile Rome. In 1309 he moved his court to
Avignon, where it would remain for the next seventy years. There was
nothing unusual, at that point, about popes residing outside Rome —
that had become fairly common in the "greatest century." War, riots,
plague, or general poverty sealed Rome off from pope after pope, who
preferred to stay in Orvieto, Perugia, Viterbo, Spoleto, Anagni, or some
other perch of opportunity. But to take the papacy entirely out of Italy
was to distance it from the shrines of the apostles which had been the
source of papal charism in the first place, and saintly people would
spend over half a century pleading for the popes to leave their French
embrace and return to Rome.

Distance from Rome did not, at first, solve the problem of getting
new popes elected. Later there would be too many popes trying to rule
at the same time, but at the outset there were intervals without a pope.
It took a year to elect Clement. It would take two years to elect his successor, John XXII (1316–1334), the strongest and most controversial of
the Avignon popes. From 1319 on, John tried to organize the Guelf
(pro-papal) forces in Italy to crush the Ghibelline (pro-imperial) influence, centered in Milan. He resorted to the by now tired devices of holy
war, interdict, and excommunication, declaring the Ghibellines heretics for their insubordination to himself:

> Heresy: this was the eventual gravamen in which all other charges cul-
> minated. Canon law in matters of heresy was so unfavorable to the de-
> fendant that once a person was *suspectus de haeresi* his condemnation
> could be made practically inevitable . . . Political remarks, such as the
> denial that Ferrara was a part of the Papal State, were thought an ade-
> quate basis for heresy persecution . . . Over 800 of the 1,400 or so per-
> sons cited before the Inquisition in the Ghibelline heresy cases were
> Milanese. (P 314–15)

John made it clear that Avignon was not going to be just a brief interlude when he began building a huge fortress-palace for the papacy
in 1316, an act that dismayed many Christians. The Spiritual Franciscans came to despise John almost as much as they had Boniface. The
Franciscan theologian William of Ockham revived the tale of Pope
Joan (a legend born in the middle of the "greatest century") to show
that invalidly elected popes could go undetected.[24] The dynamic that
had worked to depose Boniface now came into play against John. As

Philip the Fair had concentrated papal foes in France for a propaganda war at the beginning of the century, the emperor Louis the Bavarian now gave haven in Germany to refugees from John's wrath — Ockham, Marsiglio, and the superior of the Franciscans, Michael of Cesena. Louis called a council to try the pope. John responded by deposing the emperor, a favor Louis returned before crowning his own pope in Rome, Nicholas V.

John XXII gave hostages to his foes by his willingness to promote doctrinal novelties:

> The pope was called a heretic not only by political opponents, but also by properly qualified theologians. On his deathbed the nonagenarian renounced his erroneous opinions concerning the so-called beatific vision. There also seemed to be some substance in the charge of heresy committed by this pope, who was, nevertheless, one of the best canonists and a most acute expert in jurisprudence. This accusation concerned his views on the poverty of Christ [which he denied], which were at least theologically debatable.[25]

Things did not improve under the next Avignon pope, Benedict XII (1334–1342). Ockham called him just as heretical as his predecessor.[26] Petrarch called him the church's "drunken helmsman" (K 219). Benedict responded with defiance, appointing only six cardinals, five of them French. After a Spanish cardinal who was also a military genius, Gil de Albornoz, had regained or neutralized much of the former papal state, Pope Urban V (1362–1370) returned briefly to Rome in 1367, but was driven back to Avignon in 1370. It was another six years before Gregory XI (1370–1378) finally ended the "Babylonian captivity" (as Petrarch called it) of Avignon. Many felt a vast relief at the pope's return to Rome. They did not know that even worse trouble lay ahead.

The Great Schism (1378–1417)

When Gregory died, rioters in the street demanded that a Roman pope be chosen, to prevent any return to Avignon. A safely secluded conclave defied the clamor and, ignoring what had happened with Celestine V, chose a Neapolitan outsider, a dark horse, to be Pope Urban VI. Though the cardinals proclaimed his legitimacy and supported him at the outset, it soon became clear, to their horror, that the man was deranged (K 227). Since there was no provision for deposing a crazed pope, the cardinals confected a story that they had been intimidated in choosing him (though they had actually refused to accede to the crowd's demand for a Roman), declared his election invalid, and chose a new pope, Clement VII (1378–1394). "The remarkable feature of this double election was that one and the same college of cardinals had elected two popes within a few months. In the numerous previous schisms this contingency had never occurred. The cardinals had acknowledged Urban VI as the rightful pope through the five months following his election."[27] But Urban, in Rome, defied the college, which had withdrawn to Anagni to make its choice; and Clement was forced to flee — first to Naples and then back to Avignon. Now there were popes in both places. Dismay gradually mounted to panic.

> How was the ordinary Christian to decide who was the legitimate pope? The result was that some monasteries had two abbots and two priors, some parishes had two parish priests, and so on. Europe was split into two halves: France, Scotland, Aragon, Castille and Navarre adhered to Clement VII, while the larger part of Italy, Germany, Hungary, England, Poland and Scandinavia followed Urban VI; Portugal could not make up its mind for a long time; the Neapolitan kingdom was swayed from Clement to Urban and back again, after a number of Urbanist cardinals had migrated to Clement's curia.[28]

Each pope excommunicated the other, and neither was willing to yield. The erratic Urban became weirder, informing others that past popes in the Lateran series of portraits had frowned before his election, but now they were all smiling (Sch 220). "His main preoccupation was a petty, endlessly shifting struggle, punctuated by explosions indicative of his mental instability, over the kingdom of Naples, which he wished to secure for a worthless nephew" (K 228). In his paranoia he had cardinals tortured and murdered. He died in Rome, despised, having reduced the city to anarchy. He is the pope, out of this confused scramble, counted authentic in the Roman tradition.

Since neither Urban nor Clement would give way, the only solution to the schism that men of good will could come up with was to call a council to decide between them. An explosion of writings picked up where Marsiglio had left off, arguing that the whole people of the church are the true sovereign and could legislate for the papacy. Learned theologians spelled out this doctrine — Pierre d'Ailly, chancellor of the College of Navarre; his famous student Jean Gerson, chancellor of the University of Paris; Dietrich of Niem, the curial official pressing for councils; and the great canonist Cardinal Francis Zabarella.[29] None of these men was an outsider or a wild radical. They were at the very center of responsible reform efforts in the church, which antedated Luther's and Calvin's criticisms. Under their intellectual and practical guidance, a council was held in 1409 at Pisa, where they chose a new pope, Pietro Pilarghi, the Franciscan archbishop of Milan, who had helped bring the council into existence. Pilarghi took the name Alexander V, and asked the other popes to step down. Since neither did, there were now three popes competing for increasingly confused allegiances.

The early death of Alexander V did not reduce the number of popes, since the reform forces of Pisa chose a successor to him, John XXIII, keeping the number of competing rulers at three. King Sigismund, trying to break the impasse, persuaded John XXIII that he had the credentials to call a new council, one that would probably support him, as the choice (through Alexander) of a council *and* (in his own election) a conclave. A new council would dispose finally of his competitors. So John issued a bull for a council to gather in the German town of Constance (Konstanz) in 1414. He expected the majority at Constance to be made up of Italian bishops, who supported him. But when large numbers from the north appeared, council fathers decided to vote by "nations," according to the University of Paris system — which diluted the Italian vote. John recognized that this was a runaway council, so he ran away himself.

The council deposed all three popes then in play, and started from scratch with their own choice — Martin V (1417–1431). This was the great triumph of the conciliarist movement. It had seen the papacy reduced to a nullity, unable to relaunch itself from its own resources. Only the council could do that — which was a final proof that it was the pope's superior. After all, Martin could not challenge the legitimacy of what the council did without undermining his own authority, given him by the council fathers. It was a case of no valid council, no valid pope. Nor did Constance simply elect this pope. It did so conditionally, imposing on him and his successors the duty of calling regular councils — the first in five years, the next in seven, and one every ten years after that. Martin had to swear to observe this ruling in order to get himself elected.[30] There seemed, at this point, no way for the papacy to regain its independence. But, amazingly, it would.

13

Renaissance and Reformation

WHEN THE PAPAL COURT came back from Avignon, it was a changed institution. Earlier, when it had been fixed in Rome or drifting from city to city in Italy, it was a comparatively open operation. When the pope was in Rome, his palace was at the Lateran, but he processed from station church to station church for public feasts, often ending up at Peter's Vatican shrine, which did not originally include a bishop's palace. A residence was built there in the sixth century, as we have seen, only because Pope Symmachus had to stay somewhere while a rival pope held the Lateran. The Vatican territory was not, after that, always friendly to the pope, since forces hostile to him could and did make a stand in the nearby Castel Sant'Angelo. After Symmachus, the Lateran resumed its place as the center of curial activity in a larger network of movable feasts. But the papacy in Avignon made popes familiar with a castle complex sealed in on itself. The castle routine was contained, moated off, and secretive.

> This change from [papal life as] a municipal liturgy into [life as] a palace ceremonial was to leave its mark for over five hundred years on the papacy's conception of itself and on the form in which it was represented. Henceforth the pope was a ruler removed from the people; the average cleric and pilgrim got a glimpse of him in Avignon only when he went — surrounded by bodyguards — to a cardinal's residence as an honored guest, when he took in the fresh summer air at Chateauneuf-du-Pape, among other places; or when he was transported to the cathedral as a corpse. (Sch 201)

The popes, on their return to Rome, made their headquarters in the Vatican, expanding its palace, toughening its walls with all the latest techniques of fortification, binding it more closely with Castel Sant'Angelo, which was also given new bastions, creating an encloseable complex like the Avignon redoubt.[1] The popes rarely went out to the pilgrim stations, or even to the basilica within their walls. "The huge papal chapel took the place of the station churches. Even St. Peter's basilica was now used for just a few big celebrations, under Leo X for only three. And just as in Avignon, the traditional processions only moved through the palace" (Sch 240).

The papacy at Avignon had been run as a tight ship, with significantly improved management techniques, especially in the collection of money from taxes, exemptions, benefices, and indulgences (Sch 204–9). Indeed, the banking and mulcting policies of the Avignon papacy set standards that would tempt Renaissance popes, after the return to Rome, to ever more exigent methods of financing their grandiose new mode of self-presentation. This, according to Father Schatz, was the evil legacy of Avignon:

> The ultimate step toward a systematic reservation [to the papacy] of the appointment of bishops was taken by the Avignon papacy in the fourteenth century, primarily for financial reasons. In the meantime, the appointment of bishops had become a lucrative source of income for the papal curia. Institutions and customs had been developed that were nothing but simony under a papal cloak. Notorious among these were the "annates" (the first year's income from a benefice whose occupant had been named by the curia had to be paid to Rome) and the "expectancies" (a candidature for a benefice for which annual payments were made). As it gradually came about that in more and more cases the appointment was reserved to the curia, Pope Urban V drew the line in 1363 by reserving all archbishoprics, bishoprics, and abbacies with incomes above a certain sum to the curia. The "free election" of bishops — fought for in the Gregorian period, founded on and protected by the highest spiritual and theological arguments — was thus abolished almost silently by the papacy itself, not for pastoral reasons, but purely on financial grounds. (S 99–100)

Renaissance

The ethos of Avignon caused the court to close in on itself, making it less and less part of the healthy circulatory system of the city's shrines and processional avenues. The new palace in Rome became the great court of a Renaissance prince, with typical courtly activities — as when "Innocent VIII had his daughters married in the palace courtyard with great pageantry" (Sch 240). The artistic decoration of the palace spared little expense, with results we still marvel at. Chesterton once said that the lights of Broadway in New York would be a paradise for one unable to read the advertisements' words. In the same way the Vatican is a wonderland for anyone too innocent to be able to read its iconography. Renaissance Rome in general is full of huge sculpted symbols of the popes' families — stone bees as big as buzzards, acorns like cannon balls, tiaras like beehives. All these emblems reach a climax in the Vatican itself. The facade has a huge inscription celebrating Pope Paul V, not Saint Peter. Inside, the Barberini bees crawl all over the baldachino above Peter's altar — just as the della Rovere acorns are scattered across the Sistine Chapel ceiling.

Raphael's masterpieces in the Vatican, his rooms (*stanze*), are shameless propaganda for the popes who commissioned them. He gives Julius II's portrait to leading figures in four of his large frescos — presenting Julius as Saint Gregory the Great in the *Disputa*, as Gregory IX in the *Delivery of the Decretals*, as Sixtus IV in the *Miracle at Bolsena*, and as himself in the *Expulsion of Heliodorus*. Then, when Leo X succeeded to the throne, Raphael celebrated *him* with portraits in five frescos — as Leo I in the *Repulse of Attila*, as Leo III in the *Oath of Leo III* and the *Coronation of Charlemagne*, and as Leo IV in the *Fire in the Borgo* and the *Battle at Ostia*. The scenes with Leo III celebrate two forgeries. The *Oath* recasts the humiliation of Leo's "oath of purgation" after the trial authorized by Charlemagne, making it a triumph of the principle enunciated in the False Decretals — that popes are subject to no earthly judges (the forgery is paraphrased in the inscription on the painting). The *Coronation* shows Charlemagne kneeling to Leo, in accord with the idea that Charlemagne accepted the terms of the Donation of Constantine, whereas (as we saw in Chapter 10) Leo prostrated himself full length before Charlemagne.

All these obsequious pictures were mere prelude to what Raphael began before his death — a whole room devoted to the fraudulent myth of the Donation. His pupil Giuliano Romano, working from Raphael's sketches, completed these frescos in the Sala di Costantino, showing the emperor's miraculous cure from leprosy and his gift of temporal realms to the pope. Another fresco cycle telling the same story was painted for the Lateran Palace by 1585.

These brazen trumpetings of a fraud were mounted without any reference to the fact that Lorenzo Valla had proved conclusively in 1440 that the Donation was forged. No matter. The Donation would continue to be a theme of Vatican art into the Baroque period, when it was commemorated by Bernini in the grand staircase connecting St. Peter's with the pope's palace.[2] The artists' insouciance toward historical evidence had been authorized by papal acts like that of Alexander VI in 1493 — half a century after Valla's revelation. Alexander used the Donation to authorize his apportionment of territories in the New World. The line he drew consigning separate arenas to Portugal and Spain is still reflected in the fact that Portuguese is spoken in Brazil while Spanish is the official language of the rest of South America.

Raphael was conscripted to paint forgeries and lies, but he was spared the ignominy of Giorgio Vasari, who was commissioned to celebrate a crime. In 1572, when Charles IX of France authorized the infamous murder of Huguenots by the thousands (the so-called Saint Bartholomew's Day Massacre), Pope Gregory XIII rejoiced in Rome with a sung Te Deum, the striking of a medal to honor the slaughter, and a painting of the gory deed commissioned from Vasari for the Sala Regia, just off the Sistine Chapel — as Acton wrote in 1869, "The shameful scene may still be traced upon the wall, where for three centuries it has insulted every pontiff that entered the Sistine Chapel."[3]

We can, I suppose, be thankful that not all the megalomaniacal artifacts commissioned for the Vatican were completed. There can be no greater instance of the prostitution of great genius to crude idolatry than the tomb of Julius II that Michelangelo worked on for years. This temple within a temple was meant to stand in the choir of the planned new St. Peter's — a three-tiered structure with over four dozen huge statues on its four sides and a walk-through passage holding the pope's body in its inner sanctum. If it had been completed, the tomb would have cost as much as a year's work on the new St. Peter's. The architect Bramante objected that Michelangelo's monument would dwarf his choir.[4] Even when the plan was modified from a central and freestanding structure to one attached to the choir wall, it still held fifty-two statues, all over life size. The seated Moses now in Rome's San Pietro in Vincoli is one of these — and eleven of the planned statues were to have been almost twice the size of Moses. The figure of Moses represents just one of Julius's virtues, while the two bound slaves of the Louvre were part of a planned series of twelve "herms" celebrating Julius's conquests over enemy vices. The work would have cast in the shade the tomb of Peter, which was supposed to be the center of the new church. No wonder Peter, in a satirical dialogue written by Erasmus, denied Julius entry into heaven — upon which Julius stormed off to raise an army that would force the gates of heaven against Peter himself.[5] (Though Michelangelo's work never reached the choir, Bernini put another egregious monument there, the huge monstrance holding, not the eucharistic host, but the supposed throne of Saint Peter — a fake, of course.)

The crowning touch to these idolatrous exercises is provided by knowledge that much of this glorious artwork was financed by the sale of indulgences. A practice that had grown up accidentally out of the preaching of the First Crusade had proved a tempting tool the pope could put to many uses — to reward soldier-pilgrims for conquering the Holy Land, to inspire extermination raids on Cathars and others, to bribe people into opposing the pope's enemies, and to raise funds for papal self-glorification. The peddling of indulgences for pay became the systematic process Chaucer records in his Pardoner, that seller of indulgences and fake relics. "Sixtus IV had attempted to restrain the superstition, but Alexander [VI] allowed it to prevail . . . It was he who simplified and cheapened the deliverance of souls in purgatory, and instituted the practices which Arcimboldus and Prierias, in an evil day, set themselves to defend . . . Whoso questioned the rightfulness of the system was declared a heretic."[6]

By Rome's own standards, the selling of indulgences was a sin. It was simony, the trading of spiritual goods for worldly pay. Catholics themselves criticized the practice before Luther attacked it, and the papal curia had urged reform even after Luther's assault — to no avail.

Leo [X], prior to his election, had taken an oath to revoke the indulgence of Julius II, and to supply otherwise the money required for St. Peter's. The capitulation [promising to revoke the practice] was in March 1513, the breach of the capitulation in March 1515. It was not desirable to raise a controversy as to the broken oath, or to let Luther appear as the supporter of the Cardinals against the Pope, or of the Pope expecting the tiara against the Pope in possession of it. The effect was to deprive Luther of the hope that he was at issue with a too eager subordinate in Saxony, and to transfer his attack to Rome.[7]

If one reads again the Gospel passages on Peter (those cited in Chapter 5), it is hard to think of the Vatican's triumphal celebrations of the Renaissance popes as anything but an insult to the apostle's memory. What has Peter — the symbol of love, unity, and service — to do with this mélange of idolatry, blasphemy, and simony?

The Renaissance popes are the ones with the darkest reputation, since they left such vivid memorials of their extravagance. It takes no Luther to see their criminality. It was of them that Acton wrote, "Power tends to corrupt, and absolute power corrupts absolutely."[8] But the level of sordid crimes was greater in the popes of the tenth century, and the massacres of Jews and Cathars under Innocent III can hardly be topped by any single pope of the sixteenth century. Acton himself admits that the papacy was weakened in the Renaissance, and far from absolute in its power. The new secular states were challenging papal primacy at its root; the conciliar triumph of Constance threatened subsequent popes with the assertion of this superior authority. The popes' desperate search for income through indulgences and the granting of other privileges reflected the drying up of earlier sources of revenue. Even papal nepotism was a defensive measure.

Popes were normally elected in their old age, and were by legal fiction celibate, so they had no hereditary succession of a natural sort. Their short tenure gave them little time to build protection against a curia filled with rivals of the pope's family, willing to use the threat of councils to tame papal ambition (Sch 252). Trustworthy lieutenants were important to popes moving in such a hostile environment, and family ties were the toughest form of alliance. In this situation, popes felt a panicky need to promote family members to every possible position that could buttress their embattled rule. In this way they created semi-hereditary claims for their relatives:

> Innocent VIII was a compatriot of his predecessor, Sixtus IV; while Julius II was his *nipote;* Alexander VI, Pius III, and Clement VII were relatives of the earlier popes Callistus III, Pius II, and Leo X. Not counting Nicholas V, Paul II (*nipote* of Eugene IV), and Adrian VI, four families occupied the papal throne nine different times, the clique established by Sixtus IV being the most successful, with three pontificates. (Sch 243)

Acton describes the scramble for power that arose precisely from a sense of papal vulnerability. Alexander VI, whose bribes to obtain his

office soon became public knowledge, was under fire from leading figures like the future Pope Julius II, who called for his removal from office on the grounds that it had been won by simony (which is exactly
how Julius would win it after him):

> Reigning over subjects unaccustomed to obey, befriended by no power
> in Europe except the Turk, surrounded by hostile cardinals, with a flaw
> in his title which invited defiance and contempt, Alexander found
> himself in a position of the utmost danger. In the natural course of
> things, a power so wrongfully acquired, and so ill secured, would have
> fallen speedily, and the Papacy bearing the penalty of its corruption
> would have been subjugated. It was only by resorting to extraordinary
> artifice of policy, by persisting in the unlimited use of immoral means,
> and creating resources he did not lawfully possess, that Alexander
> could supply the total want of moral authority and material force. He
> was compelled to continue as he had begun, with the arts of a usurper,
> and to practise the maxim by which his contemporaries Louis XI, Fer-
> rante of Naples and Ferdinand of Aragon prevailed over the disorga-
> nized and dissolving society of feudalism, that violence and fraud are
> sometimes the only way to build up a State. He depended on two things
> — on the exchange of services done in his spiritual capacity for gold,
> troops, and political support; and on the establishment of principali-
> ties for his own family. The same arts had been employed by his prede-
> cessors with less energy and profit. It was an unavoidable temptation,
> almost a necessity of his position, to carry them to the furthest excess.[9]

Acton even finds in the friability of their position an explanation for
the popes' retention of indulgences. To give in on this subject, especially under fire from Luther, would suggest that the papacy can err,
can deceive Christians on the fate of their souls — which is exactly the
fear that would make Paul VI cling to Pius XI's condemnation of contraceptives. Acton goes so far as to blame the Reformation on those
who, neglecting church teaching before the novelty of indulgences
came into use, "sacrificed the tradition of the Church to the credit of
the Papacy."[10]

Reformation

The great historian Leopold von Ranke wrote, in the 1840s, "After the
era of the Reformation came the era of the Counter Reformation."

John W. O'Malley, S.J., has written a trenchant little book, *Trent and All That*, to show how deeply misleading is Ranke's formula.[11] Regenerative spiritual energies had been in play throughout Catholicism long before Luther commandeered the concept of reformation. Reformed religious orders and a new piety, scriptural devotion prompted by Erasmus's scholarship, missionary efforts, lay congregations, the reforming emperor Charles V, "evangelical" cardinals like Francisco Jiménez de Cisneros, Gasparo Contarini, Giovanni Morone, and Reginald Pole — all these marked what O'Malley calls Early Modern Catholicism. These forces played on through and after the Protestant breakaway, neither occasioned solely by it nor directed solely against it. To adopt Ranke's formula — Reformation and *then* Counter-Reformation — leads to profound misreadings of things like the foundation of the Society of Jesus. Many people reduce the Jesuits' mandate to support for the pope in opposition to Protestants. But Ignatius of Loyola originally wanted to lead a mission to convert infidels in the Holy Land, and he early committed his most brilliant follower, Francis Xavier, to preaching in the Far East — where he could neither refute Protestant arguments nor defend the pope against those arguments.

O'Malley entirely makes his case that a renewal of Christianity was taking place among those who remained in the Catholic church and those who broke from it, with shared goals and overlapping tactics. Some popes also tried to foster reform. A good case is Paul III, who appointed Cardinal Gasparo Contarini to form a committee for recommending papal reform measures. Contarini drew on his *spirituali* friends, men like Reginald Pole, and their report, *Advice on Church Reform* (*Consilium de Emendenda Ecclesia*), pulled no punches. In 1537, they read the pope such passages as this:

Flatterers have led some popes to imagine that their will is law; that they are the owners of all benefices, so that they are free to dispose of them as they please, without taint of simony. This conception is the Trojan horse by means of which numerous abuses have penetrated into the Church. These evils must be ruthlessly suppressed . . . All contrary curial practices must be abolished, such as the charging of a benefice with a pension in favor of a third party, who is not in need, but by which the holder of the benefice is robbed, if not of the whole of his proper revenues, at least of a great part of it; resignation of bishoprics while their revenues are retained; the right of collation to benefices and regresses, since these practices make such dioceses practically hereditary; expectatives and reservations as a result of which it often happens that deserving men are excluded, or one and the same benefice is bestowed on two candidates; the accumulation of several benefices in one hand and the concession of dioceses outside Rome to cardinals who, as the pope's official counselors, form his entourage and are therefore in no position to discharge their pastoral duties.[12]

As Contarini's biographer, Elizabeth Gleason, notes, there was only one difficulty with this report: it called, in effect, for the dismantling of the papal state. The pope was entirely dependent on just what the report condemned — a network of salable offices and privileges for the upkeep of his court, his armies, his temporal realm. Other rulers could tax their subjects directly, but most of the pope's subjects lived in other princes' realms, and their moneys could be subtracted only indirectly and on some spiritual pretext.

These abuses had now worked themselves so intimately and pervasively into the church's structure that it is difficult to see how Paul III could have freed himself from the fiscal web his predecessors had woven. Fees had become customary for many transactions, including plurality of ecclesiastical benefices, reservations, compositions, and arrangements of various sorts which came perilously close to horse-trading, especially in the granting of churches and exceptionally rich abbeys to the "temporary" supervision of well-connected clerics and laymen. There was similarly busy traffic in dispensations from vows and obligations, and a host of indulgences. All had their ultimate origin in the papacy's need for ever more money, especially from Sixtus IV on, the sale of church offices being a particularly important source of income for the Renaissance popes . . . The number of venal offices increased from 625 under Sixtus IV to 2,232 under Leo X, at which approximate level they remained under Paul III. This pope also established papal knighthoods, among them those of St. George and St. Paul, which carried only ceremonial obligations but conferred resounding titles on their holders [for substantial purchase fees] . . . With all their sources of income, traditional and innovative, the popes still had to borrow heavily to cover their current obligations. Paul III was no exception; he borrowed at high interest rates and had to channel revenues from the papal state to the repayment and servicing of his debt.[13]

In the circumstances, Paul had to take the report of his own commission as a recommendation that he dethrone himself.

If the popes feared, resented, and resisted calls for such reform when they arose from loyal Catholics, it can be imagined how testily they responded to demands issuing from Protestants. Paul III had to give in to the emperor Charles V when he called for a council of reconciliation between Protestants and Catholics to be held at Worms (immediately transferred to Regensburg) in 1541. Pope Paul sent Contarini as his delegate, since the emperor admired the cardinal's reform activities. At Regensburg, Contarini formed good relations with some of the Protestants, and maneuvered for joint measures that had no doctrinal impediments — e.g., sharing the chalice with the laity at Mass.[14] But the pope's letters to his grandson and close adviser, Cardinal Alessandro Farnese, show that sending Contarini was merely a gesture, to which he did not attach any real meaning.[15]

Though O'Malley is right to emphasize that spiritual renewal was occurring at many levels in the Catholic church, apart from the Protestant challenge, the plain fact is that the popes often resisted such reforms, without regard to whether they arose from inside or outside the church. Of the cardinals who worked with Contarini for reform, Cardinal Morone went for a time to a papal prison and Cardinal Pole was a target of the Inquisition's persecution. Gleason opines that other members of the group would have suffered the same fate had they not died early.[16] Papal edginess over any challenge was such that even the great defender of the popes, the Jesuit cardinal Bellarmino, ended up on the Index of Forbidden Books when he suggested that there might be some limits to papal primacy.

When the popes were not suspicious of reform efforts among their own, they were indifferent to it, as to most of the reform movements within the religious orders. In fact, they threw up obstacles by charging large fees for the permissions and protections the reformers needed.

Rome reacted in a similarly uninterested manner to the reforms in local churches and orders that were underway from the second half of the fifteenth century, especially in Italy and Spain, and to the new orders themselves. Rome finally took notice of the orders when the Cistercians, during Innocent VIII's pontificate, and later the Observants and the Capuchins from the Franciscan orders, or the numerous other new brotherhoods and orders, requested privileges from the pope for their own safeguard. They had to pay dearly for these privileges, however. Under Innocent VIII, a bull in favor of Cistercian reform in France cost 6,000 ducats. And so it went for the Theatines from 1524, the Capuchins from 1528–1529, the Angelicals from 1524, the Barnabites from 1533, and for the Franciscan and Dominican chapters of the order in their efforts to reform their orders from the time of Julius II. Their reform activities were made even more difficult at the papal court by the fact that, for a long time, the Sacred Penitentiary followed the letter of the law in granting dispensation to members of reform-minded orders. (Sch 258)

One reason the popes were uncomfortable with Catholic reformers is that the group shared many causes with the defenders of ecumenical councils, and for a century the breaking or taming of conciliarism had been the Vatican's priority. Only after that victory had been won did the papacy risk holding a council it could (though with great difficulty) control, the Council of Trent.

14

Trent and England

AFTER CONSTANCE, it will be remembered, the pope seemed to be a creature of ecumenical councils, since Martin V was created pope in 1417 only after council fathers had deposed all three popes then claiming office. Martin was under strict obligation to call a council in five years, and succeeding popes were to call them regularly every ten years. Martin did call for a council to meet at Pavia in 1423 (six years after his appointment), but took advantage of the delegates' slow gathering to dissolve it after it had been transferred to Siena.[1] Martin died before the second council he called — at Basle in 1431 — could assemble, and his successor, Eugene IV, followed the same tactic of dissolving the council for poor attendance. But consiliarism refused to go away, and its promoters soon numbered eminent men, including Nicholas of Cusa and Enea Silvio Piccolomini (later to be Pope Pius II). Pope Eugene was in part persuaded, in part compelled by King Sigismund of Germany (who had called the council of Constance) to recognize the legitimacy of the council at Basle.

But then Eugene played his Eastern card. The Byzantine emperor John VIII Palaeologus was threatened with conquest by the Turks. In a desperate effort to recruit help from Rome, he sent delegates to effect a reconciliation with the Western church. Eugene asked the delegates from the East to meet at Ferrara (soon transferred to Florence, where Eugene was residing after being driven from Rome by his enemies, the Colonna family). The council at Basle refused to move to this new site at the pope's bidding — in fact, it deposed Eugene for usurping its authority, and created a new pope of its own, Felix V, whose secretary Eneo Piccolomini became.

Now, however, the center of the action was in Florence, where the East was capitulating to Rome, yielding on all outstanding issues of historical disagreement between the churches — the addition of *filioque* to the creed, the mode of eucharistic reception, the doctrine of purgatory, and even papal primacy. The spectacle of the entire East finally recognizing papal primacy while the same doctrine was being denounced at Basle was a great victory for Eugene — though an illusory one. When the delegates from the East returned to Constantinople, John VIII could not get his churchmen to submit to the ignominious bargain his men had struck. The hope of reunion with the East collapsed, though the prospect of it had helped reunite the West, with Florence trumping Basle. Although the decrees of episcopal election formulated at Basle were endorsed by King Charles VII of France in his Pragmatic Sanction of Bourges (1438), Enea Piccolomini, who had deserted Felix V by now, ingratiated himself with Rome by persuading King Sigismund to recognize the legitimacy of the Council of Florence. Another conciliar crisis had been weathered by the pope.

The conciliar movement failed for lack of temporal support. Sigismund had been the sponsor for Constance and Basle; but the popes were successful in convincing monarchs that ecclesiastical councils were as dangerous to them as independent parliaments. If an elected body can depose a pope, why cannot a similar body depose a king?

The danger which brought about the alliance between papacy and theocratic rulers — the realization of this danger also partly explains the return of many conciliarists to the papacy — was the threat which conciliarism was seen to constitute to the traditional set-up of society . . . The issue, in brief, was nothing else but the preservation of the status quo against the new and rapidly rising groups, classes and sections of the people — the effective rise of the third estate. The issue, in other words, was whether monarchic government in the traditional sense could hold its own against the swelling tide of "popular" forces which included the educated layman, the educated lower clergy, the cosmopolitan and prosperous merchant, and the like. It was these new classes which drove the secular kings and princes and the papacy into one and the same camp.[2]

The papacy's stand on councils was strong enough by 1460 for Pius II to issue a bull, *Execrabilis,* forbidding any appeal from a pope to a council. Nonetheless, there was another flare-up of conciliar sympathy and writings early in the sixteenth century. Books by Jacques Almain (1512) and John Mair (1518) defended a council that had been held at Pisa, called by Louis XII of France in 1511 and supported by the emperor Maximilian I.[3] This council aimed at the suspension of Pope Julius II for his corrupt exactions and conquests. Julius formed a Holy League to counter this threat — King Henry VIII joined it in 1511 — and formed his own Lateran Council to condemn the Pisan Council. Cajetan (Tommaso da Vio) poured out denunciations of Pisa. (He had earlier, as general of the Dominicans, acquiesced in Alexander VI's destruction of his fellow Dominican Girolamo Savonarola, after Savonarola called for a council to depose Alexander.)

Trent

Given the record of papal opposition to councils, why did Paul III (1534–1549) agree, at the emperor Charles V's insistence, to call what became the Council of Trent? He could hardly resist a demand from the ruler whose troops had earlier sacked Rome and imprisoned his predecessor Clement VII, especially when the emperor was seen by many as a champion of the church. Charles wanted a council to reform the church in order to break the appeal of Luther to his German subjects. He invited the reformers themselves to attend the conference. Paul was determined to control the council in ways that would preclude any deals being made with Protestants. The only use he could see for a council was to issue solemn condemnations of Protestant doctrine. Therefore, Paul tried to make sure the council would meet in his domains — not in Rome, to be sure, but in Bologna, part of the papal states. This was unacceptable to the emperor, who could not hope to lure Protestants into the pope's parlor. So the council was inched across the Italian border at the Alps, to Trent. Yet Paul sent his delegates there with secret instructions to move the council back down to Bologna as soon as any excuse presented itself — which soon happened: a fear of plague was used to transfer the site. But Charles's delegates did not fall for this ruse; they were adamant that the council must return to Trent — as it did.

Conflict with Charles in the opening session of 1545 was over the council's primary mission. Charles wanted to reform the church and win back reformers. Paul rightly saw curial reform as an attack on his fiscal empire. He had rejected such ideas when presented in the *Consil-*

ium of his own commission. He was not going to open himself up to worse attacks addressed to the church by Luther or Calvin. His view of the church's role at this time is spelled out in the *Last Judgment* that Michelangelo painted for him on the Sistine Chapel's altar wall, a work finished almost a third of a century after the ceiling Michelangelo painted for Julius II. Michelangelo's *Judgment* departs from earlier ones in many striking ways. Those had shown a wide variety of sins committed by people of a broad range of classes and both genders, with popes and bishops, priests and nuns prominently exposed to hell's fire. On the sinners' side of his *Judgment,* Michelangelo drastically reduced his cast of characters — they are all male, all laymen, all intellectuals.[4] This is a hell solely populated with heretics.[5] Women are not educated enough to commit the sins of Luther or Calvin.

Faced with the competing agendas of the emperor Charles and the pope Paul, the delegates at Trent hammered out a compromise, by which reform and dogma were to be considered in parallel sessions, with decrees on each issued in alternating order. Things did not work so neatly to schedule, but both subjects were thoroughly worked over. The most fruitful area, in its long-term results, was that of Charles. Real reforms were mandated, mainly at the episcopal level, requiring bishops to reside in their sees, to oversee proper liturgical practices, to institute seminaries for the thorough training of priests, and to provide for basic catechetical instruction and sound preaching (much of it done by themselves). This is the program of what became known as the Counter-Reformation.

At the level of dogma, there were mixed results. The council rightly fought off the predestinarian concepts of justification by "faith alone" that would have denied free will. It also defended tradition against the idea that "Scripture alone" can save, since only tradition gives us the canon of Scripture. (The council, however, held a simplistic view of what tradition is — a secret revelation, fully formed in apostolic times and passed on orally to church leaders.)[6] The Eucharist was rightly said not to be merely "commemorative" (though its positive sense was couched in an Aristotelian definition of substance, as if orthodoxy depended on being an Aristotelian).

Much of the legislation of the council was petty and merely reactive, asserted simply to reject Protestant ways. (I am reminded of people I knew who said that the cause of civil rights in the South could not be supported because Communists also supported it.) Erasmus was rejected as well as Luther when the council stayed with the official (Vulgate) Bible in Latin, authorizing only vernacular translations from it rather than from the original languages (Hebrew and Greek). It was argued that the Holy Spirit could not have let the church use a defective Bible for so many centuries.[7] Similarly, the Mass could only be celebrated in Latin, not in the vernacular. The granting of indulgences was defended, though with some regulation of their sale. The council could not bring itself to endorse the "Protestant" practice of laymen receiving the communion cup. If that were going to be approved, the pope would have to do it.

The council — which lasted, with political and other interruptions, for almost two decades — ran through the terms of five popes, of whom some tried to cripple it and one (Paul IV) tried to cancel it. Paul III, who had opened the council, wrote a bull in 1541 taking reform of the curia out of the council's hands (reform of the pope's own household was not, as a result, ever treated at Trent).[8] Paul IV (1555–1559) took office during a recess of the council, and made it clear that he would never summon it back. His own idea of reform was to institute a harsher Inquisition in Rome (the Roman office that would burn Giordano Bruno and condemn Galileo), and to set up for the first time a broad-ranging index of forbidden books to keep people from reading anything he did not approve of. Paul, as John O'Malley says, "manifested symptoms of an unpredictable fanaticism."[9] He denied the legitimacy of the emperor Ferdinand, since the emperor's brother, Charles V, had resigned his throne and retired to a monastery without first getting the pope's permission. Paul created the Jewish ghetto in Rome and compelled Jews to wear the yellow badge. The influence of his corrupt nephews so angered the Roman populace that mobs broke open the prison of the Inquisition at his death and smashed his statue on the Capitol.

His successor, Pius IV (1559–1565), was elected on a pledge to reconvene the council. He not only did so, but gave it new steadiness and stature by freeing Cardinal Morone from the prison where Paul IV had put him and sending him to preside over the final sessions. Morone had to fend off new demands from French delegates that bishops be credited with a direct mandate from God (not one derived through the pope). Pius also profited from the advice of Carlo Borromeo, the nephew he had created a cardinal and made his secretary. Pius was far more conciliatory than Paul — he used the discretion left him by the council to grant the chalice to laymen in Lutheran areas. Almost despite the papacy, the church ended up reforming itself, to spite reformers.

England

The problems caused by the papacy's political ties are exemplified in the handling of the Reformation in England. For the beginning of this story, we must go back one papacy from Paul III, who opened the council at Trent, to his predecessor, Clement VII (1523–1534), who denied Henry VIII his desired marriage annulment. O'Malley calls Clement "an almost unmitigated disaster," whose "gift for making bad political alliances . . . indirectly helped the Reformation spread and take root."[10] As a cardinal advising his Medici cousin (Leo X), Clement had mishandled Luther's first assault on the church. When he took office himself, he tried to play the emperor Charles V off against Francis I of France. After this boxed him in to an alliance against Charles, the emperor's troops sacked Rome in 1527 and made Clement a prisoner in Castel Sant'Angelo. It was during his imprisonment that the request for an annulment of Henry's marriage to Catherine of Aragon reached Clement. The pope's captor, Charles V, was Catherine's beloved nephew and a decided opponent of the annulment.

Clement, who was always trying to keep negotiatory avenues open, at first encouraged the English king. He had some reason, admittedly, to show regard for this loyal son of the church, whom we have already met as part of Julius II's Holy League. Henry said he had joined that papal alliance to defeat those who "lacerate the seamless garment of Christ."[11] Julius, in gratitude, sent Henry a golden rose, a hundred Parmesan cheeses, and a promise to crown him "the Most Christian King of France" if he would just defeat Francis I for him.[12] Acton describes Henry's standing at the moment when he requested the annulment:

> Henry VIII had given, during a reign of eighteen years, proofs of such fidelity and attachment as had never been seen on any European throne. No monarch since Saint Louis had stood so high in the confidence and the gratitude of the Church. He had varied his alliances between Austria, France, and Spain; but during four warlike pontificates Rome had always found him at its side. He had stood with Julius

against Maximilian and Louis, with Leo against Francis, with Clement against Charles. He had welcomed a legate in his kingdom, where none had been admitted even by the House of Lancaster. He was the only inexorable repressor of heresy among the potentates of Europe; and he permitted the man to whom the Pope had delegated his own authority [Cardinal Wolsey] to govern almost alone the councils of the State.[13]

What Henry asked for was hardly unusual, as his supporters made clear:

Stafileo and Simonetta, the foremost judges of the [Roman] Rota, admitted that it [his plea] was just. Two French bishops who had visited England, and who afterwards became cardinals, Du Bellay and Grammont, persistently supported it. Cardinal Salviati entreated Clement to satisfy the English demands. Wolsey, on whom the Pope had lavished every token of his confidence; Warham, the sullen and jealous opponent of Wolsey, who had been primate for a quarter of a century, and who was now an old man drawing near the grave; Langland, the Bishop of Lincoln, the King's confessor, and a bulwark against heresy — all believed that the marriage was void. The English bishops, with one memorable exception [John Fisher], confirmed the King's doubts. The Queen's advisers, Clerk, Standish, Ridley, successively deserted her. Lee, the adversary of Erasmus, who followed Wolsey at York, and Tunstall, the Bishop of London, who followed him at Durham, went against her.[14]

Henry's situation was one that frequently recurred in the ruling circles of Europe. Dynastic marriages, since they by definition took place among the interlocking royal families, often needed dispensations from various degrees of consanguinity to be contracted in the first place. Many of these unions were plighted when the principals were minors, or still living in separate kingdoms. Then, when a male heir was not born, flaws were found in the first dispensation and a second one succeeded it. Popular religion held that God, with his regard for the safety of a kingdom, must not have blessed a marriage that did not produce an heir. In 1137, for instance, a papal dispensation was given for the wedding of Louis VII of France and his cousin Eleanor of Aquitaine — the pope even promised to anathematize anyone who alleged consanguinity against the marriage.[15] But the marriage was dis-

solved fifteen years later, after Eleanor had not given the king a son —
Saint Bernard of Clairvaux approved of the annulment.[16] Both partners were free to remarry — and Eleanor's sons by her marriage to
Henry II of England were Richard Lionheart and John Lackland. In
1193, Philip II of France married Ingeborg, the sister of the Danish king
Canute, but he put her aside the next day to scheme for a better dynastic marriage. A synod of bishops granted him a divorce on grounds of
consanguinity, but King Canute complained to the pope, who overrode
the dispensation. Nonetheless, Philip's heirs by his next marriage were
granted legitimacy by a later pope for dynastic reasons.[17]

These favors to kings in need of heirs may have been corrupt, but
they were common. (Some people claim that even current annul-
ments, for prominent Catholics like the Kennedys, are corrupt.)[18] Such
dispensations were a lucrative business for popes like Alexander VI,
whose record in the matter is cited by Acton:

> Marriage dispensations became, by careful management, productive
> sources of revenue and of political influence. Charles VIII wished to
> marry the betrothed bride of the King of the Romans, and the Pope
> was solicited on either side to permit or to prevent the match. He in-
> formed Valori that he meant to decide in favor of France, as the stron-
> ger and more useful power. But he said the thing was too scandalous
> to be done publicly, and afterward spoke of the marriage as invalid.
> Divorce served him better even than dispensations. Louis XII wished
> to marry the widow of his predecessor, whose dower was the duchy
> of Brittany. He was already married; but Caesar [Cesare Borgia, the
> pope's son, recently released from his status as cardinal] was dis-
> patched to France with the permission for the king to put away his
> wife. He [Cesare] was rewarded by a French principality, a French
> wife, and a French army wherewith to conquer Romagna. Ladislaus of
> Hungary desired to put away his wife, the widow of Mathias Corvinus.
> The Pope gave him leave, and earned 25,000 ducats by the transaction.
> He twice dissolved the marriage of [his daughter] Lucretia. The King
> of Poland had married a princess of the Greek Church, and had
> bound himself by oath not to compel her to change her religion. The
> Pope informed him that the oath was illegal, and not only absolved
> him from it, but required that compulsion should be used, if neces-
> sary, in order to convert her. But if neither ecclesiastical nor secular
> weapons should avail to subdue her obstinacy, then he commanded

that she should be punished by having her goods confiscated, and by being turned out of her husband's house.[19]

The deference to dynastic considerations was made even clearer later on, when the papacy let local bishops make the lucrative marriage dispensations for their noble patrons: "Part of this was the German bishops' struggle to maintain their power to dispense from universal Church law. In fact, this was primarily a question of money, since concretely these were dispensations that were customarily given, but required the payment of fees" (S 139).

The recent example of Alexander's wholesale dispensations helps explain why Henry VIII accepted as a matter of course Pope Clement's first expressions of sympathy, and why Henry was able to insist all along that he was acting in good conscience. He had, after all, been given a dispensation, eighteen years earlier, to marry Catherine, who was his sister-in-law, the widow of his brother — which many thought a greater obstacle than mere cousinship. Now Pope Clement sent secret missives to Henry which hinted that he would grant the annulment as soon as he could work himself free from the domination of Catherine's uncle, the emperor Charles. This strung out the appeal process for years, embittering the advocates of Henry and convincing them that the pope was playing political games with them. J. J. Scarisbrick argues that Clement wanted Henry to take matters into his own hands and present him with a fait accompli, so he could tell Charles that he had played no part in the matter.[20]

That would explain Clement's apparently contradictory actions. He sent Cardinal Campeggio to England with a bull saying that legal matters were settled and all that was needed was an inquiry into fact by an ecclesiastical court in England — but Campeggio was ordered to read the bull to the king without turning it over to him. He was, in fact, to burn it rather than surrender it. The pope was in effect provoking the king into actions for which he could deny responsibility. Campeggio was also directed to tell Queen Catherine that the pope would like for her to retire into a nunnery. This would constitute a form of "spiritual death," and the king, as a spiritual widower, could marry again without troubling the pope for an annulment.[21] Clement's stalling, his backing and filling, his gestures raising false hopes, gave a color of justification to Henry's final break. The king argued that he had followed in good faith the expected procedures, and been deceived every step of the way.

Clement's mishandling of Henry led to the unintended result that later popes were gun-shy about treating Catholic rulers intransigently. As late as the eighteenth century, according to Owen Chadwick,

> the ghost of Henry VIII walked abroad among the Catholic governments. Cardinals, who had long memories, kept reminding themselves what happened in England when a Pope too pertinaciously resisted a Catholic sovereign. Cordara, who knew much about the cardinals of those years, wrote this: "By the example of Henry VIII advisers of Popes are nowadays wont to frighten them, so that, however villainous a prince, they refuse to resist with the courage that befits a priest."[22]

Rome's wariness about rushing into disputes over royal marriages was demonstrated in 1632. Gaston, duc d'Orleans, the brother of the childless king of France, Louis XIII, defied his family and married Marguerite of Lorraine. Cardinal Richelieu, fearing that this marriage would produce an heir to the throne, appointed a royal commission to consider its validity. When the commission decreed that such a dynastic marriage required the king's assent, Gaston yielded to Richelieu; but Marguerite appealed to Rome, claiming that her marriage met all the canonical requirements. Richelieu sent emissaries to Rome to block this appeal, and they were successful in getting Urban VIII to set the matter aside indefinitely. In 1643 he had still not considered the matter thoroughly enough, but by then Louis had safely begotten his own heir, and Gaston's marriage was approved — though with a conditional remarriage, to save the authority of Richelieu's commission. The pope did not object to this ceremony.[23]

Rome's unwillingness to get involved in rulers' marriages was demonstrated again in 1810, when Emperor Napoleon I decided to change wives, leaving the childless Josephine for Marie-Louise, daughter of the Austrian emperor. Pope Pius VII had crowned Napoleon in 1804, after his church wedding to Josephine; but the emperor referred the annulment to a church court in Paris rather than to Rome:

> [Cardinal] Fesch, who had been the only clerical witness of the marriage he himself had performed, was persuaded to explain that there had been irregularities on that occasion, and that Napoleon had been pushed into it unwillingly, being pressed by Josephine; and this, indeed, was true. The lack of witnesses, lack of consent, and later lack of

children sufficed to satisfy the Parisian Ecclesiastical Court, and the annulment which it pronounced sufficed to satisfy the [Catholic] Hapsburg Emperor.[24]

Any Roman protest in Paris would have been feckless; but the pope did not enter any objection at the Austrian court, either.

After Clement VII's bad beginning with the English Reformation, popes continued to blunder in their dealings with that country, combining ignorance and arrogance in their measures. When a Catholic ruler returned to the throne, Mary I (1553–1558), Pope Julius III wanted to send a papal legate (Cardinal Pole, an English nobleman with Plantagenet blood) to restore at once Roman control of the English hierarchy, and to demand recovery of monastery properties confiscated under Henry VIII. Mary's advisers opposed such rapid and inflammatory change, especially since Mary was planning to marry Philip II of Spain. In conjunction, these steps raised the specter of foreign domination by Catholics plotting against England conjointly from Rome and Spain; so Mary refused for a while Pole's re-entry into his own country.[25] Pole was still attainted for treason, since he had opposed Henry VIII's annulment — and his mother and brother had been executed for his offense. He would look too much like an avenger come from the Vatican. Mary and Philip wanted to ease the country back into its old ways — Philip himself persuaded the pope to drop any talk of restoring monastery property.

After Pole was readmitted to England and made archbishop of Canterbury, Pope Julius died, and the fanatical Paul IV succeeded him. Paul issued a bull (*Rescissio Alienatorum*) nullifying any confiscations of church property. Pole had to maneuver for a suspension of the bull in order to placate Parliament and win a cancellation of the Protestant Act of Supremacy. It has puzzled some that Pole, a liberal and reformer, an ally of Contarini at Regensburg and a sympathizer with Luther at Trent, became Mary's supporter in the persecution of heretics during the last three years of her reign (when approximately three hundred people were sent to be burned at the stake). But all governments persecuted on principle at the time, Protestant as well as Catholic — and humanists like Thomas More and John Fisher supported the principle. What shocks is not so much the fact of this persecution as its stupidity. Pole thought that he could eliminate a few troublemakers and people would revert to the comfortable old ways of Catholic sacramental life.

He had been absent from his country for two decades, and he badly misread the depth of Protestant sympathy. The fires of martyrdom just strengthened the faith of those under persecution, especially when they were seen as importations from the Spanish and the Roman Inquisitions.[26]

What makes the situation surreal is that the mad Paul IV had decided that Spain itself was a heretical kingdom, against which he stirred up French opposition, and that Pole was a heresiarch who must be called to face the Inquisition in Rome for his Lutheran subversions. Queen Mary refused to let Pole leave her realm, but the pope deposed him from his chair at Canterbury, and replaced him with an old and unqualified man who refused to take the office. The English church was thus decapitated by Paul's whim, and its principal see was left empty while both Mary and Pole declined in health and died, within days of each other.

When Elizabeth I took the throne after Mary I, she tried to avoid the wrenching mistakes of her predecessor. She sought a *via media* between Catholic and Anglican tenets and worship while suppressing dissenters like the Puritans. But the popes (among others) made this impossible. First, Paul IV demanded enforcement of the bull *Rescissio Alienatorum*. If that had been impossible under Mary, it was simply an affront to deploy it against Elizabeth. Then, after Pius V became pope in 1566, he not only excommunicated Elizabeth but expressly freed her subjects from any duty of obedience to her.

This was a deadly blow, not only to Catholics who felt loyal to their government, but to missionary priests being trained to re-enter England. When Jesuits like Edmund Campion and Robert Southwell said that they had secretly come into England only to perform spiritual services for Catholics, not to foment rebellion against the government, their claim rang false. Insofar as they were recalling people to Rome, it was to an authority that told Catholics they should disobey their queen. That sounds like treason in anyone's language, and the Jesuits died a traitor's death. (Catholics had shown an early promptitude toward treason — when John Fisher's opposition to Henry VIII's annulment failed, he secretly approached Charles V to prepare for an invasion of England.)[27]

Things were made all the more complicated by the fact that some Jesuits in England, unlike the saintly Campion and Southwell, *were* actively plotting the queen's overthrow — Robert Persons, for instance who was conspiring with the Spanish government as it prepared to send the Armada against England. This Jesuit interweaving of political and spiritual activity would haunt and frighten England for many years to come. When the Gunpowder Plot to destroy King James and his Parliament was discovered in 1605, and Jesuits were found to be confessors to the plotters, it mattered little that the accused priests claimed not to have approved of the plot. Edward Garnet and others died on the scaffold with the lay conspirators. The same assumptions were in play when Titus Oates fabricated his "Popish Plot" of 1678. Three dozen innocent people were executed because it was so easy to charge that Catholics must, of course, be traitors. The papacy's political ties to governments opposed to England robbed Catholics of their presumption of loyalty. Not for the first time, the temporal power of the papacy was an enemy of its spiritual credibility. England, which was never as radical in its attitude toward Rome as Germany, had been in large part driven away from Rome by popes who alternated bumbling with bombast.

15

Ancien Régime and Revolution

THE SEVENTEENTH AND EIGHTEENTH centuries are known as the age of absolute monarchs in the West. The papacy had helped create this centralization. We have seen how popes recruited temporal rulers in the effort to defeat conciliarism. They endorsed the idea that monarchs should go unquestioned by representative bodies, just as popes should be free of any council's powers. But they did more than this. They bargained away ecclesiastical control within each monarch's realm.

> The states collected a great price for their support of Pope Eugene IV [against conciliarism]. This included not only the beginnings of state supervision and control of the Church (the *placet* or *exsequatur* as permission for the publication of Church edicts, *recursus ab abusu* as recourse to the state authorities against Church punishments, etc.). In addition, and of special importance, it included the right to nominate bishops, which remained in effect in almost all the major European nations well into the nineteenth century, either officially guaranteed through a concordat with Rome or simply exercised in practice. (S 110–11)

The principle so vigorously fought for in Gregory VII's attack on lay investiture was thus relinquished, quietly, in order to protect the pope against councils. Better state absolutism than church freedoms. "Perhaps we may describe this seemingly paradoxical process by saying that the papacy restored its power over the clergy by giving parts of the Church away to secular princes."[1]

This continued an old pattern. Rome escaped from the Eastern empire only by ceding power to Charlemagne and the West. It escaped the *Holy* Roman Empire to become the prey of rising *secular* states. It fled from councils into the harsh embrace of absolute monarchs. The exactions of these new masters would prove galling. The great powers were not only allowed to nominate bishops within their realms; they could force popes to accept even unsuitable candidates for office. In 1735, for instance, King Philip V of Spain, wanting to get at the riches of a benefice, forced Pope Clement XII (1730–1740) to make his nine-year-old son, Luis, the cardinal of Toledo.[2] The major powers were even given a veto over the choice of popes themselves, and their ambassadors went into the conclaves to see which candidates had to be stopped at the crucial stages of the vote.[3] Rome had to abide by policies set by the state — toward Huguenots and Jansenists in the seventeenth century, toward Jesuits in the eighteenth. Napoleon took this process to its culmination when he summoned the pope, as his lackey, to crown him in Paris as the new absolutist, one who both inherited and destroyed the Revolution that had tried to destroy the church.

A glimpse of the subservience to come was given at the very outset of the seventeenth century, when Pope Paul V (1605–1621) tried to limit the prerogatives claimed by rulers. Venice asserted an authority over the building and taxing of churches in its land realm (*terraferma*), and insisted on trying clerics for crimes of violence committed in its territory. Paul V excommunicated the Venetian senators *en bloc* and placed an interdict on the entire Venetian empire. This ban, imposed on all administration of the sacraments, had worked in the past, creating public pressure to let people return to the confessional and be absolved on their deathbeds. But Venice had long defended its independence under its lay leader, the doge, and priests as well as laymen simply defied the interdict, administering and receiving the sacraments with increased (defiant) devotion. A famous Servite friar, Paolo Sarpi, mounted an attack on the very concept of interdicts that made Paul V the laughingstock of Europe. Others had criticized interdicts in the past — notably Marsiglio of Padua — but Sarpi showed that they are not only contrary to the pastoral mission of the church but a usurpation of powers not given to Peter.

The church's mission is to bring the sacraments to people, not to withhold them. Even if withholding them is sometimes justified, this can be done only as a medical treatment, meant to cure a specific sinner of his specific sins. The sinner should be admonished, informed of his sin, and given time to repent. Then, if he defies treatment, he may be excommunicated under certain conditions, meant to bring him back to grace. But to slap a ban on all people in a realm simply to make its rulers toe the line is unjust, arrogant, un-Christian, and unaccountable to Scripture. "Do we want to see if an excommunication is valid? Let us see if Saint Peter would have imposed it. And if we see it standing far off from that apostle's love and non-assertiveness, we cannot believe that it has the force of apostolic authority."[4] Sarpi so thoroughly demolished this policy that Rome never again had recourse to it. (One can look, now, in popular manuals on Catholicism and find no mention of interdicts — this is one of those actions, overused in the past and stoutly defended by popes, that have been allowed to slip down the memory hole.)

Other rulers looked with approval on Venice's refusal to let the pope challenge its sovereignty. The new rules were, as Cardinal Richelieu put it, "to kiss the pope's feet — and bind his hands." This is what Richelieu did when he compelled Urban VIII (1623–1644) to support France even while France was using the Protestant armies of Gustavus Adolphus against the Catholic Habsburgs. Political exigency (*raison d'etat*) was the controlling consideration for the senior partner in that alliance of king and church at the heart of the established order (*ancien régime*). Richelieu was a symbol of this union of church and state, since he was both cardinal and the king's chief minister. Nor was he an anomaly. Cardinals Mazarin, Dubois, and Fleury would succeed to his office in France. Cardinal Alberoni was chief minister in Spain. This access of churchmen to great positions of power would seem to be a blessing to the church; but it more often proved to be a curse. The alliance was doubly damaging to the junior partner in the scheme. The church was blamed for the outrageous actions of the state, but it rarely won credit for a ruler's better actions.

In France, for instance, when Catherine de Medici, acting as regent for Charles IX, orchestrated the massacre of Huguenots on Saint Bartholomew's Day in 1572, the pope, who shamefully rejoiced in the act, was treated as if he had initiated it. By contrast, when Richelieu broke the armed resistance of Huguenots at La Rochelle in 1628, and set terms of religious tolerance for them, he was seen as a moderate defying the zealots of Rome. Similarly, when Richelieu took a moderate stance toward Jansenists, imprisoning their leader Saint Cyran but then freeing him, and when his successor Mazarin took a harshly repressive stand against them, Rome became the villain for opposing Richelieu but endorsing Mazarin. Of course, the state, too, suffered in the long run, since it was blamed for having such close ties with a power that looked bad in situation after situation.

The absolute rulers' attitude toward the church was patterned after the French crown's policy, since Gallicanism (royal prerogative in the church) was a deeply established principle there, ever since the Pragmatic Sanction of Bourges (1438). Now other countries could follow the French example. Not that control of religion was easily maintained in this period. French religious life, especially, was overheated and extreme, and not only as a result of the religious wars between Catholics and Protestants. The compromises of ecclesiastical politics led to a revulsion from such external embarrassments and a turn to the interior life of piety and otherworldliness. Perhaps, then, it is not surprising that the "age of absolutism" should also be called "the age of souls" in France, its deep spirituality studied lovingly by Henri Bremond.[5] Saints abounded — Benoît-Joseph Labre, François de Sales, Vincent de Paul, Jean Eudes, Jeanne de Chantal, Marguerite-Marie Alacoque. Even those who acted more openly in the political realm were often driven by spiritual devotion — the leader of the Oratorians, Pierre de Bérulle; of the Capuchins, François Leclerc du Tremblay (known as Father Joseph, Richelieu's "Gray Eminence"); of the Sulpicians, Jean-Jacques Olier. Deep intellectual affinities existed, under grating external rivalries, between *devots* (pro-papal zealots), Jansenists, Huguenots, and Quietists. Richelieu coolly played these off against each other, using Rome when it served him and defying it when necessary.

A surplus of priests and monks and nuns was accumulating — in southern Italy, there was one priest or monk for every hundred people. The governments tried to limit the number who could enter seminaries. Some priests filled their time saying commissioned masses for the souls of the dead.[6] Popes, too, retreated from their ineffectual relations with the kings, cultivating an air of otherworldliness. Yet since their realms had to be administered, popes turned temporal administration over to "cardinal nephews," who compensated for the loss of real power by taking financial advantage of their assignments. The pious Benedict XIV (1740–1758) appointed Cardinal Niccolò Coscia, whose "gang of Beneventan cronies" systematized papal graft.[7] Activities like this just convinced Catholic kings that they were right to handle the church's moneys and administration within their realms, and that their

veto was needed at the conclaves in order to keep the papacy's standards from sinking too low.[8] Another sinister favorite was Olimpia
Maidalchini, the sister-in-law of Innocent X (1644–1655), "without
whose advice the Pope would do nothing."[9]

The kings also thought it was their duty to defend doctrinal purity
— mainly as a way of eliminating theological strife from their subjects'
lives. That was the reason for continued pressure on Rome to condemn
the Jansenists of Port-Royal because of their elitism, their contempt for
ordinary Christians' lives, their high social protectors. The popes had
reason to fear meddling in this Parisian nest of enmities. For one thing,
the Jesuits and Jansenists were wrangling over the doctrine of grace, a
subject on which Rome had for years tried to impose a ban on debate.
Also, the Gallican bishops of France resented papal interference in
their arena. But persistent royal pressure brought four different popes
to issue five bulls directed at the elusive doctrines of the Jansenists.[10]
Some of these were not accepted by the Gallican French, and others
were evaded by Jansenist use of the hair-splitting tactics they condemned in Jesuits. When a secret network of Jansenist propaganda was
discovered in Belgium, the king decided he wanted just one more condemnation out of Rome, this one a crusher.

> Louis XIV, exasperated by the persistence of a problem he had ex-
> pected to solve at the start of his reign, was persuaded by [his Jesuit
> confessor] Le Tellier that this was the opportunity for a final and doc-
> trinally authoritative condemnation of all that Jansenism stood for in
> the work of its apparent leader [Pasquier Quesnel], now an exile
> among Dutch heretics in an enemy state. Ignoring an unpromising
> string of precedents, he asked the pope for one last bull. Clement XI
> was very reluctant to issue yet another bull, but he could scarcely re-
> fuse a direct request from Louis XIV.[11]

The result was the disastrous bull of 1713, *Unigenitus,* which condemned 101 allegedly Jansenist propositions. The indictment was so
sloppily drawn up that Jansenists could in good conscience say that it
did not apply to them, while orthodox Catholics found themselves in
agreement with some of the proscribed opinions. The 101 views anathematized included, among other things,

> 74. The Church, or the whole Christ, has the Incarnate Word as its
> head, but all the saints as members.
> 80. The reading of the Sacred Scripture is for all.

81. The sacred obscurity of the Word of God is no reason for the laity to dispense themselves from reading it.

83. It is an illusion to persuade oneself that knowledge of the mysteries of religion should not be communicated to women by the reading of Sacred Scripture. Not from the simplicity of women, but from the proud knowledge of men, has arisen the abuse of the Scripture by which heresies have been born.

84. To snatch away from the hands of Christians the New Testament, or to hold it closed against them by taking away from them the means of understanding it, is to close for them the mouth of Christ.

94. Nothing engenders a worse opinion of the Church among her enemies than to see exercised there an absolute rule over the faith of the faithful, and to see divisions fostered because of matters which do not violate faith or morals.

Some of these views might, at the time, have seemed questionable, but did they merit this description, appended to them all?

[These views are] declared and condemned as false, captious, evil-sounding, offensive to pious ears, scandalous, pernicious, rash, injurious to the Church and her practice, insulting not only to the Church but also the secular powers, seditious, impious, blasphemous, suspected of heresy, and smacking of heresy itself, and, besides, favoring heretics and heresies, and also schisms, erroneous, close to heresy, many times condemned, and finally heretical, clearly renewing many heresies respectively and most especially those which are contained in the infamous propositions of Jansen, and indeed accepted in that sense in which they have been condemned.

In trying to settle the argument, the pope said that the views were heretical because they were taken in a heretical sense. But that is just what the Jansenists claimed was *not* their intended sense. The discussion was not ended, but fanned to new levels of reciprocal misunderstanding, while new disputants were drawn into the discussion by the document's very vagueness and extension to areas not formerly touched.

Parallel lists were drawn up, matching the condemned propositions with verses from Scripture or passages from church fathers.[12] The Austrian emperor forbade promulgation of the bull in his territory. "In 1714 alone, around 200 books and pamphlets were published on the topic. Debates on *Unigenitus* reduced the Sorbonne to chaos. The parlement of Paris, despite spectacular threats from the enraged king, refused to register the bull until it was accepted by the bishops . . . The cardinal [Noailles, archbishop of Paris] forbade publication of the bull within his diocese."[13] For many, the encyclical revealed the pope's incapacity to speak convincingly, or even coherently, on the topics being treated. "Everywhere the battle over *Unigenitus* caused a decline in the reputation of the see of Rome as a teacher of doctrinal truth."[14]

Rome, after responding to royal pressure, now found itself accused of succumbing to the anger of the Jansenists' enemies, the Jesuits. This made popes vulnerable to the next royal aggression, which came precisely over the standing of the Jesuits. The Jesuits were the greatest defenders of the papacy, but also were confessors and advisers to some monarchs. As such they attracted enemies from diverse camps. When their missions in China adapted some Chinese religious customs, they were accused by Pascal of teaching idolatry, and Pope Benedict XIV, in his bull *Ex Quo Singulari,* ordered the practice to be stopped. "In China, the prohibitions were so effective that they destroyed a young Church almost totally . . . The interests of the Chinese Church must be sacrificed to the interests of the European Church."[15]

The next target was the Jesuit missions ("Reductions") in Paraguay. The dictatorial minister of Portugal, Pombal (Sebastião José de Carvalho), wanted to seize the lands cultivated by the indigenous people, under Jesuit superintendence, for governmental exploitation. Pombal pressured Pope Benedict XIV to condemn the Jesuits, and he seized all Jesuit property in Portugal (1759). The Portuguese Inquisition, "which Pombal used as a crown court of repression," condemned to death for heresy the popular Jesuit missionary Gabriel Malagrida (1761) — the church historian Owen Chadwick calls this an act of "judicial murder."[16] Pombal imprisoned 124 Jesuits in Paraguay, "and left forty-five of them there, without a trial, for nineteen years."[17] When the pope still refused to disband the Jesuits, Pombal expelled the papal nuncio from Portugal and recalled his own ambassador from Rome.

When the Jesuits were attacked by the French government, for not teaching the Gallican articles of state control over the church, Pope Clement XIII sent a brief (1762) defending them. French ministers forbade the brief's publication. In 1764, the Jesuits were banned in France, in response to the effective campaign against them organized by "the ubiquitous hidden hand behind Jansenist strategy, [Louis-Adrien] Le Paige."[18] In 1767, Spain expelled the Jesuits on trumped-up charges of provoking riots against the government. The pressure on Clement to dissolve the Society of Jesus was intense. France seized the papal territory of Avignon with the implicit promise that it would be returned when the Society was abolished. Naples took Benevento and Pontecorvo for the same bargaining purpose. Yet Clement refused to abandon the Society of Jesus.

This just made rulers more determined to extract a condemnation from the next pope. Knowing this, the Franciscan Lorenzo Ganganelli spoke out against Jesuits on the eve of his election as Clement XIV, maneuvering to avoid a veto from the great powers; but once elected, he hoped to placate the Jesuits' enemies by disciplining the order, by refusing to let it take in novices, and by making other gestures short of outright abolition. He cultivated Pombal in Portugal, making his brother a cardinal, though that brother had been part of the panel contriving the Jesuit Malagrida's "judicial murder."[19] But four years of stalling did not ease the governments' demands, to which Clement finally yielded in 1773, dissolving the Society in his brief *Dominus ac Redemptor*. Jesuit schools, libraries, and missions were wiped out overnight. Church outposts in India, Japan, Peru, and the Philippines were closed down. The whole system of Catholic education was disrupted. The saintly general of the order, Lorenzo Ricci, who counseled his men to submit obediently to the pope, was imprisoned without trial or charges in Castel Sant'Angelo, and left there till his death.

After sacrificing its strongest defender, the papacy gained little — except the territories that had been used for barter. "[Street talk in] Rome said that the Jesuits were the price paid for Avignon and Benevento . . . He who reads the details of the treatment of Ricci in his cell at the Castel Sant'Angelo, the maltreatment of an innocent, holy, and prayerful general, keeps being reminded of the saying then current in the streets of Rome, 'Good ends do not justify bad means.'"[20]

Chadwick, weighing the many things that contributed to the suppression of the Jesuits, thinks that not the least reason for it was "the fanatical orchestration of abuse against Jesuits" unleashed by the foolish anti-Jansenist bull *Unigenitus*. In that sense, Clement XIV was paying the price of Clement XI's folly.[21] The victory over the pope was not one that the great powers had much time to savor. They themselves were about to face a storm of revolution, in which the church could do nothing to support them or itself. Clement, having appeased his masters, "saw the prestige of the papacy sink to its lowest level for centuries" (K 301).

Revolution

When the French Revolution came, kings and priests, partners in the *ancien régime,* had to go down together, each being blamed for the sins of the other. The king (Louis XVI) could, after some hesitation and uncertainty, be beheaded with finality. The priest (Pius VI, 1775–1799) could only be captured in Rome, hauled from city to city, and asked to bargain away his church's privileges. The French nation thought that it could do without a king. It was not entirely sure it could do without religion. And if any religion would do, why not the ancestral one? After all, the monarchs had tamed the church with their Gallican rules. The people should be able to do that as well.

But Rome found it hard to trade masters. The revolutionary regime confiscated the church's extensive properties in order to stave off national bankruptcy. In compensation, the clergy were guaranteed generous wages, more for the priests than they were used to, drastically less for bishops — which struck some priests as just about right. Then the Assembly, acting on the advice of a bishop (Talleyrand), framed the Civil Constitution of the Clergy (1790), reducing the number of bishops, providing for free election of the clergy, and exacting an oath of allegiance to the state.

About a third of the priests took the oath. The rest were "refractory." There were so many of them that the state did not, for a time, try to remove them from their parishes. The pope, meanwhile, delayed any response to the Civil Constitution for a year, leaving the priests without his guidance. When he did condemn it, he denounced as well the Declaration of the Rights of Man of 1789, showing that the *ancien régime* was a package deal.[22] The papacy was so woven into the texture of the old monarchical system that it could not shift for itself but had to defend its old master against the new — and it would continue to do that long after the Revolution.

The pope's initial hesitancy was understandable. The Revolution was so new, apparently rootless, and chaotic that it was easy to hope it would prove a passing disturbance. King Louis XVI temporized from some of the same considerations, signing acts of the Assembly that he devoutly hoped were doomed. Not till his repudiation of those accommodations in his flight to Varennes (1791) did he give up his hope of preserving the *ancien régime* with only tactical reforms and adjustments to modernity. The pope showed that he, like the king, had decided to end his efforts at accommodating the new regime when he sent an exiled member of the Assembly, the Abbé Maury, a fierce enemy of the Revolution, as his envoy to the Austrians at war with France.[23] This had the same effect on Catholics in France that papal alliance with Spain had on Elizabethan Catholics. It made their loyalty suspect, and aligned them with enemies of the state.

Napoleon nonetheless hoped to recruit the church to the new order. A Rome that had deserted Constantinople for Charlemagne, and Constance for the monarchs, should have some skill at maneuver. Napoleon, from his Italian government based in Milan, proposed in 1796 that Pius learn to live with the Civil Constitution. When the pope refused, Napoleon invaded the papal states and, as the price of peace, exacted from Pius a brief, *Pastoralis Sollicitudo,* recognizing the legitimacy of the new government and calling on Catholics to obey it. But the Directory in Paris wanted more than this, and Napoleon's general, Louis Berthier, captured Rome, proclaimed a republic there, and carried the pope off into exile. He was trundled about through northern Italy and southern France until he died, at Valence, in 1799. Some predicted that this was the end of the papacy. The monarchy was dead. Why should the papacy not follow it into the grave? Yet enough cardinals were determined to hold another conclave, and Austria gave them refuge in Venice. But when Pius VII (1800–1823) was elected in the island monastery of San Giorgio Maggiore, the Austrians refused permission for him to be crowned in St. Mark's Basilica on the main island. He was installed at the monastery church.

Partly to secure his own return to French-held Rome, and partly to fend off Napoleon's threat to create a French national church entirely separated from the papacy, the new pope negotiated a concordat (1801) with Napoleon, who was now first consul. Catholic opponents of the Revolution were disheartened by what they considered this surrender. Napoleon completed the pope's humiliation by unilaterally appending new provisions (the Organic Articles) to the concordat before it went into effect. In this move, the first consul simultaneously tamed Rome and crushed the old Gallican bishops — he gave the pope an unwanted gift, the power to depose old bishops and appoint new ones (the very thing the Gallican church had considered its ancient and essential prerogative). "Neither the Pope nor Consalvi [his secretary of state] wished or intended such power in a Pope. Consalvi called it 'the massacre of a hundred bishops.' One of his intelligent colleagues in Rome saw instantly what a knock Bonaparte gave to old Gallican ideas. A Pope was forced by a half-Catholic French government, for its social and political purposes, to act in the Catholic Church like a despot."[24]

Pius VII delivered a further blow to Catholic intransigents when, against the advice of his curia, he went to Paris in 1804 to crown Napoleon emperor. Bonaparte was presenting himself now as the new Charlemagne, a defender of the church; and Pius thought he could win some concessions from him (like repeal of the Organic Articles) by his accommodation. But the four-month papal stay in Paris was fruitless.

When Pius refused to endorse Napoleon's war against England, French troops annexed what was left of the papal states in 1809, leading Pius to excommunicate those on the scene (carefully neglecting any mention of Napoleon). The excommunication led to the pope's arrest. He was sent into isolated custody in northern Italy (Savona). Napoleon wanted the pope to recognize the bishops being appointed by his government, and the cardinals sent to negotiate this point won a verbal agreement from Pius. The pope's anguish over what he had done shows that this was no man to cope with the iron will and slippery tactics of a Bonaparte: "On hearing of the departure of the delegation, he had been beside himself with remorse, thankful only that he had signed nothing. Chabrol [the prefect of Savona] thought him near to madness, and Napoleon assumed he was mad."[25]

Worse was to come. Napoleon had the pope brought to Fontainebleau in 1812 and exacted from him a new concordat surrendering all claim to the papal states. The pope tried to rescind this concession when he was returned to Savona, but Napoleon's defeat at Waterloo made the matter moot. The pope, released from prison, lived nine more years, determined to reclaim all that he had lost. Consalvi — Pius's brilliant minister, whom Napoleon had carefully kept away from him while he was in custody — now went to the Congress of Vienna, where the kings who conquered Napoleon were carving up spheres of interest. Consalvi won back most of the papal states. France and Russia preferred that this territory not be in Austria's hands, though they could not prevent Austria, which still held Lombardy and the Veneto, from having a shadow suzerainty over the pope's domains lower on the peninsula.

The pope's returned territories were a poisonous bequest. When successor popes proved unable to control these unwieldy appendages to an obsolete system, foreign garrisons had to be called in repeatedly to put down uprisings — Austrian troops in the north and French ones in the south. This foreign presence just hardened the forces seeking Italian independence and unity (the Risorgimento). The cardinals choosing a pope in 1831 had to conclude their squabbles hastily because the streets were full of rioters and a bomb had gone off in the conclave. Those choosing again in 1846 took only two days in voting, since they needed a pope who could call in Austrian soldiers at once. The man thus chosen, Pius IX (1846–1878), was later able to summon a council to Rome (in 1860) only because French troops were policing Rome's streets. Italian reaction to this state of affairs can be gauged from the fact that even a man in distant England, John Henry Newman, wrote at the time: "As to Rome, I cannot think it right that the Holy Father should be protected against his own people by foreign bayonets. It is a great scandal. Anything is better than that. When he is persecuted, he is in his proper place — not when he persecutes."[26] But the Curia that had been so brutally manipulated by the Revolution felt that it was now being given a turn as persecutors. The beaten child grows up to be a child-beater.

16

War on Democracy

A RETURN to the status quo ante was what the cardinals electing a successor to Pius VII wanted. They were counting on the support of the Holy Alliance. They seem not to have noticed that three of the four great powers were now not Catholic — Britain, Prussia, and Russia — and the fourth, the Catholic Habsburgs in Austria, would in the person of Metternich find the most high-handed manipulator of Rome. The popes threw themselves with relief into the arms of the restored monarchies. Before the Revolution, they had resisted the absolutists' Gallican control of national churches. But after it, in their retrospective gratitude to the kings for overthrowing the Revolution, they became more subservient than ever. They needed the Holy Alliance to fend off the specter of returning revolution.

> The popes were driven to a helpless dependence upon the governments which succeeded the revolution, and which held the revolution in check throughout Europe. As the [coming] revolution in Italy attacked not only the outworks of the church, but the territorial basis of its temporal power, this dependence upon the conservative governments became more abject, more panic-stricken. The weakened, but intellectually more virile, [Catholic] churches in France and Germany could make little resistance to the central organization of the hierarchy. To the papal court the conservative power in Europe, the stay of the church, was the house of Habsburg. When this power collapsed, the popes found themselves isolated from any direct political influence of the first order in Europe, and cut off by their own acts, definitions, and allegiances from the intellectual future of the rest of the Christian Church.[1]

Metternich's advice to Consalvi, when the papal states were restored, was that he should not undo everything that occurred during the time of French occupation. Italy "had suffered less and gained more than any other country from the revolution and Napoleon."[2] The Italian states ruled by Napoleon's relatives had substituted lay civil servants for clerical rulers. Apart from natural resentment of taxes and conscription, Italians had liked many aspects of the Bonapartists' regime (which lasted from one to two decades, depending on the place). The Inquisition had been abolished, the laity empowered, the economy improved. A symbol of this new orderliness is the fact that construction of the great Gothic cathedral of Milan, stalled for centuries, had been brought to completion by Napoleon.

Consalvi realized that if priests were rushed back into all the major positions of political power, the laymen ousted from those positions would create a pool of discontented talent that could be turned against the restored papacy. On this he agreed with Metternich, who was a conservative but who "disliked despotism, as the sign of incapacity."[3] Yet when Consalvi tried to keep on some lay officers from the French days, cardinals in Rome conceived a hatred for him that was self-defeating. They overrode his (and Metternich's) objections to forcing Jews back into the ghetto (whose gates had been thrown open by the French).[4] They also restored the Inquisition to new vigor.

The first urgency in the electoral conclave of 1823, after the death of Pius VII, was to choose a pope opposed to Consalvi and his policies. Metternich, through his ambassador in Rome, vetoed the first candidate put up by the conclave; but the cardinals found another enemy of Consalvi to elect as Leo XII (1823–1829). Leo wanted not only a theocratic state, but a monastic one. He angered his reacquired subjects with clerical interferences in their daily life — forbidding encores and ovations in theaters, imprisoning those who played street games on Sunday, closing bars and selling alcohol only through grilles, and prescribing "modest" dress for women.[5]

The modern state which Consalvi had been tentatively fostering reverted to a police regime infested with spies and intent on stamping out, with penalties ranging from petty clerical surveillance of private life to execution, any possible flicker of revolution. The result was inevitably economic stagnation, the alienation of the middle classes, and hatred of the personally mild pontiff, who was held to blame for making the papal state one of the most backward in Europe. (K 304)

Each of these moves made it more difficult for the pope to hold on to his temporal domains, which were seething with unrest even before his ill-judged disciplinary moves. Yet the popes were determined to maintain these realms that drained away their strength.

> It was difficult for the Roman see to think in terms unconnected with its territorial power. The states of the church could hardly be abandoned by popes who had grown to old age in the belief that the temporal power was an indispensable guarantee of the independence of the church. No machinery existed whereby this power could be surrendered. Every pope took an oath to defend it; it was a property held in trust for the church universal, for the good of Catholics in all places of the world. On a lower level, it was unlikely that the vested clerical interests would ever elect a pope who would not make it his duty to preserve so important a source of place and profit. The clerical monopoly of office was a consequence of the temporal power in fact as well as in the opinion of the clerics in possession. A government of laymen might commit the papacy to a foreign policy which endangered the security of the church. Yet the maintenance of the clerical monopoly was more and more distasteful to the governed, incompatible with the development of a competent civil service, and out of keeping with the political theory of Europe. Under such conditions there could be no question of government by consent. For this reason the popes were driven to keep on good terms with the conservative governments of Europe, and in particular with the Habsburgs; for the Habsburgs alone could be trusted not to give Italy to the revolution. The support of the Habsburgs must be paid for by the disavowal of liberalism in other countries . . . Isolated movements of revolt in Ireland or Belgium might be permitted where they could not be prevented, but in the long run the leaders of the church must condemn all that Metternich condemned. So the popes heaped anathemas upon a cause which they never understood.[6]

The anathematized cause was democracy. If "there could be no question of government by consent" in the papal realms, then the popes would declare that an illegitimate condition everywhere.

Gregory XVI (1831–1846)

After the interval of a brief reign (Pius VIII, 1829–1830), another determined conservative came to office in the person of Gregory XVI. The outbreak of guerrilla war against his regime, waged by the Carbonari, intensified a panic caused by the revolution of 1830 in France, which put the constitutional monarch, Louis Philippe, on the throne. At such a time, the pope was in no mood to hear from an idealistic young priest in France, Félicité Robert de Lamennais, that the pope should take control of the French church away from the Gallican new monarch. Gregory did not want to be appealed to as a priest. He wanted to make sure as a ruler that submission to rulers was instilled everywhere. Lamennais made things worse by begging him to support the 1831 uprising of Catholic Poland against the Russian czar, Nicholas I. The czar was one of the four pillars of the Holy Alliance, on which the pope depended for control of his own state. Pope Gregory told the Poles that revolutions are never justified:

> More than one earlier Gregory would have died in agony rather than tell a people with the history of the Poles to trust a man with the history of Nicholas I. Not so Gregory XVI. The Poles were advised to have confidence in the kindness of their most powerful emperor, and were reminded of the Christian duty of submission to divinely appointed authority. Gregory went even further in his carefulness. The draft of the apostolic brief contained the text: *bonum certamen fidei certate* — "fight the good fight of faith." Gregory thought the implications too dangerous, and erased the words with his own hand.[7]

Lamennais took more to heart the pope's rejection of the Poles than his own condemnation by Rome.[8] But that condemnation was inevitable. The pope's masters, the kings, told him that Lamennais must be silenced. He had founded an influential journal, *The Future* (*L'Avenir*), after the revolution of 1830, calling for the church's freedom from state control, with Catholicism benefiting from liberty of conscience and speech and the press. This was a challenge to the governments of the Holy Alliance, not directly to the church — except for the fact that the two were often the same entity, working through different channels. Metternich, who feared liberal ideas more than mere practical reformers, told Rome that Lamennais was a menace, and demanded that the pope, when he saw Lamennais, have others with him to stiffen his spine.[9]

Metternich's advice was followed; others were present at the interview, and they reported to Metternich. But the pope could not bring himself to rebuke Lamennais in person. He waited until he had left

Rome, then issued a hysterical public document, *Mirari Vos* (1832), which drew attention to Lamennais instead of maneuvering him into the shadows. Metternich would have preferred finesse. The pope's words merely stirred up more trouble. On liberty of conscience he wrote, "From the sewery spring of indifference [to truth] flows the ridiculous and false claim — better described as a lunacy — that anyone at all should exercise and defend freedom of opinion."[10] Freedom of the press is defined as "that retrograde printers' license, which can never be adequately cursed and despised, for turning just any old thing over to the common people."[11] Citing Acts 19.19, where Corinthian magicians burn their books, Gregory says that book burning is a church tradition often upheld by popes.[12] The freedoms of conscience and the press are denounced because of their tendency to undermine "the trust and submission due to princes." The new freedoms are "torches of treason being lighted everywhere."[13]

Lamennais was not named in the encyclical, but everyone knew it was directed against him. Through private channels, the pope demanded not only that Lamennais submit but that he publicly urge everyone else to obey *Mirari*.[14] Lamennais was actually of a submissive temper. Handled more deftly, he would probably have retired from the fray. Instead, he wrote a best-selling plea for the church and state to take up their neglected duty to the poor (*Paroles d'un croyant*, 1834). This elicited an even more intemperate denunciation of Lamennais by name in the encyclical *Singulari Nos* (1834). Here we see the papal tendency to find in every target of its wrath a complete and entire evil, comprehending every sort of heresy.

> On our own initiative, with complete knowledge of the matter, and from the fullness of our apostolic authority, we repudiate the aforesaid book, and wish and decree that it be forever after repudiated and condemned, for containing propositions that are, severally, false, defamatory, foolhardy, conducive to anarchy, opposed to God's word, irreligious, scandalous, erring, and already condemned by the Church, in the cases of Waldensians, Wycliffites, and Hussites, and similar heretics.[15]

Theologically, the popes' arsenal had no weapons of sub-nuclear caliber. And not only was this *theological* assault made on a book that dealt mainly with *political* freedoms, but it was prompted by political advisers. "From Austria, Prussia, and Russia . . . came demands

that Lamennais be severely reprimanded."[16] In fact, documents not released until John XXIII's time prove that, despite all the theatrical roar
of Rome's thunder-machine, the pope was reluctant to move against
Lamennais. He caved in to political pressure. "The dossier proves what
surprises: that Gregory XVI himself was one of those who had no wish
to condemn . . . If there was to be a condemnation of Lamennais, it
could only be because Metternich forced it upon his client state, or because the engines of the Inquisition churned away and could not be
stopped even by a pope."[17] It was the "engines of the Inquisition" that
dressed up this political judgment with "God's Word" and Hussites
and "similar heretics."

Pius IX (1846–1878)

Pius came in as a liberal, strongly distrusted by Metternich. He encouraged the idea of a united Italy, but expected it to be under his paternal
authority. Since that is not what liberals wanted, any encouragement
he gave them was (as Metternich observed at the time) self-defeating.
When Pius realized at last that the liberals meant to take away his states
and secularize them, his disillusionment caused a violent reaction, one
that puzzled his friends and infuriated his enemies. His *Syllabus of Errors* (1864), denouncing the vast left-wing conspiracy he saw taking
control of the world, was a gallant (and perfectly stupid) act of defiance. Pius spent years preparing his list of "errors," adding to it, sub-
tracting from it, as his many anxieties shifted focus. At one point he became obsessed with Charles Forbes Montalembert, the restorer of the
Dominican order after the revolution. Montalembert was suspect to
the Curia because of an early connection with Lamennais and his journal, *L'Avenir,* the object of Gregory XVI's condemnations. In 1863, at a
Catholic conference in Malines, Montalembert had called for the separation of church and state based on the freedom of conscience. This set
off alarm bells in Rome, where a Barnabite priest, Luigi Bilio, wrote an
extensive attack on Montalembert. This so pleased Pius that he made
Bilio the principal draftsman for the *Syllabus.*[18]

To understand the *Syllabus,* and the mentality behind it, we need to
look at a phenomenon that would be given a name under Pius X but
was already present in Pius IX's circle — Integrism, or Integralism. This
saw Catholicism as a systematic whole, each part connected with all
other parts, and therefore all of equal weight. Criticize one part and

you have denied the whole. Each outwork is as precious as the inner citadel. The Scholastic philosophy is as important as the Gospels, because it has perfected the defense of the Gospels' authority. The hierarchical state is as important as the monarchic papacy, since each supports the other. The ban on freedom of speech is as important as the creed, since the latter is endangered by indulgence of the former. As Pius put it in the encyclical accompanying the *Syllabus* (*Quanta Cura*): "If human arguments are always allowed free room for discussion, there will never be wanting men who will dare to resist the truth and to trust in the flowing speech of human wisdom; whereas we know, from the very teaching of our Lord Jesus Christ, how carefully Christian faith and wisdom should avoid this most injurious babbling."[19]

Those who took this position tended to see their opponents as their mirror image. They too are mounting a coordinated system, all parts of which are at enmity with the true faith, so all parts must be equally feared and rejected. What Pius was attempting in the long exercise of drawing up the *Syllabus* was to connect the many dots of this organized opposition. When they were properly connected, they would reveal the face of Antichrist, the church's vast and single foe. The face never came quite into focus, though Pius knew it was there. That is why he labored so energetically to draw and redraw the picture. But the sketch was clear enough for him to damn all parts of it with equal emphasis. As *Quanta Cura* put it: "Therefore, by our Apostolic Authority, we reprobate, proscribe, and condemn all the singular and evil opinions and doctrines severally mentioned in this letter, and will and command that they be thoroughly held by all children of the Catholic Church as reprobated, proscribed, and condemned."[20]

The views condemned included these:

15. It is open to anyone to choose and proclaim the religion that, instructed by the light of reason, he believes to be the true one.

55. The church should be separated from the state, the state from the church.

76. Abolishing the temporal domains the church possesses would greatly extend the freedom and success of the church.

77. In the present conditions, it is no longer a great advantage that the Catholic faith should be the only one recognized by the state, to the exclusion of all other beliefs.

78. Thus it is a noble provision of the law, in Catholic countries, that people entering them from abroad be allowed the public exercise of their own religions.

80. The Roman Pontiff can and ought to recognize and cooperate with progress, liberalism, and modern conditions.[21]

Before issuing the *Syllabus*, Pius IX had sheltered (in 1858) a Jewish boy kidnapped from his parents — a case that received a good deal of attention during the 1999 beatification of Pius. But the pope's attitude toward free government is revealed even more strikingly in an action he took after the *Syllabus* was published — the canonization of Pedro d'Arbus, a fifteenth-century inquisitor who presided over the forced baptisms of Jews in Spain, and who was assassinated for his dictatorial ways. Owen Chadwick says there was only one period when such a man could be declared a saint — the embittered last half of Pius IX's term.

> To make him a saint could only be accounted for by a wish in Pius IX to declare that, whatever Protestants and liberals said, the Inquisition was good . . . The Pope wanted to say as loudly as he could: the axioms of the modern world are wrong; it is right to stop error from being spread; it is right to use force to prevent error. The *Syllabus* carried more weight in the canonization of d'Arbus than research into the history of what he did and how he suffered . . . The text [of canonization] said, "The divine wisdom has arranged that in these sad days, when Jews help the enemies of the Church with their books and money, this decree of sanctity has been brought to fulfillment." There was no need to say this. It could not but offend — and must have been intended to do so. Its presence in the text is a sign that the making of d'Arbus into a saint had other motives besides commemorating a specially devout man (if that is what he was).[22]

At the same time (1867) Pius gave new support to the vicious charge that Jews commit ritual murder to obtain Christian blood for making their Passover matzoh. He decreed that the church recognize the cult of Lorenzino of Marostica, a boy "ritually murdered" by Jews in 1490. In 1870, the pope established a feast day for the child martyr, the second Sunday after Easter.[23] The cult was still being locally observed a hundred years later. In 1869, Pius gave the Cross of Commander of the Papal Order to Henri Gougenot des Mousseaux, the author of a book (*The Jews: Judaism and the Judaizing of Christian Peoples*) that repeated the myth of the ritual murder of Christian children.[24] In 1871, he addressed a group of Catholic women and — according to the Vatican's authorized account — lamented that Jews, during their ghetto days, "had been children in the House of God," but since their release from the ghetto, "owing to their obstinacy and their failure to believe, they have become *dogs*" (emphasis in the original). "We have today in Rome unfortunately too many of these dogs, and we hear them barking in all the streets, and going around molesting people everywhere."[25] Chadwick said that only a pope like Pius IX could have canonized a man like Pedro d'Arbus. I suppose that only a pope like John Paul II could have beatified a man like Pius IX.

Leo XIII (1878–1903)

Leo XIII, who replaced Pius at the end of his long reign, is often called the nineteenth century's liberal pope. He is famous for his letter endorsing labor unions (*Rerum Novarum,* 1891). But that letter has to be put in the context of Leo's general program. He yearned back toward the Middle Ages. His personal hero was Innocent III, the wager of the Cathar crusade. He had Innocent's body transferred from Perugia, where Leo had been bishop, and placed the remains in St. John Lateran, where he could be buried next to it.[26] For Leo, the thirteenth was the greatest of centuries, Innocent's century; and the greatest of its thinkers was Thomas Aquinas, whose writings he made the official philosophy of the church (*Aeterni Patris,* 1879). He praised modern unions on the misconception that they resemble medieval guilds. He believed with Innocent that the state should serve the church, and with Pius IX that the papal states should be restored. He renewed the latter pope's attacks on freedom of opinion and speech. His encyclical on church-state relations, *Immortale Dei* (1885), contrasts the ideal arrangement of the thirteenth century with the debased conditions of the nineteenth. "Look at that picture — and on this!" First, the good old days:

> Once upon a time, gospel values reigned in the polity, a time when the power and divine influence of Christian philosophy permeated the laws, structures, and popular customs, all the political classes and relations; and a time when the church established by Jesus Christ, given the assured pre-eminence that befits it, enjoyed the favor of rulers

and the legitimate preference of officials; a time when the harmony of priests and princes, and their kindly alternation of services, was most favorably united. The state thus structured bore results beyond imagining, results whose memory perdures, confirmed by numberless achievements, such as cannot be misrepresented or effaced by any hostile maneuvers.[27]

And here is the ugly brother, born of modern standards:

Of these standards this is the highest: just as all humans beings are understood to be of the same race and nature, by that very fact they should be equal in all their dealings with each other, making each the sovereign over his own acts, subject to no other authority; able freely to think whatever he wants about whatever he wants, to act as he pleases, no one having any right to command him. In a society based on such practices, there is no principle of rule except what people want — and people thus powerful can be ruled only by themselves. They will, admittedly, appoint some as their leaders, but granting them only the functions of government, not the right to govern, which can exist only by their sufferance.[28]

Anyone with Leo's concept of the medieval order must despise democracy ("the mob's whim and delusion"), freedom of opinion and the press ("unchecked power to think whatever one wants and to print whatever one thinks"), and the separation of church from state.[29] The authority of the church is superior to that of the state — it holds toward it the relation of the soul to the body.[30] There is only one true church, as men can easily find out.[31] And all authority in the church is entirely lodged in the pope: "God has willed that one man should be the ruler of everyone, should be truth's highest and surest teacher, the man to whom he gave the keys of heaven's kingdom."[32] Naturally, then, the workingmen's organizations recommended in *Rerum Novarum* should, whenever possible, be Catholic groups led by priests, who will provide the workers religious instruction. Indeed, as Leo urged on other occasions, Catholics should shun, so far as possible, all association with non-Catholics:

As a great safeguard to the faith, Catholics are obliged, unless necessity makes this impossible, to prefer association with other Catholics. And in setting up groups of their own, they should choose for leaders either priests or upright and recognized laymen, under whose leadership they should work in concord to arrive at and act on the policies that best advance their position, keeping close to the measure of the precepts I set out for them in *Rerum Novarum*.[33]

How could anyone with these views be called a liberal? Well, for one thing, Leo's letter on workers' unions *did* show real concern for the poor, and was of immense practical help to Catholics opposing the laissez-faire maxims of the industrial revolution. But we should remember that Leo was expressing a medieval distrust of commerce when he said that "capitalism's evil is increased by devouring usury" (*usura vorax*).[34] His ideal is that of the landholding peasant of the Middle Ages, and his defense of private property is related to the hope that modern workers can earn enough to acquire land and escape their wage-bondage.

People labor with more zeal and enjoyment when they know they are working on what is theirs — they come, indeed, to love the very earth they work with their own hands, with the expectation that it will yield not only enough for their own needs but a surplus for them and their children. No one can doubt that such zeal makes the soil yield more and increases the national wealth. And an extra benefit flows from this, that people will want to stay in the country of their birth and upbringing.[35]

Chesterton's glorification of the medieval peasantry, as the answer to modern capitalism's proletariat, is partly derived from this passage.

Another reason some think of Leo as a liberal is connected with his return to Scholasticism. Much later (after World War II), the neo-Scholastic revival *would* have a liberating and disciplining effect on Catholic religious training. But that work accepted developments in modern thought. Leo's aim in 1879 was to *cut off* Catholic thought from modern philosophies, to draw back into an arid citadel. The closed seminaries and disrupted education of the French Revolution had further deprived an already intellectually impoverished culture:

The contribution of Italians to Catholic thought in the eighteenth and nineteenth centuries was negligible. The Roman see did not encourage scientific thinking; the ablest of its prelates were employed in administration or diplomacy. In the papal states there was no opportunity for freedom and originality of mind; scarcely even for erudition. No Italian university outside of Rome had a proper faculty of theology. The

bishops appointed to Neapolitan sees by the Bourbon kings were unlikely to be men of intellectual power ... Döllinger, in the next generation, complained bitterly that there were more books on religious
questions published in Germany, England, or North America in one
year than in Italy during half a century. Yet these Italians controlled
the organization of the Catholic church throughout the nineteenth
century without any sense of their intellectual backwardness.[36]

Leo's praise of Thomas Aquinas as having reached a pinnacle of
thought, one from which no further advances could be made, had the
effect of denying while increasing the backwardness of Catholic seminary training. Proof of Leo's own intellectual prowess — as well as a
sample of what he thought Scholasticism proves — was given when he
assured the governments of the earth that they have no excuse for not
recognizing the one true church and excluding all others from their
realms:

> No one can have trouble identifying the true religion who will just ap-
> ply himself carefully and sincerely to the question. Proofs multiple and
> clear, the fulfillment of so many prophesies, the recurrence of mira-
> cles, the rapid spread of the faith despite active opposition or imped-
> ing circumstance, the witness of the martyrs, these and like things
> show that the only true religion is the one Jesus Christ first established
> himself and then turned over to the Church to be kept and carried to
> others.[37]

Leo took an equally simplistic view of the Bible. His encyclical on
that subject, *Providentissimus Deus* (1893), says that the entire Bible is
"a letter sent us from our heavenly Father," who would not lie to us.[38]
Therefore,

> it would be impious to confine the truth of inspiration to certain parts
> of the holy writings and to grant that the inspired author ever erred
> ... For all books accepted in the sacred canon are, throughout and in
> every part, written at the dictation of the Holy Spirit. It is so impossi-
> ble for error to insinuate itself into divine inspiration that the latter of
> itself precludes and rejects all error, by the same necessity that pre-
> vents God, the highest truth, from issuing any untruth.

That is the rule by which Galileo was silenced three centuries earlier.

A passage in *Providentissimus* that would prove especially destructive to scholarship is this:

A perverse device has been introduced, to the bane of religion, under the pretentious title of "the higher criticism." According to it, the source, soundness, and authority of any book in the Bible is established only from internal evidence (as they call it), whereas in fact it is clear that in historical matters, like the source and provenance of books, history itself provides the strongest testimony and it must be questioned and tested with precision. Internal evidence is insufficient to be used as proof unless for a degree of confirmation [of historical findings]. If this were not the case, great difficulties would be entailed. The way would be opened for the foes of religion to challenge and ravel out the authority of the sacred books, and the higher criticism now so praised would reduce itself to a matter of each critic's preference or bias in interpreting the books.[39]

What this meant in practice is (for example) that the "historical" (traditional) claim that John the Beloved Disciple wrote all the things expressly attributed to him in the Bible has to be accepted, though "internal" evidence — of style, chronological references, social assumptions — proves that one man could not have written them all.

A further implication of Leo's position is that the church, as the guardian of the historical tradition, holds a monopoly on the relevant evidence: "The uncontaminated sense of Holy Scripture cannot be discovered at all [neutiquam] without the church."[40] And laypersons cannot study Scripture on their own, since "no one can penetrate its ambiguities without moral guidance [aliquo vitae duce]."[41]

The pope did his most lasting damage to Bible scholarship when he set up the Pontifical Biblical Commission in 1902, which for decades would police Catholic thought on the Bible, threatening and punishing any exegetes who departed from its directives. These directives included, in the decades to come, that Catholic priests must be taught in their seminaries that the first five books were written personally by Moses, that Eve was literally created from Adam's rib, and that the Beloved Disciple wrote the fourth gospel. Catholic professors, thus fettered, became a laughingstock in the world of biblical scholarship.

A further indictment of Leo's liberalism comes from the fact that he invented a phantom heresy, providing a model for the heresy-hunting that would reach a fever pitch under his successor. To the long list of heresies bravely resisted by the church — Docetism, Arianism, Pelagianism, Patripassionism, and so on — a new one was added in 1899, sounding very strange in this exotic company: Americanism. It is a heresy without named heretics, one that no one was aware of professing. It can be explained only by the Vatican's long war on democracy, which made many cardinals in Rome very uneasy about a pluralist and secularist society like that of America. Four years before Leo discovered the non-existent heresy, he sent a letter of warning to American Catholics (*Longinqua Oceani*, 1895), telling them not to be proud of their odd constitutional arrangement, not to consider themselves superior to good Catholic monarchies of the sort the Vatican was still proposing as the political ideal. If they were prospering, it was because they were Catholics, not because they were Americans:

> One should not draw the wrong conclusion that America offers the model of an ideal condition for the church, or that it is allowable and advantageous to keep state and church separate and apart from each other, as in America. That Catholicism is still intact with you, that it indeed advances in prosperity, is a testimony to the innate fertility of the church's divine endowment, which expands of itself and begets offspring if no enemy opposes it, no inhibition checks, yet it would be even richer in progeny, far more so, if it enjoyed not merely freedom but state favor and political establishment.[42]

It is dangerous for the pope to tell Catholics in any country that their system is fundamentally mistaken — it encourages those who think Catholics cannot be loyal to their government (shades of Pius V and Elizabeth I). We can see how bothered Rome was with the scandal of Catholics living outside countries where theirs was the established religion from the fact that Leo could not leave the American system alone. He went on to attack Americanism as a heresy in his encyclical *Testem Benevolentiae* (1899), deploring a spirit of freedom that might loosen dependence on the authoritarianism of the church:

> License mistaken for liberty; an appetite for discussion and criticism; a readiness, ultimately, to think whatever one wants to and to publish it — these have so involved men's minds in confusion that the teaching authority of the church is more than ever needed to call people back to their beliefs and duties.[43]

Leo had been signaling his distrust of Americans even before he sent the two encyclicals there. Americans tended to mix too freely with non-Catholics. He ordered them not to join clubs like the Odd Fellows.[44] Though the Vatican had no diplomatic relations with the

United States, an apostolic delegate, Cardinal Francesco Satolli, was sent there in 1893, to warn Catholics against attending ecumenical meetings with those of other religions. With Satolli's help, the head of Catholic University in Washington was removed for being too liberal. But even in this atmosphere, the overkill of *Testem Benevolentiae* came as a surprise — mainly because it was occasioned by a chain of misunderstandings. It arose from a) a French introduction by one man of b) a translation by a French woman of c) a biography by an American man of d) an American priest, Isaac Hecker, the founder of the Paulists, whose work was seen, through these distorting filters, as far more unconventional than it was. To heresy-hunt on the basis of such flimsy accusations would become commonplace in the next pontificate, but the American bishops had not expected it from Leo XIII, whose social program they thought they were implementing.

The church in America was a very conservative body, however loyal to the American government that disturbed Rome. Most Americans were puzzled by this weird encyclical; bishops had to protect themselves by making gestures of compliance (to they knew not what), while reactionaries used it to silence the few liberal voices that had been raised in the church — principally the faculty and journal of Dunwoodie Seminary in New York. This is what made "*Testem Benevolentiae* the charter for Catholic reaction for decades to come."[45] The encyclical was still being cited a half-century later to condemn John Courtney Murray, S.J., for his praise of the American system.[46]

The final failure of Leo to live up to his reputation as a liberal has to do with the Jews. It is true that he was not as vicious in his open attacks on them as Pius IX. He even made some gestures of respect to individual Jews (including Theodor Herzl) — and that has been enough to make some call him enlightened on the subject. But David Kertzer asks what the record really shows about his relations with Jews. The greatest test of Catholic-Jewish relations during Leo XIII's pontificate was the Dreyfus affair. Alfred Dreyfus, a Jewish officer in the French army, was charged with treason and convicted by an *in camera* court-martial in 1894. Later it turned out that the evidence used to convict him had been forged. In 1899 he was re-tried, again convicted, but pardoned by the president of France. In 1906, he was entirely vindicated and returned to his army service. The attacks on Dreyfus were electric with anti-Semitic hatred, much of it generated by Catholics — some of them associated with Action Française, but even more goaded on by the

Assumptionist priests who ran the daily newspaper *The Cross* (*La Croix*). As Owen Chadwick says, "*La Croix* dedicated itself to the anti-Dreyfus cause. This was the most powerful and extreme journalism ever conducted by an otherworldly religious order during the history of Christendom."[47]

During this long campaign by *La Croix*, Pope Leo and his Curia did nothing to restrain the Assumptionists' anti-Semitic frenzy. This was not because Rome was not paying attention to *La Croix*. The pope wrote in 1899, "I love La Croix. I need a press and I am depending on you."[48] The paper was admonished by him on other grounds, especially its strong criticism of the French government; but the records in Rome show no concern at all over the journal's anti-Semitism.

In fact, far from criticizing *La Croix*, the pope's own newspaper, *L'Osservatore Romano*, lent it support. When the charges against Dreyfus were still fresh, two years before his second trial, the Vatican paper conveyed its presumption of guilt in an article called "Treason and Traitors": "The Jewish race, the deicide people wandering through the world, brings with it everywhere the pestiferous breath of treason. And so too in the Dreyfus case . . . it is hardly surprising if we again find the Jews in the front ranks, or if we find that the betrayal of one's country has been Jewishly conspired and Jewishly contrived."[49] When anti-Semitic riots broke out in response to the Dreyfus controversy, *L'Osservatore* supported them:

> The agitation that is now developing from one end of France to the other as a result of the truly detestable provocations of Judaism . . . attempting to rehabilitate a traitor . . . has neither the look nor the nature of those popular disorders motivated only by sentiments of disorder. These demonstrations are becoming ever more anti-Semitic, as the term is now used, but they are not anti-Semitic out of any hatred for the Jewish people or things Jewish, but rather out of a natural weariness of Jewish oppression . . . The anti-Semitism that is developing today — in Russia, in Germany, and in France — expresses a real concept and reflects a concrete fact . . . [Anti-Semitism is growing] among the masses who are being excessively oppressed by the Judaic spirit, a spirit which is the opposite of the Christian spirit.[50]

The other paper controlled by the Vatican — the Jesuit journal *Civilta Cattolica*, whose every article was cleared beforehand by the pope's secretary of state — was even more viciously anti-Semitic than

L'Osservatore Romano. During the decade of the Dreyfus affair, it ran no fewer than twenty-six articles endorsing the myth that Jews ritually kill Christians.[51] At the same time, the pope was asked twice to renounce this horrid charge, one of the most potent generators of anti-Semitism. Both times he refused.

The first occasion came when Cardinal Manning of England inquired in Rome about a book by a priest who "proved" the ritual murder charge and claimed papal approval for his writings. Leo's secretary of state said that the pope had merely thanked the author for receipt of the book (he also sent an apostolic blessing) without approving its contents. Nonetheless, when the author sent a second, equally objectionable book to Leo, the same thank-you and apostolic blessing were dispatched to him. There was no comment on ritual murder itself. The pope let that matter stand unchallenged, not responding to the point of Cardinal Manning's concern.[52]

The second opportunity arose in the very same year. A group of prominent Catholics in England, including Cardinal Vaughan, asked the pope to disown an article in *L'Osservatore Romano* attacking the Jews for ritual murder. The request was turned over to the Holy Office, which chose Cardinal Rafael Merry del Val to look into the matter. (He was chosen, internal documents show, because an ancient relative was a boy supposedly slain by the Jews for his blood.) Other documents at the Holy Office show resentment at "the temerity of the powerful Jews of London, who, in their unchallenged rule in Europe, have reached the point of such lunacy that they would pretend to be defended by the Holy See." The Holy Office replied that it could not clear the Jews of the charge. An internal document noted that "ritual murder is a historical certainty . . . the Holy See cannot issue the statement that has been requested, which, while it may please a few dupes in England, would trigger widespread protests and scandal elsewhere."[53] The pope who was supposed to be sensitive to Jewish concerns did nothing to slow — and certainly nothing to stop — the steady stream of anti-Semitism coming from Vatican officials and journals. It was under his pontificate, when his secretary of state was clearing every article for publication, that the editor of *Civilta Cattolica* wrote:

> The Jews — eternal insolent children, obstinate, dirty, thieves, liars, ignoramuses, pests and the scourge of those near and far . . . managed to lay their hands on . . . all public wealth . . . and virtually alone they

took control not only of all the money, . . . but of the law itself in those countries where they have been allowed to hold public offices . . . [Yet they complain] at the first shout by anyone who dares raise his voice against this barbarian invasion by an enemy race, hostile to Christianity and to society in general.[54]

I ask again, then, why this pope is considered a liberal. Well, I suppose he was — at least by comparison with the Pius who preceded him and the Pius who followed, the former lashing out at Jewish "dogs," the latter launching a reign of terror.

17

Reign of Terror

IT MAY SEEM extreme to ascribe a reign of terror to Pius X (1903–1914), the first pope of the twentieth century. He is, after all, the only modern pope to be declared a saint (by Pius XII, in 1954). I used to belong to the St. Pius X parish in Baltimore — a new church, with a statue of the pontiff prominent at the side of the well-traveled York Road. My children attended St. Pius X School. But despite the canonization of Pius, a surprising array of people are willing to call his heresy-hunting a form of terrorism. The theologically conservative scholar Marvin O'Connell says it was "what Loisy called, with justice, 'the black terror,'" one conducted by "a ragtag crew of informers and fanatics."[1] Gabriel Daly, of the Order of Saint Augustine, calls it the church's equivalent of McCarthyism.[2] The sociologist Lester Kurtz says it was a time, for Rome, when "the whole world outside of a narrow circle was defined as the enemy."[3] The sober historian Owen Chadwick describes it as "in some ways the worst time for the church in the modern epoch."[4] The Jesuit André Blanchet referred to the "terrorist" days.[5] Cardinal Maffi of Pisa called it a new Inquisition, and Cardinal Ferrari of Milan said it was a witch hunt.[6]

Historians have trouble, now, defining just what Pius meant by the heresy of Modernism. He, like most nineteenth- and twentieth-century popes, was disturbed by the discoveries of modern science, which was often described by them as an exercise in pride, an attempt to assert a Faustian control over the world. Anxiety here was understandable; it was widely shared by many Christians in the nineteenth century, when geological discoveries, Darwinism, and textual criticism cast doubt on prior views of the Bible. Empiricism seemed to mock miracles, apparitions, and relics. Modern epistemology seemed to narrow the knowable to its physical materials. Psychiatry reduced the soul to unconscious urges and conscious responses. The pope was not wrong to fear science. He was just wrong in thinking that the Modernists, those bogeymen of his nightmare, were in thrall to science.

Actually, the Catholic Modernists were trying to escape the apparent bind that science was putting them in. They should be read, in the broadest sense, as part of the romantic movement that rebelled against the way science was draining the world of mystery, spiritual depth, and aspirations to the eternal. They resemble in some way the American Transcendentalists — though the pope would make their crime the denial of the transcendent! The starting point for some of them was Maurice Blondel's philosophy of the act, in which he distinguished between a willing-what (*volonté voulue*) and a willing-that (*volonté voulante*). In each human drive to achieve something specific there is a drive that reaches through and beyond everything specific.[7]

Joseph Lemius, the procurator general of the Oblates of Mary Immaculate and the principal author of Pius X's encyclical against the Modernists (*Pascendi*, 1907), thought this kind of thinking "subjective" and "relativist." By relying on immanent drives within man's psyche, he felt, Blondel and his followers were giving up on that direct access to the transcendent that Scholasticism made possible, with Aristotle's agent intellect grasping timeless essences. The Modernists were taking an "agnostic" stance on such assured truths, and the agnostic is, for the Vatican mentality, just a half-hearted atheist. That is why the Modernists, theists all (with the probable exception of the mysterious Alfred Loisy), were attacked for atheism in *Pascendi*. There was no halfway house for Pius. By that inversion of Integralism that had become a reflex in the Vatican, error on one point entails error on all things. So Pius called Modernism not only a (vaguely defined) heresy but "the compendium of every other heresy" (*omnium haereseon conlectum*).[8]

In order to make this omnium-gatherum charge, Pius resorted to a device that had failed twice before — when Pius IX issued the *Syllabus of Errors* and when Clement XI issued *Unigenitus*. In connection with his encyclical, Pius X issued a laundry list of condemned propositions (in a letter called *Lamentabili*). Here were sixty-five heretical statements, meant to cover the waterfront of Modernist enormities. Like the earlier lists, this one proved too scattershot — it missed some of the intended targets, while individual items hit innocent bystanders. John

Henry Newman, for instance, arguably held Number 25: "The assent of faith ultimately rests on a piling up [*congerie*] of probabilities."[9] The simple list of statements allowed Modernists to claim they never held anything so crudely put as this or that thesis.

Many of the theses would be held by any decent Bible scholar of our time — e.g. (Number 13), that the evangelists gave an artful arrangement to their parables, and (Number 33) that Jesus preached that the End Time was soon. Modern dogmatic theologians would agree that some sacraments were a development of the church, not an institution of the New Testament (Numbers 40, 43, 44, 46, 49, 51). Some of the propositions demand agreement on questionable historical facts. For instance, the following statement is branded as heretical: "The church has exposed itself as hostile to advances in natural and theological science" (Number 57).[10]

The encyclical (*Pascendi*) was supposed to furnish the background and connections for the separate items on the list (*Lamentabili*). But the first and longest part of *Pascendi* is just an elaboration of Lemius's lectures claiming that "immanentism" is a form of atheism, something insecurely, if at all, attached to the propositions in *Lamentabili*. George Tyrrell, the Irish Jesuit who was one of the encyclical's targets, wrote: "When the encyclical tries to show the Modernist that he is no Catholic, it mostly succeeds only in showing him that he is no Scholastic — which he knew."[11] Loisy, another target, said that *Pascendi* invented "a pretend school of thought" (*un système fictif*), and tried to fit all the widely differing Modernists within it.[12] A net so loosely woven did not land many of those it was fishing for — mainly Loisy and Tyrrell, who were excommunicated. Close associates of theirs, like Baron Von Hugel and Maude Petre, were spared — as Acton had been earlier in the century — because they were highborn Catholics with many connections among the influential. The "immanentist" Henri Bremond, who in Lemius's eyes may have started it all, lived on to be praised by later popes.

But if the encyclical convicted few, it indicted many, involving them in tissues of suspicion and whispers, of accusations half made, and of clearances dubiously hinted. This was because the last part of *Pascendi*, written by an inquisitorial Spanish Capuchin, Cardinal Calasanz Vives y Tuto, called for a vigilante movement throughout the church.[13] The first task was to keep Modernists and their writings away from Catholics, especially from Catholic students and seminarians: "Those with the slightest tincture of Modernism are, without respect for any special circumstance, to be deprived of any guiding or teaching role."[14] The pope echoes ancient ritual bans (*Procul, procul esto*) in saying that no modern views can be admitted to the seminaries: "Cast, O cast far off from our holy company any inclination to the new [*novitatum amor*], for God himself despises a proud and willful attitude."[15]

It is equally the task of bishops to prevent the reading of published works, or prevent the publication if possible, of Modernists or of those with any whiff of Modernism or any tendency to favor it. Seminarians and students are not to have access to any books, papers or journals of this sort, which are no less deleterious than salacious reading — in fact they are more so, since they distort the faith at its foundation.[16]

Nor are the young the only ones to be protected from such writings: "More broadly, revered bishops, we order you to deal with this great threat by banning in your dioceses, even by decree of excommunication, any published books that are dangerous to read." The bishops are not to rely on Rome to put such books on the Index, since there are too many of them for the central authority to keep up with. Each diocese must set up its own board of censors and report to the pope how many books they have banned. "Nor should any of you think he has fulfilled this duty by reporting one or two banned books to us, when many more are put in circulation."[17] They should not let books into their diocese just because they have authorization (the imprimatur) from some other diocese, since some poisons work better in one place than in another. *Every* book must be vetted by the censors.

Since Modernists had aired some of their views at theological congresses, "bishops must no longer allow priests to hold meetings, or only rarely," and those strictly supervised — priests from other dioceses, for instance, were not to be admitted without passports signed by their own bishops. Each diocese must, moreover, set up a "lookout" (*vigilantia*) committee, to spot "any false doctrines [that] are insinuating themselves, and by what artful means they are doing so."[18] The pope sets strict rules for these committees. They are to meet every other month, with the bishop attending, and their sessions are to be kept secret. They should protect verified local cults, apparitions, and relics from being ridiculed: "Finally we order these lookout committees to keep a sharp eye on political practices (*socialia instituta*) and writings on political subjects lest they harbor some form of Modernism, and to make sure they meet papal standards."[19] The bishops must report to Rome every three years on the activities of the vigilance committees — and bishops should not be intimidated by any criticism of vigilantism. "Admittedly, enemies of the church will take advantage of these measures to spread again the pestilential lie that brands us as enemies of human progress."[20] To put a stop to that calumny, the pope says he intends to set up a special papal institute for the advancement of science. This promise is as vague about times, procedures, and goals as the vigilante groups' instructions are specific, binding, and regulated.

The pope's official but secret vigilantism, mandated everywhere, would be enough to breed suspicion, stifle research, and incite mutual recriminations. But it was supplemented by private vigilantism, open and secret, informal and organized. One such network was so secret that its operation was not fully understood until a cache of its coded letters was found in Belgium during World War I. The Germans who discovered it thought at first that it was part of a spy network — and, in its way, it was. It was one outpost of the vast secret operation organized out of the Vatican by Monsignor Umberto Benigni, a member of the Secretariat of State, and carried on by him until Pius X left office.

Benigni had a secret society for discovering news or rumor through informers and used his own codes to write to his correspondents. He called the Pope "Mama," and used the pronoun "she," and intentionally misdated letters or put a wrong place of dispatch. The society was called the League of Pius V, or in secret slang La Sapiniere ("the copse of firs") . . . It was not only modernists who were under suspicion, it was anyone scholarly. He headed what has been called "a sort of ecclesiastical secret police" . . . He hated the German Center Party because it was Catholic but pretended that it was undenominational; Christian trade unions because they had to compromise; anything ecumenical (which he called "interconfessional"); Archbishop Fischer of Cologne because he was a moderate among the German bishops; Archbishop Amette of Paris because he was not so rigid against the French State as he ought to be; all feminists; all democrats because they were ruled by demagogues; the "Jewish-Masonic sects"; and most of the Jesuits because they were well educated and they argued, and argument was a form of compromise.[21]

When Pius X's canonization was being prepared, his ties with Benigni's operation were scrutinized, but not, according to Emile Poulat, thoroughly enough.[22] Benigni was, all of his life, a famously outspoken anti-Semite, a fact that did not slow his rise to influence in the Vatican of either Leo XIII or Pius X. Maria Teresa Pichetto devoted a whole book to the two Italians, Benigni being one, who created the "roots of hatred" in Italy by energetically promoting as authentic *The Protocols of the Elders of Zion*.[23] Benigni was even more virulent than the other man, Giovanni Preziosi, because Benigni specialized in "authenticating" the ritual murder charge. He also attacked the reversal of Dreyfus's conviction as the result of a secret war waged by the Jews.[24] In 1893 he was warning that "either Judaism will be checked by something resembling (with adjustments to our time) the medieval legislation that checked their unquenchable instincts for oppression and exploitation or they will be subject to a reaction of popular fury that will make the night of Saint Bartholomew fade from memory."[25] The Jews and the Masons were in secret league to take over the world, "the Sanhedrin and the Triangle, rabbis and Kadosh knights . . . to entangle the whole of humanity in their tentacles."[26] Bankers, of course, were in on the plot: "Liberalism has replaced the landed aristocracy with a lenders' aristocracy, the landed estate with the ghetto."[27]

Benigni's organization, the Sodalitium, was not finally suppressed until 1921, and he was never formally rebuked for any of his activities, anti-Semitic or otherwise. In particular, his charge that Jews commit the ritual murder of Christian children was not disowned by anyone in the Vatican, even though Saint Pius X had a perfect opportunity for doing this in 1913. We have seen how Leo turned down two pleas to renounce the ritual murder charge. An even more urgent plea came to Pius during the most famous ritual murder trial of the twentieth century. During a Russian wave of anti-Semitism, Mendel Beilis was tried for murdering a Christian boy in Kiev. One of the witnesses at the trial was Justinus Pranaitis, a Roman Catholic priest, a professor of theology, who swore that the Jewish record of ritual murders was an established fact, one that no pope had ever questioned. In England, some Jewish leaders pleaded with the duke of Norfolk, a prominent Catholic, to approach the Vatican for a refutation of this historical lie. They asked for verification that Pope Innocent IV in the thirteenth century and the Holy Office in the nineteenth had repudiated "the blood libel."

Cardinal Merry del Val, Pius's secretary of state, responded that the instances cited had dealt only with the specific guilt of individuals, not with the general charge that Jews commit ritual murder. When Norfolk tried, at the very least, to show that *individuals* had been cleared by Rome, the court in Kiev said it could not accept any such assurance unless it came from Rome itself. Merry del Val would not send such an assurance, informing Norfolk that Rome could not intervene in any other government's procedures: "I sincerely regret to have to say that it is quite impossible for me to take the initiative of addressing any communication to Kieff."[28] A papacy that was willing to sniff out any suspicion of "Modernism" anywhere and pursue it implacably would not take the slightest step to deny that Jews kill Christian children as a matter of long-established policy.

The Silent Terror

Other unfortunate encyclicals did their damage over a comparatively short run. *Quanta Cura* and the *Syllabus* were quietly ignored as soon as that became decently feasible. *Unigenitus* died away when its target, Jansenism, did. But *Pascendi* had a long shelf life, spanning the whole first half of the twentieth century. Pius X saw to that. He instituted a practice that was not abandoned until the Second Vatican Council — the imposing of a loyalty oath on everyone advanced to clerical orders in the Catholic church (and even on some of the laity — they tried to make Maude Petre take it). As Father Daly says, "It, more than any other document, kept alive the memory of modernism in the Roman Catholic Church long after modernism had ceased to be seen as an actual threat."[29] The oath was meant, Pius said in imposing it, as an antidote to "the poisonous views being injected into the veins of the Christian people by Modernists."[30] The pope even commanded that the oath be placed in large frames and hung in every bishop's office and those of all the Roman congregations, as if it were a cult object.[31]

The oath was a powerful tool in the hands of anyone in the church — not merely the clerical authorities, but any conservative watchdogs over their own rigid formulas — for saying that any liberal or scriptural scholar was breaking his solemn vow if he entertained new ideas. It was a long document that each would-be priest had to swear to. It included an explicit promise to abide by the vague *Pascendi* and the scattershot *Lamentabili*, to reject "immanentism," and to rely for proof of the faith on prophecies and miracles. It quashed the notion of the development of doctrine:

I accept without equivocation [*sincere*] the doctrinal content of the faith as passed down to us in unbroken sequence [*usque*] from the apostles through the orthodox fathers, *always with the same meaning and the very same interpretation of that meaning.* I therefore reject outright the heretical notion that dogma evolves, in the sense that it changes to a new meaning different from what the church held from the outset [emphasis added].[32]

This oath, and the documents to which it bound men (*Pascendi* and *Lamentabili*), would be used against every scholar who became suspect in the pre-conciliar modern era — including many whose views were authorized by the fathers at Vatican II.

The ordeal of these men is hard to describe, since they were disciplined in secret, under orders to keep silent about being silenced. But correspondence in the 1950s between John Courtney Murray and his Jesuit superiors allows us to reconstruct, in one case, the way Rome handled what it considered dissidence. Murray was considered dangerous, early on, because he took part in and praised ecumenical gatherings with non-Catholics (against the clear teaching of Leo XIII and Pius X). Even his Jesuit superior in Rome, Vincent McCormick, who was trying to protect him from papal wrath, thought he should steer clear of this compromising openness to others. The papal position was that "error has no rights," and that Catholicism, the only true religion, should alone be recognized as a religion of state. So when Murray submitted for censorship a chapter he had written for an American armed forces anthology of writings by representatives of various religions, McCormick wrote to him: "Why should you . . . take space to pay tribute to the spiritual influence of Jew and Protestant religion? Personally I do not see." Murray should restrict himself to showing "what and how the Catholic religion helps the country."[33]

In this same letter, of 1955, McCormick refuses to give permission for a new article Murray had written on church-state relations. The Society's censors, McCormick assures Murray, "have your interests at heart," and do not want to provoke the Holy Office ("just now it is rather on edge"). "It seems to me a mistake to wish to carry on with that controversial question under present circumstances . . . provoking those who will not be appeased. Fr. General agrees with the final verdict, although not with every comment of the censors. Leave Spain out of it. So, *fiat.* Time will bring changes."[34] This shows why it is so hard to trace the disciplinary regime of the period. Knowing how easily Rome could be provoked, men were afraid to venture anything new or original. Self-censorship, or restraint by one's friends, made overt silencing unnecessary.

The reason the Holy Office was "on edge" in 1955 was that Murray had criticized a 1953 speech by its presiding officer, Cardinal Alfredo Ottaviani, who had restated the traditional position on church-state relations — that only the true religion should be recognized, since all others are subject to the rule that "error has no rights." If toleration is unavoidable, it should be accepted as a bad second-best (a "hypothesis") to the ideal arrangement (the "thesis"). By this rule, Franco's Spain was an ideal Americans should someday hope to achieve in their own country. (This is what prompted McCormick's warning, "Leave Spain out of it.")

Speaking extemporaneously at Catholic University on March 25, 1954, Murray said that Ottaviani's speech was inconsistent with a later speech by Pope Pius XII, *Ci Riesce,* an address to Italian jurists. Murray's position was minimalist, in the sense that he explained it to his friend John Tracy Ellis: "I do not indeed want the American situation canonized as 'ideal.' It would be enough if it could be defended as legitimate in principle, as standing *aequo jure* with the Spanish situation — each representing an important realization of principle in divergent concrete historical contexts. Are we to suppose that 30,000,000 Catholics must live perpetually in a state of 'hypothesis'?"[35]

Though Murray claimed to be advancing nothing beyond what the pope had said in *Ci Riesce,* Ottaviani reacted to the reported criticism of him. (He had to rely on informants, since his name was not mentioned in the newspaper report of the speech.) Ottaviani wrote to New York's Cardinal Francis Spellman, a member of the board of Catholic University, asking him to inquire why that school gave a priest the opportunity for criticizing the Holy Office. Spellman promised to take the matter up with the university's rector.[36] Father Joseph Fenton, the editor of the *American Ecclesiastical Review,* who had been conducting a feud with Murray over church-state theory, quickly reproved Murray in print for his Catholic University speech. Then, in the next issue of his journal, he ran another man's article calling Murray "disrespectful" of the authority of Rome. Pressures from Rome began to mount, and Murray found his outlets for publishing and lecturing cut off. A book with an article by him was canceled by the University Press of Notre Dame. The head of the Holy Cross order in Rome was asked to have Murray "disinvited" from an appearance at Notre Dame, which is run by that order. Murray's friend and ally Father Joseph Ellis, invited to Rome to give an address about the American situation at the Tenth International Congress of Historical Sciences, was refused permission to attend by his bishop — the bishop had consulted with the rector of Catholic University, who was still smarting from the attacks on Murray.[37]

By 1955 Murray had given up hope of pursuing his long-term studies in the history of church-state relations. He wrote to McCormick in Rome:

> All the books on church and state and on allied topics have been cleared from my room, in symbol of retirement, which I expect to be permanent. When Frank Sheed [of the Sheed and Ward Catholic publishing house] returns, I shall cancel the agreement I had with him to edit and revise the articles on church and state for a book. Fortunately, my gloomy prescience impelled me to refuse an invitation to give the Walgreen Lectures at the U. of Chicago. And all other practical measures will be taken to close the door on the past ten years, leaving all their mistakennesses to God. (At that, I do not believe that I was mistaken on the central issue — the need for a unitary theory.)[38]

This submission cheered Murray's superior, who wrote him: "I suppose you may write poetry. Between harmless poetry and church-state problems, what fields are taboo I don't know; but ordinary prudence will give the answer. We'll try to keep out of controversy for the present."[39]

In 1957, Murray was told that he could not give permission to a German publisher to reprint one of his articles. He discouraged people trying to study his work on church-state history. An article he prepared for *Thought* magazine was quashed. Even when he stayed off the forbidden subject, he was watched and pounced on. Bishop William Scully of Albany wrote to complain to Murray's superior that a speech he gave on censorship would weaken the authority of the Legion of Decency (which banned certain movies for Catholics "under pain of mortal sin").[40] In 1958, Murray thought he saw a way to bring up again the church-state issue in terms that would show respect for past tradition, and he proposed this to Father McCormick, who threw cold water on the idea:

> I am afraid you do not know the Rome of today. I very seriously doubt that there would be any chance of the [Jesuit paper] *Civilta* accepting an article by you on the subject of church-state relations. No; we must be patient; some people never forget; if the possible political situation in the USA should put the *Civilta* et al. on the defensive, then would be the time for some explaining to be done over here, and a clearer and perhaps authoritative statement of the church's essential teaching on the matter might be made. I really think that you must wait for that, not expose yourself by trying to hasten it. In the end what is correct in your stand will be justified. Meanwhile be content to stay on the sidelines, unless the hierarchy forces you into play: deepen and clarify your own position, and be ready with your solution approved, when the opportune time comes. That is not coming in the present Roman atmosphere.[41]

This blanket of silence thrown over Murray was kept invisible to the public at large. I was in a Jesuit seminary at the time, and though there were rumors that Rome did not like some of the things he had written, my fellows and I had no idea of the extent to which he had been silenced. That is the perfection of the art of repression — that outsiders cannot see it occurring. But then the very possibility McCormick had suggested came true — the political situation in America threw Roman officials onto the defensive. John Kennedy ran for president, and all the charges of Paul Blanshard were renewed — that the church did not believe in tolerance, that the error of Protestants and others "has no rights," that the American Constitution is a second-best "hypothesis" to be corrected toward the "thesis" of church establishment.

Catholics did not want to see these old dogmas aired again, to shoot down Kennedy, on whose victory they were staking so much. Fenton, trumpeting the Ottaviani line, was now the embarrassment. Moreover, it was known that Theodore Sorensen consulted with Murray on what answers Kennedy might make to charges against the church. It would be doubly embarrassing to church authorities if the condemnation of Murray were now seen as a condemnation of Kennedy. So the screws had to be loosened on Murray. In 1960 he published *We Hold These Truths,* which — while avoiding direct argument with all the old papal documents — praised the American Constitution lavishly and showed just how patriotic Catholics could be. Murray appeared on the cover of *Time* magazine a month after Kennedy's election, as the symbol of a new spirit in American Catholicism.

Many in Rome were not happy with this sudden reversal of Murray's position, and they were able to get him "disinvited" from the first session of the Vatican Council in 1962.[42] By contrast, Father Fenton was in attendance as Cardinal Ottaviani's consulting expert (*peritus*) on church-state matters. But Murray was now too important to Catholics' status in John Kennedy's world to be shoved aside permanently. It was the conservative Cardinal Spellman himself who demanded that Murray be invited as a *peritus* to the second session — as Murray put it, Spellman "pried me in."[43] Even then, when Murray's comments at a press conference were quoted in the papers, Cardinal Egidio Vagnozzi, the apostolic delegate to Washington, tried to get his Jesuit superior in America to silence him — unsuccessfully.[44]

In the changed atmosphere created by the two Johns — John Kennedy in Washington and John XXIII in Rome — Murray could not only resume his work on church-state relations but begin it anew, without the clogs and fetters that he had worn in his earlier work. We have to remember that he, like his compeers, had taken the anti-Modernist oath, swearing that there can be no development of doctrine. That meant he had to find elements in the past that he could expound as allowing for the American position on religion and politics. The great obstacle to this was Leo XIII's condemnation of the separation between church and state, which was written precisely with the United States in mind. Murray had to argue, not very convincingly, that Leo was condemning the autonomy only of nineteenth-century *anti-clerical* states. Father Charles Curran, who would have his own troubles with Roman authority, was justified in remarking, "I do not think Leo XIII would recognize himself in the picture drawn by Murray."[45] But Curran was not surprised: "In Murray's day there were practically no Catholic theologians publicly maintaining that the official hierarchical teaching could and did make mistakes."[46] I have already mentioned the angry reaction that William F. Buckley, Jr., experienced around this same time by suggesting that a pope could be wrong — and Buckley had not even taken the anti-Modernist oath.

Murray was forced into a cramped and artificial way of doing theology — bringing in the real arguments (freedom of conscience, the competence of secular authority, the eschatological role of the church) only after preliminary hair-splitting about the shades of emphasis in this or that papal effusion. A good example of this is the use Murray tried to make of Pius XII's *Ci Riesce*. He said its emphases were different from those of Ottaviani, and he had a point — but only a small one.

Pius's address to Italian jurists took up international relations, those between states, not the internal structure of states, and he said that Catholic countries can co-operate in international arrangements with non-Catholic states — the principle on which Vatican concordats with many countries were founded. Admittedly, Pius repeats, error has no rights in itself. But "first: That which does not correspond with the truth or with moral right has, considered objectively, no right to exist or to spread itself or to be free to act. Second: Nonetheless, not to suppress it by positive legislation or by informal compulsion *can be justified in the name of some higher and even more inclusive good* [emphasis added]."[47] Murray got a lot of mileage out of the italicized words, saying the pope was no longer treating tolerance as a necessary evil but as something serving a higher and more inclusive (*piu vasto*) good.

Still, as Fenton replied, Pius repeated that the "objective" order should be observed when it can be, and he expressly renewed the thesis-hypothesis language that Murray objected to in Ottaviani's exposition of the problem. "Opposition to everything that is false in religion or degraded in morality must be unconditional — on this there has never been in the past and there is not now anything tentative or negotiable on the church's part, either in theory or in practice . . . The church cannot approve in principle, cannot approve as a thesis [*in thesi*], a complete separation of church and state."[48]

To see the level of make-believe in Murray's quote-trading with Fenton, we have to remember that the whole thesis-hypothesis distinction was created as a dodge to get around the horrors of Pius IX's *Syllabus of Errors*. Faced with its condemnation of freedom of conscience, expression, and the press, Archbishop Félix Dupanloup said that the pope was only condemning these things in an absolute sense (freedom to do whatever you like), not in the qualified forms found in the real world. He was stating an ideal (the thesis), which has to be adapted to various real conditions (the hypothesis). The document therefore condemned the thesis, but not (necessarily) the hypothesis. It was a smooth piece of evasion: "By the time Dupanloup had finished with the *Syllabus,* it was almost as though it had never been."[49] But the dodge for escaping one trap became a trap itself in the hands of

Ottaviani and his ilk. "Thesis-hypothesis" stayed around to paralyze thinking for a whole century.

The endless bowing toward papal texts imposed on priests in the era of the anti-Modernist oath is part of that texture of pressures I called structures of deceit in my earlier book. Murray had to pretend, to compliment, to stretch texts, to equivocate, to "find" things that were not in the papal documents, in order to inch the debate over toward reality. As he admitted in 1957: "You will tell me (and I shall agree) that this is no way to carry on theological argument. However, that's the way it is."[50]

Most of these fetters on him were suddenly struck off by Vatican II, where Murray could argue honestly (and successfully). The ordeal he had undergone was shared by scholars throughout Europe — Henri de Lubac, Marie-Dominique Chenu, Yves Congar, Karl Rahner, Jean Danielou. "Yves Congar, O.P., was exiled from Le Saulchoir to Cambridge, and Henri de Lubac, S.J., was forbidden to teach and even to live in a house where there were students."[51] These and other men had been in disgrace with Rome, working under suspicion, responsive to superiors' anxieties for them, forced to trim or qualify or retract, choosing between silence and compromise, pecked at and harassed by petty men like Joseph Fenton, their scholarship mocked by men incapable of it, called traitors to their oath. They had kept to their posts as obediently as Murray had. Like him, they were excluded from the council's preparatory sessions. But when bishops found they needed their expertise, these men came to Rome and were welcomed at last, recognized for the very positions the Curia had deplored. Their emergence reminds me of the scene in Chesterton's poem "Lepanto" where the galley slaves of the Muslim fleet are released from their chains:

> Breaking of the hatches up and bursting of the holds,
> Thronging of the thousands up that labor under sea,
> White for bliss and blind for sun and stunned for liberty.[52]

The reign of terror was over.

IV

THE VATICAN II CHURCH

The Second Vatican Council was, for Catholics, as much the principal church event of the twentieth century as Vatican I was of the nineteenth century. It has been as controversial, as loved and detested. But it has been even more powerful in its effect on the church. Vatican I's teaching on infallibility did not produce infallible statements. It boosted the status of the pope, which strengthened long-standing tendencies in the hierarchy and the priesthood. It made it much easier for Pius X to impose his reign of terror on the clergy. But the council's impact on laypeople was slight, and their perception of that impact was even slighter. If you had asked the average Catholic, at the end of the nineteenth century, what difference Vatican I had made in his or her life, there would have been a lot of vague fumbling for some kind of an answer, which would have added up to "Effectively, no difference."

That is not the case with Vatican II. Some would say that the council ruined the liturgy, undermined church authority, and caused a widespread crisis of faith. Others would say that it brought honesty and renewal into their lives. Only the most apathetic Catholics, only those barely Catholic at all, would say that the council made no difference. We are not only living in the church of Vatican II; we are aware that we do so, for good or ill. Being a Catholic is not quite the same since the council occurred. Thank God.

18

The Great Rebirth

IN 1972, the economist John Kenneth Galbraith told me, "Of all the changes I have seen in my lifetime, the greatest by far is the one in your church." Thirty years later he would probably agree that changes in the status of women have been even greater; but his statement was very likely true at the time when he made it. I presume he knew something of the forces at work in Rome and elsewhere from his close participation in John Kennedy's presidential campaign of 1960, when Rome had to back off from its censoring of John Courtney Murray — when, that is, centuries of solemn teaching on church-state relations were muted overnight. Galbraith saw how Murray and others went from pariahs to prophets in the course of the Second Vatican Council (1962–1965).

Anyone familiar with the papal teachings being enforced right up to the opening of the council — on Jews, on freedom of conscience, on disciplines imposed under pain of mortal sin, on ways of worshiping, on the nature of revelation, on the tools of biblical interpretation, on the role of bishops, on relations with other churches, on the competence of secular authority, on the promise of science and progress, on the centrality of Scholasticism — must think the reversals across a broad front almost miraculous. Many of these subjects were affected, as well, by the release of Pope John XXIII's two principal encyclicals, *Mater et Magistra* (1960), while the council was being prepared, and *Pacem in Terris* (1963), between the council's first and second sessions. The encyclicals and the council amounted to a one-two punch by the prime mover behind them both, Pope John XXIII. So effective was this initiative that it was sustained even after John died. It was as unthinkable for Paul VI to renounce the work of the pope who preceded him as it was for Lyndon Johnson to desert the aims of the president he followed.

But the eventual record of the council was far from what was expected when John announced, in 1959, his intention of summoning it. Conservative officials in Rome, not happy with such a venture, were nonetheless confident that they could contain any undesirable effects. And liberals were even more certain of that. John, they felt, was naïve in his hopes. He turned the planning of the event over to the canny bureaucrats of the papal court, the Curia, of which he had little experience. Those bureaucrats went to work in their obscure quarters rigging the outcome. Every advantage was on their side. They knew the turf, the language (ecclesiastical Latin, in which the world's scattered bishops were rusty or entirely non-functioning), the procedures (which the Curia had invented), and the church's record (which it tended as its prerogative). The last two councils (Trent in the sixteenth century and Vatican I in the nineteenth) had been conservative slam-dunks. In the Middle Ages, the popes feared councils and tried to avoid them. Now they had become Rome's playthings. The only anxiety the Curia had was that this pope might want to play a game different from theirs. Fortunately, they felt, he was too dumb to get away with that.

The Curia let superiors of liberal theologians know that such troublemakers were to be kept away — and, at least during the planning sessions in Rome, they were. The gloom in progressive quarters was uniform. Curialists prepared in secret an avalanche of drafts (schemata), seventy-two of them, more (they felt) than could be digested by the bishops when they arrived, strangers in Rome, to have "the locals" usher them through the documents and end the council with nothing essentially changed. Pope John said the schemata should be sent ahead of time so the bishops could review them in their dioceses; but only seven were sent ahead (four prepared by Cardinal Ottaviani and the other three vetted by him).

Some bishops, in need of theological help and fearing that they were being manipulated, called for informal advice from some of the theologians the preparatory bodies had deliberately snubbed. Cardinal Franz König of Vienna asked Karl Rahner to look at the draft on the liturgy, and Rahner sent off four hundred or so mimeographed copies of his remarks on the draft's inadequacy. Cardinal Bernard Alfrink of Utrecht asked Edward Schillebeeckx to evaluate the schemata, and two thousand copies of his criticism (especially on the Tridentine idea that tradition is a source of revelation separable from Scripture) were circulated to the bishops and *periti*.[1] Cardinal Shehan of Baltimore, in whose diocese John Courtney Murray lived, consulted Murray on the church-state schema. The draft made Murray fear the worst from a council he was still forbidden to attend:

> Ottaviani's "two standard" theory (what I call the disjunctive theory) will remain on the books, untouched, as the essential and pure Catholic doctrine (he holds that it is *proxima fidei* [all-but-defined-infallible] and Ruffini agrees). And the Council's "practical" statements will look like sheer concessions to "today's circumstances" — a matter of expediency, or, in a word, the thing called "hypothesis" again affirmed, to the joy of the curial Right, who will have triumphed in what will have been in effect no more than an affirmation by the Council of their own doctrine.[2]

The theologians saw what was wrong with the documents that had been prepared, but had no hope of defeating them. The more knowledgeable the observer, the less hopeful he could feel. The "nice guy" pope, up against his supposed underlings, would finish where nice guys normally do:

> [Marie-Dominique] Chenu reported on a meeting between Yves Congar and Hans Küng, both of whom were pessimistic. When Chenu met Jean Daniélou, the latter launched into a severe criticism of "the doctrinal schemas, devoted to academic discussions, and lacking any evangelical perspective and any sense of the needs of the present time." In the preparatory material Karl Rahner saw nothing that could be salvaged; Joseph Ratzinger [a liberal at the time] thought it incapable of speaking to the Church. Edward Schillebeeckx was no more sympathetic than the others, and Henri de Lubac saw no room for [their] intervention . . . The concern of these men was not simply that Vatican II might prove to be a ceremonial council, intended to ratify what the preparatory commission had produced, and thus a useless event. Their deeper fear was that the Council would utterly disappoint the expectations of the faithful, the other Christian communities, and public opinion.[3]

Dom Helder Camara of Brazil said at the time, "No good can come out of the Council unless the Holy Spirit can produce a miracle."[4] The liberals felt themselves in such disarray that Cardinals Julius Döpfner of

Munich and Joseph Frings of Cologne begged the pope to postpone its opening.[5]

First Session (October 11–December 8, 1962)

But the "nice guy" pope was not going to be the pushover both liberals and conservatives expected. His touch was obvious on the night of the council's opening day, when a great torchlight procession wended its way across Rome. At its arrival in St. Peter's piazza, the pope appeared at his window and delivered a spontaneous greeting that came to be known as "the moonlight address." He said:

> Even the moon may be said to have hastened on this evening . . . When you return home you will find your children: Caress them and tell them, "This is a caress from the pope." You will find some tears to dry. Speak words of comfort to the afflicted. Let the afflicted know the pope is with his sons and daughters, especially in hours of sadness and bitterness . . . It is a brother who speaks to you, a brother who, by the will of Our Lord, has become a father. But fatherhood and brotherhood are both of them gifts of God. Everything is! Everything![6]

Did afflicted theologians take heart from such words? The first business meeting of the bishops indicated that they might have. To make sure the digestion of the schemata would be supervised by themselves, the curial officials had drawn up a slate of candidates to be elected as heads of the commissions considering separate subjects. They knew that the convening bishops would not have the knowledge of their colleagues — or the time to sound each other out — to come up with other candidates. Electing their own slate meant, in effect, that any motion to redraft the schemata would send them back to substantially the same men who wrote them in the first place. But when Cardinal Eugene Tisserant, the dean of the Curia who presided over the opening session, called for a vote on the slate, Cardinal Achille Lienart of Lille moved for a delay until the bishops could propose their own candidates. Tisserant said that this was against the rules, and Lienart answered, in effect, that he would just have to break the rules. The bishops applauded his move (which was also against the rules). The pope would later thank Lienart for his initiative.[7] But Father Joseph Fenton, Father Murray's old enemy, bustling about Rome on errands for Ot-

taviani, was disheartened: "I always thought this Council was dangerous. It was started for no sufficient reason."[8]

An important principle had been asserted — but not established. It
would have to be fought for over and over, this principle that the bishops themselves were the masters of the council. The manipulation of
the rules would be a powerful weapon in the hands of the Roman
clique. The draft schemata had all to be fought over, one by one, since
they showed — as the pope himself noted in his diary — "the dominant
influence of the fixed ideas of one man" (Cardinal Ottaviani of the
Holy Office).[9] At times, only the pope's intervention could thwart the
undemocratic procedures of those trying to keep the bishops from de-
veloping their own views — as when the conservatives tried repeatedly
to quash the consideration of the deicide charge against the Jews.
When they could not do that, they tried to wrest it away from the liberal Cardinal Augustin Bea, to whom the pope had expressly entrusted
it. When they could not do that, they tried (with partial success) to di-
lute the text dealing with the charge.[10]

The council's first session was largely devoted to ground-clearing
operations, beating down the suggested schemata and trying to introduce fresh ideas. No decrees were promulgated, and the one closest to
final form (on the media) was unsatisfactory — it would remain so. But
before the bishops reassembled for the second session, the death of the
pope and the rapturous reception given his encyclical *Pacem in Terris,*
with its bold defense of freedom of conscience and its call for a confident co-operation with the world, had set a bracing tone of optimism.

The curial officials, as so often in this period, misread the situation.
Many were relieved at John's death. Cardinal Ottaviani said that now
he could die a Catholic. Cardinal Tisserant amused people at his dinner table with ridicule of John.[11] Monsignor Amleto Tondini, the official Latinist of the Curia, had the traditional task of composing John's
funeral eulogy. He made it as cold, formal, and unfeeling as the ornate
style of such things allowed.[12] Tondini also gave the address to the assembled cardinals before they were sealed up in conclave to choose
John's successor — and he showed the conservatives' foolish overreach
by turning the occasion into an attack on John. He admitted that the
world applauded John — even Khrushchev did — and then turned that
into an accusation: "Doubt should be cast [on the enthusiastic ap-
plause] . . . one wonders whether the enthusiasm came from people

who were true believers, who accepted all the dogmatic and moral teachings of the church." The pope about to be chosen should abandon John's foolish optimism and suspend the Council, in order to "let the questions mature for some time."[13]

Tondini badly misread his audience, and the conclave chose a man who was known to be close to John, Giovanni Battista Montini, whom Pius XII had humiliated and John had made a cardinal. Montini had written a confidential plan for making the council a success, and John had shown him special favor. The new pope had no choice in any case — the world had accepted John and his council with a warmth that could not be ignored. Paul VI, as Montini now became, would have forged ahead even if it had been possible to give up on the council. Nonetheless, he lacked John's sunny temperament, and he treated with excessive fear such intransigence as Tondini showed. Though the Latin stylist would never become a cardinal, Paul gave important assignments to the man who had defiled John's memory.[14]

Second Session (September 29–December 4, 1963)

The most emotional issue engaged in the second session concerned the nature of the bishops' own office. At the Council of Trent, late in its sessions, the pope's representatives had beat back an attempt to say that bishops were given their authority directly by Christ (not by Christ *through* the pope). At Vatican I, the council had been broken off just as the question of episcopal authority was coming up. Now, at Vatican II, conservatives argued that stress on the joint authority of the bishops would compromise the sole authority of the pope. Votes to rework the relevant schema (that dealing with the church) were delayed or denied by the council organizers. To break the impasse, Cardinal Leon-Joseph Suenens of Belgium, speaking for a panel of moderators Paul VI had set up in this session, brought forward five short propositions. A vote on these would establish a "sense of the assembly" to guide the rewriting of the schema. Four of these five items, taken together, gave to the whole body (the "college") of bishops the full authority of the original apostles. The conservatives hated the very word "college" and fought its use. They also challenged Suenens's proposal on procedural grounds — the rules for the council did not provide for such a "straw vote," and the language of the five propositions had not been previously vetted by the theological commission. But the conservatives could not block the vote, which went overwhelmingly against them — the articles on the bishops passed by majorities on the order of two thousand to three hundred. It was known beforehand that liberals were in a majority among the council fathers, but not that the scale was this great.[15] Cardinal Ottaviani rose to rebuke the majority, saying they should resume their rightful status, that of sheep: "It is not for the sheep to lead Peter, but for Peter to lead the sheep."[16] Conservatives left the second session badly shaken, but determined to take drastic measures to stop the revolution that was taking place before their eyes. Some already had the feelings Cardinal Giuseppe Siri of Genoa would later express: "It will take a century for the church to recover from John's pontificate."[17]

Third Session (September 14–November 21, 1964)

On the eve of the council's reconvening, a blistering letter signed by twenty prominent cardinals, several bishops, and the heads of twelve religious orders was sent to the pope. Cardinal Ottaviani, though he did not sign the letter, supported it. The letter called into question the "aims and methods" of the majority, saying their position on the college of bishops and other matters was reached in defiance of Scripture and previous councils, and reflected "non-doctrinal" motives.[18] The letter as much as said that the council's majority had become heretical, and there could be no compromise with heresy. Faced with that conviction on the part of much of his own cabinet, Paul became obsessed with proving that there *could* be a compromise, that he could soften the majority position enough to clear it of heresy in the eyes of the intransigents. (Only one of the signatories did, in fact, leave the church, Archbishop Marcel LeFebvre.)

While acting against the majority, Paul tried to cover his tracks, using cat's-paws to cancel votes or introduce new language into the drafts. Mysterious announcements were made that some "higher authority" had called for departures from what the fathers were doing. When the minority made it clear to the pope that they would not accept the decree on collegiality, the pope took steps to water it down, sending "from higher authority" an explanatory note to be appended to what the fathers had decided. This note declared four things: that

- "college" was not to be understood in a juridical sense;
- episcopal ordination gives authority to a bishop, but its exercise must be regulated by the pope;

• the college can act only with the pope; though
• the pope can act without the college.

Though these propositions went against the logic of the document to which they were appended (which is the reason the minority demanded them), the majority, over an anguished weekend, decided to submit to the pope's interference in a debate that he had said would be free. The case was made that getting any document to recognize the college (which had been anathema to the conservatives beforehand) was an important step. At least it was a development beyond Trent, where the idea of direct divine authorization of the episcopacy had been rejected. The new council's document, *Lumen Gentium,* said that the bishops' authority, "which they personally exercise in Christ's name, is proper, ordinary and immediate."[19] That was certainly an important principle to establish. But the mockery Rome would later make of collegiality gives great retrospective force to what F. X. Murphy wrote in 1968:

> The question might well be raised . . . whether it was really such a good idea, after all, to achieve quasi-unanimity, if this had to be done at too high a cost, through the promulgation of a needlessly unbalanced, disfigured document accompanied by a tortuous, ambiguous, over-subtle explanation of an explanation. In his anxiety to conciliate an unimportant [numerical] minority, Pope Paul seemed to have forgotten that he might be doing less than justice to the majority.[20]

This, of course, was the difference between the interventions made by John in the first session and Paul in the later ones — that John was acting to prevent the minority from blocking free discussion by the majority, while Paul was acting to help the minority limit the majority's freedom.

The pope did it again shortly after introducing the note on collegiality. On what came to be known as "Black Thursday," the declaration on religious freedom was scheduled for a final vote. This document had been completely rewritten, substituting the ideas of John Courtney Murray for those of Cardinal Ottaviani. The changes had been defended, during the second session of the council, in a debate before the theological commission, where Murray completely routed his old foe, the man who had silenced him. When Ottaviani, partially blind, asked who was arguing against him, Cardinal Paul-Emile Léger, sitting next to him, spared his feelings by whispering, "Just some expert or other" (*Peritus quidam*).[21] Now, in the third session, the new text was facing certain victory on the day appointed for the vote on it, when Cardinal Tisserant, presiding over the meeting, abruptly announced that the text was so new it needed maturer consideration — the vote was put over to the next (fourth) session.

The assembly broke into an uproar of protest — was the Catholic church unable to back freedom of conscience after all? Were Paul Blanshard's charges vindicated? Cardinal Albert Meyer of Chicago, who had been seated at the dais with Tisserant, walked away from him growling, "This man is hopeless." On the floor several bishops hastily composed a protest addressed to the pope. It said, in Latin, "Your Holiness: With reverence but with urgency, great urgency, maximum urgency [*instanter, instantius, instantissme*], we request that a vote on the declaration of religious liberty be taken before the end of this session of the Council, lest the confidence of the world, both Christian and non-Christian, be lost."[22] About four hundred signatures were quickly gathered, to be taken at once to the pope. (Well over a thousand names were added by the end of the day.) Cardinals Meyer of Chicago, Ritter of St. Louis, and Léger of Montreal took the petition straight to the papal apartments, where they were at first denied admission. But they insisted, and finally presented their protest. This time the pope intervened by not intervening — by saying that he could not overrule the chairman's decision on a technicality of the rules.

Fourth Session (September 14–December 8, 1965)

In the council's fourth session (fall of 1965), the pope intervened again, but this time on the side of the declaration on religious liberty. The conservatives had managed to kill the bill by a secret vote in the coordinating committee of the council. But at a "White Tuesday" session, another surprise move was announced on "higher authority," ordering a secret vote of the assembly on whether to take up the declaration after all, despite the committee's cancellation of it. The outcome was certain, and it is generally agreed that Pope Paul, who was about to make a journey to the United Nations to plead for world peace, could not afford the embarrassment of a defeat for the principle of freedom of conscience on the eve of his speech. He saved the day this time. But he made other interventions that were not on the side of freedom.

A number of bishops intended, at this session, to raise the issue of marriage for priests — *Le Monde* had even printed the text of a speech that Bishop Pedro Koop of Brazil had prepared for delivery. The pope had a letter read to the assembly saying "it is not opportune to have a public discussion of this topic," adding that "we intend to maintain this ancient, holy and providential law to the extent of our ability." Any expression of opinion on the matter should be addressed privately (and secretly) to him.[23] Only one other topic had been removed from the fathers' free discussion — contraception — and that was done by John XXIII, at the suggestion of a liberal (Cardinal Suenens) who feared that the pope's intended pastoral tone would be damaged by bitter doctrinal disputes on such a touchy matter in full session. So John quietly set up a special committee to study the matter. Paul let it be known that he was expanding this private group, so the subject was outside the purview of the assembly.

But the conservatives were not willing to let the matter alone. They demanded that a condemnation of contraceptives be included in the council documents — and the pope gave in to them. Another of those missives from an unspecified "higher authority" was read by order of Cardinal Ottaviani — four *modi* ("adjustments") to be added to the discussion of marriage, including a condemnation of "contraceptive devices" and a citation of the Pius XI encyclical that had condemned them. What was the point of the special committee's studying this matter if the council was going to anticipate its judgment? Most of the bishops had a good idea where this missive came from — and the conservative Irish cardinal Michael Browne was certain: "Christ himself has spoken to us" (*Christus locutus est*).[24] But the bishops were no longer willing to take Ottaviani's word for anything, and they directly asked the pope if *he* was telling them this. He answered that of course he was not dictating what they should decide — so they could put his *modi* in their own language. They did so, trying to minimize the glaring contrast with the rest of the document by reducing its substance to a footnote buried in other material.

The Breakthroughs

Given the intense struggles that took place over the four years of the council, during and between the sessions, in and out of St. Peter's, it is not surprising that all sides left it with a sense of inflated expectations partly deflated — of a great promise, or a great threat, not entirely carried to completion. Liberals felt it had moved in the right direction but had not gone far enough. Conservatives felt that it had gone entirely too far, but that their mining and hedging operations had left crevices for later demolition activities. This is the normal outcome of any major social change. The civil rights movement and the women's movement in America produced similar reactions. They did not go far enough for their advocates — with the result that they first stalled, and then slipped back. But the opponents felt that they had gone too far, and the swing of the pendulum against the changes only partly redressed their exaggerations.

But any sober measurement of the post-conciliar church against what preceded it is bound to vindicate Galbraith's estimate. This was a convulsive alteration of the whole religious landscape. One can quibble about the extent or meaning of each aspect of the change, but not about the general scale of change. Without considering the entire texture of interrelated considerations raised by the Council, it is easy to draw out a few strands.

1. *Laity.* The most important change effected by the council was in its way of considering and referring to the church. It was no longer a juridical body of governed and governing but "the people of God." The conservatives fought this concept as bitterly as they did the concept of collegiality; but the threat of the latter seemed more immediate to them — the bishops in their dioceses might whittle at the power of the pope's men in Rome. As usual, the Curia misread the situation. Bishops have been generally more compliant with Rome than have laypeople in the post-conciliar era. The Curia had trouble taking the laity seriously, apart from its attempt to control their participation in the liturgy.

2. *Liturgy.* Some misread the council's debates on the liturgy as a matter of mere disciplinary practices — the vernacular instead of Latin, communion under both kinds, the direction a priest faces, etc. But it was a matter of dogma, of the entire people of God constituting "a royal priesthood" (1 Peter 2.10). The laity "are in their own way made sharers in the priestly, prophetical, and kingly functions of Christ."[25] The equal dignity of all is recognized: "Neither Jew nor Greek, slave nor free, male and female — all are one in Messiah Jesus" (Gal 3.28). The Spirit dwells equally in all, and is the same in all, whatever the separate activities of members in the single body of Christ. Priests, instead of making themselves a separate caste, should "wipe out every kind of

separateness."[26] This was (or should have been) a death knell for the clericalism that was a besetting sin of the recent church.

3. *Scripture.* From the juridical language (mainly Scholastic) in which clericalism had been frozen, the council returned to Scripture and the early fathers of the church.

4. *Conscience.* The dignity of individual choice became the measure of political as well as religious freedom: "It is necessary to distinguish between error, which always merits repudiation, and the person in error, who never loses the dignity of being a person even when he is flawed by false or inadequate religious notions. God alone is the judge and searcher of hearts; for that reason he forbids us to make judgments about the internal guilt of anyone."[27] This was a formal renunciation of the long-standing Roman teaching that "error has no rights." Freedom of conscience must be honored, since "conscience is the most secret core and sanctuary of a man."[28]

5. *Church and state.* The separation of church and state is not only permissible but necessary:

> This Vatican Council declares that the human person has a right to religious freedom. This freedom means that all men are to be immune from coercion on the part of individuals or of social groups and of any human powers . . . A wrong is done when government imposes upon its people, by force or fear or other means, the profession or repudiation of any religion, or when it hinders men from joining or leaving a religious community.[29]

The views for which Father Murray was silenced were now the official doctrine of the church. The claim of the anti-Modernist oath that doctrine does not develop was refuted definitively.

6. *Other religions.* The freedom of the Spirit in leading humans to God through various paths cannot be limited by making pope or Curia the gatekeepers to every salvation transaction. Baptized Protestants are members of the body of Christ.[30] Jews, too, are "the people of God," and not mere pre-Christians or Christ-slayers.[31] Unbelievers have the rights to their own consciences. "Those also can attain to salvation who through no fault of their own do not know the gospel of Christ or his church."[32] This finally effaces all lingering vestiges of the Boniface VIII doctrine that "outside the church there is no salvation."

7. *Church teaching.* Christ teaches through his whole church, not just through one part of it. The pope leads but is within the apostolic body

of bishops; the laity share the priesthood of Christ; infallibility belongs to the whole body of Christ.

> The entire body of the faithful, anointed as they are by the Holy One, cannot err in matters of belief. They manifest this special property by means of the whole people's supernatural discernment in matters of faith when "from the bishops down to the last of the lay faithful" they show universal agreement in matters of faith and morals. That discernment in matters of faith is aroused and sustained by the Spirit of truth. It is exercised under the guidance of the sacred teaching authority, in faithful and respectful obedience to which the People of God accepts that which is not just the word of men but truly the Word of God.[33]

The people join in the entire church's witness to the truth by their acceptance of that which is proposed, showing the discernment infused by the Spirit. Newman was denounced in Rome for saying this in his essay "On Consulting the Faithful in Matters of Doctrine."

These were not insights that could be exhausted in any first statement of them, or be embodied in Christian life by any quick "implementation." They amounted to a fundamental reorientation that would take years to work into the everyday fabric of life and thought — providing that forces opposed to such a process did not abort it, reverse it, or treat it as illegitimate. Changes as deep as those suggested by the council were terrifying to many, especially those who had formed their whole notion of the Catholic church around a mystique of changelessness. And nowhere was that mystique greater than in the bowels of the Vatican (the area that used to be called The Church).

19

Born to Set Times Right

THE COUNCIL'S FOUR SESSIONS had become, as they passed, a form of slow torture for the Curia and its supporters. When it ended, the Roman professionals hoped that their church, the "real" church, would take charge again and undo the damage wrought by the bishops' four-year siege in Rome. But Pope Paul VI seemed unwilling to let that happen. He sincerely meant to fulfill the historic charge given him by John's council. He set up vehicles of consultation with bishops, priests, the laity, liturgists, missionaries, other religions, and non-believers. Though laymen and all women had been excluded from the council's delegates (significantly called "Council Fathers"), Paul expanded the all-male and all-clerical committee John had set up to reconsider the teaching on contraception. By 1965, Paul had included thirty-four lay members (in a group of fifty-eight), five of them women. In the same year, he set up a synod of bishops to hold regular meetings in Rome, for joint thinking with the head of their college.

Paul reorganized and renamed the Holy Office (the former Inquisition) as the Congregation for the Doctrine of the Faith (CDF). He reorganized the Curia and gave bishops a mandatory retirement age (seventy-five) and cardinals a cut-off age (eighty) after which they could not vote in consistory for a new pope. He authorized the reformed vernacular liturgy. He pursued ecumenical initiatives, meeting with Patriarch Athenagoras in Constantinople and the Anglican archbishop of Canterbury. His "Ostpolitik" built upon John's opening to the Soviet bloc. None of this endeared him to Roman intransigents.

Paul's Doubts

But his consultative measures soon proved hollow. When the Dutch bishops came out with their own catechism in 1966, Rome demanded that it be withdrawn until revisions were made. When the bishops defended their action in a 1967 meeting, Paul sent an emissary to spell out the limits of such gatherings.[1] This was the year when the first synod of bishops was coming to Rome; but the preparations had resurrected the control mechanisms set up before Vatican II. John Courtney Murray said it was bound to be a "ballet," not a real discussion.[2] Proof that this suspicion was justified came in two documents that Paul secretly prepared in 1967, without consulting bishops, priests, or the laity. One concerned priestly celibacy, the other contraception. This manner of formulating and promulgating church teaching was standard before the council; but the consultative bodies Paul himself had set up, in accordance with the teachings of the council, made them anachronistic — or should have done so.

The encyclical *Sacerdotalis Caelibatus* (1967) was meant to prevent the idea of priests' marrying from being considered at bishops' synods, just as Paul had removed the subject from the deliberations of the council. This had to be done *because* bishops wanted to consider it. Paul's assertions in the document are dishonest, as I argued in *Papal Sin*. He repeatedly cites a New Testament passage that has nothing to do with priestly ministry (Mt 19.11–12) and omits a passage that has everything to do with it (1 Cor 9.6). But the point here is that Paul prepared the encyclical in secret and sprang it on the world without discussing it, openly and beforehand, with those most affected by it, the priests and bishops who were part of his own teaching ministry (according to the norms of the council).

Paul had not consulted with priests about his encyclical on their status. That offered a great contrast to his deliberations on contraception, where lay men and women *were* consulted. But the outcome shows that this was window dressing, not real consultation. When early votes in the commission considering birth control revealed a majority for lifting the ban on "artificial contraceptives," Cardinal Ottaviani stepped in and stacked the commission, demoting its lay consultants and placing sixteen bishops on it as the only voting members. A single report on the final vote was to be issued, to prevent the lay members from issuing their own conclusions. But then, to Ottaviani's horror, nine of his picked sixteen bishops voted to change the Vatican's position, with only three opposing (four abstained). Now Ottaviani, who had arranged that only one report be submitted to the pope, had a second ("minority") report added, this one taking the position he had expected to be the majority report. That way Paul could claim that it was a "divided" commission, though there would have been an overwhelming majority if all the members of the commission had been allowed to report. And if the vote had gone Ottaviani's way, a majority of even one bishop would have been counted as decisive.

Luckily, the pope's men thought, the members of the commission had been sworn to secrecy — so the open discussion and consultation that the council encouraged were never envisaged, even in this comparatively "liberal" move to get advice from lay experts, women as well as men. The "findings" were considered to be so certain in favor of the old prohibition that Paul had an encyclical ready, to be issued even before the commission reported. This encyclical was based on a draft by the Jesuit Gustave Martelet.[3] The Vatican therefore panicked when a leaked copy of the majority report that favored *lifting* the ban was published in the *National Catholic Reporter*. Now it would be known that Paul was acting against the vote of his own bishops. Ottaviani's ploy, giving only the information that it was a *divided* commission, was no longer practicable. Paul told his friend Jean Guitton, "They tried to force my hand by publishing this report, but I won't give way."[4]

But now Paul had to create a new draft, addressing (so far as he could) the objections of the leaked report. He could not bring himself to change "church teaching," no matter how tortuous and contrived were the arguments he was compelled to resort to. Work on what became *Humanae Vitae* went on for two full years after the commission's report was published. His own motives were revealed to Jean Guitton:

Any attenuation of the law would have the effect of calling morality into question and showing the fallibility of the Church which then, like the Jewish synagogue, would have imposed too heavy a yoke on the people . . . Theology would then become the servant of science, *ancilla scientiae,* science's handmaid, subject to change with each new scientific discovery, so that tomorrow, for example, we would have to admit procreation without a father: the whole moral edifice would collapse, and with it the edifice of the faith.[5]

But as the bishops who voted for the change realized, it was not an "attenuation" that would call the church's authority into question, but the stubborn clinging to a discredited position. National conferences of bishops let their people know that the encyclical's ban could, after proper reflection, be rejected.[6] By ranking the affected dioceses according to the number of their inhabitants, the Benedictine priest Philip Kaufman calculated that only seventeen percent of Catholics worldwide were told by their bishops that they must submit to the encyclical unequivocally.[7] Nothing like this had happened since the *Syllabus of Errors* appeared in 1854.

It was a stunning rebuke to the pope. After it, he went into a defensive crouch that lasted through the final decade of his pontificate. Pope John had said the council would open the windows of the church. Year by year now, Pope Paul would trudge around from window to window, closing one after another. Synod meetings had to be tightly controlled, removing from their agenda, or blunting them there, the very things their participants wanted to discuss — contraception, women priests, married priests, improved dialogue, lay participation. Some of his earlier allies at the council — Cardinals Lercaro, König, and Suenens — now said that he was betraying the council's ideals. Suenens, who had warned the pope against acting alone on contraception, gave him the same advice on the subject of priestly celibacy:

> The deadlock — and deadlock there is — arises from the fact that the Pope did not allow the subject to be discussed by the fathers at the council. And this ban has been upheld in clear and repeated statements — thus excluding any collegial intervention, exactly as happened over birth control. So, with public examination and discussion blocked by authority, bishops cannot even trade thoughts on this among themselves or with the pope.[8]

The deadlock Suenens was referring to manifested itself in the 1970 synod of Dutch bishops, which concluded that lifting the celibacy requirement was necessary as a response to the shortage of priests.

Paul answered this cry for help with a weird claim that celibacy would be the solution to the shortage, a strong selling point with young men: "Celibacy, spiritually transfigured and transfiguring, is the best incentive to recruiting new vocations."[9] This bizarre argument ranks with the one he authorized for release in the 1976 document *Inter Insigniores,* on the subject of women priests — that women cannot be at the altar because they do not *look* like Jesus: "When Christ's role in the Eucharist is to be expressed sacramentally, there would not be in this the natural resemblance which must exist between Christ and his minister if the role of Christ were not taken by a man. In such a case it would be difficult to see in the minister the image of Christ. For Christ himself was and remains a man."[10]

The optimism of the conciliar period yielded to personal darknesses in Paul. Increasingly he had a haunted look. In an apocalyptic 1970 sermon, he famously said, "Through some crack in the temple of God, the smoke of Satan has entered . . . something supernatural has come into the world to destroy and strangle the very fruits of the Ecumenical Council."[11] Five months later he was brooding on the same threat: "The evil which exists in the world is the result and effect of an attack upon us and our society by a dark and hostile agent, the devil . . . the sophistical perverter of man's moral equipoise, the malicious seducer who knows how to penetrate us (through the senses, the imagination, desire, utopian logic, or disordered social contacts) in order to spread error."[12]

John Paul's Certitude

Paul's hapless air made people start calling him a Hamlet, and he did seem to have that character's feeling that "the times are out of joint — O cursed spite, that ever I was born to set them right." In this he was a perfect contrast with the man who succeeded him (after the eye blink of John Paul I's one-month pontificate). Paul VI seemed to yearn back, beyond the intervening council, to a more settled time, a kind of blissful status quo ante. John Paul II was ready to *take* people back there. O blessed times, when *he* was born to set them right! The contrast in the men's style was instantly apparent. To take just three points on which Paul had been tentative and John Paul proved decisive:

1. Paul had resented the aggressiveness of Opus Dei, the secretive religious quasi-order out of Spain, with its compromising original ties to the Franco regime. He bristled especially when the order offered to buy him out of his banking troubles, caused by Michele Sindona's crooked use of church moneys.[13] The group wanted to be given a special (independent) status, that of a "personal prelature," reporting only to its own bishop, so that it could employ what its superior called "a mobile and exceptionally well trained force" — and a wealthy one — for un-

specified secret activities for the church.[14] It was offering cash for this status, a deal that smacked of simony, as Hebblethwaite says. Paul could neither accept the deal nor discipline the order. John Paul, by contrast, who had wooed the order during his visits to Rome before becoming pope, preaching and saying Mass with its members, became its ardent patron in the Vatican, praying at the grave of its founder, canonizing that founder, and granting it the much-desired prelature. (There were enough of his addresses to Opus members for a whole book to be filled with them — *La Fede della Chiesa.*)

2. Paul had agonized over the drain of men leaving the priesthood to marry, a hemorrhage that his praise of celibacy did nothing to stop. He called these defections a personal crown of thorns, but he could not bring himself to punish those leaving. He made it easy for them to absolve themselves of the automatic excommunication they incurred. If they were going to be laymen and husbands in any case, he did not want to cut them off entirely from the church's life. Conservatives in Rome mocked this as weakness on his part; Rome's clerics said he devalued their own sacrifice in staying priests. One monsignor I interviewed in Rome, less than a year into John Paul II's reign, rejoiced that "we no longer have to pretend that Father So-and-So found Christ by screwing Sister Mary Sue." When I asked what good it does to alienate loyal Catholics, he answered, "We have to think of the morale of those who stay." When the acting head of the Jesuits at the time, Vincent O'Keefe, told the pope that many who leave want to use their talents for the church, the pope said he could not respect such men: "They broke their vow." When Cardinal Arns of Brazil brought John Paul a personal letter asking that he reconsider his ban on priests' marrying, the pope tore up the letter before the cardinal's eyes.[15] No Hamlet there.

3. Paul had worried about the liberal activism of the Jesuit order under its revered leader Pedro Arrupe (a Basque, like Saint Ignatius), and he had expressed his displeasure to Arrupe. When Arrupe suffered a stroke, Vincent O'Keefe filled in as acting general superior. When Arrupe died, the Jesuits were preparing a general congregation to choose a new leader, as was the custom. The pope, tipped off that O'Keefe was the favorite to win the election, stepped in to prevent that. For the first time in history, a pope took away the Society's right to elect its own leader, and appointed a man who would be his own personal delegate, making the Society conform to the pope's theological conservatism.

John Paul is a strong leader, and his concept of authority is seen in the models he admires. He planned to advance to sainthood the very types of pre-conciliar rigidity, Pius IX and Pius XII. He appointed a secret panel to see if he could get away with beatifying Pius IX — the pope who fumed at Jewish "dogs," imposed the *Syllabus of Errors*, and declared himself infallible ("The tradition? — *I* am it"). The secrecy of this inquiry was itself a return to old church ways.[16] Despite much opposition from Jewish groups, including relatives of the kidnapped Edgardo Mortara, he pushed this beatification through in 2000. The Vatican desire to see Pio Nono raised to the altar can be seen from the fact that the scholarly board considering his qualifications excluded the one man who knows most about Pius, Giacomo Martina, S.J., the author of the exhaustive three-volume biography of him, a project that took decades to complete. Why was he excluded? When the journalist Kenneth Woodward of *Newsweek* asked him point-blank, "Do you consider Pius a saint?" Father Martina answered, "No, I do not."[17]

Pius XII proved a more difficult case for John Paul, because of the accusation that he did not protest the Holocaust. But even aside from that, the reign of terror that Pius maintained over liberal theologians like John Courtney Murray should have given the pope pause — if that were not precisely the reason for his admiration. John Paul tried to get Pius through by a balancing act, processing his cause and John XXIII's simultaneously, one for the liberals, one for the conservatives. But John Paul's hopes for Pius XII were disappointed.

That was a striking exception in a pontificate that has canonized like crazy. This one pope has made more saints than all his predecessors put together — and he has beatified on the same scale. The saints and blessed were chosen to give a picture of the church John Paul wants to project — including Polish heroes, those from the "new church" in Africa, and especially Catholic martyrs to Nazi or Communist regimes. The desire to create a new martyrology has led to the canonization of people who did not die precisely because of their religion, according to the initial advocates of their cause — for instance, Maximilian Kolbe and Edith Stein.[18] It was John Paul who insisted on honoring them as martyrs, since he is presenting the "refounded" church of modern times as growing, like the primitive church, from martyrs' blood.[19] It is for this reason that the Vatican released the so-called third secret of Fatima, the final unrevealed part of a vision of Mary given to the Portuguese girl Lucia dos Santos in 1917 but not fully written out by her until 1944. This vision proved what the pope had been saying. In the words of Cardinal Joseph Ratzinger, issuing the Vatican's official explanation of the secret, "In the vision we can recognize the last century as a century of martyrs, a century of suffering and persecution *of the church* [emphasis added]."[20]

Fatima

The pope has even presented himself as a martyr. In 1981, when he was shot by a would-be assassin, Mehmet Ali Agca, he said that this act was "necessary" for the church, so that "the voice of God, which speaks in human history through the sign of the times, could be more easily heard and understood."[21] The church was being vindicated through his pain. But it was not only by being shot that John Paul could be martyred. When he had a hip replacement in 1994, he wrote of the event: "I have to lead Christ's church into the third millennium by prayer, by various programs, but I saw that this is not enough: she must be led by suffering, by the attack thirteen years ago *and now by this new sacrifice* [emphasis added]." When he was shot, he knew that the act had meaning for the whole church because of the date — it was the day (May 13) of Mary's first appearance to Lucia dos Santos. It was the Virgin of Fatima whose hand "guided the bullet" away from his heart.[22] (In gratitude, he sent Agca's bullet to Fatima, where it was placed in the crown on the statue of the Virgin.) But what was the mystical meaning of the date when he had his hip operation? He tells us:

> Why now, why this year, why in this Year of the Family? Precisely because the family is threatened, because the family is under attack. The pope has to be attacked, the pope has to suffer, so that every family in the world may see that there is, I would say, a higher gospel, the gospel of suffering, by which the future is being prepared . . . Understand this, understand why the pope ends in the hospital again; understand it, think it over.[23]

In case we had not "understood it," had not grasped the meaning of his suffering, the pope released in 2000 the secret meaning of the attempt on his life in 1981, explaining that the child Lucia's vision at Fatima had been a prediction in 1917 of the attempt on his life sixty-four years later. This was a new use of religious prophecy (as opposed to parlor-game prediction) — a prophecy released years after the event, not to warn ahead of time, to forestall an event, to call for prayers preceding it. The vision described was not concerned with the horrors still looming in 1917 — two world wars, the cold war, the nuclear threat. It simply foretold a fact in one man's biography. Even Cardinal Ratzinger admitted, as he explained the vision's meaning, "No great mystery is revealed; nor is the future unveiled." Though the details of Lucia's vision were sent to the pope in the 1940s, she said their final item was to be revealed to the public only after 1960. Popes Pius XII, John XXIII, and Paul VI had not seen fit to release it after that date. They did not have the key to its meaning. Only John Paul could read the mystery. Here is the text he released in 2000, with punctuation according to the Vatican's release:

We [ten-year-old Lucia and her two younger cousins] saw in an immense light that is God: "something similar to how people appear in a mirror when they pass in front of it" a Bishop dressed in White "we had the impression that it was the Holy Father." Other Bishops, Priests, men and women Religious going up a steep mountain, at the top of which there was a big Cross of rough-hewn trunks as of a cork-tree with the bark; before reaching there the Holy Father passed through a big city half in ruins and half trembling with halting step, afflicted with pain and sorrow, he prayed for the souls of the corpses he met on his way; having reached the top of the mountain, on his knees at the foot of the big Cross he was killed by a group of soldiers who fired bullets and arrows at him, and in the same way there died one after another the other Bishops, Priests, men and women Religious, and various lay people of different ranks and positions. Beneath the two arms of the Cross there were two Angels each with a crystal aspersorium in his hand, in which they gathered up the blood of the martyrs and with it sprinkled the souls that were making their way to God.[24]

Cardinal Ratzinger writes: "When, after the attempted assassination on *3 May, 1981*, the Holy Father had the text of the third part of the secret brought to him, was it not inevitable that he should see in it his own fate? [emphasis added]."[25] In other words, the pope knew in 1981 what the third vision had predicted, though he did not tell the rest of us about it until 2000, nineteen years later. Why the delay? The final release came in conjunction with the Holy Year, which the pope was trying to mark with special events. It was the beginning of a new millennium, which he dedicated to the Virgin at Fatima.

Having had two decades to reflect on the vision, John Paul published his conviction that it was "inevitable" (in Cardinal Ratzinger's word) that he interpret it as referring to the assassination attempt. Why inevitable? The assailant, Agca, was not a group, not a soldier, not shooting arrows, not aiming at a target climbing a hill, not at one "meeting corpses," not at one "half trembling with halting step." The pope was riding in the "Popemobile," his custom-made car, through the piazza of St. Peter's. And the main thing is that the bullet *did not kill* John Paul. This was a prediction of a martyrdom that did not happen.

It takes a great sense of one's own destiny for a man to twist signs so strenuously to prove that the Virgin's main message to Lucia was all about him. When previous popes privy to the third secret after 1960 did not release it, this led to feverish speculations among Fatima buffs on the apocalyptic nature of the revelation being withheld from them. A cottage industry grew up, predicting what Lucia's prediction would turn out to be. Repeated calls were made on the popes to reveal it. When Paul VI did not do so, a fervent band of Fatimites decided that he must be an imposter, someone substituted for the real pope, who had been hidden away somewhere. A real pope would do what Lucia had asked.[26] Not surprisingly, when John Paul did at last reveal that the vision concerned him, people who had spent decades predicting something more momentous felt let down. The pope was accused of a "whitewash," covering up some direr message about the church's post-conciliar deviations.[27] A 1991 interview with Cardinal Silvio Oddi was reprinted, in which he said that the secret would focus on apostasy in the church resulting from the council.[28]

The pope's interpretation of the secret is less far-fetched than those of the Marian zealots (but not enough less far-fetched). The interesting question is why the pope dignified this superstitious cult in the first place. The first two visions granted Lucia on the pivotal date of July 13, 1917, were not of the sort to inspire trust. They were not written down by her until 1941, and the third ("secret") one not until 1944. The first vision simply allowed Lucia to see souls roasting in hell. The second vision had a "prophecy" obviously based on what had happened by 1941, when she described the vision. She wrote that Mary foretold a new war unless people prayed to her, and that the war would begin (so all the praying would not, in fact, work) during the reign of Pius XI. Pius was elected five years after the vision, and the war had begun two years before Lucia wrote it down. These facts are enough, in themselves, to discredit anything Lucia ever said.

But another aspect of that second vision explains the eruption of an immense and emotional devotion to Fatima during the cold war. This is the anti-Communist connection that has much to do with John Paul's attitude toward Fatima. Mary said that she would convert Russia if the pope would consecrate that country to her Immaculate Heart. Pius XII dedicated the whole world to Mary's Immaculate Heart in 1942, but Lucia said that was not enough — the dedication had to be specifically of *Russia*. But when John Paul II dedicated the world again in 1984 (again without specifying Russia), Lucia said that was enough, and the cold war's end meant that another prophecy had been fulfilled (retrospectively).[29] Yet Russia is still not converted to Mary's (and Lucia's) church.

In some ways, it is less surprising that John Paul could believe a farrago of Fatima nonsense than that he could get an endorsement of the nonsense from a sophisticated theologian like Cardinal Ratzinger, his doctrinal czar at the Congregation for the Doctrine of the Faith. After all, Ratzinger had said in 1984 that there was nothing to be gained from revealing Lucia's final vision: "To publish the 'third secret' would mean exposing the church to the danger of sensationalism, exploitation of the content."[30] But Ratzinger, like Paul VI, has a fear of the diabolic powers: "The atheistic culture of the modern Western world is still surviving thanks to the liberation from the fear of demons which Christianity brought about . . . There are already signs of the return of these dark powers, and Satanic cults are spreading more and more in the secularized world."[31] Ratzinger seems at least as haunted as Paul was. Eamon Duffy claims that he lives in a "lurid and simplistic world of easy dualisms," amounting to "practical manicheism."[32] Perhaps, in such a place of horror, the Virgin of Fatima is our last hope — or at least the man whose life she saved is the sole person able to face the devils of our time.

Whatever one makes of the incoherencies carefully doled out at Fatima, at least we know that Lucia dos Santos is a real person. But in 1990 the pope beatified a man, Juan Diego, who seems never to have existed. And in 2002 that phantom was canonized. It was to him, supposedly, that the Virgin appeared in 1531, magically imprinting her image on his mantle, an image revered as Our Lady of Guadalupe. But people close to the date of the purported apparition — those with the best means for knowing about it and motives for recording it — are silent about this apparition. Even the first Mexican bishop, a known critic of novel images who was said, nevertheless, to have received and built a church for the miraculous cloak, left no record of doing so, though he provided bequests for his other foundations.[33] Was the exception he made for a miraculous image too unimportant to be included in these other (some minor) provisions? The respected sixteenth-century historian Toribio de Montolinía, in a record that emphasized Mexican devotion to the Virgin, does not mention Juan Diego or his mantle. The Franciscan editor of his history calls this omission inexplicable.[34] But no other sixteenth-century history of the country's religion mentions it, either.

The earliest reference to the apparition occurred in 1648, 117 years after its purported occurrence, in a highly wrought theological meditation by a Franciscan, Miguel Sanchez, who said he was relying on oral tradition since *there was no prior written record* of the apparition. This lack of earlier evidence was an embarrassment to those promoting a cult of Juan Diego, so a document was produced in 1649, a flowery account of the apparition written in the local language, Nahuatl, and supposedly composed shortly after the date (1548) when the phantom Juan Diego died. Outstanding experts on sixteenth-century Mexico have long treated this as a forgery — Juan Bautista Muñoz in the eighteenth century, for instance, and Joaquín García Icazbalceta in the nineteenth — and three modern specialists in Nahuatl have demonstrated that it depends on (and therefore post-dates) the 1643 work by Miguel Sanchez.[35] Even the Cambridge historian D. A. Brading, who is sympathetic to the symbolism of the Lady of Guadalupe, calls this last investigation "a devastating criticism of the received linguistic and textual foundations of the tradition."[36]

Though the Virgin is supposed to have appeared to an illiterate Mexican peasant, the image on the cloth is wearing European clothes, and the image is a familiar one in European iconography, reflecting European theology (of the Immaculate Conception). The Virgin's very title comes from a Marian shrine in Spain, Guadalupe, and contains sounds Nahuatl speakers could not make. The claim that the pigments are miraculous has long been abandoned, and those who say the image was formed supernaturally cannot explain amateur-painter faults in it

— e.g., why Mary's gown has arabesque patterns that do not follow its folds. None of this matters to the pope, who seems to think that a refusal to be gullible shows lack of chivalry to Our Lady. Scholars respectfully addressing to Rome their measured criticism of the historical basis of the cult have been ignored.[37] John Paul has taken an understandably popular devotion and tricked it out with the pseudo-science of investigated modern "miracles" in order to canonize a fiction. But after he has done this for the provider of the holy picture of Guadalupe, what is left for him — to canonize the architect of the Holy House of Loreto?

The pope's willingness to believe in odd things is equaled, when not surpassed, by his admirers' willingness to believe in him — nor merely in his office but in him, in his person, which is seen as redemptive. They look to him for what they call "the restoration." Paul Johnson has written: "It [the church] came into his hands just in time. There was a moment, in the mid-1970s, when the Roman Catholic Church seemed in real danger of inflicting grievous injury on itself, to the point of destroying those characteristics which are its greatest strengths: its self-confidence, its internal order, its unchangeability. With the coming of John Paul that moment passed."[38] To speak of the church as coming into the hands of a pope seems to neglect the fact that it is always in the hands of the Spirit. But Johnson believes that everything hinges on one human being. "The Roman Catholic Church is a divine autocracy. Its direction is centered in the personality of its sovereign pontiff."[39] Pope John Paul is therefore just what was needed: "He is a divine juggernaut."[40]

The pope himself seems to think the whole church depends on him — on his being saved by the Virgin of Fatima, on his living into the new millennium, on his visiting every Marian shrine, on his Stakhanovite canonizing, on his redefinitions of every truth, on his creating a like-minded episcopate. His treatises, many of great length, pour forth on every subject. When the Vatican's new catechism came out in 1994 — in answer to the liberal Dutch catechism — Saint Thomas Aquinas was quoted as an authority 58 times, Saint Augustine 85 times, Pope John Paul II 128 times.[41] Other Vatican documents depend as abjectly on the reigning pontiff. When Cardinal Ratzinger released his criticism of ecumenism, Dominus Jesus, it cited John Paul thirty-two times. It is as if the pope had to undo personally all the damage done in recent decades by the council, by John XXIII, by Paul VI, by errant theologians, by defecting priests, by noisy nuns, by what are called "contracepting" couples. This one-man rescue operation is a staggering assignment.

Back-Door Infallibility

To effect the total re-foundation of the church, the pope feels he must use all his powers. Though he has not formally defined an infallible new doctrine, he has put a stamp of quasi-infallibility on position after position. He and his doctrinal alter ego, Cardinal Ratzinger, have called the bans on women priests, on contraceptives, on homosexual acts "definitive" or "irreformable" or "already infallible." To reinforce Paul VI's pronouncement on women's ordination, John Paul wrote: "Wherefore, in order that all doubt may be removed regarding a matter of great importance, a matter which pertains to the church's divine constitution itself, in virtue of my ministry of confirming the brethren, I declare that the church has no authority whatsoever to confer priestly ordination on women, and that this judgment is to be definitively held by all the church's faithful."[42] Asked to explain the force of that statement, Cardinal Ratzinger said: "In this case, an act of the ordinary Papal Magisterium, in itself not infallible, witnesses to the infallibility of the teaching of a doctrine already possessed by the church."[43] He gives as an example of such ordinary-magisterium infallibility the papal statement that Anglican ordinations to the priesthood are "absolutely null and utterly void."[44] Ratzinger's deputy in the CDF, Tarcisio Bertoni, with whom he sometimes issues joint statements, wrote in L'Osservatore Romano for December 1996 that such papal teachings are infallible, even though not defined as such.[45] Discussion of them is not permissible to Catholics, and the Vatican has ordered priests and nuns not to treat them as open for consideration.

Practically everything the pope has said on the moral questions causing major controversy has been colored with this perfumey tint of quasi-infallibility. Yet Catholics at large refuse to accept his statements as dispositive. Perhaps that is what is meant by the "smoke of Satan" pervading the church. It must be very frustrating to speak infallibly and still be treated as fallible. The pope might like to make a formal definition — exercise his "extraordinary magisterium" — condemning, for instance, the ordination of women as priests; but how can he, when polls show majority support for the idea, among priests and nuns as well as the laity? One of the hard facts of life, for a modern pope, is that there is not much use for the power Pius IX fought so hard to give him. Newman had predicted this would be the outcome of Pius's act — the weapon would be too unwieldy to use: "Some people think the [Vatican I] decree lessens the Pope's *actual* power" (emphasis in original).[46]

The great truths of salvation — the Trinity, the Incarnation, the Resurrection — are infallible by reason of conciliar and other church declaration. A new papal definition of them would look supererogatory or plain silly — which is why they are not even considered for papal intervention. They are truths too far above the threshold of papal action. The moral rules so agitating people now are far below that threshold. The pope would expose himself to widespread repudiation by the church if he tried to define (not just declare) that contraception is infallibly forbidden. So he weasels, treating it as infallible *de facto*, though not *de jure*. That leaves little room for any more *de jure* defining, outside the heaping of more titles on the Virgin — a comparatively safe course pursued in the popes' only two infallible definitions. But the popes are running out of new titles they can definitively add to Mary, and the one title John Paul has set a commission to studying — that she is the co-redeemer of the human race — would be a mortal blow to relations with Protestants, who rightly assert that there can be only one redeemer, Jesus. It might even strain the formerly endless capacity of Catholics to keep upping the Marian ante.

The pope must take comfort in his satisfyingly frequent exercise of "back-door infallibility," the power to say with certainty that this or that person is a saint in heaven. Ever since canonizing became a papal monopoly (in the seventeenth century), canonization has become a matter of declared truth.[47] Earlier saints were created by popular acclamation or local custom — and those acts can be voided. When the official certifiers of the church calendar, the Bollandists, find that an early "saint" in the liturgy is dubious or non-existent, he or she can be erased from the official roster — the most famous case is that of Saint Christopher. But once a Maximilian Kolbe, who distributed *The Protocols of the Elders of Zion*, is declared a saint by John Paul II, there is no way of canceling this passport into heaven.

Kenneth Woodward found that out in the case of Maria Goretti, the twelve-year-old girl who was killed for reportedly resisting rape in 1902 and was canonized by Pius XII in 1950. When a book by Giordano Guerri, published in 1985, argued that the evidence in the Goretti case was flimsy, and that Pius XII "had deliberately set out to make a saint of Maria Goretti in order to counteract the sexual immorality of the American troops, most of them Protestants, who had liberated Italy in 1944," the Vatican denounced the book and its author's morals.[48] The pope's concern over Allied troops' sexuality was real. The British minister to the Holy See had relayed it to his superiors in 1944: "The Cardinal Secretary of State sent for me today to say that the Pope hoped no Allied colored troops would be among the small number that might be garrisoned at Rome after the occupation." When this request was brought up with the man in charge of promoting Pius XII's canonization, he did not deny that it had occurred, but connected it "with the case of the 'Black Shame' after the First World War in Germany, when occupying black French troops were accused of rape."[49] Woodward noticed something about this official reaction:

> What interested me most about the Guerri affair was that at no time did the congregation consider reopening the cause. To do so, I was told, would put the congregation in the untenable position of second-guessing an infallible declaration by a pope. This, then, is one important effect of papal infallibility in the making of saints: the pope's judgment is final and irrevocable, and Roman Catholics are not permitted to question the sanctity of any papally canonized saint.[50]

Up to the moment when the pope spoke, evidence was evidence, and could be considered on its own merits. After that moment, nothing else mattered but the fact that the pope had spoken.

Modern popes have become shamefaced or evasive about an earlier quasi-infallible power, that of declaring when people got out of purgatory, but this reticence on indulgences has made them compensatorily pleased at declaring who gets into heaven. While seminaries and convents have been emptying out during John Paul's reign, at least he has been filling up the rosters of the other world's population. That may be some comfort when the task of setting the times right in this nether world labors under many difficulties.

20

Fighting Vatican II

IN 1985, Cardinal Ratzinger, the director of the CDF, gave a long interview to Vittorio Massori. It was released as a book, in which the cardinal says, "I want to emphasize that I don't like the terms pre- or post-
conciliar. To accept them would be tantamount to accepting a rupture
in the history of the church."[1] He is emphatic (and repetitive): "There
is no pre- or post-conciliar church."[2] He belittles Karl Rahner's description of the council as a "caesura" in Catholic history. But elsewhere in
the same interview he says that "after the council a new theological situation had arisen," and he describes post-conciliar conditions as a dark
departure from an ideal pre-conciliar church. There were "abuses associated with the post-conciliar years."[3] A decade after the council, he
said, "It is incontestable that the last ten years have been decidedly un-
favorable for the Catholic church."[4] There was an embrace of the world
that could only be corrected by a renewed flight from the world (*fuga
seculi*): "Now after long wanderings it is being discovered that the urgent task is to find again a connecting link with the ancient spirituality
of flight from the world."[5] This escape from the world has to be total:
"Today more than ever the Christian must be aware that he belongs to
a minority and that he is in opposition to *everything* that appears good,
obvious, logical to 'the spirit of the world' as the New Testament calls
it" (emphasis added).[6] This is not only a pre-conciliar position. It is
Pius IX's position in the *Syllabus* — denouncing the seductive fallacies
of progress, humanism, democracy, all of them fatally infected with
secular values.

Luckily — Ratzinger would say providentially — Pope John Paul II
came along to oppose "those who wanted to continue along a road

whose results would have been catastrophic."[7] The pope did this by going back beyond the post-conciliar interruption to the pre-conciliar church, since "there is only one church." The post-conciliar mood was a temporary fit of amnesia about this fact, a fit during which Paul VI rashly appointed liberal bishops:

> In the first years after Vatican II, the candidate for the episcopate seemed to be a priest who above all was "open to the world" . . . After the turn of 1968 [a key date for Ratzinger, as we shall see] and with the aggravation of the crisis, it was understood that the characteristics associated with this [openness] did not alone suffice. Thanks to bitter experience, it was realized that bishops "open to the world" were indeed needed but ones who at the same time were capable of opposing the world . . . The criterion for selection, therefore, gradually became more realistic.[8]

John Paul's bishops would almost all be men who passed various loyalty tests: "It is also necessary that all be in agreement on fundamental points."[9]

> Opposition to contraceptives, to the ordination of married men and even the discussion of the ordination of women has been made the criterion for becoming a bishop. One who so much as finesses on such questions has not the slightest chance of being chosen. The result is that John Paul has created an intellectual desert and called it peace. Bishops and theologians have been cowed into silence. Synods have been reduced to papal rallies. Heads that pop up above the parapet are lopped off.[10]

Closely connected with Ratzinger's claim that there is no pre- and post-conciliar church is his assertion that there is no pre- and post-conciliar Ratzinger. Though he is in disagreement with — and often investigating — the liberal theologians in whose company he began his career, he asserts that "it is not I who have changed, but others."[11] But he has changed his position on many issues, and has been opposed to developments inspired by Vatican II in many areas. As the 1960s began, Ratzinger (born in Bavaria in 1927) was serving on the board of the journal *Concilium,* and was friendly with the circle of those writing for it — Karl Rahner, Edward Schillebeeckx, Hans Küng, Johann Baptist Metz. At Vatican II he was a *peritus* for Cardinal Joseph Frings, a leader of the progressive majority. Ratzinger helped Karl Rahner create a new text to be substituted for the Curia's schema on the nature of the church — what became the document *Lumen Gentium*. Yves Congar, another of the progressive *periti*, actually feared that the Ratzinger-Rahner document was "too advanced" to be accepted by the council.[12]

But when Ratzinger returned to teach at the University of Tübingen, he resented the noisy student activists who were disrupting academic life. He later referred to them as espousing "ideologies that were tyrannical, brutal, and cruel," so that "anyone who wanted to remain a progressive in this context had to give up his integrity."[13] In the fatal year 1968, radicals invaded his classroom, and he was never the same. He left Tübingen for the more sedate new university at Regensburg and helped form a new theological journal, *Communio*, which was as conservative as *Concilium* was liberal. Almost all the theologians investigated or rebuked by Ratzinger as head of the CDF have been connected with *Concilium*, Ratzinger's original home base.[14] The Dominican priest Fergus Kerr says that the journal has become "certainly his bête noire."[15] According to Kerr, the cardinal's style has gone back to a preconciliar tradition of "panic-mongering hyperbole."[16]

Although Ratzinger cannot openly reject an ecumenical council of the church, his latter-day program amounts to covert repudiation of it on all its major points.

1. Collegiality

The pre-conciliar Ratzinger was enthusiastic about the national conferences of bishops, who could join with their colleagues to address problems that were broader than their individual dioceses yet did not call for a worldwide meeting or set of directions from Rome. While he was still writing for *Concilium* (in 1965) he could say: "Let us dwell for a moment on the bishop's conferences, for these seem to offer themselves today as the best means of concrete plurality in unity. They have their prototype in the synodal activity of the regionally different 'colleges' of the ancient church."[17] Two years later he was saying the same thing: "The church is essentially plural . . . [so] ecclesiastical acts at national or provincial or diocesan levels have their importance."[18] As late as 1972, he was still praising the national conferences in his book *The New People of God*.[19]

But by 1985 he was singing a radically different tune, condemning all uses of the national bishops' conferences. Bishops can act only within their dioceses, or with the pope in Rome: "The decisive new emphasis on the role of the bishops is in reality restrained, or actually risks being smothered, by the insertion of bishops into episcopal conferences that are ever more organized, often with burdensome bureaucratic structures. We must not forget that the episcopal conferences have no theological basis, they do not belong to the structure of the church as willed by Christ."[20] What had happened to change Ratzinger's position so dramatically? Well, those national conferences of bishops had requested marriage for priests, to meet shortages in their parishes. They had told Catholics they could respectfully reject the ban on contraception. When the conferences did not agree with Ratzinger, they lost the very right to exist in his scheme of things.

We can almost hear conservative bishops giving Ratzinger excuses for what their conference had done:

> I know bishops who privately confess that they would have decided differently than they did at a conference if they had had to decide by themselves. Accepting the group spirit, they shied away from the odium of being viewed as a "spoilsport," as "backward," as "not open." It seems very nice always to decide *together.* This way, however, entails the risk of losing the "scandal" and the "folly" of the Gospel.[21]

The democratic procedure of voting at the conferences is itself wrong:

> Besides, it is obvious that truth cannot be created through ballots . . . Contrary to a widespread conception, the classic procedure of ecumenical councils did not deviate from this fundamental rule. At these councils only statements that were accepted with a moral unanimity could become binding.[22]

As a matter of fact, the presence of a significant minority calling for moral unanimity at Vatican I had been rejected by the pope, and Newman concluded, "There was no real moral unanimity [for papal infallibility]."[23]

Ratzinger holds that bishops must rule alone in their dioceses (that is the independent and "courageous" thing, not yielding to others), communicating with other bishops only through Rome (that is the "non-bureaucratic" way), meeting with each other only at Roman synods run by (guess who?) Cardinal Ratzinger. Peter Hebblethwaite points out that this contradicts not only Ratzinger's pre-conciliar views but Bishop Karol Wojtyla's pre-conciliar practice. Ratzinger calls for individual bishops to become "spoilsports" by defying their national conference. Imagine anyone trying to do that in pre-conciliar Poland.

> For twenty years, 1958 to 1978, Karol Wojtyla was a member of the toughest and most cohesive episcopal conference of them all. In Poland, no individual bishop dared or sought to get out of line. Because any hint of division within the church would be ruthlessly exploited by the Communist Party, arguments among the bishops — and there were some epic ones — were kept strictly under wraps. To the world, the Polish bishops presented an impressively united front. If some outsider such as the Vatican diplomat they have not had since the war were to inform them that, as a group, they have no mandate to teach, I fear they would have invited him to jump with his theory into the Vistula River.[24]

But now the pope has a double standard like that of his soulmate Ratzinger. The bishop who observed a political discipline in the church under communism became the pope who crushed the discipline of liberation theologians opposing repression in Latin America. Liberation, an imperative behind the Iron Curtain, was "too political" in Chile and El Salvador.

Though Ratzinger poses as a champion of the historical church, it is not only Wojtyla's Polish record that makes nonsense of his attack on the conferences. As his own earlier statements recognized, the early church was full of pivotal actions by local synods. In the second century, remember, Christians were told to refer their concerns to the apostolic church nearest them, in their various spheres of joint action. As Tertullian put it: "If Achaea is close by, you have Corinth. If Macedonia is not far off, you have Philippi or you have Thessalonica. If you can reach Asia you have Antioch. If however, Italy is your neighbor, you have Rome."[25] In the third century, Cyprian of Carthage used local councils to put the churches of Africa back together again after the rebaptism issue had torn them apart. In the fourth century, bishops Augustine, Aurelius, and Alypius used the same form of meetings to discipline the churches of their province, when the separate bishops — who alone should have authority according to Ratzinger in his later phase — were often uneducated or lacking in resources that only joint action could bring to them. Naturally, the post-conciliar Ratzinger would not want to admit these facts, since Augustine and his allies used a regional conference to go around Pope Zosimus, who had exonerated Pelagius, to secure the latter's condemnation.

2. Ecclesiology

While Ratzinger was trying to shove individual bishops back into their own dioceses, cut off from comradeship with their neighboring prelates, he was also undercutting their authority in that narrower sphere. He said in 1985 that bishops should "courageously" take control of their own dioceses, not depending on other bishops to help them decide what is best for their domains. But when Walter Kasper, the bishop of Rottenburg-Stuttgart (and, like Ratzinger, a former professor of theology), took him up on that, and wrote in 1999 that he had to make certain pastoral decisions for his people — e.g., the re-admission of remarried Catholics to the sacraments — Ratzinger responded to him with great asperity in an article for the *Frankfurter Allgemeine Zeitung* (December 22, 2000). Ratzinger defended a CDF document he had released in 1992, which claimed that the universal church "is a reality ontologically and temporally prior to every individual church."[26] Kasper returned fire in *Stimmen der Zeit* (December 2000), rejecting both of Ratzinger's assertions — that the universal church is temporally and ontologically prior to the local church.[27]

Ratzinger's assertion that the universal church has a temporal priority over the local ones is clearly false. The "churches" of the New Testament were not mere outgrowths of a central church at Jerusalem (Rome, of course, would not have been in play at the outset). Paul stresses that he had his gospel direct from God and did not found his churches by authority from Jerusalem (Gal 1.111–17). The term "churches" in the plural shows that the mystical body of Christ is entire in each community of the faithful. It is to "the churches" that messages are sent in Revelation. Later on, when the communities are better organized, it is to the apostolic *churches* that appeal is made for authoritative teaching, their unanimity establishing the genuine tradition, which could not be dictated to any of them from a single source. To repeat from an earlier chapter what the Jesuit historian Klaus Schatz said of the early church: "A juridical superiority of one church over another, or certainly anything like papal primacy of jurisdiction, was completely foreign to Ignatius [of Antioch], or Irenaeus, or even Augustine

. . . All kinds of thinking in categories of hierarchical subordination or superiority will lead us astray" (S 3).

If a temporal antecedence is out of the question, what does Ratzinger mean by an "ontological" priority? He speaks of the ideal church as pre-existing in God's plan of salvation — a concept that could apply to every created thing. It was all there in the mind and will of God. But that is an atemporal concept, where "priority" has no bearing. Pursued to its Platonic consequences, this would make of the whole earthly church a poor reflection of some pure archetype. But the Incarnation made all such thinking obsolete. The real Christ is fully present in the church, in each of its gatherings, truly acting in time as well as in eternity.

3. Exegesis

The key concept of the council, that the church is the people of God, has become an irritating "catchword" to Ratzinger, a concept used to introduce a false democracy into the church. In the hands of the dreaded liberals,

> the conciliar emphasis on the "People of God" is transformed into a Marxist myth. The experience of the "people" elucidates Scripture. Here "people" is the antithesis of the hierarchy, the antithesis of all institutions, which are seen as oppressive powers. Ultimately anyone who participates in the class struggle is a member of the "people"; the "church of the people" becomes the antagonist of the hierarchical church.[28]

This is not just a matter of some liberals misusing the council's words. The council itself was faulty in its use of the Bible, referring too vaguely to a Jewish concept that obscures New Testament reality:

> "People of God" in Scripture, in fact, is a reference to Israel in its relationship of prayer and fidelity to the Lord. But to limit the definition of the church to that expression means not to give expression to the New Testament understanding of the church in its fullness. Here People of God actually refers always to the Old Testament element of the church, to the continuity with Israel. But the church receives her New Testament character more distinctively in the concept of the "Body of Christ" . . . Behind the concept of the church as the people of God,

which has been so exclusively thrust into the foreground today, hide influences of ecclesiologies which de facto revert to the Old Testament, and perhaps also political, partisan and collectivist influence.[29]

The Jewish concept is merely "sociological" and political. I suppose the same thing could be said of Augustine's "City of God," or the many Christian readings of the concept of the New Jerusalem. These do not exclude the mystical body, but are variant expressions for it.

Ratzinger neglects the key scriptural passage used by the council in its document *Lumen Gentium*, which is not from Jewish scripture but from 1 Peter, a letter that refers to the churches of the Diaspora purified in the blood of Christ (1.2), who are a structure built upon the rejected Stone that is Christ (2.5–6): "You are a sector of humanity set apart, a priesthood of royal status, a sanctified nation, a population God acquired to announce the wonders of his calling you from darkness into bewildering light. For you, formerly not a people at all, are now God's people — the uncared for have become the objects of his care" (1 Peter 2.9–10). The exhaustive list of ties to the Lord — as his chosen sector of humanity (*genos*), priestly body (*hierateuma*), nation (*ethnos*), acquisition (*peripoiesis*), people (*laos*) — is not "sociologically" reductive. What Ratzinger dislikes about it is that it is inclusive — and that is why *Lumen Gentium* found it appropriate *precisely* for describing the body of Christ. There are no non-chosen parts of this people, no non-priestly parts, no non-possessed parts, nothing that is *not* set apart as special to the Lord. It is all one *hierateuma*, the Spirit animating the entire "priesthood." As the council said: "In order that we might be unceasingly renewed in him, he has shared with us his Spirit, who, existing as one and the same being in the head and in the members, gives life to, unifies, and moves through the whole body. This he does in such a way that his work could be compared by the holy fathers with the function which the principle of life — that is, the soul — fulfills in the human body."[30]

Saint Paul addressed each church as a whole, not singling out parts of it; but this approach offends Ratzinger, for whom it carries unpleasant connotations of democracy. His is always a church of rulers and ruled. "It must not be forgotten that every council is first of all a reform of the 'summit,' which then must spread to the base of the faithful."[31] The hierarchy is a necessary "service to the baptized," since "the church of Christ is not a party, not an association, not a club. Her deep and permanent structure is not *democratic,* but *sacramental.*"[32] We should think of it not as a people but as a structure, with rulers providing holy *things* to the ruled: "*Communio sanctorum* means also to have 'holy things' in common, that is to say, the grace of the sacraments."[33] This is a deeply unscriptural reading of the church's reality, and therefore at odds with *Lumen Gentium.*

4. Liturgy

Though Ratzinger rejects the concept of God's people as too much a matter of "the Old Testament," he insists that the priest must face away from the people at Mass because it is the "Old Testament" way. Everyone must face east, which is the symbol of God as origin. "Judaism and Islam, now as in the past, take it for granted that we should pray toward the central place of revelation."[34] Besides, people at table in Jesus' time did not face each other, since they were all on the same side of the table (as in Leonardo's *Last Supper*).[35] But the table was U-shaped, designed expressly to promote symposium interchanges across the central space while allowing for room to recline at table. Well, Ratzinger says, what they did at table is irrelevant anyway, since the Eucharist is not a meal:

> The Eucharist that Christians celebrate really cannot adequately be described by the term "meal." True, the Lord established the new reality of Christian worship within the framework of a Jewish (Passover) meal, but it was precisely this new reality, not the meal as such, that he commanded us to repeat. Very soon the new reality was separated from its ancient context and found its proper and suitable form . . . This new and all-encompassing form of worship could not be derived simply from the meal.[36]

So: we are all to face one way (east) because that was the Jewish practice, but we are *not* to think of the Eucharist as a meal because that was the Jewish Passover. The Mass is the sacrifice of the cross, with the priest as a stand-in for the sacrificed victim. This sets the priest apart, facing away from the community, which is not to act like people at a meal.

Ratzinger hates the busyness of the congregation at modern Masses, "assigning all kinds of liturgical functions to different individuals and entrusting the 'creative' planning of the liturgy to groups of people who like to, and are supposed to, 'make their own contributions.'"[37]

But active participation is what the council called for, emphatically, in its liturgical document *Sacrosanctum Concilium:*

> Mother Church earnestly desires that all the faithful should be led to that full, conscious, and active participation in liturgical celebrations which is demanded by the very nature of the liturgy. Such participation by the Christian people as "a chosen race, a royal priesthood, a holy nation, a redeemed people," is their right and duty by reason of their baptism. In the restoration and promoting of the sacred liturgy, *this full and active participation by all the people is the aim to be considered before all else* [emphasis added].[38]

Here, as elsewhere, Ratzinger thinks that action by a group is undesirably democratic, if not actually socialist/Marxist. He deplores, for instance, the change from the Latin *ne respicias peccata mea* ("look not on *my* sins") to the vernacular Mass's "Look not on *our* sins."[39] The latter form is scripturally sounder — the Lord's Prayer says, "Give us this day *our* daily bread, and forgive *us* our sins as we forgive those who have sinned against *us,* and lead *us* not into temptation but deliver *us* from evil."

Ratzinger is being disingenuous when he says that he objects to the new liturgy, with the priest facing the congregation, because it makes the priest too important. We see *his* face, not the symbol of Jesus. Actually, when the priest turns to the community, he joins it, expresses with it the oneness of the mystical body making this eucharistic prayer. When the priest was fenced off from the people — by rood screens and language barriers, by power to consecrate separately from the community's act — he was far more important, which is just what Ratzinger misses. (Does Ratzinger, yearning back toward the old liturgy, really imagine that when Jesus instituted the Eucharist, he turned his back on his followers, muttered in a language they did not understand, and consecrated a cup he did not give to them?)

In his astounding attack on the idea of the Eucharist as a meal, Ratzinger does not address one of the central points made in the council's liturgical document, that the Mass anticipates the eschatological meal. *Sacrosanctum Concilium* (8) puts it this way: "In the earthly liturgy we take part in a foretaste of that heavenly liturgy which is celebrated in the holy city of Jerusalem toward which we journey as pilgrims, where Christ is sitting at the right hand of God." Clearly Jesus thought of the meal in this way: "'I longed beyond longing to eat this pasch with you before my death. But I tell you I eat no more until this pasch is completed in the reign of God.' Given a cup, he gave thanks and said, 'Take and drink from it in turn, for I tell you I drink no more until the reign of God has arrived'" (Lk 22.15–18). The Lord's Prayer prays that the reign of God should arrive (Mt 6.10), and it also prays that the eschatological meal should be anticipated (6.11 — see Chapter 27). There is a depth to the concept of the eucharistic meal that makes Ratzinger's shallow dismissal of it merely embarrassing.

5. Intellectual Freedom

The council encouraged the interchange of ideas by all members of the body of Christ. In the past, the Index of Forbidden Books had protected believers from the challenge of "dangerous" ideas — as in the past the laity had been forbidden to read the Bible on their own (either in the vernacular or without authoritative guidance). The anti-Modernist oath had crippled the intellectual freedom of theologians right down to the eve of the council. *Lumen Gentium* removed the protective walls built around the believers' intellects:

> Christ, the great prophet, who proclaimed the kingdom of his Father both by the testimony of his life and the power of his words, continually fulfills his prophetic office until the complete manifestation of his glory. He does this not only through the hierarchy, who teach in his name and with his authority, but also through the laity, whom he made his witnesses and to whom he gave understanding of the faith [*sensus fidei*] and an attractiveness in speech so that the power of the gospel might shine forth in their daily social and family life. They conduct themselves as children of the promise, and thus, strong in faith and in hope, they make the most of the present, and with patience await the glory that is to come. Let them not, then, hide this hope in the depths of their hearts, but even in the program of their secular life let them express it by a continual conversion and by wrestling "against the world-rules of this darkness, against the spiritual forces of wickedness" (Eph. 6.12).[40]

The other major document of the council, *Gaudium et Spes*, brought the same message: "Only in freedom can man direct himself toward goodness . . . Hence, man's dignity demands that he act according to a knowing and free choice that is personally motivated and prompted from within, not under blind internal impulse, nor by mere external pressure."[41]

Yet when John Paul came to America in 1979 he spoke as if Catholics still needed to be protected from knowledge. Addressing a group of theologians in Washington, he said: "It is the right of the faithful not to be troubled by theories and hypotheses that they are not expert in judging or that are easily simplified or manipulated by public opinion for ends that are alien to the truth."[42] A right not to know was something that Catholics were familiar with from the time before Vatican II. It seemed an odd thing to be promoting after it. But Ratzinger, too, believed in it. Not only should the laity be protected against the danger of theological speculation. Even bishops should not be specialists in theology (though both he and John Paul had been):

> As bishops, their function is not that of also wanting to play an instrument in the concert of specialists . . . [their] task rather is to incorporate the voice of the simple faith with its simple and fundamental intuitions that precede science. Faith, indeed, is threatened with destruction every time science sets itself up as an absolute. In this sense, bishops are discharging a function that is altogether democratic; a function which, of course, does not depend on statistics but upon the common gift of baptism.[43]

The West of the Enlightenment, or of modern science, is a constant threat to simple faith:

> I have understood that a certain "contestation" of some theologians is stamped by the typical mentality of the opulent bourgeoisie of the West. The reality of the concrete church, of the humble (simple) people of God, is something altogether different from that which is imagined in the "laboratories" in which Utopia is distilled.[44]

This concern for protecting "the simple" is an old attitude in the church, expressed by Cardinal John Heenan of England: "It is a form of pastoral sadism to disturb simple faith. Those close to God are untroubled by the winds of academic controversy."[45] Obviously, then, those engaged in the academy must be *far* from God.

Ratzinger believes that exposure to modernity has infected Catholics with a Protestant virus:

> Those who speak of a "Protestantizing" of the Catholic church nowadays probably see it as an alteration in the fundamental understanding

of what is meant by "church," a different concept of the relationship between church and gospel. There is indeed a danger of this kind of alteration; it is not merely the caricature drawn by certain integralist circles . . . Protestantism arose at the beginning of modern times; and thus it is much more closely related to the inner energies which produced the modern age than Catholicism is . . . So it is that those Catholic theologians, particularly, for whom their inherited theology no longer means anything, imagine that they will find a path already blazed for the fusing of faith and modern thought.[46]

Statements like that affect one's attitude toward academic freedom. If theologians were so corrupted by exposure to modernity and Protestantism, does that not suggest that undergraduates should be protected from such contagious stuff, or should be exposed to it only under monitored conditions and clerical guidance?

John Paul's apostolic constitution on Catholic universities, *Ex Corde Ecclesiae,* issued August 15, 1990, answers that question in the affirmative. It orders that "the number of non-Catholic teachers should not be allowed to constitute a majority within that institution." This is bound to affect academic excellence. To achieve the crucial fifty-one percent of Catholic faculty, the administration may have to prefer a Catholic to an academically superior non-Catholic — unless, of course, definitional games are played. What counts as being a Catholic — childhood baptism not followed up by any Catholic activity? Nominal church membership? Might a non-believer, but one who was baptized as an infant, claim that he meets the criterion for holding a job? In that case, what happens to intellectual probity? For that matter, is there a Catholic way of teaching mathematics or chemistry? Apparently the pope thinks so: "Catholic teaching and discipline are to influence *all* university activities" [emphasis added]. This reminds me of the congressman who, during the McCarthyite hunt for Communists in universities, wanted to fire a mathematics teacher suspected of Red sympathies. But how could he give a Communist turn to mathematics? "By teaching it wrong," the congressman said, "to weaken the West."

Catholic authorities should, of course, be more concerned for what is being taught in theology classes than for what is being taught to aspiring chemists. But the pope's handling of this aspect of the matter is to require that every theologian be directly monitored by the bishop of the place where the school is located, receiving a *mandatum* that authorizes his or her teaching and can be withdrawn at the bishop's discretion. The problem with this is spelled out by the former president of Notre Dame University, Father Theodore Hesburgh: "If church or state or any other power outside the university can dictate who can teach and who can learn, the university is not free and, in fact, is not a true university where the truth is sought and taught. It is rather a place of political or religious indoctrination."[47]

Bishops have assured university presidents that they will exercise their oversight with restraint; but the record of some of them is not reassuring — and the chilling effect of ecclesiastical supervision could well inhibit scholars, especially when we remember Ratzinger's recommendation that bishops should *not* be expert in theology, but should confine themselves to safeguarding the faith of simple believers. Newman expressed what a man can feel if the church seems always ready to pounce on speculation: "Now, if I, as a private priest, put anything into print, Propaganda [the Congregation for the Propagation of the Faith] answers me at once. How can I fight with such a chain on my arm? It is like the Persians driven to fight under the lash."[48]

6. Ecumenism

Part of the argument between Cardinal Ratzinger and Bishop (at the time, now Cardinal) Kasper concerned relations with other churches. Kasper, who was engaged in dialogue with Protestants, wondered how the church can ever reach out to other believers if Ratzinger refuses to allow diversity in the local churches. How could he talk to real Protestants if Ratzinger fears and castigates even "Protestantized" Catholics? How can ecumenical dialogue flourish if academic discourse among Catholics is restricted? Ratzinger's condemnation of bishops' conferences meant, in effect, that dialogue was denied within the church, making a mockery of any attempt at *external* discussions.

Ratzinger especially dislikes ecumenical gestures in which the Catholic side admits its share of blame for past misunderstandings and division: "A certain attitude in Catholic ecumenism after the Council was perhaps marked by a kind of masochism and a somewhat perverse need to declare itself guilty for all the catastrophes of past history."[49] Nothing could be more opposed to the council's own words on the issue, which call for an examination of Catholics' own faults with regard not merely to other religions but to atheism itself:

Believers themselves frequently bear some responsibility for this situation [of atheistic advances]. For, taken as a whole, atheism is not a spontaneous development but stems from a variety of causes, including a critical reaction against religious beliefs and in some places against the Christian religion in particular. Hence, believers can have more than a little to do with the birth of atheism. To the extent that they neglect their own training in the faith, or teach erroneous doctrine, or are deficient in their religious, moral or social life, they must be said to conceal rather than reveal the authentic face of God and religion.[50]

Kasper finds in Ratzinger a slide back toward the old view that "outside the church there is no salvation," a view that Vatican II finally gave up.[51] Kasper's suspicion of Ratzinger was confirmed when the CDF issued *Dominus Jesus* in September 2000. This document begrudges other religions the very title of church or faith. Failure to arrive at the truth leaves man little but religious "experience," not real faith:

This distinction is not always borne in mind in current theological reflection. Thus, theological faith (the acceptance of the truth revealed by the One and Triune God) is often identified with belief in other religions, which is religious experience still in search of the absolute truth and still lacking assent to God who reveals himself. This is one of the reasons why the differences between Christianity and the other religions tend to be reduced at times to the point of insignificance.[52]

Dominus Jesus became instantly notorious for calling all churches or religions but the Catholic church "gravely deficient."[53] In an accompanying protocol, Ratzinger told ecumenists to stop using the term "sister churches" for anything but particular *Catholic* churches. "There is but a single church." *And even among Catholic churches, Rome is not a sister church but* "mother of all the particular churches" (emphasis in original).[54]

This seemed to go beyond what Pope John Paul was trying to say to other churches in the jubilee year of 2000, and the pope assured people that Ratzinger's text had been "misinterpreted." John Paul took an even more significant step away from it when he made Walter Kasper a cardinal in the 2001 consistory, after having appointed him to the chief ecumenical post of secretary of the Council for Promoting Christian Unity. John Paul also gave the red hat to Karl Lehmann of Mainz, who had fought his own battles with Ratzinger. The two promotions were seen as a rebuke to Ratzinger, prompting Robert Leicht in *The Tablet* to speak of "a farewell ceremony for a whole era — the era of Cardinal Joseph Ratzinger."[55]

Announcing the end of the era may be premature. But the existence of that era, stretching over the last two decades of the twentieth century, cannot be disputed. Though Ratzinger was the second most powerful man in the Vatican, he would have been nothing without the support and agreement of the most powerful man. Between them, they did much to turn back or defeat the initiatives of Vatican II. As Kasper put it in 1999, "The progressive interpretation of Vatican II as a criticism and overturning of the centralism of Vatican I is being thwarted. An attempt at restoration is working to restore the centralism which the majority at the Second Vatican Council clearly wanted to overcome."[56] This was not a selective resistance, but a blanket effort, covering all the major matters raised by the council — the nature of the church, the concept of authority, the status of bishops and laity, the use of Scripture, freedom of religious inquiry, the liturgy, and ecumenism. Such a perfect match of council and resistance to the council had to reflect a deep antipathy in the Vatican of John Paul II to John XXIII's council.

21

Living Vatican II

THE DEFENDERS of Pope John Paul and/or Cardinal Ratzinger say that they could not have been denying the authority of an ecumenical council. They were just combating abuses, excesses, misinterpretations of the council. Of course, any complex transaction like the council — any contentious process of the kind that produced the conciliar documents — is bound to leave imperfect meshings of part with part, especially when the pope was intervening to help the minority baffle majority proposals or formulations or votes. As Peter Hebblethwaite says:

> Whenever the Council faced a difficulty, it had produced a compromising text which simply set the contrasting positions alongside each other. It repeated previous doctrines, and hoped that they would be modified by being set in the context of rediscovered doctrines. Thus the papal prerogatives were reasserted, but it was hoped that the emphasis on collegiality and the "sense of the faithful" would modify the exercise of the papacy.[1]

When John Kenneth Galbraith says the scale of change coming from the council was immense, it must be remembered that the scale was made possible because it was measured against previous immobility, against a myth and mystique of changelessness, against entrenched views and practices. The council had to indicate strands of continuity as it brought up new departures, it had to use old formalities of language and protocol, it had to put its new wine in very old skins. It is possible to tease out all these remnants of the past and create from them an impression of the council that is at odds with the aspect it bore for both its friends and its foes at the time. Some of those who later promoted a "conservative" interpretation of the documents were the very people calling them radical when they were first debated.

It should be granted, then, that there are several ways of interpreting the council, which can be boiled down to two main ways. The faithful at large take the view that it called for major change. The Vatican has considered that view unjustified, an exaggeration and an extrapolation from what the documents really said.

What justifies my saying that the faithful at large have adopted the council-as-change view? A number of separate considerations, which I shall try to put in some kind of sequence.

1. One indication of the popular attitude toward the council is the way the Vatican has had to deplore it as a major crisis — Ratzinger says that the masses have adopted a pernicious "spirit of the council," which he considers a spurious interpretation of it, a "Council Non-spirit" (*Konzil-Ungeist*).[2] He and the pope could not deplore so intensely something that did not exist, something merely peripheral or trivial.

2. The fact that the pope's men are not exaggerating is confirmed by polls showing that large majorities of Catholics ignore or reject teachings that are urged on them as authoritative, essential to their faith, and of great moral significance. This is not the way Catholics behaved in the past, and it has surprised non-Catholics as well as dismayed some Catholics in our time. This is true not only for "headline" subjects like contraception, the ordination of women, the marriage of priests, but for many other issues — intermarriage or intercommunion with those of other faiths, divorce and remarriage, sterilization and *in vitro* fertilization, abortion, gay unions. The great break with the Vatican occurred over contraception. This prepared the way for other disagreements, since the "disobedience" has been so extensive on this subject, despite maximizing rhetoric on its importance from the Vatican. In 1995, the National Survey of Family Growth found that

- ninety-five percent of Catholic women who had sex had used contraceptives at some point
- seventy-five percent of Catholic women still fertile and sexually active were using contraceptives
- fewer than three percent of sexually active Catholic women used the "rhythm" method of birth control, the only authorized method. (In this area, then, the church hierarchy is legislating for, and being followed by, only three percent of its affected members.)[3]

Furthermore, the number of Catholics having abortions is the same as the number of non-Catholics. One of John Paul's rare public shows of anger was when his own Catholic country of Poland ignored his emotional pleas against legalizing abortion. "This people," he said, "worships me with its lips, but not in the depths of its heart."[4] But does this divergence mean that the faithful are relying on a "spirit of Vatican II," as Ratzinger suggests, or are they just hedonists without any moral basis for their actions? The former seems more likely, since:

3. The people disagreeing with the Vatican do not consider themselves disloyal or disobedient. They do not feel that they are "bad Catholics." They continue to go to church and to take communion, without supposing that they must confess their actions or attitudes as sinful. Women who use contraceptives, for instance, go to church on Sunday just like those who do not use them. Only four percent of these churchgoers who are fertile and active use the rhythm method.[5] They do not reject authority in general, but recognize an authority at odds, on some points, with the pope. What is that authority?

4. Ratzinger is right. Vatican II explains their actions. They are following what he calls the *Konzil-Ungeist*. This does not mean that they know the council documents in any detail or could cite chapter and verse from them to justify their position. They cannot do that (often because there is no chapter or verse they might call on). What is this amorphous "spirit of the council" that they rely on? It is an image of the church arising out of the council's deliberations and the early implementation of its decrees. In this process, a church manifested itself that they found authentic, closer to the spirit of Jesus than the image of the church they held before the council. The ethos of the council that took hold in their imagination was that voiced by John XXIII, who said that the church is called to serve the world, not condemn it. The words of his opening speech to the council struck a note that did not die out: "Today the Spouse of Christ prefers to use the medicine of mercy rather than severity. She considers that she meets the needs of the present age by showing the validity of her teachings rather than by condemnations."[6] The pope threw open windows, and Catholics breathed in a bracing new air. John said that the church, that changeless and perfect thing Catholics had relied on, needed "catching up with the times" (*aggiornamento*), what he called "a leap forward" in his opening address. Catholics who admired Pope John saw the council as his legacy to them, and they mean to be true to it.

5. Besides, some Catholics — not all, but many, including those connected with Catholic journalism or the academy — had watched as theologians played a major role in steering the debates at the council. And those men being vindicated had been harassed, rebuked, or silenced by the Holy Office under Cardinal Ottaviani. The council showed that they had been right and the Vatican wrong on issue after issue. When some of the same people or their students began to be investigated and reined in by the CDF under Cardinal Ratzinger, this attempt to go back to the status quo ante was publicized and resisted, and not only by professional theologians. The objects of suspicion did not go quietly into CDF night. Instructed not to tell anyone that they were under investigation, they refused. They asked to see the dossiers on them, to be told who their accusers were, to be represented by their own counsel.

No books were written in the 1950s about Rome's treatment of John Courtney Murray; but there has been a flood of books and articles about the processes undertaken against Leonardo Boff, Dom Helder Camara, Hans Küng, Edward Schillebeeckx, Charles Curran, and others. If the theologians silenced in the 1950s turned out to be right, could the same not prove true of their epigones? Charles Curran was fired from Catholic University for holding views on contraception that were as acceptable to most American Catholics as Father Murray's views on democracy had been in the 1950s. The presumption of orthodoxy that the Vatican enjoyed in the pre-conciliar era was no longer secure. How right had it been about the separation of church and state?

6. Questions like these changed Catholics' attitude toward criticism of church authority, especially criticism made by qualified and loyal theologians. This was not a new development, except in the degree of its acceptance by ordinary Catholics. Newman had always taken the position that the theological discipline (the *schola theologorum*, as he called it) was an important part of the church's exposition of the faith. He compared "the school" to courts that adjudicate the meaning of legislative enactments in a modern democracy:

The schola theologorum is (in the Divine Purpose, I should say) the regulating principle of the church, and, as lawyers and public officers . . . preserve the tradition of the British Constitution, in spite of King, Lords, and Commons, so there is a permanent and *sui similis* [in its proper likeness] life in the church, to which all its acts are necessarily assimilated, nay, and, under the implied conditions of its existence and action, such acts are done and are accepted.[7]

This is a view of theologians very different from the one held by authorities during Pius X's reign of terror, when suspicion of intellectual independence cowed all but the bravest. We should remember that the work of Anselm, Ockham, Abelard, Bonaventure, Albertus, and Thomas was considered radical and dangerous in their day, yet the faith grew and was deepened by their labors.

7. In fact, theologians are not the only ones who now claim the right to think freely. Laypeople, too, feel empowered to form their own opinions and conduct their affairs guided by their conscience — which, again, the council said should be the norm. What Newman wrote of them in "On Consulting the Faithful in Matters of Doctrine" has been vindicated — that they are not merely passive receptacles of teaching formed elsewhere, apart from them. They are what the council called them — witnesses of the faith, guided directly by the Spirit who is shed on the entire people of God.[8] Yet a number of people, including non-Catholics, find something new or anomalous in the fact that people can disagree with the pope and remain Catholics. And some keep up a drumbeat of demand that such people conform to directives or get out. But how new is this situation, really?

8. I grew up — and so did some of the people calling our current situation intolerable — blithely ignoring papal teaching, not conforming to what the Vatican was energetically demanding, yet without any feeling of being a bad Catholic. Paul Blanshard pointed this fact out, and we thought he was a nut. He proved from papal statements and their explicators that we could not possibly be sincere democrats and loyal Americans, that we did not truly endorse freedom of conscience, toleration of other religions, or separation of church and state. He compiled a significant record of papal positions that put us at odds with all the pluralist American values we thought we lived by. In fact, he could have made a much stronger case if he had been better informed. He neglected a huge trove of genuine papal teaching, drawing much of his evidence from secondhand conservative echoes of the primary material. This reminds me of what Acton said when William Ewart Gladstone quoted papal statements to show that Catholics could not be British patriots in the Victorian era: "Your indictment would be more just if it was more complete. If you pursue the inquiry further, you will

find graver matter than all you have enumerated, established by higher and more ancient authority."[9]

Why did we shake off Blanshard's charges so blithely, feeling them wrong even where they were not literally false? Because they did not reflect the church we lived in and were, the experience we had of what our Catholic lives meant at their deepest level. If the pope said something that claimed we could not be living that life of faith, then the *pope* would clearly have been wrong. In short, our response was then what people are saying now. Admittedly, we were not aware that the pope had said things that were in conflict with our deepest American convictions. But if we had been forced into such an awareness, would we have stopped being loyal Americans, or stopped being Catholics? No. Because we felt no real contradiction between our attitudes toward country and toward church. In the same way, a woman using contraceptives now sees no conflict between doing that and receiving the sacraments. Her behavior is not merely idiosyncratic. It is adopted along with that of other Catholics she respects, who have reached their position conscientiously. In this way, they are witnesses to the lived faith of the church. If they are told they are doing what "the church" forbids, they respond that *they* are the church, *they* are the people of God. On this matter, at least, the pope is out of step with the church.

9. Can this be? Can the pope be out of step with the church? Let us be clear that papal infallibility is not involved in this discussion. Infallibility in the strict sense applies only to the two Marian doctrines. Some will say that even non-infallible statements of the pope should be treated as if they could not be wrong, but experience rejects that proposition. Holding to it made Paul VI write *Humanae Vitae,* convinced that if the papacy admitted it was wrong on such an important matter, people would lose their faith in the church. Well, the papacy *was* wrong, and people did not lose their faith in the church. They just lost blind trust in the papacy — which is not the same thing. And to lose that kind of trust in the papacy is not to rebel against it. The people I am describing do not want to overthrow the papacy, remove it from their lives or from the church's life. They value its Petrine charism of unity. They revere it as part of the body of which they are joint members. They know it is intimately linked with their faith. It is just not identical with it.

This is the point Acton was making in his public letter to Gladstone. He proved that the papacy had held a number of revolting positions in the past — the right to depose and assassinate non-Catholic rulers, to suppress religions, to banish infidels, to kill heretics. But Catholics of Acton's time no longer believed the pope on such matters, if they ever had, even though the papal authorizations were never formally withdrawn. Acton knew he could add to the list in all kinds of ways. The papacy had condemned freedom of conscience and of the press, the toleration of other religions, the administration of the sacraments in countries that had opposed the pope. It had held many outlandish views — some of them listed in my earlier chapters. And Catholics not only ignored such "teachings" in later times. Many disregarded them when they were fresh. Acton said that few British Catholics believed it was desirable and justified to overthrow Elizabeth I, despite Pius V's authorization for doing it. The "sense of the faithful" did not endorse the pope on that action. Newman said that the *sensus fidelium* did not endorse Arianism, even though almost the whole hierarchy did so, joined (as Saint Jerome said) by Pope Liberius.[10]

There is nothing in Catholicism that says we have to suspend our common sense or honesty when faced with papal assertions like that of Paul VI that women cannot be ordained because they do not look like Jesus, or that priests cannot be married though Saint Paul told the Corinthians that he had every right to be married, like Peter. Such "teachings" are dishonest, naïve, or stupid on their face. The claim that *in vitro* fertilization is immoral because it involves masturbation is similarly weak — it affected the American bishops' condemnation of stem cell research using *in vitro* embryos. So is the assertion of the South African Bishops' Conference that condoms probably cause AIDS rather than prevent it: "Condoms may even be one of the main reasons for the spread of HIV/AIDS. Apart from the possibility of condoms being faulty or wrongly used, they contribute to the breaking down of self-control and mutual trust."[11] (This statement was issued at a time when the Vatican was admitting that African priests were raping nuns to avoid getting AIDS from prostitutes and others.)[12] The Vatican obsession with condoms is heartbreaking in its homicidal consequences where AIDS is concerned. As James Carroll says, if American planes had been dropping condoms instead of napalm in Vietnam, the bishops would have had us out of that war in no time.

10. It is time to return to the question with which this chapter began. Which interpretation of Vatican II is the valid one, that of the papacy or that of the people of God? If one returns to the list of ways Cardinal

Ratzinger whittled at or denied the teachings of the documents, one can have little trust in his interpretative skills or good faith in reading them. In fact, the papacy has focused almost exclusively on the parts of the documents that reflect the minority view of the two parties — either to placate them, or because Pope Paul insisted on their inclusion. Of course, the papalists will say that the fact that Paul insisted is the real source of authority of the document, not what the majority of mere bishops wanted. But that leaves them with the same authority that insisted on re-imposing the ban on contraceptives. How trustworthy is that?

It seems that an interpretation more in accord with the majority of the fathers than with the minority best reflects the intent of the council. Otherwise we interpret its statements in ways that please those who opposed the council, who thought it was a bad idea beforehand, who hampered its action during its progress, and who have undermined its enactments ever since. It is a rule of legislative interpretation that one should take an act's meaning from those who supported it, not those who opposed it. However one might quibble with the exact terms of each item, it is clear that the majority of the fathers in the council meant to promote the view of the church as the people of God. The majority also promoted episcopal collegiality, liturgical change, and the freedom of the individual conscience. Thus, when a Vatican spokesman like Cardinal Ratzinger says that "people of God" is an invalid term, that collegiality should not exist at the conference level, and that the liturgy should return to its old forms, he is clearly not speaking for the council, no matter what other claims might be made for his views. The people he attacks, however, are not arguing with (or about) Vatican II. They are living Vatican II.

11. Cardinal Ratzinger has said that some dissidents have hijacked the council, carried it off for their own use or misuse. A contrary case is far stronger — that he has tried to minimize what he cannot erase from the council, to ease back around it into the status quo ante. The church at large has experienced the aftermath of the council, in full acceptance of it. He is the one who is out of step with the church. In fact, the Vatican has attempted a coup, a takeover of the conciliar church it does not like. I use the term "coup" advisedly. That normally means the effort of the ruled (some of them, anyway) to overthrow their rulers, the people overthrowing the government. But that is because the government is the center of authority in a political structure. The church is different.

The church is more than a polity. Its center of authority is the Spirit, diffused through the people of God. The Vatican refuses to accept that fact. It continues to speak of "the church" teaching this or that, of "the church" being opposed to contraception. Pope John Paul says "the church" never wronged Jews; only some of its members (*not* the papal member) did so. This is a usurpation of authority. It is an attempt to overthrow the people of God.

12. Luckily, it has been a baffled attempt. "The church" (in Ratzinger's sense) has decreed this and that. It issues commands in a vacuum. It appoints compliant bishops and puts submissive subordinates on liturgical commissions. It forbids ministry to gays. It orders Poles not to legalize abortion. It repeats and repeats its condemnations, precisely because they have not worked. With what result? It has demoralized its own troops, emptied the convents of nuns, the rectories of priests. It glorifies celibacy while priest after priest is being caught in repeated crimes of pederasty, and bishop after bishop is found to have covered up the crimes. Millions of dollars are paid in damages to the devastated families of priests' victims. The sociologist Andrew Greeley says there has been a drastic falling off in contributions to the church. Some Catholics resent paying money to hush up, or compensate for, criminal activities.

We have to thank God that the attempted coup failed. If it had succeeded, the good will engendered by the council would have been dissipated. Catholics would have retreated into embattled opposition to other religions, into distrust of science and intellectual freedom, into a peculiar obsession with condoms, into a cramped view of the Spirit that treats the clergy as the only genuine carriers of the gospel message. The generous vision of John XXIII would have been betrayed. We would have the narrow and semi-Manichaean outlook of Cardinal Ratzinger, who tells us (for instance) that women cannot become Catholic priests because the religions of antiquity had priestesses.[13] We would be accepting Paul VI's arguments for clerical celibacy. We might even be taking seriously John Paul's superstition that the Fatima secret referred to him. We should be asked, on entering church, to check our brains at the door.

Pope John Paul is far more attractive than Ratzinger — a charismatic figure much admired for his personal qualities. He gave great moral support to the cause of freedom in his native Poland. But if we measure him by what he most wanted to do for his church, his pontificate has been a failure — thank God. He is not a monstrous or disastrous pope, like John XII or Boniface VIII, or a misguided one, like Innocent III or Paul VI. He is more a well-meaning failure, like the man he beatified, who was also a charming person, Pius IX. Much as John Paul is admired, young men do not want to be like him. A charismatic figure like John Paul, if he had been successful, would have had men wanting to follow him into the priesthood. His undoubted merits would have carried people over dubious matters. He would have been given the benefit of the doubt, obeyed however hesitatingly. He would *not* have been, as John Paul has been, quietly but openly defied. It is true that the church has grown more learned and pious and free and varied during his time, but that was from energies he tried partly to impede or tamp down. The church, insofar as it is living on papal momentum, is still drawing on the legacy of John XXIII. Papal rebirth will occur, but it will be a rebirth of John's church, not John Paul's.

13. The papacy is always reborn, because it has many energies to draw on. Often it is the church that comes to the pope's rescue rather than the other way around. That is how the monasteries rescued the disreputable papacy of the tenth century. That is how Constance rescued the freakish triple-headed papacy of the fifteenth century. That is how Vatican II rescued the papacy of the anti-Modernist oath's reign of terror. The Bible scholar Austin Farrar once said, not disrespectfully, that the three synoptic Gospels stagger back and forth, holding each other up, like three drunks reeling merrily along. In the same way, the church's members lurch about in mutual support. Newman described the situation:

> I think I am right in saying that the tradition of the Apostles, committed to the whole church in various constituents and functions *per modum unius* [as if to a single thing], manifests itself variously at various times: sometimes by the mouth of the episcopacy, sometimes by the doctors, sometimes by the people, sometimes by liturgies, rites, ceremonies, and customs, by events, disputes, movements, and all those other phenomena which are comprised under the name of history.[14]

Father Schatz makes a similar point:

> Any ecclesiology that simply binds the Church to the pope, and not the reverse as well, is refuted by the historical experience of the great schism and the events connected with it. The example of [the coun-

cil of] Constance itself shows that truth lies not only in Ambrose's famous saying, *ubi Petrus, ibi ecclesia* (where Peter is, there is the Church), but in the reverse, *ubi ecclesia, ibi Petrus* (where the Church is, there is Peter). It is not always the case that Peter is the more definite entity who sets norms for the less defined laity of the Church. It can also be the other way around. (S 113–14)

Sometimes it is resistance to the pope that leads to papal rebirth — just as papal rebirth can be delayed by failure to heed loyal resistance. There would have been a papal rebirth if Paul VI had heeded Cardinal Suenens when he begged the pope not to issue *Sacerdotalis Caelibatus* or *Humanae Vitae*. As Chesterton said, the loving son cries a warning when his mother nears the edge of a cliff. The church at large now supports John Paul, not by agreeing with him, but by refusing to abandon him despite his attempt to re-create a status quo ante, a different church from the one that exists. We do not leave a father whenever he proves wrong on something. That is when he needs us. The greatest service one can do for John Paul is to continue baffling his attempted coup. That coup *would* be a disaster for the papacy. The job of a loyal Catholic is to give a support that is not uncritical, or unreasoning, or abject, but one that is clear-eyed and yet loving. Newman describes what happens when any other kind of support is given to the leadership of the church — "when she [the teaching church] cuts off the faithful from the study of her divine doctrines, and requires from them a *fides implicita* [unquestioning trust] in her word, which in the educated classes will terminate in indifference, and in the poor in superstition."[15]

~⌒~

22

The Pope's Loyal Opposition

SUPPORT OF THE PAPACY is possible for the conscientious only if certain things are recognized. I believe there are a number of such conditions to be met. One must recognize, for a start, that:

1. *The papacy is a deeply flawed institution.* Saying such a thing is considered by some Catholics to be disloyal. Apparently they believe that the only real Catholic is one able and willing to deny a long history of abuses and corruption. That assertion is usually prefaced with an "of course." *Of course* there have been individual popes who were bad, certain persons' peccadilloes or individual sins, usually committed long ago — Boniface VIII's political vendettas, Alexander VI's bastards, Julius II's war crimes, and so on. Sure, Dante and others in the Middle Ages put this or that pope in hell. But these were blemishes on an essentially noble and holy record, extraneous faults not connected with the core of papal teaching.

This is an evasion, an attempt to deny that the institution itself has been at fault over long stretches of time. The record shows centuries of principled and authoritatively ordered repression, centuries in which the papacy or its agents tortured and executed people for thought crimes, persecuted Jews and other non-Christians, persecuted (for that matter) Christians who differed with Rome's doctrines, suborned or excused political assassinations, sang a papal Te Deum for the Saint Bartholomew's Day Massacre, opposed political freedoms and democracy, burned books, burned witches — and called all these actions holy, blessed by God, even commanded by God.

Admittedly, the popes have been around so long that they have lived through stupid and criminal times, and have been infected by their surroundings. And power of itself tends to corrupt, especially when a combination of maximum spiritual and temporal power tempts men to a combination of apparent opposites, fanaticism and cynicism. Although early popes were automatically canonized, and an unworthy one was canonized as recently as 1954 (Pius X), few of the popes were saints, even by the standards of powerful men. In terms of basic decency, the average president of the United States has been a better human being than the average pope.

Are we to make it a test of faith that one denies or minimizes so soiled, so incriminating a record? Are only two stands possible — defending the essential righteousness of the papacy, the only *Catholic* option; and admitting a dark legacy, an entirely *non-Catholic* option? Where, then, does an honest historian like Lord Acton stand? He took neither of those positions. He thought the government of the church, like all governments, was corrupted by the very nature of power's exercise; yet he remained a believer in the church *and the papacy.* There should be nothing surprising about this attitude when we consider the larger truth of which it is only one aspect, namely that:

2. *The church itself is a deeply flawed institution.* It was said of Acton (and I have heard it too) that if he did not like the papacy, he should go join a church without the papacy. But how would that solve the problem? Where is a church not deeply flawed? Such a thing has never existed. Some Protestants like to imagine a "primitive church" that preceded the corruptions of Rome. Some Catholics (like Leo XIII) like to imagine a golden age of benign papal supremacy in the Middle Ages, one centered on the thirteenth century. Others talk as if only the apostolic time was true to the pure gospel. None of these views is even remotely accurate.

The thirteenth century saw the vicious crusades against the Cathars and others and the rise of the Inquisition. The "primitive church" was riven with disagreement and the clash of egos — between "Hellenist" and Jewish Christians, between Gnostics and the orthodox, between Pauline and Petrine factions. Paul's own churches rang with bitter feuds and jealousies. Ignatius was thrown out of his church of Antioch. Clement of Rome had to tell the Corinthians that brother-hurting-brother was an old story in the church — even Peter and Paul were turned over to Nero by their fellow Christians. For that matter, the apostles were driven by ambition, blindness, and rivalry during Christ's life. If one wants a pure or perfect church, one must go off to search for it on some other globe.

Some think the dividing line between a pure church and an impure one was the conversion of Constantine and the rise of Christianity to worldly acceptance, entangling it in compromises with temporal power. If there is anything to this charge, it has little to do with Rome and the papacy. Constantine took the action off to the East, where he concentrated ecclesiastical discipline in himself and his court. Those who want a powerless church need look no further than Rome in the fourth and immediately subsequent centuries. Did that make it holier? Is that the golden age yearned back to by those who think Rome was corrupted by its earthly kingdom? The fact that Gregory I had to submit to rule by the emperor is not a happier one than the ability of Gregory VII to impose his own imperial will — a fact that leads us to a further point that must be made when it is said that a Catholic must agree with the papacy. *Which* papacy? The truth is that:

3. *There have been many papacies.* The papacy that Augustine defied when Pope Zosimus backed Pelagius is not the same papacy that made Boniface say that everyone must be subject to the pope. The triple-headed papacy deposed by the Council of Constance and reconstituted by appointment of a new pope on its own authority is different from the papacy of Pius IX declaring itself infallible. And the latter is different from the papacy of Honorius, condemned by a council and by subsequent popes. The papacy of rival claimants, each one accepted as genuine by intelligent and virtuous people, is different from the unchallenged papacy of more recent times. The papacy that persecuted Jews is not the papacy of John Paul II, who went to Yad Vashem to honor victims of the Holocaust. The papacy that opposed democracy is not the same as the one that endorsed the Vatican II document on religious liberty. The papacy of Pius X saying that doctrine can never change is not the papacy of Paul VI, who endorsed the Vatican Council's assertion that it can change.

There have been popes elected by the people, deposed by councils, subjected to the control of corrupt families. Indeed, there was a whole millennium when the papacy had nothing like the primacy later claimed for it. Popes were chosen or deposed by secular rulers; they themselves chose or deposed secular rulers; they let secular rulers choose bishops. None of those things would seem acceptable in the modern papacy. The papacy has at one time or another backed almost any political arrangement available in the West, and has eventually opposed the same kinds of regimes it endorsed. It has itself been collegiate, subordinate, autocratic. Since papacies have differed so widely, we must recognize that:

4. *One is obliged to differ from the papacy.* If that were not true, we would all have to honor papacies that persecuted, lapsed into heresy, or supported despotism. We would have to believe in the many frauds used in canon law to define the papacy — the Symmachan forgeries, the false Isadore, the Donation of Constantine. We would still be believing that Jews are cursed and non-Catholics damned. It is not an honest "out" to say that we must agree only with the papacy of our time, not the straying ones of the past, since the claim of papalists is precisely that the institution defies time and change, that it spans the centuries with a single truth. We can thank God that this is not true. We must differ from some forms of the papacy because:

5. *The papacy, like the church, changes.* Newman said, "In a higher world it is otherwise, but here below to live is to change, and to be perfect is to have changed often."[1] Since he thought that the church is "here below," he obviously was asserting that the church must change — and if the church (the *whole*), then how not the papacy (a *part* of the church)? Actually, he conceded too much when he said it is different "in a higher world." That view was the source of misconceptions about the church. Early views on the church drew from Greek philosophy the idea that the perfect is the immutable. God had to be above change, and so his church must be changeless as well. Well, God is above change. But he is also above changelessness, as the doctrine of the Trinity indicates (see Chapter 23). Christ promised a Spirit-guided church, not a changeless one. The Spirit is perfectly able to steer the church through changes. If she were not able to, the church would never have survived so many divagations, so many dangers, so many disasters.

Those who deny that the papacy has changed rely on two main dodges. First, they say that preceding changes were developments, all right, but they were developments toward a single final concept of the papacy, a concept implicit in it from the outset. This is what the great classical historian Moses Finley calls "the teleological fallacy" in the interpretation of historical change: "It consists in assuming the existence from the beginning of time, so to speak, of the writer's values . . . and in then examining all earlier thought and practice as if they were, or ought to have been, on the road to this realization; as if men in other periods were asking the same questions and facing the same problems as those of the historian and his world."[2] That the history of the papacy is not the unfolding of a single idea can be seen from the fact that:

6. *Change in the papacy has not been unidirectional.* There was nothing in the concord of the early apostolic churches that would have indicated, as a next and natural step, submission to an Eastern emperor — and nothing in that submission that would have made inevitable a later claim to papal primacy in temporal affairs. That very primacy did not demand as its next stage the *loss* of temporal primacy (if it had, then popes would not have rejected beforehand such loss as opposed to the very nature of their authority). The claim that no doctrinal development is possible would not have "developed," as it were, into the concept that there *is* development at Vatican II. Negation does not magically turn into assertion.

The dogma of papal infallibility is not a natural outgrowth of the non-papal processes that established the creeds and the canon of Scripture, of the councils that defined the Trinity and the Incarnation, of the council of Constantinople that anathematized Pope Honorius I, or of the council of Constance that deposed all existing popes and appointed a new one on conditions established by itself. These events do not form an arc whose obvious destination can be traced throughout their passage. There was more going on in these historical tergiversations than the development of a single idea. In fact, the core of the unchanging truths — the great saving truths, the creed — was formed by the church before the fourth century, at a time when (as Newman said) there was no papal primacy. So the link between infallibility and the popes was lacking from the very outset.

I said there were two dodges used by papists to deny the changing nature of the papacy. The second one is to "define infallibility down," so narrowing it that every challengeable papal statement is excluded from its purview. But that just demonstrates that:

7. *The historical reality of papal teaching has little to do with infallibility.* We are told by papists that the pope was infallible all through history; we just did not notice that fact because he did not exercise his gift, even where we might most expect it. What more appropriate time for using it than in condemning the heresy of Pelagius? But Zosimus failed to do that — he must have been saving up his infallibility for some other occasion. In the same way, Honorius did not use his gift of iner-

rancy to condemn Monothelitism — in fact, he advocated it and was called a heretic by a council and later popes. Boniface was not saved by his infallibility from saying that outside the church there is no salvation. The history of the papacy thus becomes a series of near misses where the pope's only saving grace was a *failure* to be infallible — a fact that is somehow used to prove that he is, in fact, infallible. Popes, it turns out, can err over and over again on matters affecting eternal salvation — consigning people to hell for mortal sins like taking interest on loans, using contraceptives, remarrying, eating meat on Friday — without calling into question their inerrant power. They can release souls from purgatory or assure the entrance of saints into heaven — all without abusing (because never using) the gift of infallibility. Then what was the gift given for? Apparently for two reasons only: the definition of Mary's immaculate conception (in 1854) and of her bodily assumption into heaven (in 1950). This is a very odd gift of the Spirit, one not vital to the life of the church for most of the first two millennia of its existence.

So infallible truths are not connected historically with the papacy. But, one may object, if the papacy is not the supreme and unerring teacher of eternal truths, what is its principle of continuity through all the disjunctions and dead ends of its past? The answer to that returns us to the point where we must always begin when discussing the pope, to Peter, since:

8. *The essence of the papacy is the Petrine charism.* Peter was told to uphold his brothers, to feed the Lord's sheep. And that flock is to be one. Peter is not the master of truth or power or government. He is the center around which the other parts of the church cohere. The saints gather here, to pray for the church and each other and their leader. Even when the popes are corrupt, the church redeems them from its own resources. The abbots of Cluny and other monasteries prayed the papacy out of its slavery to the family of Marozia. When the pope went off to Avignon, Christians gathered to pray at Peter's shrine for his return — praying in conjunction with him even when he deserted, finding each other in their concern for him. John Paul II, in apologizing to Jews for wrongs done them in the past, always said it was the "sons and daughters" of the church who were to blame, not the teaching authority; but it has often been the teaching authority that strayed, and the "sons and daughters" who brought it back to the place where it belongs. They realized that:

9. *The papacy is the sacrament of the unity of the church.* Augustine spoke of the kinds of symbols that make a religion cohere: "Human beings cannot be associated as a religious entity, a true one or even a false one, unless they are bound together by shared symbols or visible sacrednesses [*sacramenta*] — such sacrednesses have an unspeakable power, and only the irreverent treat them with disrespect. It is wrong not to respect what religion needs for its performance."[3] The visible sign of the one flock is the shepherd charged with care of it. Peter's representative performed this function even before the papacy in the modern sense existed. In Augustine's day, the pope was the symbol of the unity of the apostolic churches in their shared custody of the tradition. By historical development, guided by divine providence, the pope has become even more strikingly the symbol of unity as the apostolic churches have faded in importance (some even fallen out of existence). Now Augustine's words have a weight he never thought they would have to carry. It is worth repeating here a passage from him that was quoted earlier (Chapter 8):

> Peter, because he was the first apostle, represented the church by synecdoche. As for his merely personal characteristics, he was a man by nature, a Christian by grace, an apostle and the first apostle by grace added to grace. But when he was told, "I will give you the keys of heaven's kingdom, and what you tie on earth will have been tied in heaven, what you untie on earth will have been untied in heaven," he was standing for the entire church, which does not collapse though it is beaten, in this world, by every kind of trial, as if by rain, flood, and tempest. It is founded on a Stone [*Petra*], from which Peter took his name Stone-Founded [*Petrus*]; for the Stone did not take its name from the Stone-Founded, but the Stone-Founded from the Stone — as Christ does not take his name from Christians, but Christians from Christ . . . Because the Stone was Christ.[4]

10. *Heresy is a sin against this sacrament of unity.* The heretic has hold of a truth, the very truth with which I began this chapter: the fact that the church is a deeply flawed institution. But the heretic thinks this can be remedied by taking off a segment of the church to live a purer life, free from all the corruptions acquired by the historic church. The very term "heresy" signifies, etymologically, an elite, a "selection" or select group. The higher wisdom of the Gnostics was like the unfallen status of the Donatists. The heretic has many virtues (almost too many), but

he or she is almost always a snob — the very last thing that could be said about Peter. It is significant that the Cathars were "the pure" and Manichaeans "the elect," that Calvinists were securely predestined, that Jansenists became worthier than others by a superior sense of unworthiness — they knew they were not worthy to receive the sacraments that other Christians received only as pigs take slop. The reformers live by reform, but a reform of only one part of the Christian population. They have a narrow perfection, of the sort that Chesterton described: "A bullet is quite as round as the world, but it is not the world. There is such a thing as a narrow universality; there is such a thing as a small and cramped eternity."[5]

The fate of most heretics is, not surprisingly, to become too pure even for themselves. They are fissiparous. Having purified themselves of the larger church, they find they have to purify themselves of themselves, as they shrink into smaller and smaller centers of censoriousness. They, too, find that there is no such thing as a perfect church, even though they aimed (as the broader church did not) at perfection. They come to rely on temporal powers, on the props and impurities of living beyond the first gesture of protest, the first stance of defiance. And when reform needs reform, it often finds it more difficult to criticize its own criticism of the larger mass of the imperfect and impure. This brings us to the next point, that:

11. *The papacy, as a center of unity, has many sources of renewal.* The historic church is, compared to the reform movements, a mixed bag, but with all kinds of energies in the bag. The church is centralist where heresy is fissiparous; but what it concenters is so huge and varied that many forms of life struggle back from the periphery toward the center. The saints and the critics and the loyal opposition are constantly at hand to differ from the papacy and recall it to the Petrine charisms of unity, apostolicity, and love. The British historian Eric John noted this about the aftermath of the Reformation:

The result of the schism was everywhere to identify the separated churches more closely with particular status-groups than the church had ever been before. Those groups which rejected episcopacy altogether tied themselves more closely to the status-group that formed them in the first place. It is not without point that whatever may be said about the post-Tridentine church in terms of the social groups it included within the apostolic structure, whether groups by source of income, social standing, or even color, it was much the most comprehensive.[6]

So when people ask why I do not go in search of a popeless church, I answer sincerely that I *want* the papacy. It is a blessing, a necessity — it is a requirement for the mystical body of Christ to remain one body. In fact, I think of what Evelyn Waugh answered when asked how he could be a Christian and remain so mean and uncharitable: "Just think how much worse I would be if I were not a Christian." In the same way, as bad as the papacy has been all through its history, just think how much worse things would have been *without* it.

Even in the darkest hours of the papacy, there is more life and light within the church than in the groups that split off from it. The Murrays and Rahners and de Lubacs agree with Chesterton that "the severed hand does not heal the whole body."[7] If you want to reform the church, you need a church to be reformed. The stark alternative to Luther or Calvin is not simply Popes Pius V or Paul V. The church of the popes is more than the pope. It is their *church* that matters. Looking at it in those terms, I prefer the company of Ignatius of Loyola to that of Luther, or Charles Borromeo to Calvin, Philip Neri to Melanchthon. The church gathers around the papacy, and supplies the resources for its rebirth and continued life. And, gathered there, the Catholic church has been highly successful in preserving the great truths of the creed. It has remained trinitarian while other Christians drifted toward a vague unitarianism or vaguer pantheism. It still believes in original sin, and in its forgiveness by baptism. It preserves the truth of the Incarnation, the actual embodiment of the Lord — including belief in his fleshly resurrection, his reincarnation in his mystical body at the Eucharist, the eschatological vision of his judgment and of life everlasting. The papacy, as I said, did not formulate the creed containing these truths; but it has been essential in preserving them, while heretics "selected" this or that item from the creed.

To say that the heretical (withdrawing) churches have their problems is not to deny that the central (imperial) has them, too — as most of this book has tried to make clear. Nor is it to deny that the churches not in communion with Rome are true churches (despite what Cardinal Ratzinger said in *Dominus Jesus*). The Second Vatican Council declared that all baptized Christians are members of the mystical body of Christ. As the Christian churches should be always reforming, they should be always repenting — like Peter, the symbol of the church. Final repentance on all sides will reunite the whole Christian church around the symbol of Peter.

Several people objected to my preference for Acton over Döllinger in *Papal Sin*. They said that Döllinger was more principled; when he disagreed with the pope, he had the consistency to leave the church. But that amounted to a simple equating of the pope with the church. Acton knew the church is more than the pope. The defenders of Döllinger remind me of those blowhard Americans who say, in a presidential election year, "If So-and-So wins this race, I am leaving the country." They never do, and they should not. If the "So-and-So" is as bad as they say, then their country has greater need of them. The true lover of a country does not leave it in its time of peril. The patriot is not one who thinks a country must be perfect in order to deserve his allegiance. Patriots are often critics of their country, since they feel so deeply that it is worth protecting. "A man who says that no patriot should attack the Boer War [or the Vietnam War, as the case may be] is not worth answering intelligently; he is saying that no good son should warn his mother off a cliff until she has fallen over it."[8] A person who loves the church can have a lover's quarrel with its leadership. He can appeal from the pope to Peter. He cannot wish to do without Peter and still be true to the gospel, since it is Christ who made Peter the first of apostles, our brother with a special mission to care for us, the servant of us servants.

V

THE CREED

I was asked to address a college class that had been assigned *Papal Sin* as a textbook. One of the students asked, "What authority do you recognize for your beliefs?" My answer was brief: "The church." I hope it will be clear by now that I do not always and everywhere identify belief in the church with belief in what the pope says — though the Catholic church is not separable from the pope. The church does teach certain doctrines, which one must *believe* in order to be a Catholic.

Around those doctrines, firm and always believed in, there have been peripheral stances taken by church authorities, some of which are not only non-binding but scandalous and morally repulsive, things to be repented as well as renounced — for instance, that one can earn indulgences by killing infidels, that Jews are a cursed race, that believers should be denied access to the sacraments if their rulers oppose the pope's state, that one can assassinate non-Catholic rulers. Other teachings were just culturally conditioned and passed with those cultural conditions — for instance, the ban on taking interest for loans. Some teachings are blatantly opposed to the New Testament (that priests may not marry). Others are merely silly (the ban on contraceptives).

These teachings form a penumbra (sometimes a dark one) around the core of beliefs always affirmed, those best summarized in the creed. Christians recited this as a condition of their baptism. Its articles were elucidated in key councils. Saint Ambrose taught the creed to those about to be baptized, and said they should cherish it as their soul's seal, and treasure, and watchdog.[1] Augustine taught the creed to those about to be baptized, and said that it must be a thing pondered and lived thenceforth:

> *The creed that you have learned in company and recited back individu-*
> *ally contains the words by which the faith of your mother church is stead-*
> *ied on its firm foundation, which is Christ the Lord . . . So what you*
> *learned and recited back you must store away in your intellect and affec-*
> *tions, reciting it in bed, pondering it on your walks, not forgetting it while*
> *you eat — letting your affection keep watch over it even while your body*
> *sleeps.*[2]

In my dim way I try to do what Augustine recommends. That is what
I meditate on at Mass, or in daily recitation of the creed when I say the
rosary, or in my reading on the truths of revelation. I do not, I confess,
continually meditate on the evil of condoms, or the horror of letting
women be priests. That is not "church teaching" in the same sense that the
creed is.

The creed is not all that the church teaches, but it is the church's central
message, against which the importance of other things is measured. Some
of the other things believed are corollaries of the creed, from the Marian
doctrines to belief in the canon of Scripture. I do not mean to deny any of
those things by concentrating on the creed as a starting place for discus-
sion of Catholic belief. But I find it odd that some Catholics treat periph-
eral things as if they were more important than the essential truths. They
do not ask me if I believe in the divinity of Christ, but if I believe the pope
when he says priests cannot be married. They do not tell me to leave the
church because I do not accept its teaching on the Resurrection. (I would
have left, long ago, if I did not believe in that.)

I hold the truths of the creed in company with the pope (and the rest of
the church), and largely because of him — since I am firmly convinced
that the church would not have preserved the creed as faithfully as it has
but for the steadiness, continuity, and symbolic unity supplied to the
church by the Petrine charism. There have been plenty of popes who were
unworthy representatives of Peter, who stood in the way of unity rather
than strengthened it; but all parts of the church have been unworthy at
times. That is no reason to jettison any of its constituent members. At least
we have preserved and honored the symbol of Peter. Other Christian
churches, insofar as they lack this recognition of Peter's importance, are
omitting something that is in the gospel.

The Spirit works in other churches, which sometimes preserve aspects of
the gospel more authentically than Catholics do. But the papacy makes us
more aware of the oneness of Christ's body. It helps us resist tendencies

that some in other churches succumb to — an individualism that tugs against the feeling for community, a rationalism that dilutes the scandal of the Incarnation, a symbolic sense that dims the reality of the Resurrection. Some Catholics succumb to these trends, now as in the past; but in general we are less ready to break off from our fellows, to take our own tack, to think of ourselves as apart from the church. To disagree with one another is not seen as denying our solidarity with the great body of the faithful over the great span of our shared history.

I am about to give my own reasons for believing the creed. I feel uncomfortable about being so personal. But I am not called on to give a general theology of the church, or to convince other people to accept what I believe. The question addressed to me was "What precisely do you believe if you continue to call yourself a Catholic?" There is no way to give that question an impersonal answer. What is at issue, for the moment, is not the truth of the creed but the truth of my own profession of it. I shall try to explain what the creed means to me, and how others have helped me to accept it in that meaning. Some of these people are known only to me. Others are part of our shared Catholic heritage — especially, in my case, Saint Augustine, Cardinal Newman, and Gilbert Chesterton.

The Apostles' Creed

I believe in God, the Father almighty, creator of heaven and earth.

And in Jesus Christ, his only Son, our Lord; who was conceived by the Holy Spirit, born of the Virgin Mary, suffered under Pontius Pilate, was crucified, died, and was buried. He descended into hell; the third day he rose again from the dead; he ascended into heaven, sits at the right hand of God, the Father almighty; from thence he shall come to judge the living and the dead.

I believe in the Holy Spirit, the holy Catholic Church, the communion of saints, the forgiveness of sins, the resurrection of the body, and life everlasting.

Amen.

23

I believe in God . . .

THE CREED IS the profession of faith that was, in some form, voiced at baptism, since belief was the condition of Jesus' salvific work. "Your belief has been your healer" (Mk 10.52). The earliest Western profession developed into what was soon accepted as the Apostles' Creed, supposedly formulated by the Twelve before they left Jerusalem, each on a separate mission to his part of the world. Each clause was attributed to a specific apostle.

> *Peter* dictated: "I believe in God, the Father almighty, creator of heaven and earth"
> *Andrew* added: "and in Jesus Christ, his only son, our Lord,"
> *James the Greater* continued: "who was conceived by the Holy Spirit, born of the Virgin Mary,"
> *John:* "suffered under Pontius Pilate, was crucified, died, and was buried,"
> *Thomas:* "descended into hell; the third day he rose again from the dead;"
> *James the Lesser:* "he ascended into heaven, sits at the right hand of God, the Father almighty,"
> *Philip:* "from thence he shall come to judge the living and the dead."
> *Bartholomew:* "I believe in the Holy Spirit,"
> *Matthew:* "the holy Catholic church, the communion of saints,"
> *Simon:* "the forgiveness of sins"
> *Thaddaeus:* "the resurrection of the body,"
> *Matthias:* "and life everlasting."[1]

This tale of the apostles' collaboration on the creed was old when Rufinus put it in writing in 404, and it continued to be held as true until the seventeenth century. Thomas Aquinas, admittedly, had an objection: the creed seemed to him to have fourteen articles, not twelve.[2] In the fifteenth century, Lorenzo Valla, who proved that the Donation of Constantine was a fake, suggested that the same thing might be true of this story; but believers were so shocked that he had to recant.[3] What the story indicates is true enough — that the church held this creed as ancient, universal, and of apostolic authority. Modern scholarship traces its core to a basic form used in baptism before 100 C.E.[4] This made the creed the most important text outside the New Testament itself. It was one of the two texts "handed over" to the Christian just before baptism, to be "handed back" in the profession of faith required for the reception of the sacrament. The other text, handed over a week later, was taken from Scripture — the Lord's Prayer (Mt 6.9–13).

In the West, these texts were not revealed to the catechumens until the moment of the handing over (*traditio*) — two weeks before baptism in the case of the creed, one week in the case of the Lord's Prayer. The catechumens had to commit the words to memory for the handing back (*redditio*), and they were forbidden to write them down. A sermon of Augustine (213) indicates that some had trouble remembering them exactly, and he had to prompt them in a kindly way. The oral requirement may originally have been a matter of secret initiation (*disciplina arcani*), though it cannot have been a real secret for very long. Augustine in his sermons gives the procedure a symbolic meaning — that the words should be inscribed on one's heart, not on external pages; as a personal expression, not impersonal legislation.[5] Oral communication personalized the face-to-face nature of the Christian community.

The customary term for the creed indicated its importance. It was called "the symbol." The Greek word *symbolon* means a "putting together" (*sym-ballein*). Contracts were parted — just as later indentures were — and their binding nature was indicated by the exact fit of the two parts when they were rejoined. The Christian proved his or her commitment by this exact correspondence with what the church proposed for belief. Because the *symbolon* was an authenticating device, "symbol" also came to mean a password of admission. Augustine calls it a *signum datum* in Sermon 214 (PL 38.1072).

The creed and the Lord's Prayer were so intimately associated with baptism that Augustine says daily recitation of the Lord's Prayer will be a kind of daily re-baptism.[6] The connection of the creed with baptism was even closer, since the basic form of the creed was identical with the questions asked of the baptisand at the most important part of the ceremony. The person receiving the sacrament was stripped and went into the baptismal water. While standing in the water, he or she was asked:

1. "Do you believe in God, the Father almighty?" When the answer yes was given, the person was totally immersed in the water.
2. The next question was, "Do you believe in Christ Jesus, his son?" Once again a yes was given, with a second immersion.
3. A third immersion followed the third question, "Do you believe in the Holy Spirit in the holy church?"

I give the baptismal interrogatory in what J.N.D. Kelly argues was the core of the old Roman rite.[7] It is clearly connected with Mt 28.19: "Journey off to make disciples among all peoples by baptizing them into the honor of Father, Son and Holy Spirit."[8] The Bible text, roughly contemporary with the practice, probably reflected it rather than prescribed it. But what is clear is that the Christian believed in three persons from the outset. The later declaratory (not interrogatory) creeds built on this core profession. It had three main articles:

I believe in God, the Father almighty
And in Christ Jesus his son
And in the Holy Spirit in the holy church.

Additions to each article would be made in the second century, mainly to combat varieties of Gnosticism. The divine status and the interrelation of the three persons believed in would not be definitively explored until the fourth century. At the outset it was enough that the New Testament clearly treated of the Son sent into the world by the Father, and of the Spirit sent into the world by the Son. That was the most basic set of beliefs that one had to profess in order to qualify for baptism. Christianity was born trinitarian (however that is understood), not unitarian. The relations between the three persons in whom the Christian believed would be discussed, understanding of them deepened, formulations of them refined. But it is clear that any religion that could be called Christian had to retain all three. The doctrine of the Trinity developed, but only because it was *forced* to develop in order to

remain true to the commitment to the *three* persons while retaining
the Judaic monotheism that was Christianity's matrix.

The commonsense objection to this enterprise is obvious — that
"three into one won't go" — and Gibbon made fun of the mental con-
tortions that the trinitarian councils indulged in. For him this exercise
typified the decline of Greek philosophy into Christian sophisms. Gibbon's fellow in the Enlightenment, Thomas Jefferson, did not think
anyone could honestly believe in "the Athanasian paradox" of "a god
like another Cerberus with one body and three heads."[9] Well, honesty is
precisely the issue. I think it took great intellectual honesty for the
Christians to subject what they experienced as having overpowering
force — Jesus, the other two persons he spoke of, and the one God that
Jews were committed to — to an examination of all the contradictions
they seemed to entail. In order to assess their effort, we should keep
two things in mind: that God is above all reality that we have direct experience of, and that number is below that reality.

On the first point, the Bible assures us that we cannot know God's
ways. As Augustine put it, "Since it is God we are speaking of, you do
not understand it. If you could understand it, it would not be God."
We speak of God only in inadequate analogies, where nothing that we
say is strictly true. "Whatever you can describe will not be indescribable. But God, precisely, is indescribable."[11] Newman says the same:
"Not even the Catholic reasonings and conclusions as contained in
Confessions [creeds] and most thoroughly received by us are worthy of
the Divine Verities which they represent; but are the truth only in as
full a measure as our minds can admit it; the truth as far as they go, and
under the conditions of thought which human feebleness imposes."
Augustine says that we speak of God only in analogies, Newman that
we use "economies" of speech — limited forms of expression that are to
be accepted only if they move us partway toward the unreachable truth
rather than drift us farther off from it. God the Father is not a father.
God the Son is not a son. The Holy Spirit is not a wind. We call them
such as an approximation of the truth we only partially apprehend. We
come a little bit closer to the truth, that is, by reflecting on what the
terms suggest without their being literally true. Our creed, according to
Newman, can only be something as clumsily phraseable as this: "[God]
is truly One, if the idea of Him falls under earthly number. He has a triple Personality, in the sense which the Infinite can be understood to
have personality."[13]

If God is a mystery in one direction, number is a mystery in the opposite direction. God is too rich a reality to be apprehended by human faculties. Number is too thin a reality to be literally embodied. There is no One in nature. Everything we see and know has different degrees of unity and diversity. Plotinus's One is a mental construct like Euclid's triangle. Like the triangle, it is a more useful construct than the unicorn; but it has no more secure grounding in what actually exists. Rather less, in fact, since the animal parts of which the unicorn is fabricated do exist. Plato took the absence of the One among changeable and imperfect beings as a sign that the One is perfect, is above other realities by being realer than they are. Actually, number is only useful because it is less real. Apply number to reality and you make it more manipulable by reducing its complexity. Number the pages of a book — you make it easier to find a passage by reference to its page number. But the numbers will be different in another edition of the book, and the book will be the same.

These things had occurred to me — perhaps because my own mathematical deficiencies made me prejudiced against number — when I was pondering the Trinity during my atheistic depression in the seminary. But I can find confirmation of my bias in people who are very good indeed at mathematics — for instance: "There is no mathematics out there in the physical world that mathematical scientific theories describe."[14] Mathematics is a mental construct based largely on conceptual metaphors.[15]

So the three-into-one-won't-go problem is not as clear-cut a matter as at first it seems. We are dealing with the conjunction of two different levels of reality — the realer-than-real reality of God and the less-real-than-it-seems reality of number. The unity involved and the diversity involved, and the language we use to describe them, are not of a single conceptual order, like the body parts of Jefferson's Cerberus. It adds to the misunderstanding that so much of our inherited God-talk involves concepts of perfection and immutability. For Platonists, the highest good was unchanging, and man's highest faculty for grasping it was the intellect. The perfect is sealed in on itself; it cannot be affected by the less perfect. And the intellect can only receive the highest truth, not interact with it. The divinity arrived at was static, not dynamic. As much as Jefferson despised Plato, he agreed with him that any God who would bother to answer human prayer is not a high enough God to meet our exacting standards for him.

In Greek thought, the highest reality was impersonal. Perhaps that is why, as the Plotinus scholar Paul Henry argued, so little of classical thought was devoted to the human person.[16] Even the terms used for it are shallow: Greek *prosopon* and Latin *persona* both mean "mask," something added onto the human reality behind it. Personality is always *inter*personality, and Aristotle defined relations with others as "accidents," mere adjuncts to underlying substance. Augustine, in what Henry calls the most brilliant breakthrough in thinking about the person, turned Aristotle upside down. What if relationship could be neither substance nor accident? What if God the Father were *entirely* his relationship to God the Son and God the Spirit? This relationship is a matter neither of substance nor of accident. If it were God's substance to be Father, he would be father of himself. If his fatherhood were an accident, like a human father's, there would have been a time when he was not a father, or he could cease to be a father by losing his son. Neither happens with God.[17]

Human lovers talk as if they aspire to have their *whole being* devoted to the beloved. Our loves fall short of that aspiration. God's, Augustine claimed, does not. In him personal interrelationship is perfected: "Love is the act of a lover *and* the love given to a loved person. It is a trinity: the lover, the loved, and love itself."[18] Chesterton, as often happens, sounds as if he had read Augustine, though he had not:

> If there is one question which the enlightened and liberal have the habit of deriding and holding up as a dreadful example of barren dogma and senseless sectarian strife, it is this Athanasian question of the Co-Eternity of the Divine Son. On the other hand, if there is one thing that the same liberals always offer as a piece of pure and simple Christianity, untroubled by doctrinal disputes, it is the single sentence "God is Love." Yet the two statements are almost identical; at least one is very nearly nonsense without the other. The barren dogma is only the logical way of stating the beautiful sentiment. For if there be a being without beginning, existing before all things, was He loving when there was nothing to be loved? If through that unthinkable eternity He is lonely, what is the meaning of saying He is love? The only justification of such a mystery is the mystical conception that in His own nature there was something analogous to self-expression; something of what begets and beholds what it is he has begotten. Without some such idea, it is really illogical to complicate the ultimate essence of de

ity with an idea like love. If the moderns really want a simple religion of love, they must look for it in the Athanasian Creed.[19]

In the Book of Genesis (2.18) we read that "it is not good for man to be alone." The Christian doctrine of the Trinity means that it is not good for God to be alone. He is a society, a dialogue, a set of interrelationships that impel him out from himself toward himself. He is pure act, and the divinity is a raging field of energy, of self-emptying to fulfill the self.

Augustine reversed the tendency of "enlightened" thinkers about the divinity, who try to escape anthropomorphism by abandoning myth for philosophy. Augustine embraced anthropomorphism. In his view the noblest of created things we know on earth is the human person. Anthropomorphism is just an application of Gen 1.6: "And God said, 'Let us make man in our image.'" Augustine says that he was wrong to seek God in the external world. He turned inward to find him. "I was outside myself, and you within [*intus eras et ego foris*] . . . deeper in me than I am in me [*interior intimo meo*]."[20] The most intimate experience we have of unity and diversity conjoined is our sense of our own self. Each of us has an identity. I am not you. I am not several people. I am me. But what is that me? Augustine wanders through his own memory as if through strange caverns. We say or do things that do not express "the real me." We speak of trying to "find ourselves." We say we have been self-forgetful. We haul ourselves before ourselves, as if we had captured a hiding dog and pulled it up by the scruff of the neck to look it in the face. Even this self-inquest is a kind of mystery. He asks, "Where shall I put myself to view myself?" — and has to answer that he does not look out at himself as at a detachable object of inspection; he has to effect some startling inward turn to make the mind be both the thing looked at and the thing looking.[21] He has to make himself two in order to understand himself as one.

But more often he made himself three in order to appreciate the richness of his identity. In a dazzling series of introspective analyses, he finds over a dozen ways in which three inner activities cooperate as one within him. Take, for instance, remembering, understanding, and willing. Each of these has a twofold aspect — considered in itself, as a faculty for doing something, and as a faculty doing that (actually remembering, understanding, or willing). Each, that is, has the potential for a relationship with its object, with the thing remembered, understood, or willed, and each (in both aspects) can be that object for the others — the memory, for instance, recalling not only what was understood or willed, but what understanding and willing are. Or the will moving the memory not only to recall a specific thing but to recall what recalling means. In this rich interplay, the three activities are simultaneous, mutually comprehensive, and equal to one another.

These three things — the memory, the understanding, and the will — are not three lives, but one life; not three minds, but one mind; and therefore not three substances, but one substance.

Memory, for instance when it is called a life, or a mind, or a substance, is being identified as it is in itself. But when it is called precisely the *memory*, there is reference to something beyond itself [that is remembered].

The same holds true for the understanding and the will. When called by those names, there is reference to something beyond themselves [to be understood or willed]. But each of them is, in itself, a life, or a mind, or a substance.

So all of them are one, insofar as they share one life, one mind, one substance; and whenever they are named as such, the *singular*, not the plural, is to be used of each of them and of all together. But they are a *plural*, three, when each refers, beyond itself, to the others.

And each is *equal* to the others, taken singly or together, since each *contains* the others, either singly or together. In fact, not only does each contain the others, but each contains the totality of all three.

For I *remember* that I have memory, understanding, and will.

I *understand* that I understand, and will and remember.

I *will* that I will, and remember and understand.

And I remember all of my memory and understanding and will, all at the same time.

If there is any memory I do not remember, it is not in my memory; for nothing can be more remembered than what is in the memory. So my memory is of my *entire* memory.

Similarly, I know that I understand all that is in my understanding, and know that I will all that is in my will — and this knowledge, too, I remember.

I remember, then, the entirety of what I understand and what I will; and when I understand all three together, it is their entirety I understand. For when I do not know things that can be understood, they are not in *my* understanding. And what is outside my understanding I can neither remember nor will, since if I remember or will something understandable, it must be in my understanding.

My will in the same way contains the entirety of what I understand and what I remember, whenever I want to activate anything from my store of understanding or memory.

Since any of the three contains any of the other two, or all of them, they must be equal to any of the others, or to all of them, each to all and all to each — yet these three are one life, one mind, one substance.[22]

Augustine hedges this whole discussion around with caveats. He is not describing literally what goes on in the inscrutable Trinity. He is just trying to see how unity and diversity can be experienced together, if only in dim images of what the creed says about God's triune being. The fact that the mind is a mystery to itself just shows how appropriate it is as a pathway to God: "Our mind cannot be understood, even by itself, because it is made in God's image."[23]

. . . the Father almighty, creator of heaven and earth . . .

FEMINISTS MAY OBJECT to the patriarchal language of the creed, but it is too solidly enmeshed both in Hebrew Scripture and in Christ's rescue-message (gospel) to be forsworn. It is precisely this kind of personalist language in the Bible that saved Augustine from thinking of God in featureless neo-Platonic categories. The Father of the Bible is a passionate person, jealous, angry, loving. He has affective ties with his people, the people of God.

> As a father has compassion on his children,
>   So has the Lord compassion on all who fear him.
> For he knows how we were made,
>   He knows full well that we are dust. (Psalm 103.13–14)[1]

The great proof of his love is the sending of his Son, who comes only to do his will, and into whose humanity we are incorporated, completing our relationship to him as sons-in-the-Son. (There is that gendered language again; but the Incarnation is a specific act in human history, and one cannot simply deny that it was as a *man* that the Son came to us. Things will be different when we come to speak of the Spirit.)

The creed affirms that there was only one creator, distinguishing Christianity from polytheistic creeds that recognized several creators — Prometheus, for instance, making man, and Epimetheus making woman. But this article of the creed was aimed more immediately at Gnostic deniers of a single and beneficent creator. Some sects had a dismissive attitude toward the inferior world of matter, and gave a lower god the credit or the blame for it, a god who was not above making messy things like the intestinal tract or pointless nuisances like the flea. The Gnostic god made heaven, but he emphatically did *not* make earth.

Orthodox Christians could not take such a hostile view of matter and the flesh — Christ had, after all, assumed mortal flesh, intestinal tract and all. And Tertullian could find much sagacity in a flea:

Why should trivial creatures embarrass me? If you think the creator a bungling workman, just look at a little flower in the hedge (I call not in whole meadows of them), or a tiny shell from any beach (I cite not the Red Sea), or a single feather from a pigeon (not to mention a peacock). You ridicule the minor artifacts our major artificer has equipped with clever strategies and weapons, teaching us that the large can be lodged in the little — "strength in weakness," as the apostle says: Can you make anything that is able to build like the bee, fortify like the ant, weave like the spider, or spin like the silkworm? Can you ignore the very beasts in your bed or bedclothes — the poison of the canthar, the probings of the gnat, the trumpet and spear of the mosquito? The great things of creation must truly be great if the little things can please or annoy you so. Then how can you despise the one who made them? Or, to cap the matter, haul yourself before yourself — just look at what a man is, at his outer and inner self. This at least you must admire.[2]

Augustine, too, had to deal with attacks on the material creation in the fourth century, attacks mounted by the Manichaeans, to whom he replied with a celebration of everything that God made:

I could descant in all candor on the glories of the worm, when I look at its iridescence, its perfect corporeal rotundity, its interaction of end with middle, middle with end, each contributing to a thrust toward oneness in this lowest of things, so that there is no part that does not answer to another part harmoniously. And what of the principle of life effervescing its melodious order through this body? — its rhythmic activation of the whole, its quest for that which serves its life, its triumph over or revulsion from what threatens it, its reference of all things to a normative center of self-preservation, bearing a witness more striking than the body's to the creative unity that upholds all things in nature.[3]

This encomium to creation's beauty resembles some arguments used to prove God's existence from the marvelous concinnities of the cosmos — so many complex things, huge and minute, deftly fitting into each other. Planets are as neatly adjusted to each other's orbits as a glovemaker might fit his glove to a customer's hand. This is the so-called argument from design. Design is *purposive;* it implies a designer who has the purpose. Those who relied on this argument were panic-stricken when the theory of evolution revealed that there can be design without a designer. Instead of teleology we were left with entelechy, things with their own drive to fit into each other. The long ages implied for the work of evolution also disturbed those who had believed in the compact chronology of the Jewish Scripture. John Ruskin said of the new time spans being broken open by the geologists' hammers that his brain rang with the hammers' tapping, driving him into despondency.

But the belief in creation I imbibed with Chesterton's help had nothing to do with the argument from design. Even if nothing were to fit into anything else, the mere existence of a single thing is the miracle that is inexplicable except as an arbitrarily willed act. Not the long and gradual shaping of species but the abrupt and unmediated emergence of anything from nothingness — not that the glove can be made to fit the hand, but that there is a hand at all — is the creation that Chesterton revered. For him, as for Augustine, creation is not something that was done thousands of Jewish years ago, or scientists' billions of eons ago, but something that has to be occurring at each instant, now, for any (even the slightest) thing to exist. Without that continual flow of creative energy, the entire cosmos would blink out in an instant. This sense of the world's constant dependence on God's energy is what lay behind the mysticism of Saint Francis:

> If St. Francis had seen, in one of his strange dreams, the town of Assisi upside down, it need not have differed in a single detail from itself except in being entirely the other way round. But the point is this: that whereas to the normal eye the large masonry of its walls or the massive foundations of its watch towers and its high citadel would make it seem safer and more permanent, the moment it was turned over the very same weight would make it seem more helpless and more in peril. It is but a symbol; but it happens to fit the psychological fact. St. Francis might love his little town as much as before, or more than before, but the nature of the love would be altered even in being increased. He might see and love every tile of the steep roofs or every bird on the battlements; but he would see them all in a new and divine light of eternal danger and dependence. Instead of being merely proud of his

strong city because it would not be moved, he would be thankful to God Almighty that it had not been dropped; he would be thankful to God for not dropping the whole cosmos like a vast crystal to be shattered into falling stars.[4]

The Christians of the nineteenth century were intimidated by vast reaches of space or time. But if size is the criterion, Chesterton said, then we would all be inferior to the nearest tree. Creation is as wondrous in a tiny thing as in the vast sum of things. The instant is as improbable as the eons.

> "Elder father, though thine eyes
> Shine with hoary mysteries,
> Canst thou tell what in the heart
> Of a cowslip blossom lies?"

> "Smaller than all lives that be,
> Secret as the deepest sea,
> Stands a little house of seeds,
> Like an elfin granary."

> "Speller of the stones and weeds,
> Skilled in Nature's crafts and creed,
> Tell me what is in the heart
> Of the smallest of the seeds?"

> "God Almighty, and with Him
> Cherubim and Seraphim,
> Filling all eternity —
> Adonai Elohim."[5]

The personal nature of creation as God's act explains, for Chesterton at least, our instinct to be grateful to things simply for existing, to feel an obligation to the sunrise. Having a conscience means feeling we owe the universe something in return. Rilke said that looking at a sculpted Greek head made him feel that he should change his life. Looking at the whole of things can hardly impose a lesser duty. Who can deserve the Spring? Anyone might feel an urge to reciprocate the magnanimity of the Alps; but Chesterton did not need such grandiosity to feel grateful. He wondered, as he trudged along, that

> The stones still shine along the road
> That are and cannot be.[6]

When Chesterton calls the God of creation the "conqueror of chaos in a six-days war," he spoke as a beneficiary of that campaign. Each day in the creation narrative is a victory over nothingness, and we are in on the conquest, each moment that the world continues to exist. In "The Ballad of the White Horse," King Alfred feels indebted to the humble workers of his kingdom because they are images of the God who labors for us all:

> And well may God with the serving folk
> Cast in His dreadful lot;
> Is not He too a servant,
> And is not He forgot?
>
> For was not God my gardener
> And silent like a slave;
> That opened oaks on the uplands
> Or thicket in graveyard gave?
>
> And was not God my armorer,
> All patient and unpaid,
> That sealed my skull as a helmet
> And ribs for hauberk made?
>
> Did not a great grey servant
> Of all my men and me,
> Build this pavilion of the pines,
> And herd the fowls and fill the vines,
> And labour and pass and leave no signs
> Save mercy and mystery?[7]

The Manichaeans saw their god as at war with a counter-force of evil. There is something very winning in this idea that God himself has to overcome foes, that he is not merely our monarch but our champion, that he has dispatched his own son to the battlefront. "No mysterious monarch, hidden in his starry pavilion at the base of the cosmic campaign, is in the least like that celestial chivalry of the Captain who carries his five wounds in the front of battle."[8]

The trouble with this idea of a fighting God is that it requires an enemy, which plunges us back toward the Manichaean view of a split universe, with good and evil locked in eternal combat. Augustine escaped this system by seeing that God, as the creator of existing but limited things, is at war with non-being. At first this seems a non-answer to his problem. If the enemy is non-being, it is a non-enemy. Admittedly, non-being as such cannot be an existing foe. But neither can evil as such. Evil is by its very nature obliterative. Standing alone, it would devour itself. So God cannot be at war with a self-existing evil. Evil is a parasite on existing things, living off them while twisting them from their proper ends. Since any creature must be imperfect, unlike God, who is the sole perfect being, creatures are nearer to the edges of non-being, able to put good things in the wrong place, subordinating the better to the lesser good. The apple Eve eats is good. Even the serpent is good, and the perverted angel who tempts her had an originally good nature, one not entirely effaced or he would have been effaced along with it. The only evil arose from trying to turn these good things from the role God established for them, making them less than they are or should be, less in their being. The extreme sign of this is the murderer or the suicide, who literally tries to erase from existence one of God's creatures — Chesterton called this deserting the flag of Being. Those who "merely" hurt or maim another, physically or psychologically, are doing the same work, only not as thoroughly. They are at war with existence. They serve non-being.

Augustine puts the doctrine of divine creation this way: "What can there be that does not, in its own form and manner, bear the likeness of God, since he made everything surpassingly good? . . . Souls, in fact, strain to be like God in their very sins, with a proud, a disoriented, a (so to speak) fettered freedom."[9] Augustine often saw the mystery of creation in man's creativity. Man is made in the image of God, and never more so than when he is making. This analogy between God and humankind is a continuing thread in Augustine's thought — seeking God in the thing not only closest to us but closest to him: "Admittedly, the human mind does not have the same nature as God. Still, it is fitting that an image of His nature, than which none is higher, should be sought and found in that part of our nature, than which no part is higher."[10]

Chesterton, too, pondered the mystery of creation in works of human art. An extended example, from his book on Chaucer, may show how nuanced this search for the act of creation in created things could become:

A thousand times have I heard men tell (as Chaucer himself would put it) that the poet wrote *The Rime of Sir Topas* as a parody of certain bad romantic verse of his own time. And the learned would be willing to fill their notes with examples of this bad poetry, with the addition of not a little bad prose. It is all very scholarly, and it is all perfectly true; but it entirely misses the point. The joke is much larger than that. To see the scope of this gigantic jest, we must take in the whole position of the poet and the whole conception of the poem.

The Poet is the Maker; he is the creator of a cosmos; and Chaucer is the creator of the whole world of his creatures. He made the pilgrimage; he made the pilgrims. He made all the tales that are told by the pilgrims. Out of him is all the golden pageantry and chivalry of the Knight's Tale; all the rank and rowdy farce of the Miller's; he told through the mouth of the Prioress the pathetic legend of the Child Martyr and through the mouth of the Squire the wild, almost Arabian romance of Cambuscan. And he told them all in sustained melodious verse, seldom so continuously prolonged in literature; in a style that sings from start to finish. Then in due course, as the poet is also a pilgrim among the other pilgrims, he is asked for his contribution. He is at first struck dumb with embarrassment; and then suddenly starts a gabble of the worst doggerel in the book. It is so bad that, after a page or two of it, the tolerant innkeeper breaks in with the desperate protest of one who can bear no more, in words that could be best translated as "Gorlumme!" or "This is a bit too thick!" The poet is shouted down by a righteous revolt of his hearers, and can only defend himself by saying sadly that this is the only poem he knows. Then, by way of a final climax or anti-climax of the same satire, he solemnly proceeds to tell a rather dull story *in prose.*

Now a joke of that scale goes a great deal beyond the particular point, or pointlessness, of *The Rime of Sir Topas.* Chaucer is mocking not merely bad poets but good poets; the best poet he knows; "the best in this kind are but shadows." Chaucer, having to represent himself as reciting bad verse, did very probably take the opportunity of parodying somebody else's bad verse. But the parody is not the point. The point is in the admirable irony of the whole conception of the dumb or doggerel rhymer who is nevertheless the author of all the other rhymes; nay, even the author of their authors. Among all the types and trades — the coarse miller, the hard-fisted reeve, the clerk, the cook, the ship-miller — the poet is the only man who knows no poetry. There is in it some hint of those huge and abysmal ideas of which the poets are half-conscious when they write; the primal and elemental ideas connected with the very nature of creation and reality. It has in it something of the philosophy of a phenomenal world, and all that was meant by those sages, by no means pessimists, who have said that we are in a world of shadows. Chaucer has made a world of his own shadows, and, when he is on a certain plane, finds himself equally shadowy. It has in it all the mystery of the relation of the maker with things made. There falls on it from afar even some dark ray of the irony of God, who was mocked when He entered His own world, and killed when He came among His creatures.[11]

. . . and in Jesus Christ our Lord, the only son of God . . . He descended into hell . . .

THE ENLIGHTENMENT VIEW of Jesus, typified by Thomas Jefferson, is that he was a supremely good man on whom later theological claims were foisted. The true Jesus is discernible in the simple story of the Gospels, if only one brushes away the supernatural incrustations (mainly miracles and exorcisms). "It is the innocence of his character, the purity and sublimity of his moral precepts, the eloquence of his inculcations, the beauty of the apologues in which he conveys them, that I so much admire; sometimes indeed needing indulgence to Eastern hyperbolism."[1] To brush away the later absurdities was an easy task for Jefferson, "the work of one or two evenings," since the genuine sayings of Jesus "are as distinguishable from the matter in which they are imbedded as diamonds in dunghills."[2] In assembling his own expurgated version of the Gospels, "I separate therefore the gold from the dross . . . I found the work obvious and easy."[3]

Jefferson had the misconception of his time, that the four Gospels were the original Christian writings, to which the epistles of Paul were added later. "Paul was the great Coryphaeus [stage manager], and first corrupter of the doctrines of Jesus."[4] This is still the view of New Testament popularizers. Martin Scorsese's *The Last Temptation of Christ*, for instance, repeated the old canard, which was surprising, since the author of the script was a former student of theology, Paul Schrader.

Actually, the four Gospels, though they rely on earlier oral and written material, were given their present form after the fall of the Jewish temple in 70 C.E., and were thus written in the same period as the early creeds and liturgies. The crises of that period are reflected in these accounts, which were written four to seven decades after the death of Christ. The earliest surviving Christian documents are precisely Paul's letters, written in the fifties and sixties (two to three decades after the death of Jesus). His words are the closest to the time of Jesus of any that have come down to us, and even earlier church utterances are imbedded in his letters — baptism formulae, liturgical hymns, and what J.N.D. Kelly calls "fragmentary creeds." Some of these have the metrical shape of poems, and are community utterances, not Pauline inventions. There is, for instance, the baptismal hymn of Gal 3.26–28:

> Baptized into Christ,
>   you are clothed in Christ
> so there is no more Jew or Greek,
>   slave or free, man and woman,
> but all of you are one,
>   are the same in Christ Jesus.

One of the most interesting things about these early glimpses of a tradition from Christ's time is that they have as "high" a Christology as anything in Paul.[5] An example of this is the *kenōsis* ("hollowing out") poem at Phil 2.6–11 (c. 58 C.E.). This is the famous *Carmen Christi:*

> Since his form was always divine,
>   he did not usurp equality with God;
> yet he hollowed out his own claim,
>   taking the nature of a slave,
> and in the likeness of humans,
>   himself visibly a man,
> he lowered himself in obedience,
>   even to death, a death by the cross.
> That is why God has exalted him,
>   given him a name before all others;
> so that every knee shall bend to his name,
>   in heaven, on earth, and in the abyss;

and every tongue shall announce
that Jesus Christ is Lord, in the Father's glory.

Paul said that he stood in the great tradition, handing on what was handed to him (1 Cor 11.2); and this hymn may even have come from Jerusalem, since some scholars find an Aramaic original behind it.[6] So the Christian tradition *begins* with the things Jefferson and Paul Schrader (to name just two from thousands) think were later shoveled into it by Paul. It is the oldest chorus that makes the highest claim for Christ's divinity. At Eph 1.4–10 the author plays elegant variations on an earlier hymn:

He singled us out in Christ before beginning the world,
by love to be holy and blameless in his company,
marking us beforehand to be his sons in Christ Jesus —
such was the favor he designed —
that the splendor of his deed should be praised,
extended to us in his loved son
by whose blood we are liberated;
the account of our failings canceled
out of the richness of his favor,
overflowing with all wisdom and foresight;
revealing the secret of his design —
how he first singled out Christ for favor,
to guide time to its completion
summing all things up in Christ,
contained in him, all things of heaven,
and all things of earth.

Christianity arose from a recognition of Christ's divinity. Only then was his human career studied in the light of that faith. The Gospels are a product of the belief, not vice versa. Christianity began as the cosmos does in Genesis — first a great light, and only later the articulated planets. That is why attempts to create "the historical Jesus" or his "authentic sayings" begin at the wrong end. These things were recalled, in the attempt to say what was adequate to the Christ of faith and to the needs of his believers. The Gospel of Mark, for instance, is written to strengthen a local church in persecution — just as the song of 2 Tim 2.11–13 was sung by the persecuted.[7]

Die we in him, in him shall we live,
  stand we with him, with him shall we reign.
But deny we him, he will deny us;
  betray we him, he shall not betray —
for he is true, always, to himself.

I find the story of Christianity more convincing precisely because it begins with a great blinding light, from which men stumble only gradually, their eyes still dazzled, toward more coherent attempts to understand what has happened. In fact, in those early hymns there are insights into the meaning of the revelation that are still not widely appreciated — especially in that language of Christ "summing up" creation, and of sons being incorporated into Christ even before the world began. This points to a concept of Christ that Duns Scotus (c. 1266–1308) made popular with his fellow Franciscans, but one that goes against the general view of the Incarnation. That view, sound so far as it goes, was presented in a play by Chesterton that is a parable of the Incarnation.

The Surprise is a two-act play found among Chesterton's papers after his death. In the first act, a friar, wandering in a forest, comes across a showman's caravan. Life-size puppets are collapsed in a jumble on the traveling stage, their strings lying over them like a net. The friar admires the dolls' beauty, and when the puppeteer pops up on the roof of the caravan, the friar asks where he will be giving his next show, so he might attend. The showman says that if the friar will just sit down, he will give him a private performance — he loves the story he tells.

The curtain on the caravan's stage goes down, to let the showman arrange his dolls under their guiding strings; then it goes back up and the play-within-the-play begins. It is an old-fashioned melodrama. A young knight loves a lady who is subject to the power of an evil baron. In league with a friend, the knight plots her rescue, though his effort is discovered by the baron, who attacks the knight and is slain by him. The lady is free, the knight triumphant, the friend happy.

The friar admires the show, but wonders why the puppets' contriver looks sad after completing it. He had been all cheer and anticipation beforehand. The man says he has lived with the puppets and their tale so long that he feels he knows each character. But they can never know him. They cannot respond to him in any words he is not putting in their mouths. He is talking to himself when he would like to be talking to them. After hearing this "confession," the friar expresses his sympathy and parts from him — but we see him, just as the outer curtain begins to descend, kneeling to pray for something.

The second act of the surround-play begins as the first one had, with the puppets in a heap and their strings loose about them. But then, unprompted, they rise of their own power, shaking off their strings. The story begins again, with the same plot but no audience. This time, however, as the story progresses, little slippages occur, things just missing their mark, only a bit at first, but cumulatively throwing off the whole sequence. The hero and friend get tipsy while singing the drinking song that was so winning in the first performance. They quarrel, making them late to the showdown with the villain. The heroine turns in anger on them. The villain taunts the helpless knight. Everyone is at odds with everyone else, and about to come to blows indiscriminately. At this point the puppet master suddenly rears himself up over the roof and shouts: "Stop! I'm coming down!"

The play is typical of Chesterton — making subtle points in strokes as broad as caricature. Compressed into this little parable is his view of free will (how God cut the strings), evil (the lapses from reality through misused freedoms), and the Incarnation (God is coming down). This is quite in accord with Christian tradition, going all the way back to New Testament baptismal hymns like Ti 3.4–7:

> When the nobility and loving-kindness shone out
>   from Christ our rescuing God,
> not by any acquittal owing to our own acts,
>   but from water of rebirth he deigned to us
> our renewal in the Holy Spirit, poured out
>   profusely through Christ Jesus our rescuer;
> so that, acquitted by his favor, we might be heirs
>   to the promise of life never-ending.

This is an orthodox version of the Incarnation, of the rescue it effected after Adam's fall from grace. But Duns Scotus — unlike Thomas Aquinas — thought it was not the entire or primary explanation. It has an air of mere repair work on creation, as if conditioned on the fall of Adam. Had he not fallen, would there have been no Incarnation? No sinning Adam, no saving Jesus? Duns sees in the Incarnation not simply rescue work performed on a creation that had gone awry, but the culmination of creation, always foreseen, by which the highest of God's earthly creatures, humankind, would be united to him in the Son. This was always the aim, not to be caused by the means (Incarnation and passion) which God chose to bring it about.[8] Adam should not be given "credit" for the Incarnation, which is the goal toward which all creation was tending, as the early Christian hymns and text make clear — Col 1.15–20, for instance:

> Christ is the invisible God's visible form,
>   the first-brought-forth in the universe.
> All, in heaven or earth, was built up from him,
>   all, whether seen or unseen,
> whether thrones or dominions,
>   whether principalities or powers —
> all was built up through him as agent,
>   toward him as goal.
>
> He came before all things,
>   and all things are stabilized in him.
> He is the head of the body
>   the body being the church.
> He is the origin,
>   the first-brought-forth out of the dead.
> He is the first-honored of all things,
>   in him was decreed universal fulfillment,
> in him all things reach reconcilement,
>   pacified by his blood,
> whatever there is in heaven,
>   whatever there is on earth.

The verbs for "summing up" in Eph 1.10 (*anakephalaiō*) and for "reconciling" in Col 1.20 (*apokatallassō*) have led to a "recapitulation" (*anakephalaiōsis*) theology begun by Irenaeus, which sees Christ gathering up all the work of creation and bringing it to fulfillment.[9] This tradition has been especially strong in the Eastern church, where another clause in the creed, "he descended into hell," shows an enactment of Col 1.18. Christ goes back in time to free those who died before his coming, so that nothing in the universe shall go unredeemed. His death culminates all the pain of a universe striving to bring forth the completion of its own creation, as Paul envisioned it at Rom 8.18–23:

I count as nothing what we suffer at this time, against the glory still unfolding within us. The whole structure of things is suspended in anxious anticipation of this unfolding, since that structure has been stalled in baffled hope, not willingly but by its ruler's decree. Yet the structure too will reach freedom from the laws of decay when God's children are glorified. We realize that the whole structure shares our outcries and birth-pangs in this process. Nay, more — though we already have the first gifts of the Spirit, we still cry out for completion of our birth as God's children, with redemption of our bodies.

In this vision of the Incarnation, Christ's passion is a completion of the world's struggle out of the system of sin into the freedom of the Spirit. This is in accord with Augustine's denial that the passion was a sacrifice to the Father.[10] According to René Girard, Christ's suffering was an *exposure* of the scapegoating processes of sacrifice.[11] By not being complicitous with the violence of the world, Christ gathered into himself all the striving out from under that violence. This is very like what Paul said in Heb 2.10: "Rightly did God — for whom all was made, through whom all was made — make perfect in his pain the champion [*archēgos*] of their rescue, the one who leads a multitude of sons to glory."

It may seem odd for Paul to speak of a thing being perfected in pain but under the system of worldly violence, the one who does not return the violence, who suffers for others under its thrall, is the most perfect of humans. We get some image of that in the earthly *kenōsis* enacted by Saint Francis, of whom Chesterton (as already noted) wrote:

> We cannot follow St. Francis to that final spiritual overturn in which complete humiliation becomes complete holiness or happiness, because we have never been there . . . Whatever else it was, it was so far analogous to the story of the man making a tunnel through the earth that it did mean going down and down until at some mysterious moment he begins to go up and up. We have never gone up like that because we have never gone down like that.[12]

But Christ has descended like that, has gone ahead of us into every depth. We can never be so low that he cannot reach us. "He descended into hell."

Christ's embrace of full humanity, reconciling all things to him, even death, recalls Saint Francis's line in the *Canticle of the Sun:* "God be praised for our sister, the bodily death." Death was made our sister by our Brother. The willingness of that self-surrender is suggested, for Chesterton, in the myth of Prometheus. But this Prometheus is not tortured by Zeus. He chooses his own suffering:

> "Hailed of my hand, and by this sign alone,
> My eagle comes to tear me."[13]

I have read, over the course of my life, many prayers composed before the crucifix. None of them brings me closer to the mystery than those two lines of Chesterton.

~~

. . . conceived by the Holy Spirit, born of the Virgin Mary . . .

THE HOLY SPIRIT has been called the forgotten person of the Trinity. She is given the third and separate clause, "I believe in the Holy Spirit, the holy Catholic church . . ." J.N.D. Kelly argues persuasively that the object of "I believe" was originally "the Holy Spirit in the church."[1] That is the form in the early baptismal interrogatory of *The Apostolic Tradition,* of which the documents of Vatican II make much use.[2] The Spirit is the animating principle of the body of Christ, and so she is mentioned in the Jesus-kerygma that was added to the second main clause of the creed. The Spirit who will fill the mystical body of Christ is, before that, the agent forming his physical body. The role of the Spirit here is like that of the wind/spirit of Gen 1.2 that moves over waters of the formless dark. The words of the angel in the Annunciation (Lk 1.35) make this clear:

> The Holy Spirit will come upon you,
> the power of the Most High cloud you in light.

Raymond Brown points out that the parallelism of Hebrew poetry shows that the Most High in the second line is also the Holy Spirit (not the Father).[3] The verb "will come upon you," a characteristically Lukan term, is used again when it is said that the Spirit "will come upon the disciples" at Pentecost (Acts 1.8). The verb for "put a shadow over" is not something that *darkens,* since it is a cloud *of glory* that stands over the tabernacle at Ex 40.35 and over the transfigured Jesus at Lk 9.34.

The wind blowing over the dark waters in Genesis is heralding the creation of light.

The role of the Spirit in Christ's coming is mentioned not only in Luke's childhood narrative. In Matthew (1.20), Joseph is told in a dream, "What is conceived in her comes from the Holy Spirit." And Paul writes to the Romans (1.3–4) that Jesus was "physically descended . from the stock of David, but assigned the power of God's Son by the Spirit of Holiness."

Just as the Spirit oversaw the formation of Jesus' body in the womb, it presided over the formation of the church as a body at Pentecost. It made each disciple's tongue a tongue of fire to speak truth without fear or inhibition, with the *parrhesia* (free speech) that marks the person freed from worldly despotisms. The Spirit also fills the Christian at baptism, and early Spirit language was closely linked with that rite. In the third section of the creed, the words are "I believe in the Holy Spirit, the holy Catholic church, the communion of saints [Pentecost], the forgiveness of sins [baptism] . . ."

J.N.D. Kelly proves with a series of early texts that "forgiveness of sins" here refers to baptism and not to the (not yet existent) sacrament of penance. The regular formula was "baptism unto forgiveness of sins."[4] Paul, after listing various types of sinners, says, "Some of you were of that sort. But you were rinsed, you were sanctified, you were vindicated in the majesty of the Lord Jesus Christ and in the Spirit of our Lord" (1 Cor 6.11). The triple phrase seems to reflect the triple immersions of baptism. Jn 20.22 is also a reference to Spirit baptism: "He breathed on them and said, 'Receive the Holy Spirit. If you forgive people's sins, they are forgiven. If you confirm them, they are confirmed.'" The Spirit lifts the baptized to a new level of life: "As many as accepted him, to them he gave the privilege of being God's children, born not of a human bloodline, or flesh's desire, or a man's scheming, but of God" (Jn 1.12).

Augustine describes the Spirit as *returning* the Father's and the Son's love, completing God's conversation with himself. Within the earthly economy, this means that the outward creative energy of the Father, as articulated in the Word, is responded to by the Spirit testifying to it in us. This witness of the mystical body of Christ lifts us into the inner communication of the Trinity. The Spirit is the comforter, the strengthener, the giver of gifts. Since the Spirit is not usually gendered

(*Pneuma* is a neuter noun), it is easy to see in these activities the feminine aspect of God. This is said only by distant analogy — but the same
is true of the "masculine" Father and Son. If humanity is the best image of God on earth, it makes no sense to limit that reflective capacity to one half of the human race. A mother's care for the world and its
inhabitants is expressed in the Spirit's action — a care described by
Gerard Manley Hopkins in the lines:

> Because the Holy Ghost over the bent
> World broods with warm breast and with ah! Bright wings.[5]

It is true that John's Gospel uses the word "Paraclete" four times in
the final discourse of Jesus, and the pronoun "he" is used of it. Some
have thought that this was not the Holy Spirit, but some other "defender" of the church; and Raymond Brown says that it does not refer
to the Holy Spirit in any but a specific *role,* as active confronter of
the world. Brown thinks the Paraclete had a special mission of defending the church when the world had not come to its expected end.[6]
"When the Defender [Paraclete] comes, he will expose the world's lie
about sin, about conformity with God, and about criminal execution
— about sin, because they do not recognize me [as sinless]; about conformity with God, because I am the one who arrives at the Father
[when you lose sight of me]; and about criminal execution, because the
Prince of This World is the one convicted (Jn 15.8–11)." The usage is too
localized to invalidate a general ascription of feminine qualities to the
Spirit.

. . . born of the Virgin Mary . . .

The New Testament is a book of theology, not of obstetrics or gynecol-
ogy, though some later cultists became uncommonly curious about
Mary's hymen, arguing that it could not have been broken when Jesus
was born, or she would have lost her virginity.[7] The early Christians
could not have had such problems, since they calmly accepted the fact
that Jesus' brother James was the leader of the church in Jerusalem. We
should recall in this connection the verse from John quoted above: "As
many as accepted him, to them he gave the privilege of being God's
children, *born not of a human bloodline, or flesh's desire, or a man's*

scheming, but of God." The stress on Mary's virginity was a way of saying the same thing, but with a special emphasis reserved for Mary.

The spiritual status claimed for Mary was once, for Catholics, mired in the physical claim that she was always *intacta — ante partum, in partu, post partum.* But now Catholic exegetes are saying, with Joseph Fitzmyer, S.J., that the Gospel of Luke lacks "the affirmation of Mary's virginity, which is never presented in any biological sense."[8] Raymond Brown notices that some bad side effects followed from Catholic insistence on a literal virginity:

> All Christians should be wary of any implication that the conception of Jesus in wedlock would detract from his nobility or Mary's sanctity. In its origins, the virginal conception shows no traces whatsoever of an anti-sexual bias and should not be made to support one. For the evangelists it was a visible sign of God's gracious intervention in connection with the becoming of His Son; in no way did that intervention make ordinary conception in marriage less holy.[9]

Early on, the *reality* of Mary's flesh was what had to be insisted on against the Docetists, who thought Jesus' body a phantom. But her own purity was also stressed because Jesus, as the second Adam, was beginning a new order of creation. Adam had been formed from the "virgin earth." Jesus had to rise from a nobler element. But beyond that, the Gospels do not show him making much of his earthly ties to mother or family. Quite the opposite. Augustine rightly argued against those who try to soften his harsh response to Mary at Cana (Jn 2.4).[10] On another occasion, when Jesus is told that his mother and his brothers want to see him, he turns down their request: "My mother and my brothers are ones who hear the word of God and do it" (Lk 8.21). When a woman cries out to him, "Happy the womb that bore you," he answers, "Happy, rather, are those who hear the word of God and do it" (Lk 11.28).

But Luke, who narrates the last two encounters, makes it clear in his infancy narrative that Mary is "favored" by God (Lk 1.28), and he puts on her lips the prophecy that has certainly been fulfilled, "I shall be called happy down the generations" (Lk 1.48). Her response to the angel shows that Mary qualifies for the discipleship Jesus demands — she *does* hear his word and do it. And her very body *is* special, in ways signaled by that title of spiritual virginity. After all, that body did bring forth the savior. Insofar as we baptized Christians belong to the mystical body of Christ, we are the products of her body. Her place in the economy of salvation is assured. Whenever I say the rosary, I enter into the mysterious transaction described by Hopkins:

> Of her flesh he took flesh.
> He does take fresh and fresh,
> Though much the mystery how,
> Not flesh but spirit now
> And makes, O marvelous!
> New Nazareths in us,
> Where she shall yet conceive
> Him, morning, noon, and eve,
> New Bethlems, and he born
> There, evening, noon, and morn —
> Bethlem or Nazareth
> Men here may draw like breath
> More Christ and baffle death.[11]

The poem is very close to what Augustine said in a Christmas sermon: "You, who are astonished at what is wrought in Mary's body, imitate it in your soul's inmost chamber — sincerely believe in God's justice, and you conceive Christ. Bring forth words of salvation, and you have given birth to Christ."[12]

When I say the five glorious mysteries of the rosary, the fourth is Mary's bodily assumption into heaven — the only dogma to be infallibly defined since Vatican I set the rules for infallible pronouncements. Pius XII defined the dogma in 1950. The old view of bodily resurrection as the reassembling of parts from corruption goes against what Paul says at 1 Cor 15.50: "Flesh and blood cannot inherit the reign of God." The body that rises will be a spiritualized thing, he writes, a mystery, more different from the present body than a flower in the air is from its seed that was put in the ground (15.35–49). An identity formed by physical memories may be all that is preserved of the body. Since that is what Mary's body signifies in this dogma, there is no reason to doubt that she shares the privilege of the thief who died with Jesus, to whom it was promised, "This very day [*sēmaron*] you will be with me in Paradise" (Lk 23.43). The same must be said of all who die in the Lord. This confirms that Vatican I's grant of infallibility has proved a nugatory power. Mary was always an exemplar of the resurrection that all the faithful look forward to. The definition neither added to nor detracted from that role.

Thus Mary is closely associated with the Spirit in the activities ascribed to her in the third article of the creed — "I believe in the Holy Spirit, the holy Catholic Church, the communion of saints, the remission of sins, the resurrection of the flesh, and eternal life."

— *the holy Catholic Church:* Though Christ is the head of the mystical body of the church, and the Spirit is the animating power in that body — roles Mariolaters should not be allowed to usurp for Mary — the Virgin did bear the body of the physical Christ; and that makes her a mother to all of us in the mystical body. Many theologians make her a symbol of the church, which tends to play down the importance of the Spirit. Yves Congar noted this by quoting a fellow theologian, who said, "When I began the Catholic study of theology, every place I expected to find an exposition of the doctrine of the Holy Spirit, I found Mary."[13] But Mary, though not the guide of the church, is the most honored human citizen of the City of God, our elder sister in the faith, a model of discipleship. Christian denominations are the poorer for lack of devotion to her, for not giving her the honor called for in the gospel Magnificat — just as they are the poorer for lacking the symbol of Peter. It is one of the great achievements of the papacy to have kept honor to Mary active in the daily lives of believers.

— *the communion of saints:* The mystical body of Christ is one, and members are not cut off from us when they die. To be part of Christ is to be connected with them, and we honor them in prayers to and with them. Popes in the past policed and exploited such prayers in the indulgence racket. But that is no reason for us to desist from a practice that is as early as the church's original devotion to its martyrs. And Mary is the one we Catholics most easily and often address ourselves to in prayer.

— *the forgiveness of sins:* As we have already seen, this refers to the great answer to sin, baptism; and being reborn into Christ takes us closer to the role of Mary in Christ's original human birth. Becoming part of Christ makes us her sons and daughters.

— *the resurrection of the body:* The Feast of the Assumption, it was noticed, is a striking reminder of this general promise, fulfilled in her.

— *and life everlasting:* The woman from whom Jesus took human life took from him everlasting life. That is a truth of faith that never ceased to amaze Augustine — how the maker of the Milky Way drew milk from her breast.[14]

> Remaining with his Father, yet is he brought forth by his mother; maker of heaven and earth, yet born under heaven on the earth; unspeakably wise, yet wisely speechless [*infans*]; filling the cosmos, yet confined to his crib; ruling the stars, yet a suckling at her breast.[15]

⁓

... *shall come to judge the living and the dead* ...

CHRISTIANITY IS through-and-through an eschatological faith. It holds that the murky transactions of our sin-clouded history stand under the gaze of a divine justice that will assert itself in final confrontation at the Ultimate Moment (*to Eschaton*). This theme runs through all the Gospels, and it stands at the end of the Jesus-kerygma (the second article) of the creed: "He shall come to judge the living and the dead." It is even more central to the other main text entrusted to people at baptism, the Lord's Prayer.[1] In Augustine's Africa, this was given to the baptisands a week after their rendering back the creed. Elsewhere, too, instruction in the prayer ran through Holy Week.[2] The creed was the profession of faith that qualified one for baptism. The Lord's Prayer gave expression to the new Christian life — it was said at Mass after catechumens had left, renewing the baptized community's solidarity in hope for the coming of the Lord. The baptismal-liturgical provenance of the prayer may even be expressed in the structure of that section of Matthew's Gospel where it occurs. It comes in the middle of a "cultic instruction" (*didachē*), part of the Sermon on the Mount, and that *didachē* is itself in the middle of the Sermon.[3]

The shape of the prayer is very studied, falling into two parts, each with three petitions. The first part deals with God's plan for the Eschaton, the second with the community's participation in that plan. This much is clear even in the quite inadequate English translations used by Catholics and Protestants. The Catholic one goes this way:

> Our Father who art in heaven,
>   hallowed be thy name.
> Thy kingdom come,
>   Thy will be done,
> on earth as it is in heaven.
>
> Give us this day
>   our daily bread,
> and forgive us our sins
>   as we forgive those who have sinned against us,
> and lead us not into temptation
>   but deliver us from evil.

The two parts stand in contrast in many ways. The first is anarthrous (with no connectives between clauses), the second joins its clauses with repeated "and." The first repeats "thy" (Greek *sou*) with each clause, the second repeats "our" (Greek *hēmōn*) with each clause. The first part's clauses have similar shapes, in ways a translation cannot capture. The first three clauses begin with a verb of the same form (anaphora) — the rare third-person imperative. They are all in the aorist (timeless) tense, a once-for-all tense:

> *hagiasthētō to onoma sou,*
> *elthatō hē basileia sou,*
> *genēthētō to thelēma sou.*

The verbs of the second part are also aorists, and each is followed by a form of "us." But these verbs are second-person active ones, not third-person passive ones.

The many confusions about meaning in the prayer (e.g., is the bread "daily," does God lead people into temptation) can only be resolved by looking at its entirely eschatological theme.

Our Father of the Heavens

Joachim Jeremias claimed that calling God Father (Aramaic *Abba*) was a uniquely familiar usage of Jesus', which he extends to his followers. But critics of Jeremias have shown that Jews had similar prayers. Raymond Brown argues that Father is the title that will be promulgated at the Eschaton, when the legitimacy of the "children of God" is established. Mt 13.38 says that at the Judgment, the good will be gathered into heaven as "the children of the kingdom," admitted to "the kingdom of their father" (verse 43), while the rest (verse 38) will be branded as "sons of the Evil One" (*ho Ponēros*). Luke's Gospel says that the title of the good in heaven will be "sons of God" (Lk 20.36), "sons of the Most High" (6.35).

The "in heaven" of the normal translation is a *title* for God, the article with a prepositional phrase containing the plural (*ho en tois ouranois*), "the in-the-heavens Father." Back in the twentieth century there was a popular denunciation of the idea that one should look "up there" to find God, locating him Elsewhere, and we have seen that Augustine thinks God is to be sought within (*intus*). Perhaps that is why he takes "in the heavens" in this prayer to mean "in God's saints," and "on earth" to men "among sinners."[4] He is so personalist that he thinks God's sanctification comes in the souls of humans. But the eschatological sense would look to the moment when heaven judges earth, when Christ comes again in glory to judge the living and the dead. This coming-together of heaven and earth is enacted in the last phrase of the first part, "on earth as it is in heaven," which serves as a rhetorical "enclosure," or return of the end to the beginning in this first half of the prayer.

Your title be honored . . .

The *name* is the title by which one acts — "Stop, in the name of the law." It is the title honored by others, or whose honor is vindicated. Christians "baptized into the name of God" were admitted into the honor of God, which meant both the *title* by which they were saved and the thing they pledged themselves to honor. Augustine takes "hallowed be" to mean that the title will *increasingly* be honored by humans, since in itself the name is *always* holy.[5] But this fits neither the passive imperative nor the aorist sense. The passive imperative used of God (the so-called *passivum divinum*) is sometimes used where the petitioner does not want to be presumptuous enough to tell God directly what he should do. A vaguer formula is used: "Be it done . . ." But the prayer does not avoid second-person imperatives in the second part.

God's name will be openly vindicated at the Eschaton, which is what Brown takes the aorist to mean. It is not a process of "hallowing" but a decisive moment that the community is praying for, when God's title will blaze out in ways that all must acknowledge. Only God can bring this about. As Brown says (292), "The passive is a surrogate for the divine name, and the *Einmaligkeit* [once-for-all] of the aorist is to be given its full force. It is a prayer that God accomplish the ultimate sanctification of His name, the complete manifestation of His holiness, the last of his salvific activities." Brown argues (291) that this is what Jesus was praying for at Jn 12.28: "Father, make glorious your title [*onoma*]." There, as here, the specific title referred to is Father. That title will be vindicated by the acknowledgment of the "sons of God" who are declared saved.

Your reign arrive . . .

The parallel between this clause and the preceding one shows that the first was eschatological, since that is the *only* possible meaning for the second. God's reign comes to earth in stages — when Christ brings the gospel, when he is crucified, when he rises. Those stages are all past. The only one left to await with joyful hope is the coming in judgment. Only then will the reign be entirely vindicated, inescapably acknowledged by all. Thus, at the Last Supper, Jesus says: "I shall not from this moment drink the fruit of the vine *until the reign of God arrive*" (Lk 22.18). He is referring to the eschatological meal, the Lord's banquet that will be so prominent in the second half of this prayer.

Your design be fulfilled . . .

Some have taken "your will be done" as an acknowledgment that the person saying the prayer should be obedient to God in daily ways. That is against the once-for-all aorist of the verb. Something is to be done decisively, in a single act. It is not God's separate commandments that are at issue here. What he wills (*thelēma,* singular) means the whole plan of salvation he is bringing to completion. The exact words used here (*genēthētō to thelēma sou*) are used by Christ at the agony in the garden, where he must accept the suffering that lies before, since that is part of God's design for human salvation: "Father, if that is possible, be this cup removed from me. Yet not my design but yours be fulfilled" (Mt 26.39).

he meal still to come
rant us even today . . .

he adjective translated "daily" is unique in Greek, *epiousios*. That ad-
·ctive can have two equally valid etymologies. It is a union of the
reposition *epi* ("to") with *ousios,* which could come from the stem of
ιe verb "to be" (*einai*) or of the verb "to come" (*ienai*). That is, we
ray either for "to be" bread or for "to come" bread.

Those who translate it "daily" make "to be" bread either bread that is
ɔ be had now or bread that is necessary for being, for existence. For
ιem it is a prayer for continued earthly existence, for the means of
ιbsistence — which seems oddly pedestrian in this prayer of apoca-
ˈptic hope for the Eschaton. It reduces those praying to the literal-
ιindedness of Jesus' auditors at Jn 6.33–35: When Jesus says "The
read of your Father is coming down from heaven and giving life to the
orld," they say "Give us this bread continually (*pantote*)." He has to
ɔrrect their misconception: "I am the bread of life — whoever comes
ɔ me will hunger no more; who trusts me will thirst no more." It is
ιly in the eschatological kingdom that one hungers or thirsts no
ιore: "Those who stand before the throne of God . . . shall never again
ιow hunger or thirst" (Rev 7.14–16). Jesus at Jn 6.33 was not talking of
hysical bread. Yet the Lord's Prayer in the old translation would make
s all do precisely that.

That the eschatological meaning of bread, the bread of the great
anquet, is meant should be clear from passages like this:

"Happy whoever shall eat bread in the kingdom of God" (Lk 14.15)
"As my Father has prepared for me a kingdom, so I prepare for you to
    eat and drink at my table in my kingdom" (Lk 22.29–30)
"I promise you that many will come from the East and from the West
    and they will sit down at table [*anaklithēsontai*] with Abraham,
    Isaac, and Jacob in the kingdom of heaven" (Mt 8.11)

ɔ the "to come" bread is the bread of the coming eschatological ban-
ιet. "Bread" is, of course, a term for meal. "It is well known that both
ιe Hebrew *lehem* and the Aramaic *lahma* describe not only wheat
ɔur but any food whatsoever; in particular, the phrase 'eat bread' sim-
y means 'have a meal.'"[6] The meal to come is thus the feast on what
remias (25) calls "the great Tomorrow." We ask in the prayer that we

may anticipate the final banquet, since the kingdom is in the process of coming even now — or why was Jesus sent to us? Jesus told the disciples at the Last Supper that this was not the great final banquet. But it fore-tells it: "However many times you eat this bread or drink this cup, you are heralding the Lord's death until his return" (1 Cor 11.26).

Though some have denied that the Mass is a meal, the Lord's Prayer declares that it is:

> The expression "to give bread" [*arton didonai*] is a rare one in the gos-pels. It occurs in the Bread of Life discourse in John . . . and in two other important places: the multiplication of the loaves and the Last Supper. At the Last Supper, Mark 14.22 reports, "Taking *bread*, he blessed and broke and gave it to them." The multiplication scene in Mark 6.41 has virtually the same words, probably by way of pointing out the multiplication as Eucharistic preparation (John 6 makes that explicit). Thus, in asking the Father "Give us our bread," the commu-nity was employing words directly connected with the Eucharist. And so our Roman Liturgy may not be too far from the original sense of the petition in having the *Pater Noster* introduce the Communion of the Mass.[7]

Clear our moral account with you, as we have cleared our account against others . . .

"Dismiss our debts" is the literal translation here — the King James version rightly used the word "debts" where the Catholic versions use "sins." Of course, the debts are a metaphor for moral deficits, but the metaphor is important, since what is being referred to is the Great Day of Reckoning (Jeremias 27), modeled on the Jews' Jubilee year when all debts were canceled (Lohmeyer 163). The final judgment is compared to the Jubilee in this respect — we pray that God will cancel finally whatever we, his people, owe him (the emphasis throughout is on the community, not individuals' sins). The verbs, again, are aorist, so this is not a matter of *daily* forgiveness, but of the readiness to stand before God forgiving and forgiven in the last account. We are not bargaining with God, "Forgive us *later* because we forgive others now." The actions are simultaneous. This is a prayer to escape the whole system of debt and collection, to be free of such exactions.

And bring us not to the Breaking Point . . .

The old translation here has bothered Christians for centuries. Can God deliberately "lead us into temptation"? And if he is sadistic enough to do so, will he stop simply because we ask him to? The answer to this problem lies in the word translated "temptation." It is *Peirasmos*. In an eschatological context like this one, it refers to the Last Trial of the earth at the Eschaton, when the powers of darkness will fight against the judgment that ends their reign. Not wanting to suffer its buffetings is an appropriate response to the ordeal, as we learn from Rev 3.10, where the Lord says, "Because you have kept my counsel of perseverance, I will keep you from the hour of Trial [*Peirasmou*] that is ready to reach the whole world, putting its inhabitants to the test." As we say the Lord's Prayer, we are following the advice given by Jesus at Mk 14.38: "Be cautious and pray that you not enter into the Trial [*Peirasmon*]."

The "temptation" of Jesus in the wilderness was a trial run, a preview, of the Eschaton, that great Breaking Point of history when the devil will be finally defeated. But the devil was given his "hour and the power of darkness" when Jesus was "put to the test" in the garden of olives. The disciples could not face up to the test with him then, and we are asking for the same forgiveness he gave them. We do not rely on our strength, after all, but on his. He has been there, and won the struggle for us.

But wrest us from the Evil Power . . .

The verb used here (*eryomai*) is very strong, and often implies a necessary force, to wrench or tear something away.[8] We ask God to wrestle us free from the grasp of the great enemy at the time of Trial. The customary translation of *ponērou* as "evil" is grammatically possible — it assumes that the genitive *ponerou* comes from a neuter (*ponēron*) instead of a masculine nominative (*poneros*). But the verb, the eschatological context, and numerous parallels show that the Evil One is the meaning here. We saw above that the final judgment will separate the children of God from "the sons of the Evil One" (Mt 13.19). Jesus makes this request of the Father: "I do not ask that you release them from the world but that you guard them from the Evil One" (Jn 17.15). "Cain was a son

of the Evil One" (1 Jn 3.12), but the children of God "have overcome the
Evil One" (1 Jn 2.13). "Take up the shield of faith, fireproof against the
Evil One's flaming arrows" (Eph 6.16). "We know that a child of God
does not commit sin, since the Son of God protects him and the Evil
One cannot lay hands on him. We realize that we are God's children,
but the whole system of the world is in the power of the Evil One" (1 Jn
5.18–19).

This last statement gives a sense of the cosmic struggle that is the
background of the Lord's Prayer. We pray to be on God's side in this
battle, to survive it and reach the promised last banquet of the saved. At
Thes 5.5–9, Paul says that is the meaning of baptism:

> You are all sons of light, sons of the day,
> and none of us belongs to darkness or the night.
> Let us, then, never fall asleep,
> like the rest of the world;
> let us keep awake,
> with our wits about us.
> Night is the time for sleep, when men get drunk,
> but we men of the daylight should be sober,
> with faith and love as our body armor
> and hope of salvation our helmet.

The creed and the Lord's Prayer were the two things baptized Christians were told to meditate on and pray with for the rest of their lives.
The first-century *Didachē* (8.3) says that the believer should say the
Lord's Prayer three times a day. Those of us who say the rosary say it six
times just in the course of that. (We also say the creed, as part of it —
uniting the two prayers originally called for on the part of the baptized.) In this way the rosary, often derided by "enlightened" Catholics,
is close to ancient practices.

Brown admits that change in liturgical formulae is always resisted,
so we make our prayer together in the inadequate English translation. I
count that the most important way I pray the Our Father. But when I
say the rosary alone, I repeat the prayer in Greek, with roughly this
meaning:

> Our Father of the heavens,
> your title be honored,
> your reign arrive,

your design be fulfilled
on earth as in heaven.

The meal still to come
grant even today,
and clear our moral account with you
as we clear our account with others,
and bring us not to the Breaking Point,
but wrest us from the Evil Power.

To have an eschatological faith is to have a "synchronic" faith, one in which eternity is continually intersecting — literally, cutting across — time. We are created *now,* at every now. Christ comes now; the Incarnation is now. The great judgment is now. "The accomplishment of everything impends" (1 Peter 4.7). That is the good news Jesus came to bring. Believing it is what makes me a Catholic.

EPILOGUE

SINCE I HAVE DEPENDED so much on Chesterton in this book, I might as well give him the last word. As it turns out, he addressed the very question I have been dealing with — how one can be a member of the church while criticizing its faults. He was addressing the claim that Chaucer could not have been a real Catholic since he attacked abuses like the sale of indulgences and expressed sympathy for the heretical Lollards, whose combined poverty and piety were admirable.

A man does not come an inch nearer to being a heretic by being a hundred times a critic. Nor does he do so because his criticisms resemble those of critics who are also heretics. He only becomes a heretic at the precise moment when he prefers his criticism to his Catholicism. That is, at the instant of separation in which he thinks the view peculiar to himself more valuable than the creed that unites him to his fellows. At any given moment the Catholic Church is full of people sympathizing with social movements or moral ideas, which may happen to have representatives outside the Church. For the Church is not a movement or a mood or a direction, but the balance of many movements and moods; and membership of it consists of accepting the ultimate arbitrament which strikes the balance between them, not in refusing to admit any of them into the balance at all. A Catholic does not come any nearer to being a Communist by hating the Capitalist corruptions, any more than he comes any nearer to being a Moslem by hating real idolatry or real excess in wine. He accepts the Church's ruling about the use and abuse of wine and images; and after that it is irrelevant how much he happens to hate the abuse of them. A Catholic did not come any nearer to being a Calvinist by dwelling on the omniscience of God and the power of grace, any more than he came any nearer to being an atheist by saying that man possessed reason and free will. What constituted a Calvinist was that he preferred his Calvinism to his Catholicism. And what constituted his Catholicism was that he accepted the ultimate arbitration that reconciled free will and grace, and did not exclude either. So a Catholic did not come any nearer to being a Lollard because he criticized the ecclesiastical evils of the fourteenth century, as Leo the Thirteenth or Cardinal Manning criticized the economic evils of the nineteenth century.[1]

NOTES
ACKNOWLEDGMENTS
INDEX

NOTES

2. JESUIT DAYS

1. John Henry Newman, *Fifteen Sermons Preached Before the University of Oxford* (Christian Classics, 1966), p. 322.
2. G. K. Chesterton, *Autobiography* (Hutchison & Co., 1934), p. 91.
3. G. K. Chesterton, *Collected Poems* (Methuen & Co., 1933), pp. 277–78.
4. Ibid., p. 245 ("The Mirror of Madmen").
5. Chesterton, *St. Francis of Assisi* (Image Books, 1957), p. 75.

3. CHESTERTON

1. G. K. Chesterton, *Chaucer* (Farrar & Rinehart, 1932), p. 28.

4. ENCYCLICALS

1. John B. Judis, *William F. Buckley, Jr., Patron Saint of the Conservatives* (Simon & Schuster, 1988), pp. 325–26.
2. Buckley objected to the pope's claim that the free market is unjust to underdeveloped countries, to which the advanced nations owe support from a simple consideration of the humanity of their inhabitants. Buckley's free-market absolutism maintained that the market will do whatever can be done to increase prosperity all around. Not a Distributist position. Conservatives were also upset at the encyclical's use of the word *socialization*. Actually, the pope never used the word in his Latin text, but the English translation put out by the Vatican used it for *socialium rationum incrementa* (a thickening of social ties). Pius XII had used the German word *Sozialisierung* in an address to Austrian Catholics of September 1952 — and he condemned it as a threat to individual freedom. John XXIII saw in the increasing interwovenness of modern society a humanizing process that makes us all more responsible to and for each other. Conservatives preferred the approach of

Pius XII, which was closer to Buckley's. See Peter Hebblethwaite, *Pope John XXIII: Shepherd of the Modern World* (Doubleday, 1985), pp. 361–63.

3. Anne Fremantle, ed., *The Papal Encyclicals in Their Historical Context* (Putnam's, 1956). Fremantle begins by saying that 1 Peter in the New Testament is "the first papal encyclical" and goes downhill from there.

4. Thomas Aquinas, *Questiones Quodlibitum* 9.16.

5. Schatz (S 117) gives convincing counter-arguments to Tierney's much-bruited thesis.

PART II. CHURCH WITHOUT PAPAL PRIMACY

1. John Henry Newman, *An Essay on the Development of Christian Doctrine* (University of Notre Dame Press, 1989), p. 149.

2. Newman, *A Letter Addressed to His Grace the Duke of Norfolk,* in *Newman and Gladstone: The Vatican Decrees* (University of Notre Dame Press, 1962), p. 98.

3. Ibid., p. 101.

4. Ibid., p. 102.

5. Newman, *Essay on Development,* p. 156.

5. PETER

1. G. K. Chesterton, *Heretics* (Ayer, 1970), p. 67.

2. G. K. Chesterton, *The Everlasting Man* (Dodd, Mead, 1947), p. 227.

3. What is now commonly translated as "super apostles" is, literally, "the too excessively [*hyperlian*] apostles." C. K. Barrett explored the meaning of this term (as including Peter) in a series of articles before enshrining it in his *Commentary on the Second Epistle to the Corinthians* (Harper & Row), pp. 30–32, 277–79. See also T. W. Manson, "The Corinthian Correspondence," *Bulletin of the John Rylands Library* 26 (1941), pp. 101–20. But Barrett does not, like some, include Peter in the group of "would-be apostles" (*pseudapostoloi*) at 2 Cor 11.13.

4. Brian Stock, "Is Matthew's Presentation of Peter Ironic?" *Biblical Theology Bulletin* 18 (1989), pp. 65–66.

5. Max Wilcox, "Peter and the Rock," *New Testament Studies* 22 (1976), p. 87.

6. For a survey of such exegetes, see Arlo J. Nau, *Peter in Matthew: Discipleship, Diplomacy, and Dispraise* (Liturgical Press, 1992), pp. 29–32.

7. G. F. Snyder, "John 13.16 and the Anti-Petrinism of the Johannine Tradition," *Biblical Research* 16 (1971), pp. 5–15.

8. Elaine Pagels, *The Gnostic Gospels* (Random House, 1979), pp. 15–16.

9. Tertullian, *Answer to Marcion* 4.5, in Ernest Evans, ed., *Tertullian Adversus Marcionem,* Vol. 2 (Oxford University Press, 1972), p. 270. The "fellowship of the revealed faith" is *societas sacramenti,* where the emphasis is on the *shared* mystery, not the private illuminations of the Gnostics.

10. Tertullian, *Disqualifying Heretics* (*De Praescriptione Hereticorum*) 36, in Francis Oehler, ed., *Tertulliani Quae Supersunt Omnia* (Leipzig, 1854), p. 34. *Praescriptio* is the assertion of a prior claim invalidating a new claim being made.

Tertullian thinks that orthodoxy already occupies ground heretics have no right to intrude upon.

11. John Knox attributes the whole canon to Marcion's influence in *Marcion and the New Testament* (University of Chicago Press, 1942). But most see this as an important factor in the canon's formation, even if not its cause.

12. Irenaeus, *Answer to the Heresies* 110, ed. Norbert Brox (Herder, 1993), pp. 198–200.

13. Ernest Evans, *Tertullian's Treatise Against Praxeas* (Society for Promoting Christian Knowledge, 1948), pp. 189–91.

14. The story behind Ignatius's letters was puzzled out successfully by Percy Neale Harrison in his *Polycarp's Two Epistles to the Philippians* (Cambridge University Press, 1936), which provides the basis for William Schoedel's exposition of the letters in *Ignatius of Antioch* (Fortress Press, 1985).

15. Ignatius, *Letter to the Smyrnaeans* 1–3 (Schoedel, *Ignatius*, pp. 220–25).

16. G. K. Chesterton, "The Red Moon of Meru," *Father Brown Omnibus* (Dodd, Mead, 1951), p. 767.

17. Raymond Brown, Karl P. Donfried, and John Reumann, *Peter in the New Testament* (Paulist Press, 1973), pp. 96–97.

6. PAUL

1. R. Joseph Hoffmann, *Marcion: On the Restitution of Christianity* (Scholars Press, 1984), p. 101.

2. Walter Bauer, *Orthodoxy and Heresy in Earliest Christianity,* ed. Robert R. Kraft and Gerhard Krodel (Fortress Press, 1971), pp. 214–15.

3. Ibid., pp. 83–84.

4. Oscar Cullmann, *Le problème litteraire et historique du roman pseudo-Clementin* (Librairie Felix Alcan, 1930), pp. 253–57.

5. Bauer, *Orthodoxy,* pp. 257–64.

6. *Peter's Announcements* 2.17.

7. Cullmann, *Le problème,* pp. 243–44.

8. For "his other writings" the New English Bible gives "other scriptures." But it is not sure that this letter, which would come to be included in the canon, can already be referring to the canon.

9. Tertullian, *Answer to Marcion* 5.3, in Ernest Evans, ed., *Tertullian Adversus Marcionem,* Vol. 2 (Oxford University Press, 1972), pp. 518–26.

10. Tertullian, *Disqualifying Heretics* 2–25, in Francis Oehler, ed., *Tertulliani Quae Supersunt Omnia* (Leipzig, 1854), pp. 22–23.

11. Ibid., p. 24.

12. Tertullian, *Answer to Marcion* 4.5, in Evans, Vol. 2, p. 270.

13. Oscar Cullmann, *Peter: Disciple, Apostle, Martyr,* translated by Floyd V. Filson, 2d ed. (Westminster Press, 1962), pp. 91–100; Raymond Brown, *Antioch and Rome* (Paulist Press, 1982), pp. 122–27.

14. Cullmann, *Peter,* pp. 52–53.

15. Some take *Rome* as "the far term of the West," but Clement probably knew that Paul meant to stay in Rome only briefly before going on to evangelize Spain.

16. Irenaeus, *Answer to Heretics* 3.3, in Adolph Stieren, *Irenaei Quae Supersunt Omnia* (Leipzig, 1853), p. 428.

17. "*Dyarchy:* A government in which power is vested in two rulers or authorities"; *Webster's Third International.*

18. The catalogue of the exhibit is Angela Donati, ed., *Pietro e Paolo: La storia, il culto, la memoria nei primi secoli* (Electa, 2000).

19. Ibid., p. 73.

20. Ibid., p. 44.

21. For Paul on Christ's right hand side, see ibid., pp. 132 and 155. For Christ giving the scroll to Paul, see pp. 50, 51.

22. Ibid., p. 206.

23. P. van Moorsel, "Il miracolo della roccia nella letteratura e nell'arte paleo-cristiane," *Rivista di archeologia cristiana* 51 (Pontificio Istituto di Archeologia Cristiana, 1966), pp. 237–49. Charles Pietri denies the connection with the legend of Processus and Martinianus, arguing that the soldiers are part of the symbolic Militia Christiana led by Peter, as Moses led his troops — a suggestion rightly rejected by the curators of the Roman exhibit on Peter and Paul. See Pietri, *Roma Christiana* (Ecole Française de Rome, 1976), pp. 336–39.

24. Ibid., p. 224; Augustine, *Sermon* 352.5.

25. Bauer, *Orthodoxy,* p. 113.

7. ROME MEDIATING

1. For the doctrines of the Trinity and the Incarnation as "not primitive," see John Henry Newman, *An Essay on the Development of Doctrine* (University of Notre Dame Press, 1989), pp. 14–20, 135–44.

2. Eric John, "Papalism Ancient and Modern," in Robert Markus and Eric John, *Pastors or Princes* (Corpus, 1969), pp. 77–78.

3. Peter Brown, *The Rise of Western Christendom: Triumph and Diversity, A.D. 200–1000* (Blackwell, 1996), p. 134.

4. James S. Jeffers, *Conflict at Rome* (Fortress Press, 1991), p. 95.

5. J. E. Merdinger, *Rome and the African Church in the Time of Augustine* (Yale University Press, 1997), pp. 1136–53.

6. Augustine, Letter *22.11, in Robert B. Eno, S.S., *The Fathers of the Church,* Vol. 81 (Catholic University of America, 1989).

8. ROME MEDDLING

1. Eusebius, *History of the Church* 5.24.13.

2. Ibid., 5.24.7.

3. Maurice Bevenot, S.J., *Cyprian: "De Lapsis" and "De Ecclesiae Catholicae Unitate"* (Oxford University Press, 1971).

4. Ibid., p. 106.

5. The bishops of Asia Minor had already settled this question in a council held at Iconium c. 230; see Walker, *The Churchmanship of St. Cyprian* (Lutterworth Press, 1968), p. 31.

6. It is now generally accepted that the two editions of Cyprian's *De Unitate* were best explained by Maurice Bevenot in a series of articles in the 1930s, as summarized in his edition of the crucial works, cited in note 3 above.

7. Ibid., p. 62 (Cyprian, *The Catholic Church's Unity* 4).

8. Walker, *Churchmanship*, p. 26.

9. Bevenot, *Cyprian*, pp. 62, 64 (*De Unitate* 4–5).

10. Ibid., p. 109.

11. Cyprian, Letter 75.

12. Cyprian, Letter 74.

13. J. E. Merdinger, *Rome and the African Church in the Time of Augustine* (Yale University Press, 1997), pp. 127–28.

14. Ibid., p. 128.

15. Ibid., p. 129.

16. Ibid., pp. 120–26.

17. Ibid., pp. 191–92.

18. R. A. Markus, *Saeculum: History and Society in the Theology of St. Augustine* (Cambridge University Press, 1970), pp. 129–30.

19. By synecdoche: *figurata generalitate*, "the whole represented in a figure." Augustine the rhetorician took such tropes in a technical sense.

20. To make his point that no mere man can be the foundation of the church, Augustine relies on the Latin text of Matthew to note that *petra* and *petrus* are not the same word. *Petrus* is "stone-related," not "stone," and means founded on the stone, not itself a stone of foundation. He did not know that the two words are the same in Aramaic: "You are *Kephas,* and on this kephas I will build up . . ."

9. ROME AND THE EAST

1. J.N.D. Kelly, *Early Christian Creeds,* 3d ed. (David McKay, 1972), p. 258.

2. Ibid., pp. 258–59.

3. Ibid., p. 258.

4. Henry Chadwick, *Boethius* (Oxford University Press, 1981), p. 32.

5. Ibid.

6. John Moorhead, *Theodoric in Italy* (Oxford University Press, 1992), pp. 122–23, p. 121.

7. Ibid., p. 121.

8. John Moorhead, *Justinian* (Longman, 1994), p. 81.

9. John W. Barker, *Justinian and the Later Roman Empire* (University of Wisconsin Press, 1946), p. 109.

10. Moorhead, *Justinian*, p. 82.

11. Barker, *Justinian*, p. 111.

12. R. A. Markus, *Gregory the Great and His World* (Cambridge University Press, 1997), p. 128.

13. Ibid., p. 102.

14. Ibid., pp. 88, 95.

15. Ibid., p. 94.

16. Ibid.

17. Lord Acton, "The Vatican Council" (1870), in Harold Acton, *Selected Writ-*

ings, ed. J. Rufus Fears, Vol. 3 (Liberty Classics), p. 309. John Henry Newman was so upset by the Honorius precedent that he prompted a friend, Peter le Page Renouf, to publish a booklet on the eve of Vatican I called *The Condemnation of Pope Honorius.* See John R. Page, *What Will Dr. Newman Do?* (Liturgical Press, 1994), p. 45: "Though Newman disagreed with Renouf's conclusions, it was generally known that he had encouraged Renouf to write his pamphlet. This would come back to haunt him as the controversy over the pamphlet unfolded."

18. John Henry Newman, "On Consulting the Faithful in Matters of Doctrine," ed. John Coulson (Sheed and Ward, 1961), p. 76.

19. Victor Saxa, "Il culto degli apostoli Pietro e Paolo dalle origine all epoca Carolingia," in Angela Donati, ed., *Pietro e Paolo: La storia, il culto, la memoria nei primi secoli* (Electa, 2000), pp. 80–81.

20. John Henry Newman, "Letter to His Grace the Duke of Norfolk," in Alvan S. Ryan, ed., *Newman and Gladstone* (University of Notre Dame Press, 1962), p. 100.

10. ROME TURNS WEST

1. Anthony Grafton, *Forgers and Critics* (Princeton University Press, 1990), pp. 224–25.

2. John Moorhead, *Theodoric in Italy* (Oxford University Press, 1992), pp. 121–23.

3. The great scholar of the forgeries, Horst Fuhrmann, sums up his findings on Pseudo-Isidore in the *New Catholic Encyclopedia* (1967), s.v. "False Decretals."

4. I cite the Donation from the authoritative edition by Horst Fuhrmann, *Das Constitutum Constantini* (Hannsche Buchhandlung, 1968), pp. 56–98.

5. Luitpold Wallach, *Alcuin and Charlemagne* (Cornell University Press, 1959), pp. 169–77.

6. Robert Folz, *The Coronation of Charlemagne, 25 December, 800,* trans. J. E. Anderson (Routledge and Kegan Paul, 1974), p. 95.

7. Ibid., p. 96.

8. Wallach, *Alcuin and Charlemagne,* pp. 147–55.

9. Edward Gibbon, *The Decline and Fall of the Roman Empire,* Vol. 6, Chap. 60, J. B. Bury ed. (Methuen, 1912), p. 382.

10. Folz, *Coronation,* pp. 115–16.

11. Ibid., p. 125.

12. Ibid., p. 138.

13. Ibid., p. 148.

14. Robert Browning, *The Ring and the Book* 10.81–92.

11. FORGERIES AND POPULISM

1. Domenico Maffei, *La Donazione di Costantino nei giuristi medievali* (Giuffre Editore, 1964), pp. 17–18.

2. Ibid., pp. 16–17.

3. Uta-Renate Blumenthal, *The Investiture Controversy: Church and Monarchy from the Ninth to the Twelfth Century,* trans. by the author (University of Pennsylvania Press, 1982), p. 113.

4. H.E.J. Cowdrey, *Pope Gregory VII, 1073–1085* (Oxford University Press, 1998), p. 41.

5. Blumenthal, *Investiture Controversy,* p. 117.

6. Ibid.

7. Cowdrey, *Gregory VII,* p. 533.

8. R. A. Markus and Eric John, *Pastors or Princes* (Corpus, 1969), p. 67.

9. Ibid., pp. 27–29.

10. Cowdrey, *Gregory VII,* pp. 502–3: "Popes from Victor III to Innocent II in their letters and official documents provide only occasional parallels with them; when they do, the succcinctness and challenge of their wording are reduced."

11. Maffei, *Donazione,* p. 18.

12. Cowdrey, *Gregory VII,* p. 645. And cf. pp. 20–21, 481, 640, 643.

13. Markus and John, *Pastors or Princes,* p. 70.

14. Hans Eberhard Mayer, *The Crusades,* 2d ed., trans. John Gillingham (Oxford University Press), p. 39.

15. Ibid., p. 9.

16. Ibid., pp. 15–16.

17. Ibid., pp. 223–37, 293–95.

18. Ibid., p. 96.

19. Jacques Le Goff, *The Birth of Purgatory,* trans. Arthur Goldhammer (University of Chicago Press, 1981), p. 289.

20. Ibid., pp. 216–17.

21. R. W. Southern, *Scholastic Humanism and the Unification of Europe* (Blackwell, 1995), p. 305.

22. Ibid., pp. 301–2.

23. Walter Ullmann, *A Short History of the Papacy in the Middle Ages* (Methuen, 1972), pp. 217–18.

24. Jane Sayers, *Innocent III: Leader of Europe, 1198–1216* (Longman, 1994), pp. 148–49.

25. Richard Kieckhefer, "The Office of Inquisition and Medieval Heresy: The Transition from Personal to Institutional Jurisdiction," *Journal of Ecclesiastical History* 46 (January 1991), pp. 36–61.

26. Mark Gregory Pegg, *The Corruption of Angels: The Great Inquisition of 1245–1246* (Princeton University Press, 2001), p. 33.

27. James J. Walsh, *The Thirteenth, Greatest of Centuries* (Catholic Summer School Press, 1913), pp. 350–63.

28. Alain Erlande-Brandenburg, *Quand les cathédrales étaient peintes* (Gallimard, 1993).

29. Walter Ullmann, *A Short History of the Papacy in the Middle Ages* (Methuen, 1972), p. 257.

12. RISE OF THE SECULAR STATE AND CHURCH COUNCIL

1. T.S.R. Boase, *Boniface VIII* (Constable, 1933), p. 178.

2. Alain Boureau, *The Myth of Pope Joan,* trans. Lydia G. Cochrane (University of Chicago Press, 2001).

3. Boase, *Boniface VIII,* p. 169.

4. Walter Ullmann, *Law and Politics in the Middle Ages* (Cornell University Press, 1975), pp. 267–78.

5. D. E. Luscombe, "The State of Nature and Origin of the State," in Norman Kretzmann et al., eds., *The Cambridge History of Later Medieval Philosophy* (Cambridge University Press, 1982), pp. 757–70.

6. Ullman, *Law and Politics,* p. 277. Cf. Oliver O'Donovan and Joan Lockwood O'Donovan, *From Irenaeus to Grotius: A Sourcebook in Christian Political Thought* (Eerdmans, 1999), pp. 397–412.

7. The book is conventionally dated c. 1309–1313, but see counter-arguments in Prue Shaw, *Dante, "Monarchia"* (Cambridge University Press, 1995), pp. xxxvii-xli.

8. Ibid., 1.12.8, p. 30.

9. Ibid., 3.8.6–11, p. 120.

10. Ibid., 3.10.1–17, pp. 126–31. For a curse on Constantine's gift, "which the original rich father [Pope Silvester] snatched from you," see Dante, *Inferno* 19.116–17.

11. Marsiglio of Padua, *The Defender of Peace,* ed. and trans. Alan Gewirth, Vol. 2 (Columbia University Press, 1955), Discourse I, Chap. 12, Par. 3, p. 45. By the "weightier part" (*valentior pars*) of the community, Marsiglio means to exclude only "children, slaves, aliens, and women" — the "democratic" position down to the nineteenth century.

12. Jean Dunbabin, "The Reception and Interpretation of Aristotle's *Politics,*" in Kretzmann, *Later Medieval Philosophy,* pp. 725–35.

13. Quentin Skinner, *The Foundations of Modern Political Thought,* Vol. 1 (Cambridge University Press, 1978), pp. 62–65.

14. Walter Ullmann, *Medieval Political Thought* (Penguin, 1975), p. 217.

15. Luscombe, "The State of Nature," pp. 759–60.

16. See the chapter on John of Paris in Brian Tierney, *Foundations of the Conciliar Theory* (Cambridge University Press, 1955), pp. 157–78.

17. Marsiglio, *Defender of Peace,* Discourse II, Chap. 2, Par. 3, pp. 103–4.

18. Marsiglio of Padua, *Defensor Minor,* in *Writings on Empire,* trans. Cary J. Nederman (Cambridge University Press, 1993), *Defensor Minor* 7.3, p. 21.

19. Ibid., 7.1, pp. 20–21.

20. Ibid., 10.2, pp. 30–32.

21. Ibid., 7.4, p. 22.

22. Marsiglio, *Defender of Peace,* Vol. 1, p. 286.

23. Walter Ullmann, *A Short History of the Papacy in the Middle Ages* (Methuen, 1972), p. 282.

24. Alain Bourneau, *The Myth of Pope Joan,* trans. Lydia G. Cochrane (University of Chicago Press, 2001), pp. 153–56.

25. Ullmann, *Short History,* p. 286.

26. Arthur Stephen McGrade, *The Political Thought of William of Ockham* (Cambridge University Press, 1974), pp. 68–77.

27. Ullmann, *Short History,* p. 295.

28. Ibid., pp. 295–96.

29. Tierney, *Foundations,* pp. 220–37.

30. Ullmann, *Short History,* p. 302.

13. RENAISSANCE AND REFORMATION

1. Deoclecio Redig de Campos, *I palazzi Vaticani* (Cappelli Editore, 1967), pp. 42–44.

2. Bernini's great statue the *Conversion of Constantine* was recognized as a reference to the Donation at its unveiling in 1670; see T. A. Marder, *Bernini's Scala Regia at the Vatican Palace* (Cambridge University Press, 1997), p. 209. Pope Silvester's cure of the emperor's leprosy is shown in a roundel-relief on the stairway itself.

3. Lord Acton, "The Massacre of St. Bartholomew," in J. Rufus Fears, ed., *Selected Writings of Lord Acton*, Vol. 2 (Liberty/Classics, 1985), p. 227.

4. Giulio Carlo Argan and Bruno Contardi, *Michelangelo, Architect,* trans. Marion L. Grayson (Abrams, 1993), pp. 49, 53.

5. Desiderius Erasmus, *Julius Excluded from Heaven,* in *"The Praise of Folly" and Other Writings,* trans. Robert M. Adams (Norton, 1989), p. 173.

6. Acton, "The Borgias and Their Latest Historian," in Fears, *Lord Acton,* pp. 252–53.

7. Harold Acton, "Luther," in *Lectures on Modern History* (Meridian, 1961), pp. 97–98.

8. Acton, "Acton-Creighton Correspondence," in Fears, *Lord Acton,* p. 383.

9. Acton, "The Borgias," p. 349.

10. Acton, "Acton-Creighton Correspondence," p. 380.

11. John W. O'Malley, S.J., *Trent and All That: Renaming Catholicism in the Early Modern Era* (Harvard University Press, 2000), p. 20.

12. *Consilium de Emendenda Ecclesia,* quoted in Hubert Jedin, *A History of the Council of Trent,* trans. Dom Ernest Graf, O.S.B., Vol. 1 (Thomas Nelson, 1957), pp. 424–25.

13. Elizabeth G. Gleason, *Gasparo Contarini: Venice, Rome, and Reform* (University of California Press, 1993), pp. 144–46.

14. There is no doctrinal reason for denying the chalice to the laity. In fact, the infant baptism rite of the eleventh century included communion for the baby, to signify the total union with Christ effected by baptism, and since the toothless child could not chew bread, the sacramental wine was rubbed on its lips (M 493).

15. Ibid., pp. 201–8.

16. Ibid., p. 195.

14. TRENT AND ENGLAND

1. Hubert Jedin, *A History of the Council of Trent,* trans. Dom Ernest Graf, O.S.B., Vol. 1 (Thomas Nelson, 1957), p. 17.

2. Walter Ullmann, *A Short History of the Papacy in the Middle Ages* (Methuen, 1972), pp. 312–13. Cf. John Hine Mundy, "The Conciliar Movement: Monarchy and the Councils," in Mundy et al., eds., *The Council of Constance* (Columbia University Press, 1961), pp. 14–21.

3. Translations of their works are in J. H. Burns and Thomas M. Izbicki, eds., *Conciliarism and Papalism* (Cambridge University Press, 1997).

4. Vasari's myth that there is one clergyman in the painting — shown as Midas,

with a serpent twined about him biting his testicles — has been definitively refuted by Leo Steinberg's "Michelangelo's 'Last Judgment' as Merciful Heresy," *Art in America* 63 (1975), pp. 49–63.

5. The painting's two slight references to the traditional deadly sins — the grab at one sinner's testicles, and the money bag — simply show that heretics' sins were not *exclusively* intellectual.

6. Jedin, *Council of Trent*, Vol. 2, pp. 91–92.

7. Ibid., p. 92.

8. Ibid., pp. 128–30.

9. John W. O'Malley, *Trent and All That: Renaming Catholicism in the Early Modern Era* (Harvard University Press, 2000), p. 59.

10. John W. O'Malley, S.J., "The Renaissance Papacy," in Paul Johnson, ed., *The Papacy* (Weidenfeld and Nicolson, 1997), p. 135.

11. J. J. Scarisbrick, *Henry VIII* (University of California Press, 1968), p. 29.

12. Ibid., pp. 27, 33–34.

13. Lord Acton, "History and the Divorce of Henry VIII," in J. Rufus Fears, ed., *Selected Writings of Lord Acton*, Vol. 2 (Liberty/Classics, 1985), p. 280.

14. Ibid., pp. 281–82.

15. Amy Kelly, *Eleanor of Aquitaine and the Four Kings* (Harvard University Press, 1950), p. 71.

16. Ibid., p. 79.

17. Ibid., pp. 313–14, 368–69.

18. Sheila Rauch Kennedy, *Shattered Faith* (Pantheon, 1997).

19. Acton, "The Borgias and Their Latest Historian," in Fears, *Lord Acton*, pp. 251–52.

20. Scarisbrick, *Henry VIII*, p. 206.

21. Ibid., pp. 213–14.

22. Owen Chadwick, *The Popes and European Revolution* (Oxford University Press, 1981), pp. 345–46.

23. G.R.R. Treasure, *Cardinal Richelieu and the Development of Absolutism* (Adam and Charles Black, 1972), pp. 219–20.

24. E.E.Y. Hales, *Revolution and Papacy, 1769–1846* (Doubleday, 1960), p. 204.

25. D. M. Loades, *The Reign of Mary Tudor: Politics, Government, and Religion in England, 1553–1558* (Ernest Benn, 1979), p. 431.

26. Ibid., pp. 446–48.

27. J. J. Scarisbrick, "Fisher, Henry VIII, and the Reformation," in Brian Bradshaw and Eamon Duffy, eds., *Humanism, Reform, and the Reformation: The Career of John Fisher* (Cambridge University Press, 1989), pp. 156–68.

15. *ANCIEN RÉGIME* AND REVOLUTION

1. John Hine Mundy, "The Conciliar Movement and the Council of Constance," in Mundy et al., eds., *The Council of Constance* (Columbia University Press, 1961), p. 17.

2. Owen Chadwick, *The Popes and European Revolution* (Oxford University Press, 1981), pp. 314–15.

3. Ibid., pp. 264–73.

4. Paolo Sarpi, *Istoria dell'interdetto e altri scritti editi ed inediti*, ed. Manlio Duilio Busnelli and Giovanni Gabarin, Vol. 6a (Giuseppe Laterza & Figili, 1940), p. 26.

5. Geoffrey Treasure, *Mazarin* (Routledge, 1995), pp. 285–91.

6. Chadwick, *Popes*, pp. 96–102.

7. Ibid., p. 291.

8. Ibid., p. 297.

9. Ibid., p. 303.

10. The popes were Urban VIII (*In Eminenti*, 1643), Innocent X (*Cum Occasione*, 1653), Alexander VII (*Ad Sacram*, 1656, *Regiminis Apostolici*, 1665), and Clement XI (*Vineam Domini*, 1705).

11. William Doyle, *Jansenism* (St. Martin's, 2000), pp. 44–45.

12. Ibid., p. 49.

13. Ibid., p. 46.

14. Chadwick, *Popes*, p. 285.

15. Ibid., p. 289.

16. Ibid., p. 351.

17. Ibid., p. 350.

18. Doyle, *Jansenism*, p. 72.

19. Chadwick, *Popes*, p. 369.

20. Ibid., pp. 375, 383.

21. Ibid., p. 384.

22. François Furet, "Civil Constitution of the Clergy," in Furet et al., eds., *A Critical Dictionary of the French Revolution* (Harvard University Press, 1989), pp. 449–57.

23. Chadwick, *Popes*, p. 448.

24. Ibid., p. 488.

25. E.E.Y. Hales, *Revolution and Papacy* (Doubleday, 1960), p. 209.

26. John Henry Newman to Charlotte Ward, Oct. 29, 1870 (*Letters and Diaries* 25.217).

16. WAR ON DEMOCRACY

1. E. L. Woodward, *Three Studies in European Conservatism* (Constable, 1929), p. 235.

2. Ibid., p. 91.

3. Ibid., p. 29.

4. David I. Kertzer, *The Popes Against the Jews* (Knopf, 2001), pp. 31–37.

5. Owen Chadwick, *The Popes and European Revolution* (Oxford University Press, 1981), pp. 567–69.

6. Woodward, *Three Studies*, p. 246.

7. Ibid., p. 266.

8. Meriol Trevor, *Prophets and Guardians* (Hollis and Carter, 1969), pp. 150–51.

9. Woodward, *Three Studies*, pp. 265–66. For Metternich's view on intellectuals as troublemakers, see pp. 48–52, and for theological troublemakers in particular, p. 56.

10. Gregory XVI, *Mirari Vos*, in H. Denzinger, ed., *Enchiridion Symbolorum*

(Herder, 1963), p. 549: *Atque ex hoc putidissimo indifferentismi fonte absurda illa fluit ac erronea sententia, seu potius deliramentum, asserendam esse ac vindicandam cuilibet libertatem conscientieae.*

11. Ibid.: *deterrima illa, ac numquam satis execranda et detestabilis, libertas artis librariae ad scripta quaelibet edenda in vulgus.*

12. Ibid.

13. Ibid.

14. Trevor, *Prophets and Guardians*, pp. 154–55.

15. Gregory XVI, *Singulari Nos: Motu proprio, et ex certa scientia, deque Apostolicae potestatis plenitudine, memoratum librum, propositiones respective falsas, calumniosas, temerarias, inducentes in anarchiam, contrarias Verbo Dei, impias, scandalosas, erroneas, jam ab Ecclesia, praesertim in Valdensibus, Wicflefitis, Hussitis, alliisque generis hereticis domnatas continentem, reprobamus ac pro reprobato et damnato in perpetuum haberi volumus et cernimus.*

16. Woodward, *Three Studies*, p. 265.

17. Owen Chadwick, *A History of the Popes, 1830–1914* (Oxford University Press, 1998), pp. 20, 22.

18. Giacomo Martina, *Pio Nono (1851–1866)* (Editrice Ponteficia Universita Gregoriana, 1985), pp. 321–30.

19. Pius IX, *Quanta Cura*. Here the pope is quoting the fifth-century pope Leo I (Epistle 14).

20. Ibid.

21. Pius IX, *Syllabus Errorum*, in Denzinger, *Enchiridion Symbolorum*, pp. 579–84.

22. Chadwick, *Popes*, pp. 555–56.

23. Kertzer, *Popes Against Jews*, p. 128.

24. Ibid.

25. Ibid., p. 130.

26. Chadwick, *Popes*, p. 280.

27. Leo XIII, *Immortale Dei*, ASS 18 (1885), p. 169.

28. Ibid., p. 170.

29. Ibid., pp. 168, 170.

30. Ibid., p. 166.

31. Ibid., p. 164.

32. Ibid., p. 165.

33. Leo XIII, *Longinqua*, ASS (1895), p. 396.

34. Leo XIII, *Rerum Novarum*, ASS 23 (1891), p. 642.

35. Ibid., p. 663.

36. Woodward, *Three Studies*, pp. 240–41.

37. Leo XIII, *Immortale Dei*, ASS 18, p. 164.

38. Leo XIII, *Providentissimus Deus*, ASS 26 (1893), p. 289.

39. Ibid., p. 285.

40. Ibid., p. 282.

41. Ibid., p. 281.

42. Leo XIII, *Longinqua Oceani*, ASS 28 (1895), p. 390. The narrowness of Leo's concerns is shown at the end of this letter (p. 399), where he addresses the plight of American Indians and Negroes — by which he means their continued "superstition," as if the only thing they needed was conversion to Catholicism.

43. Leo XIII, *Testem Benevolentiae*, AAS 31 (1899), p. 470.

44. Frank J. Coppa, *The Modern Papacy Since 1789* (Longman, 1998), p. 136.

45. Martin Marty, *Modern American Religion*, Vol. 1 (University of Chicago Press, 1986), p. 198.

46. Donald E. Pelotte, S.S.S., *John Courtney Murray: Theologian in Conflict* (Paulist Press, 1975), pp. 158–68.

47. Chadwick, *Popes*, p. 384.

48. Kertzel, *Popes Against Jews*, pp. 171–72.

49. Ibid., p. 184, citing *L'Osservatore Romano* for December 2, 1897, p. 2.

50. Ibid., p. 184.

51. Ibid., pp. 216–17.

52. Ibid., pp. 214–18.

53. Ibid., pp. 219–20.

54. Ibid., pp. 136–37, citing Giuseppe Oreglia, S.J., *Civilta Cattolica*, 1880.

17. REIGN OF TERROR

1. Marvin R. O'Connell, *Critics on Trial: An Introduction to the Catholic Modernist Crisis* (Catholic University of America Press, 1994), pp. 364, 361.

2. Gabriel Daly, *Transcendence and Immanence: A Study in Catholic Modernism and Integralism* (Oxford University Press, 1980), p. 218.

3. Lester R. Kurtz, *The Politics of Heresy: The Modernist Crisis in Roman Catholicism* (University of California Press, 1986), p. 161.

4. Owen Chadwick, *A History of the Popes, 1830–1914* (Oxford University Press, 1998), p. 355.

5. Emile Poulat, *Integrisme et Catholicism integral* (Casterman, 1969), p. 7.

6. Frank J. Coppa, *The Modern Papacy Since 1789* (Longman, 1998), p. 147.

7. Daly, *Transcendence*, pp. 33–34.

8. Pius X, *Pascendi*, AAS 40 (1907), p. 632.

9. Pius X, *Lamentabili*, AAS 40 (1907), p. 47.

10. Ibid., p. 478.

11. O'Connell, *Critics on Trial*, pp. 343–44.

12. Daly, *Transcendence*, pp. 204–5.

13. Ibid., p. 232.

14. *Pascendi*, p. 641.

15. Ibid., p. 642.

16. Ibid.

17. Ibid.

18. Ibid., p. 647.

19. Ibid., p. 649.

20. Ibid., p. 650.

21. Chadwick, *History*, pp. 357–58.

22. Poulat, *Integrisme*, pp. 45–55. Kenneth Woodward wrote in 1990, while doing research on the process of advancing people to sainthood, that he could not study the process of Pius X's canonization because "the documents on his cause — or at least the last, clinching *positio* [plea for advancement] — were embargoed by the

Vatican because some of the material is still considered sensitive"; see Woodward, *Making Saints* (Simon and Schuster, 1990), p. 311.

23. Maria Teresa Pichetto, *Alle radici dell'odio: Preziosi e Benigni antisemiti* (Franco Angelo Editore, 1983).

24. Ibid., pp. 113–14.

25. Ibid., p. 113.

26. Ibid., p. 115.

27. Ibid., p. 113.

28. David I. Kertzer, *The Popes Against the Jews* (Knopf, 2001), p. 231.

29. Daly, *Transcendence*, p. 235.

30. Pius X, *Sacrorum Antitistum*, AAS 2 (1910), p. 655.

31. Ibid., p. 669.

32. Ibid., p. 670.

33. Donald E. Pelotte, S.S.S., *John Courtney Murray: Theologian in Conflict* (Paulist Press, 1975), p. 52.

34. Ibid., p. 252.

35. Ibid., p. 38.

36. Ibid., p. 47.

37. Ibid., pp. 49–50.

38. Ibid., p. 51. By a unitary theory he meant one not based on the thesis-hypothesis dualism.

39. Ibid., p. 151.

40. Ibid., p. 55.

41. Ibid., p. 59.

42. Ibid., p. 77.

43. Ibid., p. 82.

44. Ibid., pp. 85–86.

45. Charles Curran, *American Catholic Social Ethics* (Notre Dame University Press, 1982), p. 229.

46. Ibid., p. 228.

47. Pius XII, *Ci Riesce*, AAS 45 (1953), p. 799.

48. Ibid.

49. Chadwick, *History*, p. 178.

50. Pelotte, *Murray*, p. 56.

51. Peter Hebblethwaite, *The Runaway Church* (Collins, 1975), pp. 113–14.

52. G. K. Chesterton, *Collected Poems* (Methuen, 1933), p. 120.

18. THE GREAT REBIRTH

1. Gerald P. Fogarty, "The Council Gets Underway," in Giuseppe Alberigo, ed., *History of Vatican II*, Vol. 2 (Orbis, 1997), pp. 72–73.

2. Donald E. Pelotte, S.S.S., *John Courtney Murray: Theologian in Conflict* (Paulist Press, 1975), pp. 79–80.

3. Andrea Riccardi, "The Tumultuous Opening Days of the Council," in Alberigo, *History*, pp. 1–2.

4. Peter Hebblethwaite, *Paul VI: The First Modern Pope* (Paulist Press, 1993), p. 305.

5. Peter Hebblethwaite, *John XXIII: Pope of the Century,* rev. ed. (Continuum, 2000), p. 214.

6. Ibid., p. 225.

7. Riccardi, "Tumultuous Opening Days," pp. 28–29.

8. Fogarty, "Council ets Underway," pp. 28–29.

9. Riccardi, "Tumultuous Opening Days," p. 67. Pope John told his secretary that, in delivering his opening address to the council, the one that called for an "updating" (*aggiornamento*) of the church, he had glanced nervously at "my friend on the right (Ottaviani)"; ibid., p. 18. This was no doubt when he said (according to his own Italian draft of the speech), "In the everyday exercise of our pastoral ministry, greatly to our sorrow, we sometimes have to listen to those who, although consumed with zeal, do not have very much judgment or balance. To them the modern world is nothing but betrayal and ruination"; see Hebblethwaite, *John XXIII,* p. 223.

10. Riccardi, "Tumultuous Opening Days," pp. 44–45, 55; Xavier Rynne (F. X. Murphy), *The Third Session* (Farrar, Straus and Giroux, 1965), pp. 261–62; Evangelista Vilanova, "The Intersession (1963–1964)," in Alberigo, *Vatican II,* Vol. 3, pp. 430–32.

11. Hebblethwaite, *Paul VI,* p. 533.

12. Francis A. Burkle-Young, *Passing the Keys: Modern Cardinals, Conclaves, and the Election of the Next Pope* (Madison Books, 1999), pp. 154–55.

13. Hebblethwaite, *Paul VI,* pp. 325–26.

14. Ibid., p. 504.

15. Xavier Rynne (F. X. Murphy), *Vatican Council II* (Orbis, 1968), pp. 213–15.

16. Joseph Fameree, "Bishops and Dioceses," in Alberigo, *Vatican II,* Vol. 3 (Orbis, 2000), p. 133.

17. Hebblethwaite, *Paul VI,* p. 590.

18. Ibid., pp. 384–85.

19. Vatican Constitution, *Lumen Gentium* 27, in *The Sixteen Documents of Vatican II* (Pauline Books, 1999), p. 155. All council documents are in the translation of the National Catholic Welfare Conference.

20. Rynne, *Vatican Council II,* p. 414.

21. Ibid., p. 228.

22. Ibid., p. 419.

23. Ibid., pp. 520–21.

24. Ibid., p. 555.

25. *Lumen Gentium* 31, in *Sixteen Documents,* p. 150.

26. Ibid., 28, p. 158.

27. Pastoral Constitution, *Gaudium et Spes* 28, in *Sixteen Documents,* p. 650.

28. *Gaudium et Spes* 16, p. 615.

29. Declaration, *Dignitatis Humanae* 2, 5, in *Sixteen Documents,* pp. 492, 496.

30. *Lumen Gentium* 15, pp. 139–40.

31. Declaration, *Nostra Aetate* 4, pp. 397–98.

32. *Lumen Gentium* 16, p. 141.

33. Ibid., 12, p. 136.

19. BORN TO SET TIMES RIGHT

1. Peter Hebblethwaite, *Paul VI: The First Modern Pope* (Paulist Press, 1993), p. 489.

2. Donald E. Pelotte, S.S.S., *John Courtney Murray: Theologian in Conflict* (Paulist Press, 1976), p. 104.

3. Hebblethwaite, *Paul VI*, p. 488.

4. Ibid.

5. Ibid., p. 472.

6. John Horgan, ed., *"Humanae Vitae" and the Bishops: The Encyclical and the Statements of the National Hierarchies* (Irish University Press, 1972).

7. Philip Kaufman, *Why You Can Disagree and Remain a Faithful Catholic* (Crossroad, 1991), pp. 72–83.

8. Hebblethwaite, *Paul VI*, p. 553.

9. Ibid., p. 550.

10. *Inter Insigniores*, in Leonard and Arlene Swidler, eds., *Women Priests: A Catholic Commentary on the Vatican Declaration* (Paulist Press, 1977), Par. 27, pp. 43–44.

11. Paul VI, General Audience, June 29, 1972.

12. Paul VI, General Audience, November 15, 1972.

13. Hebblethwaite, *Paul VI*, p. 624.

14. Jonathan Kwitny, *Man of the Century: The Life and Times of Pope John Paul II* (Holt, 1997), p. 305.

15. Eamon Duffy, "Urbi, but Not Orbi — the Cardinal, the Church, and the World," in *The New Blackfriars* 66 (March 1985), p. 277.

16. Kenneth L. Woodward, *Making Saints* (Simon and Schuster, 1990), p. 309.

17. Ibid., p. 333.

18. Neither of these was initially presented as a martyr, since Kolbe died as a substitute for a family man, where no religious test was at issue, and Edith Stein because her killers thought she was a Jew; ibid., pp. 139–47.

19. The cult of modern martyrdom is promoted by John Paul's admirers in the Commission for New Martyrs, on which see Robert Royal, *The Catholic Martyrs of the Twentieth Century* (Crossroad, 2000).

20. Congregation for the Doctrine of the Faith (CDF), *The Message of Fatima,* May 13, 2000, p. 24. The twentieth century was a time of many genocidal acts and ethnic cleansings, but the vision of Lucia sees only deaths for the church as plaguing the century. Like many of John Paul's canonizations, this one tends to downgrade the Holocaust.

21. Peter Hebblethwaite, *Pope John Paul II and the Church* (Sheed and Ward, 1995), p. 287.

22. CDF, *Message of Fatima*, p. 24.

23. Hebblethwaite, *The Next Pope* (Harper/San Francisco, 1995), pp. 159–60.

24. Ibid., p. 13. If one wonders at Lucia's use of terms like "aspersorium," it should be remembered that this is not the ten-year-old girl of 1917 describing her vision, but a thirty-seven-year-old nun writing it down in 1944.

25. Ibid., p. 25.

26. For various strands of sedevacantism ("empty-chair-of-Peterism"), see Mi-

chael W. Cuneo, *The Smoke of Satan* (Oxford University Press, 1997). The school thrives not only on the Fatima cult but on the belief that the Second Vatican Council must have been fraudulent, since the true church could not have endorsed changes in its doctrine and practice. Some think the late conservative Cardinal Siri was the real pope, shoved aside by the heretical John XXIII. More — including the Society of Saint Pius V and the Bayside Movement — have been attracted to the false Paul thesis. Some attacked John Paul II during the first two decades of his pontificate, when he had not revealed the third secret.

27. "Third Secret 'Commentary' [by Ratzinger] Raises Concerns over Whitewash," *Fatima News,* June 27, 2000.

28. Oddi's interview with *Il Sabato* was reprinted by *Our Lady's Library* on the Fatima Network.

29. Cuneo, *Smoke,* pp. 134–36.

30. Joseph Cardinal Ratzinger with Vittorio Messori, *The Ratzinger Report,* translated by Salvator Attanasio and Graham Harrison (Ignatius Press, 1985), p. 110.

31. Ibid., p. 139.

32. Duffy, "Urbi," pp. 273–74.

33. Stafford Poole, C.M., *Our Lady of Guadalupe* (University of Arizona Press, 1995), pp. 34–36.

34. Francis Borgia Steck, et al., *Motolinía's History of the Indians of New Spain* (Academy of American Franciscan History, 1951), p. 103.

35. Lisa Sousa, Stafford Poole, and James Lockhart, *The Story of Guadalupe* (Stanford University Press, 1998).

36. D. A. Brading, *Mexican Phoenix* (Cambridge University Press, 2002), p. 359.

37. Author's communication with Stafford Poole, the Vincentian priest and historian of Mexico, on Rome's repeated refusals to respond to the critics' objections.

38. Paul Johnson, *Pope John Paul II and the Catholic Restoration* (Weidenfeld and Nicolson, 1982), p. 124.

39. Ibid., p. 3.

40. Ibid., p. 117.

41. *Catechism of the Catholic Church* (Liguori, 1994), Index to Citations, pp. 751–52, 742–43, 732–34.

42. John Paul II, *Ordinatio Sacerdotalis,* May 22, 1994.

43. Citation in John L. Allen, Jr., *Cardinal Ratzinger: The Vatican's Enforcer of the Faith* (Continuum, 2000), p. 186.

44. Ibid., p. 230.

45. Ibid., p. 207.

46. John Henry Newman, Letter to Lavinia Wilson, Oct. 20, 1870, in John R. Page, *What Will Dr. Newman Do?* (Liturgical Press, 1994), p. 159 (*Letters and Diaries* 25.216).

47. Woodward, *Making Saints,* p. 75: "It was only during the pontificate of Urban VIII (1623–1644) that the papacy finally gained complete control over the making of saints. In a series of papal decrees, Urban defined the canonical procedures."

48. Ibid., pp. 123–24.

49. John Cornwell, *Hitler's Pope: The Secret History of Pius XII* (Viking, 1999), pp. 319–20.

50. Woodward, *Making Saints,* p. 124.

20. FIGHTING VATICAN II

1. Vittorio Messori, *The Ratzinger Report: An Exclusive Interview on the State of the Church* (Ignatius Press, 1985), p. 113.

2. Ibid., p. 35.

3. Ibid., p. 125.

4. Ibid., p. 20.

5. Ibid., p. 116.

6. Ibid., p. 115.

7. Ibid., p. 40.

8. Ibid., p. 65.

9. Ibid., p. 64.

10. Peter Hebblethwaite, *Pope John Paul and the Church* (Sheed and Ward, 1995), p. 222.

11. Ibid., p. 18.

12. Andrea Riccardi, "The Tumultuous Opening Days of the Council," in Giuseppe Alberigo, ed., *History of Vatican II*, Vol. 2 (Orbis, 1997), p. 86.

13. John L. Allen, Jr., *Cardinal Ratzinger: The Vatican's Enforcer of the Faith* (Continuum, 2000), p. 117.

14. Nicholas Lash, "Catholic Theology and the Crisis of Classicism," in *The New Blackfriars* (March 1985), p. 286.

15. Fergus Kerr, O.P., "The Cardinal and Post-Conciliar Britain," in *The New Blackfriars* (March 1985), p. 306.

16. Ibid., p. 300.

17. Joseph Ratzinger, "The Pastoral Implications of Episcopal Collegiality," in *Concilium*, 1965, p. 30.

18. Joseph Ratzinger, "Announcements and Prefatory Notes of Explanation," in Herbert Vorgrimler, ed., *Commentary on the Documents of Vatican II*, Vol. 1 (Herder, 1967), p. 300.

19. Joseph Ratzinger, *Das neue Volk Gottes* (Dusseldorf, 1971), p. 67.

20. Messori, *Ratzinger Report*, p. 59.

21. Ibid., p. 62.

22. Ibid., p. 61.

23. John Henry Newman, Letter to Emily Bowles, Aug. 12, 1870 (*Letters and Diaries* 25.178).

24. Hebblethwaite, *Pope John Paul*, p. 139.

25. Tertullian, *Disqualifying Heretics* 36.

26. An account of the interchanges is given by Robert Leicht, "Cardinals in Conflict," *The Tablet*, April 28, 2001, pp. 607–8.

27. A translation of Kasper's article appeared in *The Tablet* as "On the Church," June 20, 2001, pp. 927–30.

28. Messori, *Ratzinger Report*, p. 181.

29. Ibid., p. 47.

30. Dogmatic Constitution, *Lumen Gentium* 7, in *The Sixteen Documents of Vatican II* (Pauline Books, 1999), p. 129.

31. Messori, *Ratzinger Report*, p. 42.

32. Ibid., p. 49.

33. Ibid.

34. Joseph Ratzinger, *The Spirit of the Liturgy* (Ignatius Press, 2000), p. 75.

35. Ibid., p. 78.

36. Ibid.

37. Ibid., p. 80.

38. Constitution, *Sacrosanctum Concilium* 14, in *Sixteen Documents,* p. 53.

39. Messori, *Ratzinger Report,* pp. 50–51.

40. Dogmatic Constitution, *Lumen Gentium* 35, in *Sixteen Documents,* pp. 163–64.

41. Pastoral Constitution, *Gaudium et Spes* 17, in *Sixteen Documents,* p. 639.

42. Garry Wills, "The Pope in America," *Columbia Journalism Review* (January 1980).

43. Messori, *Ratzinger Report,* pp. 65–66.

44. Ibid., pp. 19–20.

45. Peter Hebblethwaite, *The Runaway Church* (Collins, 1975), p. 106.

46. Messori, *Ratzinger Report,* p. 156.

47. Peter Hebblethwaite, *John Paul II,* p. 165.

48. John Colson, ed., *Newman: On Consulting the Faithful in Matters of Doctrine* (Sheed and Ward, 1961), Introduction, p. 44.

49. Messori, *Ratzinger Report,* p. 159.

50. Pastoral Constitution, *Gaudium et Spes* 19, in *Sixteen Documents,* p. 641.

51. Leicht, "Cardinals," p. 608.

52. CDF, "On the Unicity and Salvific Universality of Jesus Christ and the Church," in *Dominus Jesus* (Pauline Books, 2000), p. 15.

53. Ibid., p. 43.

54. CDF Protocol Number 121'99–1095, pars. 10–11.

55. Leicht, "Cardinals," p. 607.

56. Ibid.

21. LIVING VATICAN II

1. Peter Hebblethwaite, *The Runaway Church* (Collins, 1975), pp. 103–4.

2. Vittorio Massori, *The Ratzinger Report* (Ignatius Press, 1985), p. 34.

3. National Survey of Family Growth, 1995, available on Web site of Catholics for Contraception, www.cath4choice.org.

4. Carl Bernstein and Marco Politi, *His Holiness* (Doubleday, 1996), pp. 487–88.

5. National Survey of Family Growth, 1995.

6. John XXIII, "Opening Address to the Council," quoted in Peter Hebblethwaite, *John XXIII: Pope of the Century* (Continuum, 2000), p. 224.

7. John Henry Newman, Letter to Lord Blachford, Feb. 5, 1875 (*Diaries and Letters* 27.211–12).

8. Apostolic Constitution, *Lumen Gentium* 12, in *The Sixteen Documents of Vatican II* (Pauline Books, 1999), p. 136.

9. Lord Acton, "Letter to Mr. Gladstone" in *The Times of London,* Nov. 9, 1874, in J. Rufus Fears, ed., *Selected Writings of Lord Acton,* Vol. 3 (Liberty Classics, 1988), p. 365.

10. John Coulson, ed., *On Consulting the Faithful* (Sheed and Ward, 1961), pp. 81–82.

11. Teresa Malcolm, "African Bishops Reject Condoms to Counter AIDS," *National Catholic Reporter,* August 10, 2001, p. 13.

12. "Sex, Power and Priesthood," *The Tablet,* March 24, 2001.

13. Massori, *Ratzinger Report,* p. 94.

14. Coulson, *On Consulting,* p. 63.

15. Ibid., p. 106.

22. THE POPE'S LOYAL OPPOSITION

1. John Henry Newman, *An Essay on the Development of Christian Doctrine* (University of Notre Dame Press, 1989), p. 40.

2. M. I. Finley, *Ancient Slavery and Modern Ideology* (Penguin Books, 1980), p. 17.

3. Augustine, *Answer to Faustus* 19.11 (PL 42, col. 355).

4. Augustine, *Interpreting John's Gospel* 124.5.

5. G. K. Chesterton, *Orthodoxy* (Image Books, 1959), p. 20.

6. Eric John and Robert Markus, *Pastors or Princes* (Corpus Books, 1996), p. 87.

7. G. K. Chesterton, *Chaucer* (Farrar and Rinehart, 1932), p. 303.

8. Chesterton, *Orthodoxy,* p. 69.

PART V. THE CREED

1. Ambrose, *Exposition of the Creed* 7 (PL 17, 1193).

2. Augustine, Sermon 215.1 (PL 38.1072).

23. *I BELIEVE IN GOD . . .*

1. J.N.D. Kelly, *Early Christian Creeds,* 3d ed. (David McKay, 1972), pp. 1–6.

2. Thomas Aquinas, *Summa Theologiae,* II-II.1.8 respond.

3. Kelly, *Early Christian Creeds,* p. 5.

4. Gregory Dix, *The Treatise on the Apostolic Tradition of St. Hippolytus of Rome,* with corrections by Henry Chadwick (Morehouse, 1992), pp. xl–xliv.

5. Augustine, Sermon 212.2 (PL 38.1060).

6. Augustine, Sermon 213.8 (PL 38.1065).

7. Kelly, *Early Christian Creeds,* pp. 131–66.

8. For "name" (*onoma*) as "honor," see Chapter 27.

9. Thomas Jefferson, Letter to James Smith, Dec. 8, 1822, in Dickinson W. Adams, ed., *Jefferson's Extracts from the Gospels* (Princeton University Press, 1983), p. 409.

10. Augustine, Sermon 117.5 (PL 38.663).

11. Ibid. 7 (PL 38.665).

12. John Henry Newman, *Fifteen Sermons* (Christian Classics Reprints, 1966), p. 350.

13. Ibid.

14. George Lakoff and Rafael E. Nunez, *Where Mathematics Comes From: How the Embodied Mind Brings Mathematics into Being* (Basic Books, 2000), p. 365.

15. Ibid., pp. 6–7.

16. Paul Henry, S.J., *Saint Augustine on Personality* (Macmillan, 1960), pp. 1–7.

17. Augustine, *The Trinity* 5.6.

18. Ibid., 8.14.

19. G. K. Chesterton, *The Everlasting Man* (Dodd, Mead, 1947), p. 282.

20. Augustine, *Confessiones* 10.39, 3.11.

21. Augustine, *The Trinity* 14.8.

22. Ibid., 10.18.

23. Augustine, Sermon 398.2.

24. . . . THE FATHER ALMIGHTY, CREATOR OF HEAVEN AND EARTH . . .

1. Translation from the New English Bible (Oxford University Press, 1970), p. 701.

2. *Answer to Marcion* 1.13, in Ernest Evans, ed., *Tertulliani Adversus Marcionem* (Oxford University Press, 1972), pp. 34–36.

3. Augustine, *The True Religion* 77.

4. G. K. Chesterton, *St. Francis of Assisi* (Image Books, 1957), pp. 74–75.

5. G. K. Chesterton, "The Holy of Holies," in *The Collected Poems* (Methuen, 1927), pp. 343–44.

6. Chesterton, "A Second Childhood," ibid., p. 82.

7. Chesterton, "The Ballad of the White Horse," ibid., p. 261.

8. G. K. Chesterton, *The Everlasting Man* (Dodd, Mead, 1947), p. 303.

9. Augustine, *The Trinity* 11.8.

10. Ibid., 14.11.

11. Chesterton, *Chaucer* (Farrar and Rinehart, 1932), pp. 11–12.

25. . . . AND IN JESUS CHRIST OUR LORD . . .

1. Thomas Jefferson, Letter to William Short, Apr. 13, 1820, in Dickinson W. Adams, ed., *Jefferson's Extracts from the Gospels* (Princeton University Press, 1983), p. 392.

2. Jefferson, Letter to Francis Adrian van der Kemp, Apr. 25, 1816, ibid., p. 369.

3. Jefferson to Short, p. 392.

4. Ibid.

5. Raymond E. Brown, *An Introduction to the New Testament* (Doubleday, 1997), pp. 490–93.

6. Ibid., p. 492.

7. For Mark as a gospel for a persecuted local community, see Joel Marcus, *Mark 1–8* (Doubleday, 2000), pp. 25–39.

8. Duns Scotus, *Ordinatio (Opus Oxiense)* 3.7.3. See Richard Cross, *Duns Scotus* (Oxford University Press, 1999), pp. 127–31.

9. See Irenaeus, *An Answer to All Heretics* 1.3, 1.10, 3.22.

10. Augustine, *The Trinity* 4.3.17–18.

11. On Girard, see Garry Wills, *Papal Sin* (Doubleday, 2000), pp. 303–8.

12. G. K. Chesterton, *St. Francis of Assisi* (Doubleday/Image, 1957), p. 73.

13. G. K. Chesterton, "The Monster," in *The Collected Poems* (Methuen, 1933), p. 7.

26. . . . CONCEIVED BY THE HOLY SPIRIT, BORN OF THE VIRGIN MARY . . .

1. J.N.D. Kelly, *Early Christian Creeds,* 3d ed. (David McKay, 1972), p. 91.

2. Gregory Dix, *The Treatise on the Apostolic Tradition of St. Hippolytus of Rome,* with corrections by Henry Chadwick (Morehouse, 1992), p. 37.

3. Raymond E. Brown, *The Birth of the Messiah* (Doubleday, 1977), p. 290.

4. Kelly, *Early Christian Creeds,* pp. 160–61.

5. Gerard Manley Hopkins, "God's Grandeur," in Catherine Phillips, ed., *Gerard Manley Hopkins* (Oxford University Press, 1986), p. 128.

6. Raymond E. Brown, *The Gospel According to John,* Vol. 2 (Doubleday, 1966), pp. 135–43.

7. Jaroslav Pelikan, *The Christian Tradition,* Vol. 3 (University of Chicago Press, 1978), pp. 72–73. And see Brown, *Birth,* pp. 517–18.

8. Joseph A. Fitzmyer, S.J., *The Gospel According to Luke,* Vol. 1 (Doubleday, 1979), p. 340. The change in church scholarship is suggested by the fact that Fitzmyer's book has the *Nihil obstat* and *Imprimatur.*

9. Brown, *Birth,* p. 530.

10. Augustine, *Explaining John's Gospel* 8.9.

11. Hopkins, "The Blessed Virgin Compared to the Air We Breathe," in Phillips, *Gerard Manley Hopkins,* p. 159.

12. Augustine, Sermon 191 (PL 38.1011).

13. Yves Congar, O.P., *I Believe in the Holy Spirit,* trans. David Smith, Vol. 1 (Crossroad, 1997), p. 163.

14. Augustine, Sermon 191 (PL 38.1010).

15. Augustine, Sermon 187 (PL 38.1001).

27. . . . SHALL COME TO JUDGE THE LIVING AND THE DEAD . . .

1. The eschatological interpretation of the Lord's Prayer is now the dominant one, as seen in the basic agreement of exegetes like the three I rely on here, Jeremias, Lohmeyer, and Brown: Joachim Jeremias, *The Lord's Prayer,* trans. John Reumann (Fortress Press, 1964); Ernst Lohmeyer, *"Our Father": An Introduction to the Lord's Prayer,* trans. John Bowden (Harper & Row, 1965); Raymond E. Brown, "The *Pater Noster* as an Eschatological Prayer," in *New Testament Essays* (Doubleday/Image, 1968), pp. 275–320.

2. Jeremias, pp. 1–5; Brown, pp. 280–83. Augustine's Sermon 56 (PL 38.377–86) teaches the prayer as part of his baptism instruction.

3. Hans Dieter Betz, *The Sermon on the Mount* (Fortress Press, 1995), pp. 330–35,

373. I use Matthew's version of the prayer, not Luke's shorter one. These are not now taken to be editings, the one of the other, but liturgical variants of the ancient hymn-prayer in different communities, of which Luke may represent the earlier numbering of petitions and Matthew the earlier wording of them. Brown sees in Luke a dilution of the eschatological emphases better retained in Matthew.

4. Augustine, *The Sermon on the Mount* 2.17 (PL 34.1276–77).

5. Ibid., 2.19 (PL 34.1277–78).

6. Lohmeyer, p. 139.

7. Brown, p. 307.

8. Lohmeyer, p. 211; Brown, p. 319.

EPILOGUE

1. G. K. Chesterton, *Chaucer* (Farrar and Rinehart, 1932), pp. 257–58.

ACKNOWLEDGMENTS

I am grateful to the Sheil Center as my conduit of Christian life; to my colleague Robert Lerner for his medieval expertise; to Terry Dosh of Bread Rising for his encyclopedic knowledge of Catholicism. Also to my editor Eric Chinski, and my agents, Andrew Wylie and his assistant, Zoe Pagnamenta.

INDEX

© STEVE KAGAN

Garry Wills, one of our most distinguished historians and critics, is the author of numerous books, including the Pulitzer Prize–winning *Lincoln at Gettysburg, Saint Augustine,* the bestsellers *Why I Am a Catholic* and *Papal Sin,* and, most recently, *"Negro President."* A regular contributor to the *New York Review of Books,* he has won many awards, among them two National Book Critics Circle Awards and the 1998 National Medal for the Humanities. He is a professor of history at Northwestern University and a member of the American Philosophical Society.

NIXON AGONISTES

"Astonishing . . . a stunning attempt to possess that past, that we may all of us escape it." — *New York Times Book Review*

By analyzing some of the thirty-seventh president's opinions, Wills comes to the controversial conclusion that Nixon was actually a liberal. Reaching far beyond its assessment of the president, this classic dissection of Richard Nixon becomes an incisive and provocative analysis of the American political machine. With a new introduction by the author.

ISBN 0-618-13432-8, $15.00

INVENTING AMERICA

"A scintillating tour de force of historical detective work." — *Time*

An adept and controversial analysis compares Jefferson's original draft of the Declaration of Independence with the final, accepted version, thereby challenging many long-cherished assumptions about both the man and the document. With a new introduction by the author.

ISBN 0-618-25776-4, $15.00

THE KENNEDY IMPRISONMENT

"The ultimate Kennedy book." — *New Republic*

This is the definitive historical and psychological analysis of the Kennedy clan and its crippling conception of power, from one of America's foremost historians. Wills offers "a brilliant and troubling study of the Kennedy era in American politics" (*Philadelphia Inquirer*). With a new introduction by the author.

ISBN 0-618-13443-3, $14.00

FORTHCOMING IN HARDCOVER, FALL 2003

"NEGRO PRESIDENT": *Jefferson and the Slave Power*

The best-selling historian Garry Wills explores a controversial and neglected aspect of Thomas Jefferson's presidency: it was achieved by virtue of slave "representation," and conducted to preserve that advantage. Probing the heart of Jefferson's presidency, Wills reveals how the might of the slave states was a concern behind Jefferson's most important decisions and policies, including his strategy to expand the nation west.

ISBN 0-618-34398-9, $25.00